D1571084

THE ORGANIZATIONAL FRONTIERS SERIES

The Organizational Frontiers Series is sponsored by the Society for Industrial and Organizational Psychology (SIOP). Launched in 1983 to make scientific contributions to the field, the series has attempted to publish books that are on the cutting edge of theory, research, and theory-driven practice in industrial/organizational psychology and related organizational science disciplines.

Our overall objective is to inform and to stimulate research for SIOP members (students, practitioners, and researchers) and people in related disciplines, including the other subdisciplines of psychology, organizational behavior, human resource management, and labor and industrial relations. The volumes in the Organizational Frontiers Series have the following goals:

1. Focus on research and theory in organizational science, and the implications for practice
2. Inform readers of significant advances in theory and research in psychology and related disciplines that are relevant to our research and practice
3. Challenge the research and practice community to develop and adapt new ideas and to conduct research on these developments
4. Promote the use of scientific knowledge in the solution of public policy issues and increased organizational effectiveness

The volumes originated in the hope that they would facilitate continuous learning and a continuing research curiosity about organizational phenomena on the part of both scientists and practitioners.

Managing Knowledge for Sustained Competitive Advantage

Designing Strategies for Effective Human Resource Management

Susan E. Jackson

Michael A. Hitt

Angelo S. DeNisi

Editors

Foreword by Neal Schmitt

 JOSSEY-BASS
A Wiley Imprint
www.josseybass.com

CABRINI COLLEGE LIBRARY
610 KING OF PRUSSIA ROAD
RADNOR, PA 19087

#51172293

Copyright © 2003 by John Wiley & Sons, Inc. All rights reserved.

Published by Jossey-Bass
A Wiley Imprint
989 Market Street, San Francisco, CA 94103-1741   www.josseybass.com

No part of this publication may be reproduced, stored in a retrieval system, or
transmitted in any form or by any means, electronic, mechanical, photocopying,
recording, scanning, or otherwise, except as permitted under Section 107 or 108 of
the 1976 United States Copyright Act, without either the prior written permission
of the Publisher, or authorization through payment of the appropriate per-copy fee
to the Copyright Clearance Center, Inc., 222 Rosewood Drive, Danvers, MA 01923,
978-750-8400, fax 978-750-4470, or on the web at www.copyright.com. Requests to
the Publisher for permission should be addressed to the Permissions Department,
John Wiley & Sons, Inc., 111 River Street, Hoboken, NJ 07030, 201-748-6011,
fax 201-748-6008, e-mail: permcoordinator@wiley.com.

Jossey-Bass books and products are available through most bookstores. To contact
Jossey-Bass directly call our Customer Care Department within the U.S. at 800-956-7739,
outside the U.S. at 317-572-3986 or fax 317-572-4002.

Jossey-Bass also publishes its books in a variety of electronic formats. Some content that
appears in print may not be available in electronic books.

Library of Congress Cataloging-in-Publication Data

Managing knowledge for sustained competitive advantage : designing
strategies for effective human resource management / Susan E. Jackson,
Michael A. Hitt, Angelo S. DeNisi, editors.
    p. cm.
Includes bibliographical references and index.
  ISBN 0-7879-5717-8 (acid-free)
  1. Knowledge management. I. Jackson, Susan E. II. Hitt, Michael A.
III. DeNisi, Angelo S.
  HD30.2.M3646 2003
    658.4'038—dc21

                                                    2002154863

Printed in the United States of America
FIRST EDITION
HB Printing   10 9 8 7 6 5 4 3 2 1

The Organizational Frontiers Series

SERIES EDITOR

Neal Schmitt
Michigan State University

EDITORIAL BOARD

Robert L. Dipboye
Rice University

Fritz Drasgow
University of Illinois

Jennifer George
Rice University

Katherine J. Klein
University of Maryland

Cheri Ostroff
Teachers College-Columbia University

Richard D. Pritchard
Texas A&M

Neal Schmitt
Michigan State University

Contents

Foreword

This is the eighteenth book in a series published by Jossey-Bass that was initiated by the Society for Industrial and Organizational Psychology in 1983. Originally published as the Frontiers Series, the SIOP executive committee voted in 2000 to change the name to the Organizational Frontiers Series in an attempt to enhance its identity and visibility. The purpose of the publication of series volumes in a general sense has been to promote the scientific status of the field. Ray Katzell first edited the series. He was followed by Irwin Goldstein and Sheldon Zedeck. The topics of the volumes and the volume editors are chosen by the editorial board. The series editor and the editorial board then work with the volume editor in planning the volume, and occasionally, in suggesting and selecting chapter authors and content. During the writing of the volume, the series editor often works with the editor and the publisher to bring the manuscript to completion.

The success of the series is evident in the high number of sales—now over forty-five thousand. Volumes have also received excellent reviews, and individual chapters as well as entire volumes have been cited frequently. A recent symposium at the SIOP annual meeting examined the impact of the series on research and theory in industrial and organizational psychology. Although such influence is difficult to track, and volumes have varied in intent and perceived centrality to the discipline, the conclusion of most participants was that the volumes have made a significant impact on research and theory in the field and are regarded as representative of the best the field has to offer.

Another purpose of the series has been to bring scientific research from other disciplines to bear on problems of interest to industrial/organizational psychologists. This volume, edited by

Susan E. Jackson, Michael A. Hitt, and Angelo S. DeNisi, provides an in-depth examination of how organizations—not individuals—can find, recruit, and manage knowledge. I/O psychologists certainly train individuals and are often involved in educational efforts that enhance the knowledge of organizational members, but we do not often look at how the whole organization harnesses knowledge to strategic advantage. This is the focus of the current volume. Even thinking about knowledge in this way represents a departure for organizations that have traditionally considered their resources as commodities such as oil, gas, or other raw materials. Because the book considers different strategies by which organizations can use knowledge effectively, it also brings macro-organizational thinking to a discipline that is usually most concerned with the behavior of individuals. The very first chapter, by DeNisi, Hitt, and Jackson, describes the manner in which the knowledge, skills, abilities, and other characteristics (KSAOs) familiar to I/O psychologists are related to the broader conception of knowledge as that term is used in the strategy and organizational theory literatures.

The book is organized in six parts. The first part, consisting of the chapter by DeNisi, Hitt, and Jackson, lays the basis for the rest of the book; the authors discuss the nature of different types of knowledge, how knowledge-based competition is affecting organizations, and how these ideas relate to innovation and learning in organizations. They also lay out the questions addressed by the authors in the remainder of the book. Part Two consists of three chapters in which the authors describe different strategies by which organizations can acquire important knowledge (David Deeds), what organizational structures promote the flexibility and network building that facilitate the acquisition and development of knowledge (Marlene Fiol), and how organizations design work and what demands are placed on workers in knowledge-based organizations (Susan Mohrman).

In Part Three the authors discuss the manner in which organizations make human resource decisions about knowledge resources (David Lepak and Scott Snell), how organizations attract, recruit, and select individuals into knowledge-based organizations (Elaine Pulakos, David Dorsey, and Walter Borman), and what types of nontraditional employment contracts can be used and how they affect the protection of an organization's knowledge resources

(Alison Davis-Blake and Pamsey Hui). Part Four discusses the manner in which continuous knowledge acquisition and innovation is promoted and developed among individuals and teams (Raymond Noe, Jason Colquitt, Marcia Simmering, and Sharon Alvarez) and how innovation and creativity may be fostered as a means of creating new knowledge (Greg Oldham). The chapter by Edward Lawler examines how performance is measured and rewarded at the individual, team, and organizational levels to realize short- and long-term goals in knowledge-based organizations. Finally, the last chapter in Part Four addresses the retention of employees and knowledge (Steven Maurer, Thomas Lee, and Terence Mitchell). In Part Five the focus is on measurement. Here the authors examine how to assess the culture and climate for organizational learning (Lois Tetrick and Nancy Da Silva), as well as how to measure and monitor knowledge resources at the organizational level (John Boudreau). In the last part of the book, the editors conclude with a summary and integration of the ideas offered in earlier chapters, and they highlight several research issues that deserve attention in the future.

Our target audiences include graduate students in industrial/organizational psychology, human resource management, business strategy, and organizational behavior as well as doctoral level researchers and practitioners who want to learn about the most up-to-date data and theory on the important role knowledge plays in organizations and how organizations can acquire, develop, retain, and use that information strategically to be more productive. I believe that the topics and issues discussed in this book will be novel to many I/O psychologists and human resource practitioners. Although we have read about these topics in our literature, there has not been a similar focus on how they change for organizations whose main resource is knowledge, not raw physical materials. As is obvious from the chapters of the book and the authors chosen by the editors, researchers who do not often interact with each other because of their very different interests can all make interesting and important contributions to our understanding of knowledge-based organizations. To the degree that this book fosters interaction among these researchers and stimulates interest among other I/O researchers and practitioners it will meet the primary goals of the Organizational Frontiers Series stated earlier.

The chapter authors deserve our gratitude for attempting to communicate clearly the nature, application, and implications of the theory and research described in this book. Production of a volume such as this involves the hard work and cooperative effort of many individuals. The chapter authors and the editorial board all played important roles in this endeavor. All royalties from the series volumes are used to help support SIOP financially; none of the individuals involved received remuneration. They deserve our appreciation for taking on a difficult task for the sole purpose of furthering our understanding of organizational science. We also express our sincere gratitude to Cedric Crocker, Julianna Gustafson, Matt Davis, and the entire staff of Jossey-Bass. Over many years and several volumes, they have provided support during the planning, development, and production of the series.

January 2003   Neal Schmitt
                                                   Michigan State University
                                                   Series Editor, 1998–2003

Preface

Traditionally, organizations sought to gain and sustain competitive advantage by acquiring critical resources such as oil or gas supplies. More recently, management scholars have come to appreciate the importance of human resources as a source of competitive advantage. According to this perspective, which is a resource-based view of the firm, firms acquire critical human resources and then establish HR systems that enhance the potential of these human resources. Because both the people and the systems developed are difficult for competitors to copy, they provide a source of sustainable competitive advantage.

Human resources are especially valuable to knowledge-based firms because of their ability to create, use, and share knowledge. Firms need to acquire and retain both tacit and explicit knowledge to be competitive. Once knowledge assets are acquired, organizations and HR systems must be designed in a way that enables employees to use the knowledge and make the firm competitive. Involved in all of these tasks are processes familiar to I/O psychologists, but to date the field has not applied its own knowledge and expertise to the problem of competing through knowledge. One reason may be that I/O psychologists are not sufficiently familiar with the relevant theory, research, and practice to see how they can apply their expertise.

We developed this volume in the hope that it would encourage I/O psychologists to enter the ongoing discussion about how to manage knowledge-based organizations more effectively. We were also convinced that the expertise of I/O psychologists could be applied to enrich future research in the fields of strategic management and organization theory. That is, we were guided by a desire for more two-way interactions between the relatively "micro" research being conducted by many psychologists and the more "macro" research conducted by scholars in management, economics, and sociology. At first, we envisioned this volume serving as a foundation for a grand thoroughfare of such interactions. The final achievement is more modest, however; we might liken it instead to a swinging footbridge, with plenty of construction work left for others to complete.

For us, the editors, the creation of this volume has been a stimulating and enjoyable learning experience. We thank the authors who accepted the challenge of holding a conversation among people who seldom gather at the same party. We also thank Neal Schmitt and the editorial board of SIOP's Organizational Frontiers Series for encouraging us to have the conversation, and for giving us the opportunity now to invite others to join in it. We hope this is the beginning of a party that lasts long into the night.

January 2003   Susan E. Jackson
                                               New Brunswick, New Jersey

                                               Michael A. Hitt
                                               Tempe, Arizona

                                               Angelo S. DeNisi
                                               College Station, Texas

The Contributors

Susan E. Jackson is professor of human resource management in the School of Management and Labor Relations at Rutgers University, where she also serves as graduate director for the doctoral program in industrial relations and human resources. A fellow and active member of the Society of Industrial and Organizational Psychology, and the Academy of Management, her primary area of expertise is the strategic management of human resources and her special interests include managing team effectiveness and workforce diversity. Among her publications on these topics are several books, including *Managing Human Resources through Strategic Partnership* (with R. S. Schuler), *Management* (with D. Hellriegel & J. W. Slocum, Jr.), *Strategic Human Resource Management* (with R. S. Schuler), and *Diversity in the Workplace: Human Resource Initiatives,* and most recently, *Managing Human Resources in Cross-Border Alliances* (with R. S. Schuler and Y. Luo). She is a member of several editorial boards and previously was editor of the *Academy of Management Review.*

Michael A. Hitt is professor and Weatherup/Overby Chair in Executive Leadership at Arizona State University. He has authored or coauthored over two hundred publications. Some of his most recent books are *Strategic Entrepreneurship: Creating a New Integrated Mindset, Creating Value: Winners in the New Business Environment, Mergers and Acquisitions: A Guide to Creating Value for Stakeholders,* and *Handbook of Strategic Management.* He is a fellow and past president of the Academy of Management and former editor of the *Academy of Management Journal;* he currently serves on the board of the Strategic Management Society. Among his many awards are the 1996 Award for Outstanding Academic Contributions to Competitiveness, the 1999 Award for Outstanding Intellectual Contributions to Competitiveness Research from the American Society for Competitiveness, and the 2001 Distinguished Service Award from the Academy of Management.

Angelo S. DeNisi is the Paul M. and Rosalie Robertson Chair in Business Administration and the head of the Department of Management at Texas A&M University. He received his Ph.D. in industrial/organizational psychology at Purdue University, is a fellow of SIOP and APA, and has served as SIOP president. He has also served as one of SIOP's representatives to APA Council, chaired several SIOP committees, and is a recipient of SIOP's William Owens Scholarly Achievement Award. He is a fellow of the Academy of Management, where he has been an active member and served as editor of the *Academy of Management Journal.* He has served on over a dozen editorial boards and has published a scholarly book— *Cognitive Approach to Performance Appraisal: A Program of Research*— as well as a textbook on human resource management with Ricky Griffin.

Sharon A. Alvarez is assistant professor of entrepreneurship in the Department of Management and Human Resources at The Ohio State University. Her research interests include high-technology alliances between entrepreneurial firms and larger established firms, and theory development for entrepreneurship. She has published in the *Academy of Management Executive and Journal of Management* and regularly presents her work at national conferences. She has been active with venture capital and entrepreneurship activities in the Columbus, Ohio, area. In addition to several years of experience working in large corporations, she started and owned a small business, has served on the board of directors for small businesses, and consults in the biotechnology industry.

Walter C. Borman received his Ph.D. in industrial/organizational psychology from the University of California, Berkeley, and is currently CEO of Personnel Decisions Research Institutes (PDRI) and professor of psychology at the University of South Florida. He has published more than 250 books, book chapters, articles, and conference papers in such areas as performance measurement, job analysis, and personnel selection. Borman is a fellow of the Society for Industrial and Organizational Psychology (SIOP) and served as SIOP president in 1994–95.

John W. Boudreau is professor of human resource studies at Cornell University, where he also directs the Center for Advanced Human Resource Studies (CAHRS). His research, which addresses strategic human capital measurement, decision-based HR, executive mobility, HR information systems, and organizational staffing and development, has received the Academy of Management's Organizational Behavior New Concept and Human Resource Scholarly Contribution awards. Boudreau is an active member of the Academy of Management and Society for Industrial and Organizational Psychology and is a fellow of the National Academy of Human Resources. He has published more than forty books and articles, including *Human Resource Management.*

Jason A. Colquitt is assistant professor of management at the University of Florida's Warrington College of Business. He earned his Ph.D. in business administration at Michigan State University's Eli Broad Graduate School of Management. Colquitt's research interests focus on organizational justice, team effectiveness, and personality influences on learning and task performance. He has published articles in these and other areas in the *Academy of Management Journal, Journal of Applied Psychology, Personnel Psychology,* and *Organizational Behavior and Human Decision Processes.*

Nancy Da Silva is assistant professor of industrial/organizational psychology at San Jose State University. She received her Ph.D. in industrial/organizational psychology at the University of Houston. Her research interests include organizational learning, creativity in the workplace, and entrepreneurship.

Alison Davis-Blake is professor of management and Eleanor T. Mosle Fellow at the Red McCombs School of Business, University of Texas at Austin. She received her Ph.D. from Stanford University's Graduate School of Business. Her research interests include the determinants and consequences of workforce externalization, the use of labor market intermediaries, and the outsourcing of professional services. Her current research, funded by the Russell Sage

Foundation and the Rockefeller Foundation, examines the attributes and effectiveness of professional employer organizations and temporary agencies.

David L. Deeds is assistant professor of entrepreneurship at The Weatherhead School of Management at Case Western Reserve University. His research interests include management of strategic alliances, entrepreneurial finance, the process of going public, the biotechnology industry, and management of high-technology ventures. He received the Mescon Award for best empirical research in entrepreneurship at the National Academy of Management meeting in 1996, was awarded the NASDAQ Fellowship in Capital Formation in 1997, and received the Fast Company Award for best paper on high-growth firms at the National Academy of Management meeting in 2000. He is on the editorial boards of *Journal of Business Venturing, Venture Capital: The Journal of Entrepreneurial Finance,* and *Entrepreneurship Theory and Practice,* and is an active consultant to new venture firms.

David W. Dorsey is a research scientist with the Washington, D.C., office of Personnel Decisions Research Institutes (PDRI). He received his Ph.D. in industrial/organizational psychology with a graduate minor in computer science from the University of South Florida. His research and consulting interests cover a range of topics, from information technology and computational modeling to performance management and job analysis. He has served as an invited speaker on issues such as advanced information technologies and his work has been highlighted in professional journals such as the *Journal of Applied Psychology* and *Personnel Psychology.*

C. Marlene Fiol is professor of strategic management at the University of Colorado at Denver. She received her Ph.D. in strategic management from the University of Illinois at Urbana-Champaign. Her research interests include organizational cognition and interpretation, organizational learning, knowledge management, and entrepreneurship.

Pamsy P. Hui is a doctoral candidate in management at the University of Texas at Austin. Her research interests include contracting, interorganizational relationships, organizational learning, and information systems management. Her dissertation research examines the impact of human and social capital on Internet start-up survival chances.

Edward E. Lawler III is Distinguished Professor of Business and Director of the Center for Effective Organizations in the Marshall School of Business at the University of Southern California. He has been honored as a top contributor to the fields of organizational development, human resources management, organizational behavior and compensation. He is the author of over three hundred articles and thirty-five books. His most recent books include *Rewarding Excellence, Corporate Boards: New Strategies for Adding Value at the Top,* and *Organizing for High Performance.*

Thomas W. Lee is professor of organizational behavior and human resource management and the GM Nameplate Endowed Faculty Fellow at the University of Washington Business School. His primary research interests include job embeddedness, voluntary employee turnover, and work motivation. Lee has published over fifty academic articles and is author of *Using Qualitative Methods in Organizational Research.* He has served on eight editorial boards and currently is editor of the *Academy of Management Journal.* He is also an active member of the Academy of Management.

David P. Lepak is assistant professor in management and organization in the Robert H. Smith School of Business at the University of Maryland, College Park. He received his Ph.D. from Pennsylvania State University in human resource management. His research interests focus on the strategic management of human capital. His research has been published in *Academy of Management Journal, Academy of Management Review, Journal of Management, Human Resource Management Review, Journal of Management Studies,* and *Research in Personnel and Human Resource Management.*

Steven D. Maurer is professor of management at Old Dominion University. He conducts research focusing on recruitment, selection, and retention of knowledge workers. He has published in journals such as the *Academy of Management Review, Personnel Psychology* and *Journal of High Technology Management Research,* and in a variety of anthologies and refereed proceedings. He is on the board of the *Academy of Management Journal* and has worked as an AT&T project engineer and engineering employment manager. He also has extensive experience as a course instructor, lecturer, and HR consultant on managing high-technology workforces.

Terence R. Mitchell is the Edward E. Carlson Professor of Business Administration and Professor of Psychology at the University of Washington. He received his Ph.D. in social psychology from the University of Illinois. He is a fellow of SIOP and the Academy of Management and a member of the Society for Organizational Behavior. His research interests are decision making, leadership, motivation, and retention. He received the Scientific Contribution Award from the Society of Industrial/Organizational Psychology, and is a charter gold member of the Hall of Fame of the *Academy of Management Journal.* He has over a hundred publications to his name, including both journal articles and books.

Susan Albers Mohrman is senior research scientist at the Center for Effective Organizations in the Marshall School of Business at the University of Southern California. Her research, publications, and consulting focus on organizational design, human resource management, and organizational change and capability development. Her latest books include *Designing Team-Based Organizations*; *Creating a Strategic Human Resources Function; Tomorrow's Organization: Crafting Winning Capabilities in a Dynamic World;* and *Organizing for High Performance.* She has served on the board of governors of the Academy of Management and is on the board of the Human Resource Planning Society.

Raymond A. Noe is the Robert and Anne Hoyt Designated Professor of Management in the Department of Management and Human Resources at The Ohio State University. He conducts research, teaches, consults, and writes textbooks in human resource management, training and development, and organizational behavior. He has published articles in many academic journals, including *Journal of Applied Psychology, Academy of Management Journal,* and *Personnel Psychology,* and has served on the editorial boards of

Personnel Psychology, Journal of Organizational Behavior, Academy of Management Learning and Education, Journal of Business and Psychology, and *Human Resource Management Review.* A fellow of the Society for Industrial and Organizational Psychology, he received the 2001 American Society for Training & Development Research Award.

Greg R. Oldham is C. Clinton Spivey Distinguished Professor of Business Administration and professor of labor and industrial relations at the University of Illinois at Urbana-Champaign. He received his Ph.D. in organizational behavior from Yale University. His current research focuses on the contextual and personal conditions that prompt the development and expression of creative ideas in organizations. He is a fellow of the Society for Industrial and Organizational Psychology and a fellow and past president of the Academy of Management.

Elaine D. Pulakos is vice president and director of Personnel Decisions Research Institutes' Washington, D.C., office. Pulakos has been president, secretary, member-at-large, and program chair for the Society for Industrial and Organizational Psychology. Her research and consulting interests are focused in the areas of staffing and performance management, and her research has appeared in several scholarly journals. She has recently coedited two books: *The Changing Nature of Performance: Implications for Staffing, Motivation and Development* (with Dan Ilgen), and *Implementing Organizational Interventions: Steps, Processes, and Best Practices* (with Jerry Hedge). Pulakos is a fellow of the American Psychological Association and the Society for Industrial and Organizational Psychology.

Marcia J. Simmering received her doctorate in management from Michigan State University. She is currently assistant professor of management in the College of Business Administration at Louisiana State University. Her research in the area of training has been published in the *Journal of Applied Psychology* and has been presented at several national conferences, including SIOP and the Academy of Management. Simmering has developed and evaluated Web-based applications for several universities and business organizations.

Scott A. Snell is professor of human resource studies and director of executive education in the School of Industrial and Labor Relations at Cornell University. He received his Ph.D. from Michigan State University. His research interests combine strategic management, knowledge management, and human resources. His research has appeared in *Academy of Management Journal, Academy of Management Review, Human Resource Management, Journal of Management, Personnel Psychology,* and *Strategic Management Journal.* He has served on the editorial boards of *Journal of Managerial Issues, Human Resource Management, Human Resource Management Review, Human Resource Planning,* and *Academy of Management Journal.*

Lois E. Tetrick is professor of psychology at the University of Houston. She received her doctorate in industrial/organizational psychology from the Georgia Institute of Technology. She is a fellow of the American Psychological Association, the Society for Industrial and Organizational Psychology, and the American Psychological Society. She has served as chair of the human resources division of the Academy of Management and associate editor of *Journal of Applied Psychology* and is currently an associate editor for *Journal of Occupational Health Psychology.* Her research has focused primarily on individuals' perceptions of the employment relationship and their reactions to these perceptions, including issues of the exchange relationship between employee and employer, occupational health and safety, occupational stress, organizational commitment, and organizational learning.

Managing Knowledge for Sustained Competitive Advantage

PART 1

Introduction

CHAPTER 1

The Knowledge-Based Approach to Sustainable Competitive Advantage

Angelo S. DeNisi
Michael A. Hitt
Susan E. Jackson

In the twenty-first-century landscape, firms must compete in a complex and challenging context that is being transformed by many factors, from globalization, technological development, and increasingly rapid diffusion of new technology, to the development and use of knowledge (Hitt, Keats, & DeMarie, 1998). This new landscape requires firms to do things differently in order to survive and prosper. Specifically, they must look to new sources of competitive advantage and engage in new forms of competition. This, in turn, requires a clear understanding of the nature of competition and competitive dynamics.

One popular approach to understanding competitive dynamics is the resource-based view of the firm. According to this view, the explanation for why some firms ultimately succeed and others fail can be found in understanding their resources and capabilities. A firm's resources and capabilities influence both the strategic choices that managers make and the implementation of those chosen strategies. (The recent debate over this model suggests there are challenges involved in applying it; see Priem & Butler, 2001; Barney, 2001.)

To understand why certain competitive strategies are more effective than others, one must consider the distribution of resources in competing firms. Although a given firm may possess more or less of any particular resource, only those resources that are rare, valuable, and difficult to imitate provide a sustainable competitive advantage (Amit & Schoemaker, 1993; Barney, 1991; Schoenecker & Cooper, 1998). When the strategies employed are successful in leveraging the firm's rare, valuable, and difficult-to-imitate resources, that firm is likely to gain an advantage over its competitors in the marketplace and thus earn higher returns (Hitt, Nixon, Clifford, & Coyne, 1999). Competitive advantages that are sustained over time lead to higher performance (Peteraf, 1993).

These arguments are somewhat clear when we consider tangible resources such as buildings, machinery, or access to capital. And in the more traditional competitive landscape, these tangible resources were the most important potential sources of competitive advantage. Thus, if a firm could modernize its plant, or develop a more efficient distribution process, or access cheaper credit, it could compete successfully and prosper. But firms employ both tangible and intangible resources in the development and implementation of strategies, and as the nature of work and competition changes, intangible resources are becoming more important. Examples of intangible resources are reputation, brand equity, and—for our purposes the most important of these—human capital. In fact, in any competitive landscape it has been argued that intangible resources are more likely to produce a competitive advantage because they often are truly rare and can be more difficult for competitors to imitate (see Black & Boal, 1994; Itami, 1987; Rao, 1994).

Among a firm's intangible resources, human capital may be the most important and critical for competitive advantage because it is the most difficult to imitate. For example, Miller and Shamsie (1996) discussed the role of stars, or "talent," in the success of the Hollywood studios in their heyday, the 1930s and 1940s. The stars were developed so that each had a unique reputation or image that was difficult for a rival studio to imitate. Yet as Miller and Shamsie note, rival studios often *did* try to develop their own versions of other studios' stars by trying to imitate their "image"—for example, Warner Brothers developed Tyrone Power to compete with MGM's Clark Gable. But this approach was generally unsuccessful because it focused on the star alone.

In the competitive environment of the motion picture industry at that time, imitating only the star was rarely enough to create similar value. This was because the star's value to the studio was enhanced through integration with other studio resources. Thus, having a great musical talent was an important resource for a studio. But in order for the studio to turn that talent into a competitive advantage, it also needed people who could successfully write musicals, someone to direct them, and still others who could costume a star in a musical, design the right makeup, and film the movie in the best way. In other words, the star's value was partly a function of the others at the studio with whom he or she worked. Therefore, social complexity and ambiguity is created, making the integration of these resources difficult to imitate.

A firm's access to such bundles of integrated resources and the difficulty of imitating them are the ultimate source of competitive advantage. Any organization that seeks a competitive advantage through human resources thus must both acquire the "right" resources and take the steps required to leverage them.

Generally speaking, human capital is more mobile than other intangible resources (see Teece, Pisano, & Shuen, 1997). Therefore, it may seem an unlikely source of sustained competitive advantage. The Hollywood studios sought to reduce the mobility of human capital by signing their stars to long-term exclusive contracts. Such contracts are no longer feasible in the movie industry, nor are they usually feasible elsewhere. Yet the mobility of human capital is less a threat to competitive advantage than it would first seem to be. Once an organization integrates human capital with other complementary resources (as explained earlier) and uses this integration to create organizational capabilities (that is, leverages them), losing one or a few individuals may not lead to a loss of competitive advantage. Instead, a competitor would have to gain access to all of the resources and the system in place to leverage those resources. Thus, returning to the studio example, a rival studio would have had to lure away the star, the writer, the director, the costume designer, and the cameraperson in order to gain a sustainable advantage—an extremely difficult task. As a result, despite the mobility of talented employees, human capital is now seen as one of the most important sources of competitive advantage.

Human Capital as a Strategic Resource

Human capital is a general term that refers to all of the resources that individuals directly contribute to an organization: physical, knowledge, social, and reputational. However, we need to understand what it is about human capital resources that helps individuals contribute to gaining and sustaining a competitive advantage. During the industrial age, human capital was valued because of physical resources such as strength, endurance, and dexterity—these were the aspects of human capital that were most likely to lead to competitive advantage. But as new machinery and technology were introduced, these characteristics became less important. In the current economic landscape, human capital is more likely to be valued for intellect, social skills, and reputation.

For example, Miller and Shamsie (1996) noted that the studios' reliance on long-term contracts with well-developed stars (or "properties," as they called them) was successful only as long as the competitive environment was predictable and stable. When the studios lost their movie theaters, the stars gained more power, and the television grew as an entertainment alternative for the general public, this approach to gaining competitive advantage was no longer successful. In the more dynamic environment, managing knowledge-based resources, or intellectual resources, became the key. In today's competitive environment, where there is even more uncertainty and dynamism, these knowledge-based resources are even more important than they were in the past.

The term *knowledge-based resources* refers to skills, abilities, and learning capacity. People can develop these through experience and formal training. *Social resources* (now sometimes referred to as *social capital*) include the personal relationships that bind together members of an organization as well as relationships that link organizational members to other external sources of human capital. Through social capital, individuals can gain access both to other human resources (the physical and intellectual capital, for example) and to other forms of capital (financial, for example). *Repu-

tational capital is less personal. Often it accrues through associations with prestigious organizations. For example, people with degrees from the more respected educational institutions have greater access to valued resources simply because of the reputation of their alma maters.

We must emphasize again, however, that it is not enough to acquire individuals who have such attributes. It is also necessary to develop structures, systems, and strategies that allow the organization to exploit the resources and gain competitive advantage. For example, a football team that acquires a strong passing quarterback only gains a competitive advantage when it shifts its offensive strategy to focus on passing. Professional baseball teams often have groundskeepers cut the grass closer (or not) depending on whether the team currently includes players who tend to hit ground balls into the infield. In these ways, the teams leverage their resources to gain an advantage.

Professional service firms leverage their human capital by forming project teams led by senior experienced professionals, often partners in the firm. The other members of the project teams usually are younger, less experienced associates. In this way, they leverage their most valuable human capital to complete projects for clients. Working together on the project also allows the associates to gain some of the tacit knowledge possessed by the more senior partners; they learn by doing (Hitt, Bierman, Shimizu, & Kochhar, 2001).

Of course, some scholars and practitioners have always understood the role of human capital in creating an organization's success. Carly Fiorina, CEO of Hewlett-Packard, emphasized the role of human capital in an address she made to MIT graduates: "The most magical and tangible and ultimately the most important ingredient in the transformed landscape is people. The greatest strategy . . . , the greatest financial plan . . . , the greatest turnaround . . . , is only going to be temporary if it is not grounded in people" (Fiorina, 2000). The field of I/O psychology has also recognized the important role human capital plays in organizational effectiveness and performance, and has long suggested better ways to select and develop employees.

Nevertheless, I/O psychology has traditionally been concerned only with the acquisition and development of these resources.

There has been little concern with how to integrate them into an overall strategy that would enable a firm to leverage the resources it acquires or develops. Furthermore, I/O psychologists have been primarily concerned with improving individual performance, and more recently, work group performance. They assume that improving performance at these levels will lead to improvement at the organizational level, but this assumption is seldom tested. For example, psychologists have recommended hiring "better" employees, which often means employees with greater intellectual or knowledge resources, but mostly because these employees could be expected to perform their jobs with greater proficiency. The assessment of performance has been almost exclusively at the level of the individual or the team, and little attention has been paid to the processes or structures by which individual or team-level performance could be translated to organizational-level performance or competitive advantage (for example, DeNisi, 2000).

Utility analysis (see Boudreau, 1991; Cascio, 1987) has allowed the fields of I/O psychology and human resource management to demonstrate further how these increases in performance can be expressed in real dollars. Usually, work in this area (for example, Huselid, 1995) calculates the value of human resource practices rather than the value of the human resources themselves. Research in other areas, however, has demonstrated how human resources can produce higher organizational performance (Wright, Smart, & McMahon, 1995; Pennings, Lee, & van Witteloostuijn, 1998), especially when these resources are used explicitly in the implementation of a firm's strategies (Hitt, Bierman et al., 2001).

This brings us to one of the primary purposes of this volume: to encourage I/O psychologists to think more about the implications of their work for firm performance and competitive advantage. Some I/O scholars *have* begun to think about their work in these broader terms, but it is still the exception rather than the rule (for example, Jackson & Schuler, 2001; Klein, Dansereau, & Hall, 1994; Klein & Kozlowski, 2000; Schuler & Jackson, 1987; Schweiger & DeNisi, 1991). We hope to change that. We also want to focus attention on a specific but very important subset of human capital resources: knowledge-based resources. As noted earlier, in the new competitive landscape knowledge-based resources are the most critical for gaining sustained competitive advantage.

We also believe it is important for I/O psychologists to appreciate that organizations do not achieve and sustain a competitive advantage simply by possessing knowledge-based (or any other unique) resources. The firm must effectively manage those resources in ways that allow it to leverage and exploit them. *Capabilities* refer to a firm's ability to integrate and deploy its resources to achieve a desired goal (Hitt, Ireland, & Hoskisson, 2001). Thus, we also have created this volume to help I/O psychologists understand how they can work with organizations and assist them in developing the strategic capabilities they need to gain and sustain a competitive advantage. We begin by discussing in more detail exactly what we mean by knowledge-based resources.

Knowledge-Based Resources

Knowledge-based resources include all the intellectual abilities and knowledge possessed by employees, as well as their capacity to learn and acquire more knowledge. Thus, knowledge-based resources include what employees have mastered as well as their potential for adapting and acquiring new information. For several reasons, these resources are seen as being extremely important for sustaining competitive advantage in today's environment.

First, the nature of work has been changing over the past several decades, so that many jobs require people to think, plan, or make decisions, rather than to lift, assemble, or build. This kind of work requires both tacit and explicit knowledge (see the following section) and the ability to apply that knowledge to work. I/O psychologists have traditionally been capable of determining the levels of knowledge possessed by job applicants and helping organizations select people based on their knowledge. Psychologists and HR specialists have also been successful in identifying an individual's potential to learn specific material through the use of aptitude tests. Furthermore, these groups have been adept at designing training programs that provide employees with the knowledge they presently lack (assuming they have the aptitude to learn).

But work continues to change, and in unpredictable ways. It is often difficult to state exactly what kinds of knowledge a person needs to succeed on the job, and it is almost impossible to predict what types of knowledge he or she will need in the future. Change and unpredictability in organizations mean that knowledge-based resources such as the ability to learn and personality traits such as adaptability are extremely important, and some organizations have begun rewarding employees financially when they demonstrate an ability to acquire and master new knowledge (see, for example, Jenkins & Gupta, 1985; Gerhart, 2000; Lawler, Chapter Ten, this volume).

Still, it is not enough to select employees who have knowledge resources, or even to help them to acquire such resources by providing training or offering rewards for increasing their knowledge. Organizations must also find new ways to leverage these resources to gain competitive advantage. For example, the literature includes a fair amount of work describing the resources that must be available to teams in order for them to be successful. Some studies have examined the resources that should be possessed by the team as a whole, such as expertise, collectivism, and flexibility (for example, Campion, Medsker, & Higgs, 1993) whereas others have focused on individual resources, such as general mental ability and conscientiousness (for example, Barrick, Stewart, Neubert, & Mount, 1998). An organization might select highly conscientious individuals or train a team to develop more collectivist values, but neither of these routes would lead to sustained competitive advantage. Competitive advantage is gained only when the organization selects or develops these resources *and* structures work tasks and the reward system in ways that motivate the team to perform well and thereby contribute to organizational effectiveness (see, for example, Guzzo & Shea, 1992). Team effectiveness may be enhanced through selection and training, but competitive advantage comes only when the organization structures rewards and work to leverage those effective teams to improve organizational performance (see, for example, Jackson & Schuler, 2002).

Many knowledge (and other) resources may be acquired by hiring new individuals, and these resources may improve performance of a job or even the performance of a team or work unit. In order to become sources of competitive advantage, however, such individual resources must increase performance at the organizational level. We shall return to a discussion of ways in which individual resources can be used to improve organizational performance later. First, though, we consider alternative methods for acquiring valued knowledge resources.

Acquiring Knowledge-Based Resources

Although selection and training (or development) are reasonable means by which to acquire knowledge-based resources, they are time consuming and may be inefficient. For example, to select a number of highly intelligent employees an organization would have to convince a large number of such employees to apply for available jobs. Assuming the organization could then identify the "most" intelligent among the applicants and make offers to these individuals, it would then be necessary to convince them to accept these jobs.

Developing needed competencies may not be simple either. The development of some specific knowledge-based competencies may actually require that employees possess other abilities or characteristics (for example, aptitudes) that are absent in a firm's current workforce. Fortunately, there are other ways for a firm to acquire valuable resources, such as with mergers, acquisitions, and strategic alliances.

Firms frequently acquire or merge with other firms in order to gain access to new products or other specialized knowledge (for example, Hitt, Hoskisson, Johnson, & Moesel, 1996; Barkema & Vermeulen, 1998). Merger and acquisition (M&A) targets are often chosen because of their complementary resources and knowledge bases.

Alternatively, a firm may decide that a permanent relationship with the target firm is not desirable. For example, there may be a special project that requires knowledge resources not available to the firm but that are available elsewhere. Although it might be possible to acquire or merge with the other firm, the project, and therefore the need for those resources, may have a limited time horizon. In such cases, instead of forming an entirely new entity or acquiring the new firm, a firm may decide simply to form a strategic alliance, such as some type of joint venture. In either case, however, the goal is to acquire (even if temporarily) the valued resources of the other firm; partners are chosen in much the same ways as targets for mergers and acquisitions (Hitt, Dacin, Levitas, Arregle, & Borza, 2000; Kogut & Zander, 1992, 1996).

Acquiring knowledge from external sources and internalizing it can be difficult. Internalizing new knowledge requires adequate *absorptive capacity*, or the ability to identify, assimilate, and use additional knowledge (Cohen & Levinthal, 1990). Normally, individuals or groups cannot "absorb" additional knowledge that is too different from their current knowledge base (Grant, 1996) because they cannot identify or understand it. Thus, firms that engage in M&A activity can benefit by developing their capability for assessing the extent to which the other firm's knowledge base is similar or complementary to their own. They can also benefit from developing routines to integrate new knowledge (Levitt & March, 1988). For example, some firms have special units that identify new valuable knowledge in the organization and then find ways to diffuse (communicate) it throughout the organization. As is true for any method of acquiring knowledge resources, this method has its own challenges. Issues of culture clash and the inability of employees to adapt to new ways of doing things are serious threats to the effectiveness of this approach to acquiring knowledge-based resources (Schuler, Jackson, & Luo, 2003).

Aggregating Knowledge-Based Resources

Whatever resources are acquired, no matter the manner in which they are acquired, they need to be aggregated to the highest level of use or application. That is, if a firm acquires individual-level knowledge resources through selection or training, it must find a way to "leverage up" those resources to the team level and eventually to the organizational level. Even if a firm acquires a special expertise through a merger, it is necessary to diffuse that expertise throughout the entire organization. Otherwise, the effects of these knowledge-based resources on competitiveness will be limited.

This problem is the same one facing scholars interested in relating human resource practices to firm performance. For example, if hiring "better" people results in higher productivity, how exactly does the selection of individuals translate into improved organizational performance? The performance improvements that come with each new person hired do not simply add up to greater productivity and competitiveness. Several scholars have proposed models to explain how individual performance is transformed into team and eventually firm performance (see, for example, Ostroff & Bowen, 2000), but there is little empirical documentation on the validity of these models.

Empirical work on the processes through which firms aggregate and leverage the knowledge-based resources of individuals to create a competitive advantage also is scarce. Nevertheless, it seems reasonable to assert that leveraging individuals' knowledge requires an organization to develop systems and processes by which individuals who have the critical knowledge transmit this information to others in the organization who can use it (see, for example, Iles, Yolles, & Altman, 2001, for a model of how this might be accomplished).

In addition to implementing structures for effective communications, organizations must encourage employees to try new ideas. A recent study (Edmondson, 1999) demonstrated the importance of a supportive climate for increasing creativity and innovation in organizations. Employees are not likely to disseminate their knowledge and try to leverage it if they are afraid of failing. Organizations must make employees feel that it is safe to fail before effective knowledge transfer and innovation will occur. Cultures and climates that clearly signal the value of knowledge sharing and communication contribute to a firm's s ability to leverage its knowledge-based resources. Indeed, Pfeffer and Sutton (2001) view this as one of the most important aspects of leadership, noting that a leader's task "is to help build systems of practice that produce a more reliable transformation of knowledge into action" (p. 261). These authors also suggest that successful companies have management practices that create an environment and culture "valuing the building and transfer of knowledge" (p. 261). When a firm combines its knowledge resources with management practices such as these, it creates the knowledge-based capabilities it needs to compete successfully in a knowledge-intensive economy.

Knowledge-Based Capabilities

Strategic capabilities refer to those systems or processes that an organization creates to leverage its resources to produce a competitive advantage. In the context of knowledge-based resources we have discussed issues relating to the acquisition or development of these resources and ways in which we can carry these resources up to higher levels of analysis. Increasingly, knowledge-based capabilities are recognized as among the most strategically important capabilities for creating a sustainable competitive advantage (Grant,

1996; Marsh & Ranft, 1999; Nonaka, 1994; Simonin, 1999). Proponents of a knowledge-based approach to competitive advantage argue that the primary purpose of a firm is to create and apply knowledge (DeCarolis & Deeds, 1999).

Two important types of knowledge are tacit knowledge and explicit knowledge. *Tacit knowledge* is grounded in experience and difficult to express through mere verbal instruction; individuals know it but cannot articulate it. Because tacit knowledge is difficult to codify, it is passed along to others through direct experience (Polanyi, 1973; Reed & DeFillippi, 1990). Therefore, it is sometimes termed *subjective knowledge, personal knowledge,* or *procedural knowledge.*

Explicit knowledge, in contrast, can be formalized, codified, and communicated. Explicit knowledge has also been referred to as *objective knowledge* and *declarative knowledge* (Kogut & Zander, 1992). Explicit knowledge is often gained through formal education and training programs, but it can also be gained through experience on the job. Indeed, an important objective of many electronic information-sharing systems is to ensure that the organization captures the explicit knowledge that employees gain through their experience on the job. However, it must be emphasized that some of the experience may entail explicit knowledge that can be transferred in this way, but other experience produces tacit knowledge that cannot be transferred in this way.

Designing and effectively implementing an electronic information system for storing and distributing knowledge is one of the more familiar approaches to developing a capability for managing knowledge, but there are many others. Electronic knowledge management systems focus mostly on information storage and distribution. Other approaches focus more on knowledge creation (for example, through research and development) and continuous change that reflects new knowledge (for example, organizational learning).

Research and Development

World-class research and development activities (R&D) represent a knowledge-based capability that serves as a competitive advantage for firms pursuing innovation. The primary intent of R&D is to develop new ideas about products, processes, or services. Both knowledge and social capital contribute to the success of R&D efforts. Innovations often build on cutting-edge knowledge. To convert such knowledge into important innovations usually requires individuals in the organization to combine the knowledge with an understanding of the market, collectively use the results of the research to build a new product, and then work to commercialize it (Hitt, Hoskisson, & Nixon, 1993; Hitt, Nixon, Hoskisson, & Kochhar, 1999). Thus, the ability to combine existing knowledge to generate new applications and exploit the unrealized potential of existing knowledge is another knowledge capability that can contribute to a firm's ability to achieve sustainable competitive advantage.

Organizational Learning

Miller (1996) defined organizational learning as the acquisition of knowledge by individuals and groups who are willing to apply it in their jobs in making decisions and influencing others to accomplish tasks important for the organization. Whereas a single instance of organizational learning (that is, a single change event) may be relatively easy for other organizations to imitate, *continuous* organizational learning has cumulative effects that are much more difficult to imitate. Thus, continuous learning is an important capability that can serve as a source of sustainable competitive advantage. As a result, many highly competitive organizations now invest in developing the capability for continuous organizational learning.

Training and development programs are commonly used to promote organizational learning. Such programs seek to increase the knowledge capital, and to a lesser extent, the social capital of employees. Most training and development programs focus on ensuring that employees have the most up-to-date, explicit knowledge in their respective areas of specialization. Because explicit knowledge is well known, programs for its dissemination can be easily imitated. Although it is necessary to maintain competitive parity, explicit knowledge usually cannot serve as the basis for a sustainable competitive advantage.

But tacit knowledge is not easily disseminated. Tacit knowledge must be learned by using it, and this often requires extended periods of social interaction. Because tacit knowledge is learned by experience, the transfer of such knowledge is generally a slow and complex process (Teece et al., 1997). Thus, management practices aimed at leveraging tacit knowledge are more difficult for outsiders to understand and imitate successfully. A strategic alliance such as a joint venture can be useful for transferring tacit knowledge because it allows partners' employees to get close enough to transfer tacit knowledge (Lane & Lubatkin, 1998). Another approach to transferring tacit knowledge is to assign more experienced professionals to lead a team of less experienced professionals (Baron & Kreps, 1999; Sherer, 1995). Over time, the less experienced professionals learn the more experienced professionals' tacit skills (Hitt, Bierman et al., 2001). Organizations with significant learning capabilities understand the importance of both tacit and explicit knowledge and are able to ensure that both types of knowledge are used to promote learning.

Knowledge-Based Competition and I/O Psychology

We believe that competing on the basis of knowledge will be critical for organizational success in the coming years. Although many of the activities that organizations can use to enhance and leverage their knowledge resources occur at the level of individuals and work teams, organizational effectiveness also requires developing organizational capabilities for leveraging and exploiting knowledge. I/O psychologists can help firms achieve a knowledge-based competitive advantage in several ways. First, many programs initiated at the strategic level are designed to affect individuals. I/O psychologists can contribute, then, by providing models and theories of how these programs are likely to influence the behavior of individuals and groups. Second, I/O psychologists can examine how traditional I/O interventions may be used to increase the knowledge resources of the organization. Third, I/O psychologists can help design organizational programs and systems that help firms leverage and exploit the knowledge they hold.

A merger or acquisition is a strategic action that is not likely to succeed unless it is implemented in a manner that ensures individual employees behave as anticipated. As noted earlier, mergers and acquisitions do not guarantee that a firm's knowledge will increase. Although the knowledge of the acquired firm becomes the property of the acquirer, knowledge resides primarily in individuals, making it quite mobile. Often there is substantial turnover of key professionals and top-level executives (Schweiger & DeNisi, 1991; Walsh, 1988, 1989). If key employees in the acquired firm leave before the firms are successfully combined (or even shortly thereafter), important human capital (and knowledge) is lost. Thus, controlling turnover can be critical for successful knowledge acquisition and future learning. Even if all the human capital is retained, problems of integrating the acquired firm into the acquiring firm also can create barriers to learning (Hitt, Harrison, & Ireland, 2001). For example, different compensation systems for managers in the two original firms can lead to jealousy and hinder cooperation between managers of the two firms. Thus, expertise about how to design compensation systems that encourage collaboration can also be useful to firms that need to retain knowledge resources after a merger or acquisition.

Human capital may be important in firm expansion strategies. For example, firms that desire to expand their operations into new geographic locations can use the social capital of key employees through their relationships with customers and suppliers. Professional service firms may open offices in new cities where their current customers have operations. In so doing they can more effectively serve their current customers, but they can also use their current customers to identify and serve new customers. They may use their current employees to manage the new office and social contacts to hire new professional employees to staff the new office. Finally, they expand the use of their top employees' knowledge in serving customers in the new geographic regions (Hitt, Bierman et al., 2001). Likewise, firms may learn from the new markets that they enter. For example, a firm may enter a new geographic region where a new technology has been developed and used. The firm entering this market may learn the new technical capabilities by hiring employees with this knowledge to staff the new operation (Zahra, Ireland, & Hitt, 2000).

Decisions about organizational design are another arena in which I/O psychologists should be (and sometimes are) actively involved in applying psychological models and theories to improve the ability of organizations to develop and manage new models of employment effectively. For example, it is becoming increasingly common to use contract workers instead of permanent employees, in part because of the economic flexibility associated with this approach (see, for example, Pearce, 1993). Employing contract workers provides access to needed skills but does not commit a company to the costs and obligations associated with hiring permanent employees. But because contract workers only provide their knowledge to the firm for a limited time and often receive no incentives to help others learn their skills, usually very little organizational learning occurs. In fact, it may be to their disadvantage to help an organization learn the knowledge they hold unless they are given special incentives to do so. If the organization acquires their knowledge, it may have little need of their services in the future.

I/O psychologists can improve the learning occurring in organizations that rely heavily on contract workers by helping to design work settings and incentive structures that support knowledge sharing and learning. I/O psychologists know a fair amount about how to improve commitment (for example, Shore & Wayne, 1993) and how to translate commitment into extra-role behaviors (for example, Williams & Anderson, 1991). It may be premature to surmise that conclusions from past research, conducted mostly with permanent employees, generalize to contract workers. Nevertheless, this knowledge base provides a strong foundation for additional research that would position I/O psychologists to help organizations better leverage the knowledge resources of contract employees.

There are numerous ways in which I/O psychologists might contribute to a firm's capability to gain a sustainable competitive advantage by more effectively leveraging its human capital and developing its knowledge capabilities. In fact, there have been some attempts to describe, in general terms, how outcomes might result (see, for example, Jackson & Schuler, 2000, 2001). But there are many other possibilities as well. For example, performance appraisal and performance management systems can be designed to encourage employees to learn and share their knowledge with others. The organizational culture can be developed to encourage innovation and learning. Selection systems can be built to assess tacit knowledge and learning capacity effectively. The purpose of this volume is to stimulate additional thinking, new research efforts, and the sharing of practical experiences relevant to the intersection of knowledge-based competition and I/O psychology. Specifically, our primary goals in this volume are the following:

- To increase awareness among I/O psychologists of the dynamics of knowledge-based competition
- To increase awareness among I/O psychologists of the ways in which organizational-level variables and processes affect the development and use of knowledge in organizations
- To present some alternative ways for I/O psychologists to use their expertise to improve our understanding of and the implementation of knowledge-based strategies
- To encourage I/O psychologists to conduct research that can help firms more effectively compete in a knowledge-based economy

Secondarily, we also intend for this volume to increase awareness among scholars outside the I/O arena of the potential contributions that I/O psychologists can make to this field of study.

By adapting I/O psychology's models and approaches to achieve competitive advantage through knowledge, organizations and I/O psychologists will gain. We believe that I/O psychology research can become highly relevant to the problems and issues that top management in organizations is facing. We also believe that other management scholars can gain by learning more about the ways in which I/O research models and theories can contribute to the processes underlying knowledge-based competition. Certainly, organizations will gain from these I/O psychology contributions, because their competitiveness and overall performance should be enhanced. As the volume emphasizes, knowledge ultimately resides in individuals. It is therefore critical that scholars with the expertise in dealing with human phenomena focus on knowledge management. This expertise can help top management to understand better how to use their knowledge-based resources to gain competitive advantage.

Plan for This Volume

This book is composed of six main sections and fourteen chapters. The introductory and concluding chapters—which represent Parts One and Six, respectively, and were prepared by the editors—are wrapped around the primary contributions of the book. Part Two is composed of three chapters that address the structuring of knowledge development and application in organizations. Part Three focuses on the human resource management architecture facilitating knowledge management and acquiring knowledge through hiring employees and contract workers. Part Four examines means of developing, diffusing, applying, and retaining knowledge through human resource management systems. Part Five discusses approaches to assessing culture, climate, and knowledge-based resources in organizations. Following are concise descriptions of the chapters' content.

Work and Organizational Designs for Knowledge-Based Competition

Chapter Two, authored by David Deeds, deals with macro strategies that firms use to acquire knowledge. The chapter is based on the proposition that firms that effectively acquire knowledge are able to create and sustain a competitive advantage. Deeds examines several means for acquiring knowledge from external sources, including strategic alliances, joint ventures, licensing, and mergers with or acquisitions of other firms. He also explores the importance of social relations across firm boundaries for acquiring knowledge (that is, transferring knowledge across firm boundaries). The biopharmaceutical industry is used as an example to illustrate the need for and means of transferring knowledge across company boundaries. Deeds also notes some of the risks involved in acquiring knowledge from external sources. In short, firms that open their knowledge to acquisition by other firms risk losing their competitive position to these firms in future competition. Therefore, he argues, the success of such transactions between firms depends on their ability to maintain a strong positive relationship.

Chapter Three, written by Marlene Fiol, highlights three important premises for knowledge-based competition. Fiol argues that knowledge exists at both individual and organizational levels in both explicit and tacit forms and that the competition for knowledge is universal. Finally, no single competitive advantage is sustainable in the current hypercompetitive environment. Knowledge must be continuously changed and new knowledge developed in order to survive and succeed. Fiol uses metaphors about pipelines and rivers to explain the diffusion of knowledge in organizations. The pipeline view of knowledge transmission is based on the assumption that knowledge can be manipulated, stored, and disseminated like water in a pipeline. In contrast, the assumption that knowledge exists as a process among people suggests that it is more like a river. In other words, knowledge is embodied and only has meaning that is assigned to it by people, much like the boundaries of a river that are defined by the water running through it. Knowledge transmission in this form is more difficult to manage than in a pipeline. Changing the volume and direction of a river is challenging and must be well planned and implemented. Fiol discusses some of the means of managing knowledge (for example, information technology) along with their limitations. She suggests that a number of these knowledge management techniques are based on the assumption of knowledge flowing through a pipeline rather than a river. As an alternative to this approach, she recommends using technology to support work that requires knowledge creation, dissemination, and application. Furthermore, she recommends improved organizational structures (configurations of positions, job duties, and lines of authority) to facilitate knowledge management. Her discussion includes top-down management and flattened structures along with the role of trust in managing knowledge in organizations. Fiol's work is creative and thought-provoking.

The third and final chapter in this section (Chapter Four) was authored by Susan Mohrman. It examines designing work to manage knowledge better for a competitive advantage. Mohrman argues that new organizational forms and designs of work are necessary to manage knowledge effectively in current organizations. She describes an historical perspective on work design but especially emphasizes a framework for a knowledge-based work design. In particular, she argues for several principles to guide the design of knowledge-based work. First, she suggests the design of work for systemic performance. Essentially, she suggests that work be designed to connect elements of a system, thereby differentiating and clarifying accountability and responsibility for each of the parts. All employees share responsibility for their part of the system but also for the performance of the system as a whole. Second, she recommends creating dynamic work designs. She notes that because of the dynamic environment in which organizations exist, no work designs should be permanent. Rather, continuous evaluation and revision may be necessary. Third, she suggests focusing on sequences of assignments rather than on jobs. In this scenario, individuals do not have stable jobs; instead, there are dynamic knowledge processes and tasks on which people with various skills and types and levels of knowledge are deployed. Fourth, she suggests that the distinction between managerial and knowledge work should be blurred. In fact, she argues that managerial and leadership work is simply one form of knowledge-based work. Fifth, she recommends the design of work to enable processes that cut across boundaries, such as disciplines, functions, geographic areas, and product and service groupings, as well as sets of customers, so that the design of work is independent of individuals' "home base" in the organization. Next, she recommends designing work to develop talent; development should not be seen as separate from work but rather as an integral part of it. Finally, she recommends emphasizing the employment relationship. The organization's expectations for employee performance and contribution should be related to the outcomes employees experience from their performance and contribution. Mohrman's chapter provides an interesting and forward-thinking view of designing work in a knowledge-based environment.

Staffing Organizations for Knowledge-Based Competition

Chapter Five, by David Lepak and Scott Snell, examines the management of human resource architecture to facilitate and enhance knowledge-based competition. Essentially, Lepak and Snell discuss how organizations acquire, allocate, and manage the human capital needed to be successful. Their architectural perspective views the firm as a portfolio of human capital; employees contribute to a firm's competitive advantage based on the knowledge they possess and the jobs they perform. Firms must understand the knowledge base of their employees and establish mechanisms whereby these employees can apply and share that knowledge. Lepak and Snell describe the types of knowledge that individual employees may hold and concerns about the mobility and retention of these employees (and thereby their knowledge). They suggest that the mobility of employees is directly related to the degree of transferability of their knowledge and skills to different organizational contexts. In addition, Lepak and Snell examine the management of knowledge with employees working as cohorts or groups. The strategic value and uniqueness of the knowledge held by both individuals and groups of employees create contingencies for how organizations manage this knowledge. Finally, they explore managing knowledge at the organizational level, focusing specifically on managing the portfolio of human capital competencies. In this discussion, they examine how knowledge can be leveraged across the human resource management architecture. Their goal is to enhance employee contributions to organizational performance.

Chapter Six, by Elaine Pulakos, David Dorsey, and Wally Borman, examines how firms can use staffing practices to acquire knowledge resources. The authors focus on the more traditional I/O psychology approach of recruiting and hiring individual talent to enhance human capital and the base of knowledge, and they discuss the competition for star performers and their recruitment to build the firm's competitive advantage. In particular, they recommend recruiting strategies that emphasize the person-organization fit because of the fluidity of jobs and the continual movement of key organization members from team to team and project to project. They assert that organizations can develop a competitive edge in attracting star performers by developing and communicating organizational images and reputations that are attractive to them. They recommend offering creative compensation packages (for example, luxury cars, club memberships, and so on). The authors also examine the sources of recruiting knowledge workers, professionals who have ties to their occupations. They recommend using channels such as professional associations and societies, conferences, and publications. They suggest using the Internet for advertising and recruiting because it increases reach to many of these individuals. The authors suggest careful examination of competitors' workforces to approach high-quality employees. The next phase in this process is to select the workers who will be the best performers and thereby contribute to a competitive advantage for the organization. Obviously, a first step is to determine what is required to perform effectively in the organization (for example, creative problem solving, learning new tasks and technologies, dealing with uncertainty and stress, demonstrating cultural adaptability, and so on). Then, candidates who have been recruited can be assessed for their skills and capabilities to meet the appropriate challenges and requirements. One important requirement is their ability to help build and apply new knowledge, a critical element examined in this book. Another important element is sharing knowledge, diffusing it throughout the organization; thus, employees who have strong social skills and an ability to network may be important to support the sharing of knowledge. Two other important characteristics are relevant experience and domain-specific knowledge. The authors also examine more sophisticated selection tools such as biodata measures and high-fidelity job simulations. They conclude that firms can improve their competitive advantage by effective hiring practices.

The final chapter in this section is written by Alison Davis-Blake and Pamsy Hui. The authors explore the recent phenomenon of contract workers and their contribution to building and applying knowledge in organizations to increase their competitive capabilities. Davis-Blake and Hui describe research that shows that outsourcing has increased considerably in the last decade; contracting for knowledge-intensive activities also has grown at a rapid rate during this time. These trends create the need for human resource management systems that manage contract employees so that they contribute to organizational knowledge and performance. Davis-Blake and Hui note that firm-specific knowledge cannot be contracted for in the external labor market; this is a significant issue because of the contribution of firm-specific knowledge to competitive advantage. However, contract employees can hold and contribute valuable explicit and tacit knowledge to the accomplishment of important projects for the firm. The authors examine several human resource management activities relevant to managing contract employees, including selection, training, compensation, and retaining those who make important contributions. Finally, Davis-Blake and Hui offer a number of ideas for future research on contracting for talent.

Developing and Motivating Employees for Knowledge-Based Competition

The first chapter in this section (Chapter Eight) examines the process of developing intellectual and social capital in organizations to facilitate the management and transfer of knowledge. The authors, Ray Noe, Jason Colquitt, Marcia Simmering, and Sharon

Alvarez, discuss the development of intellectual and social capital at the individual, group, and firm levels. Specifically, they describe how social and intellectual capital are developed through knowledge management, teams, and entrepreneurial firms. Noe and his colleagues explore how knowledge management facilitates the development of intellectual capital in individuals. They also examine the types of behavior that foster the development of new knowledge, such as constructive controversy, creativity, and adaptation. They suggest that teams with moderate stability, high task interdependence, and high member openness are better able to develop intellectual capital. The firm-level focus in the chapter is on knowledge created through entrepreneurial activities. Noe and his colleagues also explore how training and development support the relationship between social capital and intellectual capital. In short, social capital facilitates the transfer of knowledge that is developed in training programs and thereby leads to the development of intellectual capital. Much like Mohrman, they recommend a dynamic approach to measuring and developing intellectual capital. They explore the processes of knowledge transfer and the potential effects of individual factors on the development of intellectual capital. Research questions on knowledge transfer, teams, and development of social and intellectual capital in organizations are offered to guide future empirical work.

Chapter Nine, by Greg Oldham, explores how organizations stimulate and support creativity. The development of new knowledge requires creativity. Oldham explores several mechanisms that facilitate the sharing of creative ideas in the organization. He presents and explains a theoretical framework that suggests how personal and contextual conditions influence creativity and the sharing of creative ideas. Oldham effectively explains that ideas must be made public and available to others in the organization if they are to contribute substantially to organizational knowledge and thereby to performance. He explores several potential contextual effects on the development and sharing of creative ideas, such as employee mood states (positive and negative), job complexity, performance goals and deadlines, supervisor and coworker support, along with the physical configuration of the workspace. He notes that individual differences can affect the development of creative ideas as well. Oldham suggests that a nonjudgmental climate and encouragement to share ideas can enhance the development and sharing of creative ideas in organizations. Therefore, this chapter deals with a critical element in the knowledge management process.

In Chapter Ten, Ed Lawler explores how performance management affects knowledge management in organizations. Specifically, he focuses on the reward systems designed to promote knowledge development and use in organizations. Lawler argues that traditional organizations were not designed to manage knowledge but rather to emphasize efficiency in the management and control of products and services. In these more traditional organizations, employees were (and are) rewarded for the size of their job, the length of their service, and their individual performance. However, Lawler argues, effectively managing knowledge in organizations requires different organizational behavior. The newer organizations need reward systems that emphasize development of new knowledge, transmission of that knowledge, and use of that knowledge to develop and improve products and services. In short, Lawler suggests that the reward system needs to attract and retain individuals with the right knowledge, motivate individuals to learn what is critical for gaining a competitive advantage, and motivate individuals to develop and use knowledge that helps create that competitive advantage. He argues that job-based pay has several risks and suggests that skill-based pay is more effective in promoting knowledge management. He believes that skill-based pay is particularly effective in situations where multiple skills are needed but may not be used all the time. This is because it is important that the skills be available for use when needed and thus represent a critical asset for the organization. Furthermore, individuals with multiple skills often can work on multiple projects simultaneously. Therefore, Lawler concludes, reward systems can play an important role in the management of knowledge in organizations.

Chapter Eleven, by Steve Maurer, Tom Lee, and Terry Mitchell, examines the importance of retaining technical professionals in order to retain knowledge in organizations. Although it is important to retain knowledge workers in order to retain knowledge, these workers are likely to be more mobile than many other competitive resources. Maurer and his colleagues argue that the ability to retain the creators of technical knowledge is of critical importance to knowledge-based organizations, and their chapter examines a variety of HR alternatives to help achieve this objective. They note that educational preparation, professional standards, and labor market factors affect technical professionals' decisions to stay or leave. The key issue is that firms must take positive actions to retain their technical professionals in order to retain the knowledge they hold. This is critical to managing knowledge in these organizations.

Measuring Knowledge-Based Resources

Chapter Twelve, by Lois Tetrick and Nancy Da Silva, examines the means by which organizations can evaluate their culture and climate in order to determine how well it supports organizational learning. Organizational learning is a critical component of knowledge management. An organization's culture and climate can have a significant effect on the amount and type of learning that occurs. Therefore, it is important to understand how cultures and climates affect organizational learning and how they can be assessed relative to learning. Given the assumption that generative learning or double-loop learning is more likely to lead to competitive advantage than adaptive or single-loop learning, Tetrick and Da Silva explore means by which the organizational culture and climate facilitate organizational learning. They examine knowledge development and acquisition through reinventive learning, adjustive learning, formative learning, and operative learning. They present a model that suggests several important issues in the measurement of these constructs, including level of analysis (individual, group, or organization), level of culture-climate (artifacts and behaviors, cognition and beliefs, and assumptions and values), and methods of data collection. They conclude that research is needed to understand better the mechanisms and context in which knowledge management and organizational learning affect individuals, groups, and organizations.

In the second and final chapter of this section (Chapter Thirteen), John Boudreau explores approaches to measuring knowledge. Whereas previous research has focused on measuring knowledge at the individual level (skills, abilities, and so on), Boudreau examines the measurement of knowledge at higher levels of aggregation, emphasizing the use of knowledge to create value. Because of the importance of knowledge management, this chapter on the ability to measure knowledge accurately and to show its relationship to organizational success makes a critical contribution to this book and to the field. Boudreau's primary goal is to explain strategically appropriate measures of knowledge that access its role in the organization's value chain. In addition to aggregate measures of knowledge, Boudreau focuses on the role of knowledge of talent pools, with specific emphasis on pivotal roles—where performance differences between individuals have the greatest effect on the organization's achieving a competitive advantage. From a research standpoint, Boudreau examines knowledge measures as higher-level dependent variables and as moderator or mediator variables that explain the effects of human resource innovations on knowledge and thereby on organizational performance. Finally, Boudreau categorizes knowledge measures in terms of stocks (existing level of knowledge at a point in time), flows (movement of knowledge between individuals, units or organizations), and enablers (creating the capability for action).

Conclusion

The last chapter, written by the editors, emphasizes the critical contributions made by the chapters of this volume and the challenges to human resource professionals to build HR systems and processes to facilitate knowledge management in organizations. But in keeping with the overall goals of the SIOP Frontiers Series, the final chapter pays special attention to the research questions and issues that still need to be addressed before we can understand exactly how to build these systems. Thus, this final chapter attempts to summarize what we know about each area discussed in the volume and what we still need to learn. An integrative model of how organizations need to acquire, share, apply, and update knowledge is used to help generate research questions and issues at a higher level of analysis than is done in the individual chapters.

It is clear that organizations will need to acquire, develop, and use knowledge-based resources if they are to gain competitive advantage in the future. We believe that I/O psychology can help organizations accomplish these goals, but that the field has not yet paid enough attention to these issues. We hope that this volume convinces some I/O psychologists to look beyond their typical dependent variables (that is, individual and team performance) and consider how their own knowledge-based resources can be used to help organizations improve effectiveness at the organizational level. We also hope this volume introduces I/O psychologists to some new and different ways of thinking about competencies and performance, showing them how some members of our scientific community have already begun to think about the larger implications of their work. The ultimate goal is help move the field of I/O psychology to the next level of analysis and to generate research programs that show how I/O psychology can help firms compete effectively in the knowledge age.

References

Amit, R., & Schoemaker, P.J.H. (1993). Strategic resources and organizational rent. *Strategic Management Journal, 14,* 33–46.

Barkema, H. G., & Vermeulen, F. (1998). International expansion through startup or acquisition: A learning perspective. *Academy of Management Journal, 41,* 7–26.

Barney, J. B. (1991). Firm resources and sustained competitive advantage. *Journal of Management, 17,* 99–129.

Barney, J. B. (2001). Is the resource-based "view" a useful perspective for strategic management research? Yes. *Academy of Management Review, 26,* 41–56.

Baron, J. N., & Kreps, D. M. (1999). *Strategic human resource: Frameworks for general managers.* New York: Wiley.

Barrick, M. R., Stewart, G. L., Neubert, M. J., & Mount, M. K. (1998). Relating member ability and personality to work-team processes and team effectiveness. *Journal of Applied Psychology, 83,* 377–391.

Black, J. A., & Boal, K. B. (1994). Strategic resources: Traits, configurations, and paths to sustainable competitive advantage. *Strategic Management Journal, 15,*131–148.

Boudreau, J. M. (1991). Utility analysis for decision making in human resource management. In M. Dunnette & L. Hough (Eds.), *Handbook of industrial and organizational psychology* (Vol. 2; pp. 621–745). Palo Alto, CA: Consulting Psychologists Press.

Campion, M. A., Medsker, G. J., & Higgs, A. C. (1993). Relations between work group characteristics and effectiveness: Implications for designing effective work groups. *Personnel Psychology, 46,* 823–850.

Cascio, W. F. (1987). *Costing human resources: The financial impact of behavior in organizations* (2nd ed.). Boston: PWS-Kent.

Cohen, W. M., & Levinthal, D. A. (1990). Absorptive capacity: A new perspective on learning and innovation. *Administrative Science Quarterly, 35,*128–152.

DeCarolis, D. M., & Deeds, D. L. (1999). The impact of stocks and flows of organizational knowledge on firm performance: An empirical investigation of the biotechnology industry. *Strategic Management Journal, 20,* 953–986.

DeNisi, A. S. (2000). Performance appraisal and performance management: A multilevel analysis. In K. Klein & S. Kozlowski (Eds.), *Multilevel theory, research, and methods in organizations* (pp. 121–156). San Francisco: Jossey-Bass.

Edmondson, A. (1999). Psychological safety and learning behavior in work teams. *Administrative Science Quarterly, 44,* 350–383.

Fiorina, C. (2000, May). Speech to graduating MBA class, Massachusetts Institute of Technology, Cambridge, MA.

Gerhart, B. (2000). Compensation strategy and organizational performance. In S. Rynes & B. Gerhart (Eds.), *Compensation in organizations: Current research and practice* (pp. 151–194). San Francisco: Jossey-Bass.

Grant, R. M. (1996). Toward a knowledge-based view of the firm. *Strategic Management Journal, 17,* 109–122.

Guzzo, R. A., & Shea, G. P. (1992). Group performance and intergroup relations in organizations. In M. D. Dunnette & L. M. Hough (Eds.), *Handbook of industrial and organizational psychology* (Vol. 3; 2nd ed.; pp. 269–313). Palo Alto, CA: Consulting Psychologists Press.

Hitt, M. A., Bierman, L., Shimizu, K., & Kochhar, R. (2001). Direct and moderating effects of human capital on strategy and performance in professional service firms: A resource-based perspective. *Academy of Management Journal, 44,*13–26.

Hitt, M. A., Dacin, M. T., Levitas, E., Arregle, J. L., & Borza, A. (2000). Partner selection in emerging and developed markets: Resource-based and organizational learning perspectives. *Academy of Management Journal, 43,* 449–467.

Hitt, M. A., Harrison. J. A., & Ireland, R. D. (2001). *Mergers and acquisitions: A guide to creating value for stakeholders.* New York: Oxford University Press.

Hitt, M. A., Hoskisson, R. E., Johnson. R. A., & Moesel, D. D. (1996). The market for corporate control and firm innovation. *Academy of Management Journal, 39*(5), 1084–1119.

Hitt, M. A., Hoskisson, R. E., & Nixon, R. D. (1993). A mid-range theory of interfunctional integration: Its antecedents and outcomes. *Journal of Engineering and Technology Management, 10,* 161–185.

Hitt, M. A., Ireland, R. D., & Hoskisson, R. E. (2001). *Strategic management: Competitiveness and globalization.* Cincinnati, OH: South-Western.

Hitt, M. A., Keats, B. A, & DeMarie, S. M. (1998). Navigating in the new competitive landscape: Building strategic flexibility and competitive advantage in the 21st century. *Academy of Management Executive, 12,* 22–42.

Hitt, M. A., Nixon, R. D., Clifford, P. G., & Coyne, K. (1999). The development and use of strategic resources. In M. A. Hitt, P. G. Clifford, R. D. Nixon, & K. P. Coyne (Eds.), *Dynamic strategic resources: Development, diffusion, and integration* (pp. 1–15). New York: Wiley.

Hitt, M. A., Nixon, R. D., Hoskisson, R. E., & Kochhar, R. (1999). Corporate entrepreneurship and cross-functional fertilization: Activation, process, and disintegration of a new product design team. *Entrepreneurship Theory and Practice, 23,* 145–167.

Huselid, M. A. (1995). The impact of human resource management practices on turnover, productivity, and corporate financial performance. *Academy of Management Journal, 38,* 635–672.

Iles, P., Yolles, M., & Altman, Y. (2001). HRM and knowledge management: Responding to the challenge. *Research and Practice in Human Resource Management, 9,* 3–33.

Itami, H. (1987). *Mobilizing invisible resources.* Cambridge, MA: Harvard University Press.

Jackson, S. E., & Schuler, R. S. (2000). Managing human resources for innovation and learning. In R. Berndt (Ed.), *Challenges of Innovations/Innovative Management* (pp. 327–356). Zurich: GSBA.

Jackson, S. E., & Schuler, R. S. (2001, January 15). Turning knowledge into business advantage [Mastering Management Supplement]. *Financial Times,* pp. 8–10.

Jackson, S. E., & Schuler, R. S. (2002). Managing individual performance: A strategic perspective. In S. Sonnentag (Ed.), *Psychological management of individual performance.* New York: Wiley, 372–390.

Jenkins, C. D., & Gupta, N. (1985). The payoffs of paying for knowledge. *National Productivity Review, 4,* 121–130.

Klein, K. J., Dansereau, F., & Hall, F. J. (1994). Levels issues in theory development, data collection, and analysis. *Academy of Management Review, 19,* 195–229.

Klein, K. J., & Kozlowski, S.W.J. (2000). *Multilevel theory, research, and methods in organizations.* San Francisco: Jossey Bass.

Kogut, B., & Zander, U. (1992). Knowledge of the firm, combinative capabilities, and the replication of technology. *Organization Science, 3,* 383–397.

Kogut, B., & Zander, U. (1996). What firms do? Coordination, identity, and learning. *Organization Science, 7,* 502–518.

Lane, P. J., & Lubatkin, M. (1998). Relative absorptive capacity and interorganizational learning. *Strategic Management Journal, 19,* 451–477.

Levitt, B., & March, J. G. (1988). Organizational learning. *Annual Review
of Sociology, 14,* 319–340.

Marsh, S. J., & Ranft, A. L. (1999). An empirical study of the influence of
knowledge-based resources on new market entry. In M. A. Hitt,
P. G. Clifford, R. D. Nixon, & K. P. Coyne (Eds.), *Dynamic strategic resources: Development, diffusion, and integration* (pp. 43–66). New York:
Wiley.

Miller, D. A. (1996). A preliminary typology of organizational learning:
Synthesizing the literature. *Strategic Management Journal, 22,* 484–505.

Miller, D. A., & Shamsie, J. (1996). The resource-based view of the firm
in two environments: The Hollywood film studios from 1936 to
1965. *Academy of Management Journal, 39,* 519–543.

Nonaka, I. (1994). A dynamic theory of organizational knowledge creation. *Organization Science, 5,* 14–37.

Ostroff, C., & Bowen, D. E. (2000). Moving HR to a higher level: HR practices and organizational effectiveness. In K. J. Klein & S.W.J. Kozlowski (Eds.), *Multilevel theory, research, and methods in organizations*
(pp. 211–266). San Francisco: Jossey-Bass.

Pearce, J. L. (1993). Toward an organizational behavior of contract laborers: Their psychological involvement and effects on employee
co-workers. *Academy of Management Journal, 36,* 1082–1096.

Pennings, J. M., Lee, K,. & van Witteloostuijn, A. (1998). Human capital,
social capital, and firm dissolution. *Academy of Management Journal,
41,* 425–440.

Peteraf, M. A. (1993). The cornerstones of competitive advantage: A
resource-based view. *Strategic Management Journal, 14,* 179–191.

Pfeffer, J., & Sutton, R. I. (2001). *The knowing-doing gap: How smart companies turn knowledge into action.* Boston: Harvard Business School
Press.

Polanyi, M. (1973). *Personal knowledge: Towards a postcritical philosophy.* New
York: Routledge.

Priem, R. L., & Butler, J. E. (2001). Is the resource-based "view" a useful
perspective for strategic management research? *Academy of Management Review, 26,* 22–40.

Rao, H. (1994). The social construction of reputation: Certification
process, legitimization, and the survival of organizations in the
American automobile industry, 1895–1912. *Strategic Management
Journal, 15,* 29–44.

Reed, R., & DeFillippi, R. S. (1990). Causal ambiguity, barriers to imitation, and sustainable competitive advantage. *Academy of Management
Review, 15,* 18–102.

Schoenecker, T. S., & Cooper, A. C. (1998). The role of firm resources and organizational attributes in determining entry timing: A cross-industry study. *Strategic Management Journal, 19,* 1127–1143.

Schuler, R. S., & Jackson, S. E. (1987). Linking competitive strategies with human resource practices. *Academy of Management Executive, 1,* 207–220.

Schuler, R. S., Jackson, S. E., & Luo, Y. (2003). *Managing Human Resources in Cross-Border Alliances.* London: Routledge.

Schweiger, D. M., & DeNisi, A. S. (1991). The effects of communication with employees following a merger: A longitudinal field experiment. *Academy of Management Journal, 34,* 110–135.

Sherer, P. D. (1995). Leveraging human resources in law firms: Human capital structures and organizational capabilities. *Industrial and Labor Relations Review, 48,* 671–691.

Shore, L. M., & Wayne, S. J. (1993). Commitment and employee behavior: Comparison of affective commitment and continuance commitment with perceived organizational support. *Journal of Applied Psychology, 78,* 774–780.

Simonin, B. L. (1999). Ambiguity and the process of knowledge transfer in strategic alliances. *Strategic Management Journal, 20,* 595–623.

Teece, D. J., Pisano, G., & Shuen, A. (1997). Dynamic capabilities and strategic management. *Strategic Management Journal, 18,* 509–533.

Walsh, J. A. (1988). Top management team turnover following mergers and acquisitions. *Strategic Management Journal, 9,* 173–183.

Walsh, J. A. (1989). Doing a deal: Merger and acquisition negotiations and their impact upon target company top management turnover. *Strategic Management Journal, 10,* 307–322.

Williams, L. J., & Anderson, S. E. (1991). Job satisfaction and organizational commitment as predictors of organizational citizenship and in-role behaviors. *Journal of Management, 17,* 601–617.

Wright, P. M., Smart, D. L., & McMahon, G. C. (1995). Matches between human resources and strategy among NCAA basketball teams. *Academy of Management Journal, 38,* 1052–1074.

Zahra, S. A., Ireland, R. D., & Hitt, M. A. (2000). International expansion by new venture firms: International diversity, mode of market entry, technological learning, and performance. *Academy of Management Journal, 43,* 925–950.

PART 2

Work and Organizational Designs for Knowledge-Based Competition

CHAPTER 2

Alternative Strategies for Acquiring Knowledge

David L. Deeds

Over the last thirty years the basis of competition in many segments of the economy has shifted from the acquisition and control of tangible critical resources, such as ores and fuels, to the acquisition, control, and creation of knowledge-based resources or assets, such as internal research capabilities, patents, product development processes, and so on (Hill & Deeds, 1996). This trend has corresponded with a dramatic increase in the specificity, complexity, and size of the knowledge bases that firms competing in the modern economy are forced to draw on (Dasgupta & David, 1994). The revolutions in information technology, electronics, genetics, materials science, and numerous other areas have had a profound impact on most of today's firms. At the same time, this explosion in technological and scientific knowledge has dramatically decreased their ability to internalize all of the knowledge required to build and sustain competitive advantage over time.

The inability of firms to develop internally all the knowledge that today's competitive environment demands is forcing them to employ alternative strategies to reach beyond their boundaries to acquire knowledge. Acquisition of knowledge from beyond the boundaries of the firm is an economic process heavily embedded in the social relationships that exist between the parties to the transaction. However, for all the risks and challenges of acquiring and assimilating knowledge from outside the firm, it is an increasingly critical competitive activity in the modern economy. This leads to the basic proposition of this chapter: *Firms that are effective in acquiring knowledge will be able to create and sustain a competitive advantage in the knowledge-based economy. Those that are not will have difficulty maintaining their competitive position.* The primary tools for acquiring knowledge from beyond a firm's boundaries are hybrid organizational forms, such as licensing, alliances, joint ventures, and acquisitions and mergers. Therefore, understanding these tools and employing them effectively is essential to creating and sustaining competitive advantage. Because these strategies depend heavily on social relationships both outside and inside the organization, social psychology can add significantly to our understanding of them.

Until recently, alternative strategies for acquiring knowledge were generally limited to noncritical projects with relatively little complexity and uncertainty. Projects that were extremely important and had high levels of uncertainty and complexity were internalized because organizations feared opportunism on the part of partners (Williamson, 1975; Teece, 1986). However, technological uncertainty and the rate of change have increased the risks and difficulties of relying solely on internal development. The hybrid forms, or alternative strategies, may have actually become lower risk, essentially functioning as real options in today's highly uncertain environment.

The various alternative knowledge acquisition strategies expose firms to different types and levels of risk, as well as to different levels of managerial challenge and resource commitment. Because there is a particular profile for each strategy, there are also conditions under which certain strategies should work better than others. This chapter will attempt to develop a model that guides the choice among the alternative knowledge strategies under varying conditions. In particular, it will examine the impact of the characteristics of the knowledge being acquired—stock versus flow, tacit versus explicit, distant or close to the firm's current knowledge base, and strategic importance—on the appropriate choice of strategy.

For example, over the last thirty years the biopharmaceutical industry has seen the technologies employed to develop drugs evolve from experimentation looking for bioreactive naturally occurring compounds, the bread molds on which penicillin is based, to monoclonal antibodies, anti-sense technologies, gene therapy, genomics, combinative chemistry, proteomics, bioinformatics, X-ray crystallography, and many other technologies. Organic and physical chemistry were the knowledge bases on which the large pharmaceutical companies were founded, but today the core skills involve genetics, computer science, biochemistry, biomechanics, and several other fields. Where the core skills will reside in the future is being determined by the complex and unpredictable processes of scientific research being carried out by researchers working in universities and research laboratories, outside the for-profit pharmaceutical companies.

In this environment it is unclear what skills and capabilities will be required to compete in the near future, making it risky to invest heavily in the acquisition of a single set of skills or technologies and improbable that a firm will be able to continue to develop internally all the skills, knowledge, and capabilities necessary to sustain a competitive advantage. Firms in this industry have responded to the rapidly evolving knowledge base by reaching beyond their boundaries to access the knowledge required to sustain and enhance their competitive positions. This can be seen in the explosion of the use of alternative strategies in the pharmaceutical-biotechnology industry. In 1991 Barley, Freeman, and Hybels (1992) documented over nine hundred active alliances. Recently, Rothaermel and Deeds (2002) have documented over twenty-two hundred active alliances in the same field, and there has also been a high level of merger and acquisition activity in the industry. Numerous mergers among the big pharmaceutical firms have taken place, as have acquisitions of biotechnology firms by pharmaceutical companies and the merger or acquisition of one biotechnology firm with another.

When knowledge is transferred across a firm's boundaries, the process is generally ambiguous and uncertain. The quality and usefulness of the knowledge being acquired is often difficult to judge ex-ante. Unanticipated changes in the environment may alter the incentives of the parties to the agreements ex-post. Intangible personal, organizational, and cultural attributes will influence the relationships between the contracting organizations and the ability of a firm to acquire the knowledge it desires. In addition, during the process of acquiring knowledge externally firms frequently open themselves up to the risks of degrading their competitive position by transferring their core skills, capabilities, and knowledge (Anand & Khanna, 2000). Cross-boundary collaboration usually requires that both parties bring skills and knowledge to the project and work together closely.

The interactions between the participants during this period create opportunities for learning and knowledge transfer, but the learning and transfer are difficult to limit to the knowledge covered by the agreement alone. Biotechnology firms working with a pharmaceutical partner during the process of guiding a drug through critical regulatory trials can learn a significant amount about the process of managing FDA trials, a key skill in the pharmaceutical industry. At the same time, the pharmaceutical partner gains access to key research personnel. Through their interactions, the researchers are able to gain key insights into the technical knowledge that the biotechnology firm has used to create the product. As the partners attempt to learn as much from each other as possible, knowledge does not simply transfer through osmosis or the ether; it is carried between the organizations by individuals. The actual process and conditions under which learning and the transfer of knowledge occurs, and the types of structures and relationships that either encourage or inhibit this type of transfer, are areas that cry out for study. In fact, these are critical issues for small technology ventures. Recent research has shown that a significant percentage of smaller entrepreneurial firms believe they have been exploited by larger partners seeking to gain new knowledge and skills (Alvarez & Barney, 2001).

Given all the challenges, uncertainties, and ambiguities involved, it is unlikely that the parties to the transaction can specify all contingencies, making contractual methods of deterring opportunistic behavior and ensuring cooperation questionable at best. *This leaves the success of the transaction dependent on the ability of the parties to the agreement to develop a strong relationship that can react and adapt to changing circumstances.* In fact, in most of these arrangements it will not be the contract and its deterrents that will make the partnership successful but rather the personal and organizational relationships that develop across boundaries (Deeds & Hill, 1999). As the former CEO of one of the largest biotechnology firms has said, "It's not the contract but the people that make an alliance work. Once the contract is finished it goes in a drawer and if I ever have to refer to it again I know the relationship is over and I'm simply looking for a way out" (Deeds, 1994, p. 68). Developing and maintaining trust and strong relationships across organizational boundaries and the role of individual organizational members in developing and maintaining this trust are important areas for future research.

This chapter is divided into four main sections. The first section will discuss strategic alliances and joint ventures. The second section will examine organizational learning through mergers and acquisitions. The chapter will then discuss how the characteristics of the knowledge being acquired affect the choice of strategy. Finally, the chapter will conclude with a discussion of the implications of the model for human resource managers and researchers and some additional thoughts on where interesting research opportunities might exist.

Hybrid Forms of Organization

According to Williamson (1991) hybrid forms of organization structure are contractual forms that entail bilateral dependence among the parties but maintain ownership autonomy. These structures are seen as encouraging adaptation and cooperation among the partners while still maintaining strong market incentives for performance. Hybrid forms run from simple comarketing agreements to complex alliances in which several parties cross-license technologies and contribute to R&D and to multiparty ventures in which a jointly owned organization is established to pursue a new market or technology. However, in general, hybrid forms fall into two categories: strategic alliances and joint ventures.

Licensing in its most basic incarnation is a simple market transaction through which one party sells the right to use a piece of intellectual property (brand name, patent, piece of music, software program, manufacturing process, and so on) to another and entails no bilateral dependence. Therefore, a pure licensing transaction—such as my agreement with Microsoft allowing me to use the software with which I'm writing this chapter—is not a hybrid structure but simply a market transaction. However, as the complexity of the knowledge being transferred and the contract governing the ongoing interaction between the parties changes to accommodate

---

the need for continual monitoring, information exchange, resource exchange, and so on, the interaction moves beyond the bounds of a simple market transaction and becomes a hybrid form.

The contract governing the hybrid structure generally commits the parties to a long-term, complex, uncertain relationship (Leblebici & Salancik, 1982; Pfeffer & Salancik, 1978) in which both parties are exposed to the risk of opportunistic behavior by the partner. The parties to this type of exchange will be required to continue to interact well beyond the signing of the agreement. It will probably be months or years before they can judge if their partner has lived up to their commitments and contributed to the success of the agreement. The actual transfer of the knowledge will probably entail multiple interactions between the technical staff of the two companies, and possibly an exchange of personnel for a period of time.

Joint ventures are viewed as a distinct subset of hybrid structures. A joint venture creates a jointly owned organization to achieve the goals of the alliance. This creation of a distinct intervening organization by the parties to the transaction substantially alters the dynamics of their relationship. This fact is supported by previous research, which has found differences in the performance of joint ventures and alliances (Anand & Khanna, 2000).

There are numerous definitions of strategic alliances in the literature. They have been defined as formal nonequity arrangements between independent firms (Singh & Mitchell, 1996) and as interorganizational relationships in which the parties maintain autonomy but are bilaterally dependent to a nontrivial degree (Williamson, 1991). Gulati (1995) defined an alliance as any independently initiated interfirm link that involves exchange, sharing, or codevelopment. Strategic alliances have also been defined as the pooling of specific resources and skills by partnering organizations in order to achieve common and firm-specific goals, such as accessing new markets, broadening product lines, learning new skills, and sharing R&D, manufacturing, or marketing costs (Varadarajan & Cunningham, 1995; Sakakibara, 1997). For our purposes we will define strategic alliances as hybrid organizational forms in which two or more entities partner to operate in a cooperative way to create value that neither could create on its own (Jorde & Teece, 1989; Borys & Jemison, 1989). This definition can be applied to a wide range of interorganizational linkages, including everything from simple comarketing or coproduction agreements to complex joint ventures between several owners.

When entering a strategic alliance the incentives for mutual cooperation may be strong because of the potential to create value. However, over time the parties' goals are likely to diverge. The value of the alliance to one party may decrease because of external events or because it has acquired the knowledge that it desired. Miscommunication and misunderstandings between the parties because of cultural differences or divergent goals are also frequently the basis for dissolving an alliance. Managing joint processes to ensure that your firm benefits while maintaining cooperation among the partners is what makes strategic alliances so inherently unstable and difficult. In fact, research has found that an alliance's performance shows strong evidence of a liability of adolescence, in a pattern very similar to that of marriages (Deeds & Hill, 1999).

Strategic Alliances and Firm Performance

Several streams of research in the literature examine outcomes from strategic alliances. One stream has focused on the relationship between strategic alliances and R&D productivity. In general, this research has found a positive relationship between the use of alliances in the R&D process and the rate of new product development (Deeds & Hill, 1996; Rothaermel & Deeds, 2002; Shan, Walker, & Kogut, 1994; Stuart, 2000). These results appear to support the hypothesis that strategic alliances can be an effective means of accessing new knowledge.

Another research stream has focused on the consequences of alliance activity for the performance of the partnering firm (Hamel, 1991; Hagedoorn & Schakenraad, 1994; Doz, 1996; Mitchell & Singh, 1996; Singh & Mitchell, 1996). The results of these studies have tended to emphasize the importance of interorganizational learning for the outcome of alliances and for a firm's performance and competitive position. The results generally support the contention that the partners often benefit from alliance activity but also stress the risks of capability transfer and dependence for the partners (Mitchell & Singh, 1996; Singh & Mitchell, 1996; Khanna, Gulati, & Nohria, 1998).

Strategic Alliances and Capability Development

In a related research stream, scholars have begun to explore the role of alliances in capability development and interorganizational learning (Lane & Lubatkin, 1998; Dussuage, Garrette, & Mitchell, 2000). The evidence appears to indicate that alliances allow firms to increase the speed of capability development and minimize uncertainty by acquiring and exploiting knowledge developed by others (Grant & Baden-Fuller, 1995; Lane & Lubatkin, 1998). When learning becomes central to an alliance, the issue of how to create conditions that are conducive to the successful exchange of knowledge becomes critical. Lane and Lubatkin (1998) found that the ability of firms in an alliance to learn from one another was strongly influenced by the similarity between their knowledge bases and their internal knowledge processing structures. Simonin (1999) found that the characteristics of the knowledge—tacitness and complexity—being transferred were important determinants of its transferability across boundaries. Dussuage et al. (2000) also found that different types of alliances led to different opportunities for learning and different alliance outcomes as a result of the diversity of the knowledge being transferred. These findings indicate that the context in which the alliance operates and the type of knowledge (that is, tacit or codified) being transferred, as well as its complexity and ambiguity, affect its transfer among the parties.

In sum, the research to date has established a link between research productivity and strategic alliances and has begun to develop an understanding of the impact of some of the contextual factors in which an alliance operates. We will now turn to a discussion of mergers and acquisitions before attempting to organize and extend our understanding of the role of these contextual factors and their implications for acquiring knowledge.

Mergers and Acquisitions

Since 1990 there has been a substantial increase in merger and acquisition activity, particularly in technology-based industries. The dollar value of completed mergers, acquisitions, and divestitures in 2000 jumped 22.6 percent to more than $1.7 trillion and set a record for the sixth successive year (Sikora, 2001). The volume was powered in particular by a barrage of megadeals linking larger players in consolidating or deal-conditioned industries, such as health care, telecommunications, media, financial services, food, and information technology.

Indications are that the rationale for this activity is also changing. During the 1990s and continuing today, the focus of M&A activity has shifted from horizontal or vertical mergers and acquisitions in the traditional manufacturing sectors to what has been called the knowledge industries, such as software, pharmaceuticals, biotechnology, electronics, and telecommunications (Ranft & Lord, 2000). In contrast to acquisitions used to achieve economies of scale, gains in market power, or geographical expansion, many of these mergers seem to be driven by the desire to acquire new skills, knowledge, capabilities, and expertise (Ahuja & Katila, 2001; Kozin & Young, 1994).

The definition of a merger or acquisition is fairly straightforward. An acquisition occurs when one firm acquires a controlling interest in another firm. A merger occurs when two firms join together by combining their operations and assets under a single ownership structure. These transactions have distinct implications, mergers being viewed as voluntary combinations of approximate equals, and acquisitions, whether hostile or not, implying the purchase and subsequent control of the acquired firm by the acquirer. However, for purposes of knowledge acquisition these distinctions probably have more to do with the relative size of the firms involved. Following the general conventions in the literature, these two types of transactions will be treated as equivalent in the remainder of this chapter. It should be noted, though, that the general tenor of the two is distinct and this probably has implications for the ability of the firms involved to benefit from the integration of knowledge bases. The implication of hostile versus nonhostile takeovers on successfully acquiring and integrating knowledge is an area that should be researched further. In fact, there are several potential research topics, such as employee attitudes and differences in HR systems between the firms, that may affect the ability to acquire knowledge through acquisition.

Recent research on M&A as a tool for acquiring knowledge has generally focused on two areas: empirical attempts to determine the relationship of M&A to research outputs, organizational change, and the introduction of new products, and the determinants and impact of retaining human capital in the acquired firm, particularly the top management team but also the technical and highly skilled employees.

Firm Performance and M&A Activity

The research on the relationship between M&A and knowledge acquisition begins with the perspective that market failure due to the imperfect tradability of knowledge resources motivates knowledge-based acquisitions. Because the knowledge, skills, routines, and capabilities of a firm are inseparable, acquiring firms are motivated to acquire the entire target firm in order to realize the value from redeploying these assets (Karim & Mitchell, 2000). The history of research on firm performance and acquisitions has led to inconclusive results and driven recent research toward a contingent approach to the problem (Ahuja & Katila, 2001). There have also been conflicting results in the research on the role of acquisitions in the expansion of a firm's knowledge base. Granstrand and Sjolander (1990) found that large firms in Sweden were able to develop and exploit their internal capabilities by trading small firms. A follow-up piece (Granstrand, Bohlin, Oskarsson, & Sjoberg, 1992) found that large multinational technology companies were able to augment and develop their knowledge base through external acquisitions.

But empirical studies have had a much more difficult time finding a positive relationship between acquisition activity and research productivity. Several studies in the governance literature (Hitt, Hoskisson, Ireland, & Harrison, 1991; Hitt, Hoskisson, Johnson, & Moesel, 1996) found a negative relationship between acquisition activity and the postacquisition innovative output of the acquiring firms. This has been attributed to agency problems and absorption of managerial energies into the integration process at the expense of ongoing innovation. According to more recent research, the relationship between acquisitions and research productivity varies depending on several factors, including the size of the knowledge base being acquired in both absolute and relative terms and the relation of that knowledge base to the firm's current knowledge base (Ahuja & Katila, 2001). Recent results highlight the role of acquisitions in deepening the firm's current knowledge base but also in extending it into new areas (Karim & Mitchell, 2000; Vermeulen & Barkema, 2001) as well as decreasing organizational inertia and enhancing the viability of later ventures by the acquiring firm (Vermeulen & Barkema, 2001). In fact, Vermeulen and Barkema found evidence of a knowledge-leveraging strategy among their sample, with firms first using a merger or acquisition to access new knowledge and then leveraging that knowledge through a later Greenfield start-up. These results indicate that under the right conditions acquisitions are valuable tools for acquiring knowledge.

Employee Retention and Acquiring Knowledge Through Mergers and Acquisitions

Another stream of research on knowledge acquisition through M&A has its roots in the literature on top management teams and problems in integrating the acquisition. Implementation problems often arise because of the clash of cultures, systems, and strategies or the loss of key leaders in the acquired firm (Ranft & Lord, 2000). A fairly extensive stream of research has focused on the causes and consequences of top management team turnover after acquisitions (Hambrick & Cannella, 1993; Krug & Hegarty, 1997; Very, Lubatkin, Calori, & Veiga, 1997; Walsh, 1988, 1989; Walsh & Ellwood, 1991). The loss of top managers after acquisitions is considered to be one of the reasons for the poor performance of many of them (Hambrick & Cannella, 1993). This stream of research has found that managerial retention is influenced by events prior to the acquisition that signal the intent of the acquirer to retain current management (Schweiger & DeNisi, 1991). Top managers are also more likely to leave when the acquired firm has been in bankruptcy or is financially distressed or underperforms the market (Walsh & Ellwood, 1991; Walsh & Kosnick, 1993). Executives are more likely to leave if there has been a period of hostile negotiations between the firms or as a result of culture clashes (Hambrick & Cannella, 1993; Lubatkin, Schweiger, & Weber, 1999). This stream of research has also found that poor social integration of the acquired firm's managers leads to increased turnover (Ancona & Caldwell, 1992; Michel & Hambrick, 1992). Finally, recent research has found that loss of autonomy is positively related to top manager turnover (Lubatkin, Schweiger, & Weber, 1999).

Researchers have also begun to focus on the role of the retention of key technical people in the success of acquisitions. In recent years leaders in high-technology fields have used acquisitions of small private companies to acquire key technical skills, such as with Cisco Systems' pursuit of optics capabilities through the acquisition of several private companies (Wysocki, 1997). These firms are not interested in the smaller firms' tangible products or assets but rather in the knowledge, skills, and talents of their technical team in order to achieve critical mass in an area of strategic importance rapidly (Ranft & Lord, 2000). In fact, there is evidence that in these circumstances retention of the management team is less critical to the acquirer's evaluation of the success of an acquisition than the retention of key technical employees (Ranft & Lord, 2000).

There is clearly a need for further study of the causes and consequences of the turnover of scientific and technical talent in technology acquisitions. What role do changes or differences in HR policies and practices have on the level of turnover? What types of policies, procedures, or training can be implemented to minimize the loss of technical talent or at least mitigate the damage done by the loss of talent? Are there contingencies based on the age and size of the technical talent pool in the acquired firm, the size difference between the acquiring firm and the acquired firm, the distance between the acquiring firm's knowledge base and the knowledge of the technical employees in the acquired firm?

In the end, the current research tells us a fair amount about the conditions that lead to high levels of turnover in the top management team but significantly less about the conditions that lead to successful knowledge transfer or integration. Managers are using acquisitions as tools to acquire new knowledge, but the context in which this tool is effective is still open to conjecture. The actual process of knowledge integration and transfer during an acquisition is still somewhat mysterious and open for additional research. Finally, the impact of the type of knowledge being acquired on the transfer and integration process, as well as on the overall success of these acquisitions, demands further study.

Characteristics of the Knowledge and Choice of Strategy

The model presented in this section is based on four characteristics of the knowledge being acquired by the firm. First, is the knowledge a stock or a flow? Second, is the knowledge predominately tacit or explicit in nature? Third, what is the strategic importance of knowledge to the acquiring firm? Finally, how close is the knowledge base to the acquiring firm's current knowledge base? The impact of these four characteristics on the knowledge transfer allows for the development of a model that can help guide a firm's choice between the alternative strategies.

This section will discuss each of these characteristics and its impact on the choice of strategies. It will then attempt to bring this discussion together in coherent fashion and present the model and some examples of the guidance it provides in the choice of alternative strategies. Implicit in all of this discussion is the trade-off between internally developing new knowledge and externally acquiring knowledge. However, as the opening paragraphs noted, in today's rapidly changing environment the ability to develop all of the specific knowledge a firm is likely to require is becoming rare.

Tacit and Explicit Stocks and Flows

Organizational knowledge is a firm-specific asset that is not easily imitated and difficult to trade (Barney, 1986). People are endowed with firm-specific skills and values that they accumulate through on-the-job training and learning. Recent research has highlighted how important the human resources of a company are to firm performance in a knowledge-based environment (Hitt, Bierman, Shimizu, & Kochhar, 2001). Although there may exist knowledge at the organizational level, much of the critical knowledge exists not in some theoretical blueprint of activities but in the knowledge, skills, and talents of the organization's members. In fact, it is becoming increasingly clear that competitive advantage in resource- or knowledge-based competition depends heavily on the human resources and human resource practices of a firm.

The idiosyncratic nature of knowledge makes it difficult to trade or move across boundaries. Knowledge assets are not only difficult to trade but are accumulated through a number of mechanisms over time and in specific contexts (Dierickx & Cool, 1989). The underlying knowledge of a firm may be conceptualized as both stocks and flows of knowledge that contribute to the firm's superior performance. Stocks of knowledge are accumulated knowledge assets that are internal to a firm or organization, and flows of knowledge are knowledge streams into the firm or various parts of the firm that may be assimilated over time and developed into stocks of knowledge.

Asset stocks are accumulated over time by choosing appropriate paths for both internal development and tying into external flows over a period of time and converting these flows into knowledge stocks by developing organizational routines, gaining patents, or incorporating these flows into products and services. The bathtub metaphor (Dierickx & Cool, 1989) illustrates the differences and connections between asset stocks and flows.

At any point in time, the stock of water in a bathtub is indicated by the level of water in the tub. This stock of water is the cumulative result of flows of water into the tub (through the tap) and out of the tub (through leaks). With respect to firm capabilities, the amount of water in the tub may represent the stock of knowhow at a particular point in time. Current R&D spending, knowledge acquired through an ongoing alliance, or a recent acquisition is represented by the water flowing into the tub, and the water leaking out illustrates knowledge depreciation over time or knowledge that is simply not retained by conscious choice or because of personnel turnover. Flows like water coming into and leaking out of the tub may be adjusted through the use of such tools as we have discussed—hybrid structures and mergers and acquisition. HR practices that improve the retention of critical knowledge workers or enhance the ability of the firm to protect knowledge from leaking out through alliances can affect the outward flow of knowledge. Over time these flows can be used to adjust the stock of knowledge that a company retains by embedding the knowledge into procedures, activities, products, patents, and other forms. Also over time the firm's stocks of knowledge can be adjusted if it decides to stop offering certain product lines or services or if patents lapse or are licensed out. A firm's stock of knowledge can be thought of as similar to its available cash balance. Although these balances can be adjusted, they are fixed at any specific point in time.

Knowledge flows may have several sources. Different labs in a single university or in several universities or even several regions and countries may contribute to a flow of knowledge about a specific subject. However, to maintain the water metaphor, it is generally not possible to license the entire river but only the small streams that are the sources of the river. Monitoring these various sources and selecting partners or acquisition targets from among them can pose a significant challenge. As we move forward in our discussion, we are working on the assumption of a single source of the flow, but in the real world the selection of that source is likely to be a difficult and important challenge.

Although the characteristic of the knowledge being acquired as a stock or a flow has important implications for knowledge acquisition strategies it cannot be considered in isolation. The tacit versus explicit component of the stock or flow of knowledge must also be considered. The idea of tacit versus explicit knowledge is dealt with in other chapters of this volume. What is important for this discussion is the amount of learning by doing, close interaction training, and observation required to complete the transfer of the knowledge or skill across the organizational boundaries.

By combining these two sets of characteristics, we gain four basic knowledge classes: tacit-stock, explicit-stock, tacit-flow, and explicit-flow. These classes form the basis for the first set of decision criteria for the model. Before we move on, let us acknowledge that there are few pure forms and that the decision needs to be based on the predominant characteristics of the knowledge a firm is attempting to acquire.

Explicit-stock knowledge is perhaps the simplest type of knowledge to acquire from outside a firm's boundaries. Examples of this type of knowledge are patented chemical formulas, algorithms, software code, and so on. These are easily transferred because they are easily codified—that is, turned into written, executable instructions. It is also fairly easy to judge the quality of knowledge with these characteristics from the start, and in general this type of knowledge has strong intellectual property protection. These characteristics make it amenable to simple licensing agreements. More complex processes could be employed, but these processes require investment of greater resources in the management of the process. Therefore, the most appropriate tool for the acquisition of this type of knowledge is a simple licensing agreement.

In contrast, tacit-stock knowledge creates several challenges for an acquiring firm. An example of tacit-stock knowledge might be the artistry of a chef who can prepare stunning cuisine. Although this chef can write out and transmit his recipes, the knowledge of the exact color of the sauce or the specific taste he is trying to achieve or an eye to select the highest-quality ingredients is not easily translated. The acquisition of his stock of knowledge will require significant direct interaction or perhaps even the acquisition of the chef himself. Acquiring tacit-stock knowledge poses several challenges. First, the transaction will require significant interaction among the parties, and the ultimate success of this transaction will depend on the quality of this interaction. Essentially, acquiring this type of knowledge requires at a minimum a substantial training process, which increases the dependence of the acquiring firm on the other organization. This dependence raises the risks for the acquirer, and accordingly, increases the need for a more complicated governance structure for the transaction in order to mitigate those risks. Acquiring tacit-stock knowledge will require at minimum a strategic alliance, but depending on some of the other characteristics it could call for a joint venture or even that the transaction be internalized through an acquisition. These increasingly complex structures place greater demands on the managerial resources of the organization and are much more dependent on the development and maintenance of a strong relationship between the parties.

Explicit-flow knowledge poses a monitoring and access challenge for the firm acquiring it. Although the output of the knowledge flow is easily transferred across boundaries because of its explicit nature, the ongoing development of new knowledge in the flow is of significance to the acquiring firm. An example of explicit-flow knowledge would be the continual development and refinement of a series of software techniques and algorithms to sort through the increasingly large database of gene sequences and proteins. It has important implications and is likely to be protected intellectual property but is easily communicated and monitored because of the explicit nature of the software. Therefore, the acquirer has to monitor the source of the flow continually and maintain access to the knowledge being produced. One possible solution is simply to monitor the flow, and as interesting new knowledge is created enter into a license agreement for that specific knowledge. For example, a company might monitor the activities of a bioinformatics lab in a university and enter into licenses for any interesting new algorithms that are discovered. This would limit the firm's investment in the stream simply to monitoring the outflow and committing additional resources only when something interesting is developed. However, if the flow has significant strategic value, a more formal long-term contractual arrangement—a strategic alliance—becomes the appropriate governance mechanism. In these circumstances alliances generally allow for provision of resources and funds on the part of the firm attempting to acquire the knowledge in exchange for a contractual right of first refusal to an exclusive license of any products of the knowledge flow, generally a series of patents or intellectual property, but perhaps new information about the workings of a particular process in the human body. Strategic alliances are the preferred choice in these circumstances. They allow a firm to guarantee exclusive rights to a potentially valuable flow, but because it is explicit and easily transferred across boundaries the firm can avoid the expense and resource commitment of an acquisition. It is the next category, tacit-flow knowledge, that poses the greatest challenge for the firm acquiring knowledge.

Tacit-flow knowledge is the most difficult and frequently the most critical type of knowledge to acquire. These types of flows are frequently the leading edge of thought and development in a specific area of science or technology. The quality, value, and applications of such knowledge are highly uncertain, but the competitive implications are also potentially very significant. An example would be the current leading edge of thought in optics and microelectrical mechanical systems. The experts believe that these two streams are likely to converge to create the first fully optical router for computer networks, including Internet and intranet applications. This breakthrough will dramatically increase the speed at which information can be transferred over computer networks. The firm that creates the breakthrough is likely to have a significant and sustainable competitive advantage in a multibillion dollar market. It will become the next Cisco Systems. This research is being carried out in numerous small and large companies, as well as in numerous university labs and research institutes. The challenge combines basic ideas of physics, optics, engineering, materials science, and many other fields. But the complexity and ambiguity of the discovery and development process in this field makes it difficult information to transfer across organizational boundaries. A similar situation is occurring in the biopharmaceutical industry as it moves from mapping the genome to developing processes that will allow scientists to understand which genes in what combinations produce which proteins—the challenge of *proteomics.*

In each of these situations a combination of alliances and acquisitions is being used to acquire knowledge. In situations where the value and quality of the knowledge flow is highly uncertain, strategic alliances are useful in gaining access to the technologies. Alliances allow a firm that is acquiring knowledge to stake a claim to the flow and position it to gain additional knowledge about the potential value and quality of the knowledge flow. Strategic alliances in these circumstances frequently allow the acquirer to place a member of the organization on the research team, where she has close access to the tacit-flow knowledge and the team creating it. Thus the firm acquiring the knowledge has an option; if the tacit-flow knowledge appears very valuable the firm can exercise an option to acquire the other firm or the team and internalize the flow. If the flow's value remains uncertain the alliance can be maintained, and if its value appears low the option can be allowed to expire and the alliance dissolved. In situations where the potential importance of the flow is deemed to be high, then an immediate acquisition is the appropriate strategy. Cisco Systems, Intel, and Microsoft have all become masters of these techniques, using alliances and acquisitions to maintain their knowledge advantage. Cisco alone acquired over thirty technology companies between 1994 and 1997, mostly small software or hardware ventures with fewer than one hundred employees; CEO John Chambers states that the company makes these acquisitions to obtain critical technologies and to retain the best skilled knowledge workers (Wysocki, 1997). It is not the firm's stock of assets that Cisco is interested in acquiring but the flow of tacit knowledge that the technical team in the firm is capable of developing.

Strategic Importance

Another important characteristic of the knowledge a firm is attempting to acquire is its strategic importance. How critical is it to the firm's future competitive advantage or to sustaining its current competitive advantage? These are key questions that determine how important it is to maintain control of the knowledge. If the knowledge being acquired has significant strategic importance, then its control is critical because lack of control opens the firm to opportunistic action and threatens the firm's future. In conditions of high strategic importance the tool of choice is acquisition. Acquiring the owner of the knowledge—or if it is held by a nonprofit organization, acquiring exclusive rights to the knowledge through an alliance and also hiring team members or perhaps postdocs or graduate students from the facility—will allow the firm to gain as much control over the knowledge as possible. The problem of relying on an alliance or licensing agreement in these circumstances is that the knowledge, particularly explicit-stock or explicit-flow knowledge, is easily transmitted to other competitors, risking the loss of competitive advantage. In contrast, if the knowledge is useful but not critical to a competitive advantage then simple licenses or alliances are the preferred tools. Licenses and alliances minimize the commitment of managerial resources and the financial expense that would be necessary in an acquisition, allowing the firm to focus its resource expenditures on the knowledge that is strategically important.

Distance of the Knowledge Base

The final characteristic of the knowledge being acquired that has a bearing on choice of strategy is its distance from the firm's current knowledge base. Previous theory and empirical research have established that an organization's ability to learn or absorb new knowledge is based on its current knowledge base (Cohen & Levinthal, 1989). Recent work has found that both acquisitions (Ahuja & Katila, 2001) and strategic alliances (Lane & Lubatkin, 1998) have been more successful when the partner's or target's knowledge base is different from but not unrelated to that of the knowledge-acquiring firm. In fact, in their study of acquisitions Ahuja and Katila found an inverse U-shaped relationship between the relatedness of the acquired firm's knowledge base and the acquiring firm's knowledge base. Building and extending on this research, I argue that when knowledge bases are closely related, simple licenses or alliances are the preferred mode of knowledge acquisition. The knowledge-acquiring firm has significant absorptive capacity in the area and simply needs to access the knowledge in order to assimilate it. In situations where the knowledge bases are only moderately related, alliances or acquisitions are the appropriate tools, depending on the strategic importance of the knowledge. Because there is some overlap in the knowledge base, the knowledge-acquiring firm is in a position to judge the quality of the knowledge and to assimilate the knowledge. However, when the knowledge-acquiring firm is attempting to expand into a new area, then its lack of prior related knowledge hinders its ability to judge the quality of the knowledge base of the target firm and to assimilate the new knowledge easily. In these circumstances an alliance or perhaps a joint venture will allow the firm to learn and expand its knowledge base without risking a difficult-to-manage acquisition of uncertain quality. This strategy leaves open the possibility of an acquisition at a later date, or dissolution if the wrong partner was chosen or the knowledge is found to be of little value.

A Model of Contingencies

Exhibit 2.1 summarizes the previous discussion. The model has three key contingencies: type of the knowledge being acquired (tacit-stock, explicit-stock, tacit-flow, explicit-flow), strategic importance of the knowledge to be acquired, and distance of the knowledge from the firm's current knowledge base. When making a decision about which tool to use to acquire knowledge outside a firm's boundaries, the manager needs to weigh each of these contingencies. In fact, a decision process based on looking at the strategic importance first, followed by considering the distance from the current knowledge base, and finally thinking through the type of knowledge that is being acquired will lead to the appropriate choice. Strategic importance needs to be the first decision point because of the risks of getting it wrong. A firm that attempts to access critically important knowledge through an alliance exposes itself to

Exhibit 2.1. The Model and Contingencies.

| | Type of Knowledge | | | | Strategic Importance | | Distance from Firm's Current Knowledge Base | | |
| | Stock | | Flow | | | | | | |
	Tacit	Explicit	Tacit	Explicit	High	Low	Close	Medium	Far
Characteristics of Knowledge	Difficult to judge and transfer—not amenable to pure market transaction.	Easy to judge and transfer—amenable to market transaction.	Difficult to judge and transfer. Requires continual interaction since new knowledge is continually being developed.	Easy to judge and transfer but requires continual interaction since new knowledge is continually being developed.	Needs to control knowledge—pressure to internalize in order to avoid risk of opportunism.	Doesn't need to control knowledge—minimal risk of opportunistic action.	Easy to assimilate. Capable of judging quality of target's knowledge base.	Capable of judging quality. Moderate difficulty in assimilating knowledge.	Difficult to judge quality and difficult to assimilate knowledge.
Acquisition Strategy	Acquisition or strategic alliance	License	Exclusive alliance or acquisition, depending on the strategic importance and the source of the flow	Alliance	Acquisition, exclusive license	License, alliance	License or alliance based on type of knowledge	Alliance or acquisition, depending on the strategic importance	Alliance, learning opportunity, option strategy

risks of opportunistic action by its partner. As already noted, this has been a significant problem for small technology ventures dealing with large established firms. Recent research has questioned the benefit of alliances with large firms for technology ventures (Alvarez & Barney, 2001). These results maybe due to an overreliance on alliances to access critical strategic knowledge, such as marketing or regulatory know-how, that leaves them open to exploitation by opportunistic partners.

Once its strategic importance has been determined, then an accurate assessment of the distance of the knowledge from the firm's current knowledge base must be made. The distance of the knowledge affects the firm's ability to judge its quality and to assimilate it, both of which are critical to success. The more distant the knowledge the greater the learning potential but the higher the probability of failure; these are the conditions under which an options-based strategy using alliances will provide the greatest benefit. Finally, as discussed, the type of knowledge being acquired will have an impact on the structure of the transaction because of its effect on the level of interaction needed to acquire it.

Conclusion

In this chapter I have argued that the context in which knowledge acquisition takes place is an important determinant of how to govern the transaction. However, all such transactions are heavily embedded in a social context. What we lack currently is a real understanding of how this social context influences the personal interactions of the participants and how it influences the outcomes of these transactions. Are there other contingencies that need to be considered based on cultural distance between the organizations and the individuals? Are there dynamics at the level of the individual champions managing the alliances or acquisitions that are relevant to our understanding of these mechanisms? How does prior individual and organizational experience play into knowledge acquisition? Finally, assimilation of the knowledge being acquired is a critical and poorly understood process to which social psychologists may be able to add a great deal of insight. Attention to the microlevel processes of these types of transactions is critical and lacking in the current research. The role of HR practices in assessing, selecting, and retaining employees during acquisitions and the circumstances that are likely to influence turnover during acquisitions are particularly important. Research into the appropriate incentives, reward structures, and training for members of the organization involved in the management of strategic alliances or joint ventures would be helpful. Further understanding of the alternative strategies for knowledge acquisition requires the participation of social psychologists and organizational behaviorists in this area.

References

Ahuja, G., & Katila, R. (2001). Technological acquisitions and the innovation performance of acquiring firms: A longitudinal study. *Strategic Management Journal, 22,* 197–220.

Alvarez, S. A., & Barney, J. B. (2001, February). How entrepreneurial firms can benefit from alliances with large partners. *Academy of Management Executive.*

Anand, B., & Khanna, T. (2000). Do firms learn to create value? The case of alliances. *Strategic Management Journal, 21,* 295–315.

Ancona, D. G., & Caldwell, D. F. (1992, December). Bridging the boundary: External activity and performance in organizational teams. *Administrative Science Quarterly, 37*(4), 634–665.

Barley, S. R., Freeman, J., & Hybels, R. (1992). Strategic alliance in commercial biotechnology. In N. Nohria & R. G. Eccles (Eds.), *Networks and organizations.* Boston: Harvard Business School Press.

Barney, J. B. (1986, October). Strategic factor markets: Expectations, luck, and business strategy. *Management Science, 32*(10), 1230–1241.

Borys, B., & Jemison, D. B. (1989, April). Hybrid arrangements as strategic alliances: Theoretical issues. *Academy of Management Review, 14*(2).

Cohen, W. M., & Levinthal, D. A. (1990, March). Absorptive capacity: A new perspective on learning and innovation. *Administrative Science Quarterly, 35*(1), 128–152.

Dasgupta, P., & David, P. (1994). Toward a new economics of science. *Research Policy, 23,* 487–521.

Deeds, D. L. (1994). *An examination of the deterrents to opportunistic action in research alliances in the biotechnology industry.* Unpublished doctoral dissertation, University of Washington.

Deeds, D. L., & Hill, C. (1996). Strategic alliances and the rate of new product development: An empirical study of new biotechnology firms. *Journal of Business Venturing, 11*(1), 41–58.

Deeds, D. L., & Hill, C. (1999). An examination of social embeddedness as a deterrent to opportunistic action in a research alliance. *Journal of Business Venturing, 14*(2).

Dierickx, I., & Cool, K. (1989, December). Asset stock accumulation and sustainability of competitive advantage. *Management Science, 35*(12), 1504–1511.

Doz, Y. (1996). The evolution of cooperation in strategic alliances: Initial conditions or learning processes? *Strategic Management Journal, 17,* 55–83.

Dussuage, P., Garrette, B., & Mitchell, W. (2000). Learning from competing partners: Outcomes and durations of scale and link alliances in Europe, North America, and Asia. *Strategic Management Journal, 21,* 99–126.

Granstrand, O., Bohlin, E., Oskarsson, C., & Sjoberg, N. (1992, April). External technology acquisition in large multitechnology corporations. *R&D Management, 22*(2), 111–133.

Granstrand, O., & Sjolander, S. (1990, June). The acquisition of technology and small firms by large firms. *Journal of Economic Behavior and Organization, 13*(3), 367–386.

Grant, R. M., & Baden-Fuller, C. (1995). A knowledge-based theory of inter-firm collaboration. *Academy of Management Best Paper Proceedings, 1995,* pp. 17–21.

Gulati, R. (1995). Does familiarity breed trust? The implications of repeated ties for contractual choice in alliances. *Academy of Management Journal, 38,* 85–112.

Hagedoorn, J., & Schakenraad, J. (1994). The effect of strategic technology alliances on company performance. *Strategic Management Journal, 15,* 291–309.

Hambrick, D. C., & Cannella, A. A. (1993, August). Relative standing: A framework for understanding departures of acquired executives. *Academy of Management Journal, 36*(4), 733–762.

Hamel, G. (1991). Competition for competence and inter-partner learning within international strategic alliances. *Strategic Management Journal, 12,* 83–103.

Hill, C., & Deeds, D. L. (1996). The importance of industry structure for the determination of firm profitability: A neo-Austrian perspective. *Journal of Management Studies, 33*(4), 429–451.

Hitt, M. A., Bierman, L., Shimizu, K., & Kochhar, R. (2001). Direct and moderating effects of human capital on strategy and performance in professional service firms: A resource-based perspective. *Academy of Management Journal, 44*(1), 13–28.

Hitt, M. A., Hoskisson, R. A., Ireland, R. D., & Harrison, J. S. (1991). Effects of acquisitions on R&D inputs and outputs. *Academy of Management Journal, 34*(3), 693–706.

Hitt, M. A., Hoskisson, R. A., Johnson, R. A., & Moesel, D. D. (1996). The market for corporate control and firm innovation. *Academy of Management Journal, 39*(5), 1084–1119.

Jorde, T., & Teece, D. J. (1989, Spring). Competition and cooperation: Striking the right balance. *California Management Review, 31*(3).

Karim, S., & Mitchell, W. (2000). Path-dependent and path-breaking change: Reconfiguring business resources following acquisitions in the U.S. medical sector, 1978–1995. *Strategic Management Journal, 21*(10/11), 1061–1081.

Khanna, T., Gulati, R., & Nohria, N. (1998). The dynamics of learning alliances: Competition, cooperation, and relative scope. *Strategic Management Journal, 19,* 193–210.

Kozin, M. D., & Young, K. C. (1994, September-October). Using acquisitions to buy and hone core competencies. *Mergers & Acquisitions,* pp. 21–26.

Krug, J. A., & Hegarty, W. H. (1997, September). Postacquisition turnover among U.S. top management teams: An analysis of the effects of foreign vs. domestic acquisitions of U.S. targets. *Strategic Management Journal, 18*(8), 667–675.

Lane, P. J., & Lubatkin, M. (1998). Relative absorptive capacity and interorganizational learning. *Strategic Management Journal, 19,* 461–477.

Leblebici, H., & Salancik, G. (1982). Stability in interorganizational exchanges: Rule-making processes in the Chicago board of trade. *Administrative Science Quarterly, 27,* 227–242.

Lubatkin, M., Schweiger, D. M., & Weber, Y. (1999). Top management turnover in related M&As: An additional test of the theory of relative standing. *Journal of Management, 25*(1), 55–73.

Michel, J. G., & Hambrick, D. C. (1992, March). Diversification posture and top management team characteristics. *Academy of Management Journal, 35*(1), 9–37.

Mitchell, W., & Singh, K. (1996). Survival of businesses using collaborative relationships to commercialize complex goods. *Strategic Management Journal, 17,* 169–195.

Pfeffer, J., & Salancik, G. (1978). *The external control of organizations.* New York: HarperCollins.

Ranft, A. L., & Lord, M. D. (2000). Acquiring new knowledge: the role of retaining human capital in acquisitions of high-tech firms. *Journal of High Technology Management Research, 11*(2), 295–319.

Rothaermel, F. T., & Deeds, D. L. (2002). More good things are not necessarily better: An empirical study of strategic alliances, experience effects, and innovative output in high technology start-ups. In M. A. Hitt, R. Amit, C. Lucier, & R. D. Nixon (Eds.), *Creating value: Winners in the new business environment* (pp. 85–103). Oxford, UK: Blackwell.

Sakakibara, M. (1997, Summer). Heterogeneity of firm capabilities and cooperative research and development: An empirical examination of motives. *Strategic Management Journal.*

Schweiger, D. M., & DeNisi, A. S. (1991, March). Communication with employees following a merger: A longitudinal field experiment. *Academy of Management Journal, 34*(1), 110–135.

Shan, W., Walker, G., & Kogut, B. (1994). Interfirm cooperation and startup innovation in the biotechnology industry. *Strategic Management Journal, 15,* 387–394.

Sikora, M. (2001). Uncertainties cloud the M&A outlook in 2001. *Mergers & Acquisitions, 36*(2), 4–8.

Simonin, B. L. (1999). Ambiguity and the process of knowledge transfer in strategic alliances. *Strategic Management Journal, 20,* 595–623.

Singh, K., & Mitchell, W. (1996). Precarious collaboration: Business survival after partners shut down or form new partnerships. *Strategic Management Journal, 17,* 95–115.

Stuart, T. E. (2000). Interorganizational alliances and the performance of firms: A study of growth and innovation rates in a high technology industry. *Strategic Management Journal, 21,* 791–811.

Teece, D. (1986). Profiting from technological innovation: Implications for integration, collaboration, licensing and public policy. *Research Policy, 15,* 285–305.

Varadarajan, P. R., & Cunningham, M. H. (1995, Fall). Strategic alliances: A synthesis of conceptual foundations. *Academy of Marketing Science Journal.*

Vermeulen, F., & Barkema, H. (2001). Learning through acquisitions. *Academy of Management Journal, 44*(3), 457–476.

Very, P., Lubatkin, M., Calori, R., & Veiga, J. (1997, September). Relative standing and the performance of recently acquired European firms. *Strategic Management Journal, 18*(8), 593–614.

Walsh, J. P. (1988, March-April). Top management turnover following mergers and acquisitions. *Strategic Management Journal, 9*(2), 173–183.

Walsh, J. P. (1989, July-August). Doing a deal: Merger and acquisition negotiations and their impact upon target company top management turnover. *Strategic Management Journal, 10*(4), 307–322.

Walsh, J. P., & Ellwood, J. W. (1991, March). Mergers, acquisitions, and the pruning of managerial deadwood. *Strategic Management Journal, 12*(3), 201–217.

Walsh, J. P., & Kosnick, R. D. (1993, August). Corporate raiders and their disciplinary role in the market for corporate control. *Academy of Management Journal, 36*(4), 671–700.

Williamson, O. E. (1975). *Markets and hierarchies: Analysis and antitrust implications.* New York: Free Press.

Williamson, O. E. (1991). Comparative economic organization: Analysis of discrete structural alternatives. *Administrative Science Quarterly, 36,* 269–296.

Wysocki, B. Jr. (1997, October 6). Why an acquisition? Often, it's the people. *Wall Street Journal.*

CHAPTER 3

Organizing for Knowledge-Based Competitiveness
About Pipelines and Rivers
C. Marlene Fiol

Knowledge management in organizations is concerned with creating, mobilizing, and applying knowledge for competitive advantage. As noted in the first chapter of this volume, there is a growing consensus among practitioners and researchers that knowledge is one of a firm's most important strategic assets. Managing this asset is becoming both more important and more difficult. The amount of information inside companies is increasing by 2 percent each month (Jensen, 1998). This means that every eleven hundred days there will be twice as much information, and everyone's ability to transform information into work will become twice as important and twice as complicated. To maintain competitiveness in such an environment, astute management of knowledge is imperative (Pinelli & Barclay, 1998).

There is also agreement that knowledge can be created and managed to enhance competitiveness. In a 1997 survey, 94 percent of respondents said they believed they could leverage the knowledge in their organization more effectively through deliberate

Note: Many thanks to Ed O'Connor and Ray Zammuto for their helpful comments on earlier versions of this chapter.

management. U.S. companies paid $1.5 billion for knowledge management services in 1996, and it was estimated they would spend $5 billion a year by 2001 (Blumentritt & Johnston, 1999).

In contrast, there is little consensus about *how* organizations should be designed for effective knowledge management. This chapter provides a brief review of what we know about designing knowledge management processes and identifies some of the limitations of current approaches. It then proposes a way to address those limitations.

Three Premises About Knowledge

Before presenting my arguments, I highlight the three premises on which they are built. First, knowledge exists as both an individual and an organizational phenomenon in explicit and tacit forms. Second, knowledge competition is universal, rather than relating to select groups of firms or market niches. And third, no single competitive advantage is sustainable in today's hypercompetitive environment, no matter how inimitable. So, letting go of old knowledge is as important as creating the new.

Premise 1: The Nature of Knowledge

Knowledge exists in organizations as both an individual and an organizational phenomenon, and in both explicit and tacit forms. *Explicit knowledge* is knowledge that can be transmitted to others in a relatively straightforward manner. Although it may belong to individuals, it may be transferred to the organizational level in written documents, contracts, and formal presentations, for example. *Tacit knowledge* is more difficult to articulate, including skills that others may learn by doing and mental models or schemas that others may learn through interaction (Lubit, 2001). It may belong to individuals—when people know more than they can say (Polanyi, 1966)—and exist at the level of organizations—when organizations know more than contracts can say (Kogut & Zander, 1992). Examples include the individual and organizational routines and beliefs Boudreau refers to in Chapter Thirteen of this volume. Whereas formal and problem- or goal-focused interactions are useful for sharing explicit knowledge in organizations, casual and nondirected interactions among people are more likely to result in the sharing of tacit knowledge (Lubit, 2001). Noe, Colquitt, Simmering, and Alvarez in Chapter Eight similarly refer to the personal discussions needed to transfer "communication codes" not amenable to explicit encoding.

Premise 2: Knowledge Competition Is Universal

Knowledge competition is often referred to as competition among *knowledge-intensive firms* (KIFs) (Starbuck, 1992). The term KIF imitates economists' labeling of firms as capital-intensive or labor-intensive. Labeling a firm as knowledge-intensive implies that knowledge has more importance for it than other inputs.

Because people define knowledge differently, discussions of KIFs lead to debates about the proper definition of such companies. Adding further fuzziness to the concept is the fact that all organizations are becoming more knowledge-intensive in the service, industrial, and governmental sectors (Boland, Tenkasi, & Ramkrishnan, 1995) because knowledge is rapidly becoming a universal source of competitiveness. The term is thus losing its specialized meaning. Managing knowledge has become a top priority for all organizations.

Premise 3: Competitive Advantage Is Not Sustainable

Larry Prusak of IBM concluded recently that "the only sustainable competitive advantage comes from what you know and how fast you can put it to use" (quoted in Cohen, 1998, p. 23). But what you know today may be of little use tomorrow. In fact, core competencies often become core rigidities in highly competitive environments (Leonard-Barton, 1992). Hamel and Prahalad (1994) suggested periodic reengineering of a company's genetic code for this reason.

It is essential to renew and cannibalize prior capabilities. A complete life cycle for knowledge management must thus not only include the creation, dissemination, and application of knowledge but also its retirement when it has outlived its usefulness (Davis, 1998). The focus of most knowledge management efforts has been on the creation and dissemination of new knowledge (Blumentritt & Johnston, 1999), and the challenges of applying knowledge are beginning to gain attention. But we know very little about knowledge destruction or undoing at the point in time when it has become old or irrelevant or otherwise no longer useful.

Pipelines and Rivers

Traditional approaches for knowledge management rest on a pipeline metaphor: knowledge is a thing that can be transmitted across locations, much like piped water. From this perspective, the volume and flow of knowledge can be managed directly, much as one can measure the flow of water in a pipeline. The complementary approach I introduce in this chapter is a river metaphor: knowing is a process that shifts and changes over time. The volume and flow of knowing can be supported by management structures and technologies only indirectly.

A pipeline view of knowledge transmission assumes that knowledge is something out there that can be manipulated, stored, and disseminated like water in a pipeline; it is disembodied. The belief is that organizations can possess it apart from individuals (Choudhury & Sampler, 1997), because the skills and insights of individuals become embedded in routines, practices, and norms that outlast their presence (Attewell, 1992).

Especially in the Western world, our focus has been on knowledge as a disembodied thing, leading to an emphasis on its management and measurement (Cohen, 1998). For example, research has modeled organizational memory as existing in storage bins, implying a concept of knowledge as separate from the social processes of knowing (Walsh & Ungson, 1991). The traditional knowledge management approaches reviewed in the following section tend to follow this logic.

In contrast, a river view of knowing assumes that knowledge exists as a process among people (Lopres & Babbitt, 2000). It is a view that Mohrman reflects in Chapter Four when she states that knowledge is relational and constructed through social interaction. From this perspective, knowledge is embodied and has no meaning apart from the meanings people assign to it—much like the boundaries of a river that are defined by the water running through them.

Although the water flowing through a river can be measured, and structures like dams can change its course, the source of inputs is far less manageable than in pipelines. Changing the volume and direction of a river requires long and detailed attention and care, and even with such care, desired outcomes are not guaranteed. In the Eastern world, the focus has long been on the attention and care that is needed to nurture the communities that are the source of knowing (Cohen, 1998). From a river perspective, technologies and structures may support but cannot create the caring communities needed for effective knowledge creation, dissemination, application, and destruction. They can generally channel the flows but cannot direct them in the sense that a pipeline can. Finally, as noted later, rivers can accommodate revolutionary changes as well as emergent new channels better than rigid pipelines can.

Teece once asked, "What are the appropriate nouns and verbs of knowledge work?" (quoted in Cohen, 1998, p. 35). I think that is a great question, one that is closely related to my metaphorical use of pipelines and rivers. If we begin with the premise that a fixed stock of knowledge can lead to sustained advantage and that the destruction of knowledge is not a critical issue, the fixed and static nature of knowledge viewed as a noun is not problematic. Given the premise of this chapter, the dynamism and change of knowing viewed as a verb is critical.

This chapter suggests that both nouns and verbs, both pipelines and rivers, are appropriate to understanding knowledge work in organizations. Both the more traditional pipeline view of information transmission and the less traditional, dynamic view of knowing as a social process refer to knowledge creation, dissemination, and application in organizations. The points of departure differ, however. From a process perspective, rather than beginning with information needs and tools, for example, one would first identify the community that cares about a topic and then enhance its ability to think together, stay in touch, share ideas, and connect with other communities. Ironically, to leverage knowledge from this perspective the focus is on the community that owns it and the people who use it rather than on the knowledge itself (McDermott, 1999).

I will argue that one can only manage *knowledge* as a noun effectively if one first understands *knowing* as a verb. If knowledge is a thing—like water in a pipeline—we will think of ways to manage and measure it like a thing, as do the traditional knowledge management approaches described later. The attention will focus on improving the efficiency of the physical assets because that is what gets measured, appraised, and evaluated by senior managers. In contrast, if knowing is like a flowing river, changing at every bend, it cannot easily be managed, and so we must find ways to support its flow. My use of metaphors thus becomes an expression of approaches for managing knowledge work.

The following sections review two traditional pipeline approaches for knowledge management and highlight some of the limitations of beginning there. From a pipeline perspective, designing the appropriate organizational conditions for effective knowledge management requires identifying appropriate technologies and structures (Volberda, 1996).

Improved Technologies for Effective Knowledge Management

Information technologies (IT) have taken center stage in discussions of knowledge management. Traditional information systems designs represent pipelines that are meant to deposit the required data at the proper time to the appropriate decision maker. Advances in IT have, in fact, greatly facilitated the dissemination and integration of explicit knowledge by increasing the ease with which it can be codified, communicated, assimilated, stored, and retrieved (Grant, 1996).

What people refer to as *knowledge management* often comes down to building an intranet (Cohen, 1998). In 1998, 62 percent of companies with over ten thousand employees had intranet-based knowledge management systems in place. Among the IT systems in existence at that time, 65 percent carried customer information, 58 percent company performance data, 54 percent product information, and 53 percent sales marketing data (Deloitte & Touche Consulting Group, 1998). Most IT systems are used to communicate internally with employees, with far fewer linking insiders with outsiders such as customers or suppliers. The most generic IT infrastructure applications include e-mail, group "calendaring" and scheduling, threaded discussions, e-forms and workflow applications, and knowledge directories (Davis, 1998).

In 1998, the industries in which IT systems were most widespread were telecommunications-media (71 percent), professional services (58 percent), and utilities (57 percent) (Deloitte & Touche Consulting Group, 1998). However, in industries as diverse as automotive manufacturing, chemical processing, electric utilities, and architectural engineering, firms are beginning to pursue IT initiatives with the stated goal of generating, facilitating the transfer of, and improving access to organizational knowledge (Marshall, Prusak, & Shpilberg, 1996).

Why the current emphasis on implementing knowledge management technologies? There are two reasons. First, as noted in the first chapter of this volume, organizational knowledge management is more essential for competitiveness now than ever before. Second, it is more feasible now than ever before. The Internet and intranet allow rapid, global transfer of information that is available twenty-four hours a day. URLs and Web sites full of new information appear or change every day; higher-speed computers provide faster and faster access. Internet technology has broken down market barriers by offering far cheaper options for enterprise-wide collaboration than existed previously. In addition, its interoperable nature allows for a flexible combination of technologies (Doyle & du Toit, 1998).

Cisco Systems provides an excellent example of a firm that is intentionally influencing knowledge flows through its management of IT. Cisco makes extensive use of its intranet to cultivate knowledge by linking together all functions in the organization as well as suppliers and customers. The company's intranet allows information to be distributed throughout the organization but centralized into one easily accessible place (Bryant, 2000). Employees use a Web browser to type in their own data, place orders for equipment, check their progress against performance targets, and get instant access to management information from PCs connected to Cisco's intranet service (Goodwin, 1999).

Limitations of a Technological Approach

Virtually every information technology—from computers to filing cabinets, standardized forms, and telephones—has been hailed as the key to dramatically improving organizational efficiency. But the benefits are usually coupled with strong disadvantages, and there is little evidence of uniform productivity growth linked to a particular technology (Nass, 1994). Research confirms a similar finding for current IT initiatives. Across the 108 companies they studied, Lucier and Torsilieri (2000) found no correlation between bottom-line results and the scope of IT initiatives. The return on investment from IT simply was not there. It appears that investment in IT, in and of itself, cannot buy a competitive edge.

Why not? I believe the answer lies partly in the fact that researchers and practitioners alike have tended to view IT as the primary driver of knowledge work, rather than simply a facilitator of the role of interacting communities of practice in generating knowledge. IT creates access to so much information that access is no longer the challenge. More pressing issues now have to do with making the information meaningful, supporting its application, and discarding it when it is no longer useful. Knowledge becomes meaningful and useful through human action and interaction. It is therefore not terribly surprising that knowledge workers still seem to want and need to work in close proximity (Blumentritt & Johnston, 1999). From a meaning-making perspective, the challenge of IT initiatives is to serve as facilitators of the human process of interpretation (Meindl, Stubbart, & Porac, 1996) rather than as primary drivers of knowledge access and flow.

A central limitation of a pipeline technology approach to knowledge management, then, is its lack of focus on interpretation and meaning (Boland et al., 1995). A lack of attention to meaning-making processes can result in incompatible "information islands," because the same information may hold many different meanings (Raitt, Loekken, Scholz, Steiner, & Secchi, 1997). The presumption of a world where decision makers can rely on a technical language as the source of organizational knowledge denies that people are important sense makers who use information in action, constantly searching for meaning and understanding. From a river perspective, we need to know the natural tides and eddies of human interaction and work with them to influence knowledge flows.

A second limitation of a pipeline technology approach to knowledge management is the loss of complexity that it often entails. Much organizational knowledge is tacit and has to be made explicit before it can be easily disseminated throughout an organization (Doyle & du Toit, 1998). This can be done through information technologies that codify and simplify knowledge in order to make it accessible to the wider organization, much like pipelines simplify the flow of water. The very process of simplification that allows easy transmission is also the process by which essential knowledge ingredients are lost (Blumentritt & Johnston, 1999). It is thus important to maintain social interactions to supplement codified knowledge with the rich depth and detail that can result from these interactions.

A third limitation of a pipeline technology approach is that its formality makes changing knowledge and discarding knowledge difficult. If it is not maintained regularly, outdated information can be as bad as (or perhaps worse than) no information. IT leaves little room for the informal, the tacit, and the socially embedded, which is where experience-based know-how lies and continuous updates occur. Thomas (2001) referred to corridor chatter as a natural information system that allows for continuous knowledge changes. Formal IT systems have in many ways replaced such informal chatter as the source of important knowledge diffusion. Formalizing knowledge work in this way is likely to limit its timeliness and its flexibility (Blumentritt & Johnston, 1999), much as pipelines limit the flexibility of water flows.

The small offshoots from a river—not accommodated in rigid pipelines—are often the beginning of new flows. Cisco's recent downturn provides a useful illustration of the fact that not all knowledge flows neatly from prior knowledge. In the aftermath of an abrupt and unexpected $2.2 billion inventory write-off in April 2001, CEO John Chambers used a river analogy when he said that the "Internet economy's all-out slump has been like a hundred-year flood" (Anders, 2001, p. 100) and that nature's ravages were being repaired as the company rebuilt its focus on virtual networks. A river perspective of the role of IT can accommodate revolutionary new knowledge creation. A rigid pipeline-type view would lead to a breakdown of knowledge, or at a minimum, to a severe backup in knowledge flows.

Finally, efforts to design technologies to support knowledge work in organizations have tended not to address the social quality of knowledge (Meindl et al., 1996). The designs have focused either on the individual as an isolated decision maker or on the group as a homogeneous decision-making unit. To support the flow of knowledge inside and between communities of users, the focus must expand to encompass the rich give-and-take among diverse participants. Every member of a community of practice has only partial knowledge. Each part does not make much sense because alone it is incomplete. It must come together with other incomplete parts to make sense (Brown & Duguid, 1998). This occurs through social interaction, which leads to forms of collective knowing that cannot be distilled down to one individual's understanding.

Knowledge, in fact, belongs to communities. People do not learn in isolation. Everyone is born into a world already full of knowledge, a world that already makes sense to other people—parents, neighbors, church members, community, and country. People learn by participating in these communities and come to embody their ideas, perspectives, prejudices, languages, and practices (McDermott, 1999). Thus, technologies must expand to support the social nature of knowledge work.

In sum, a pipeline view of technological knowledge management is the most common and familiar approach to knowledge management in organizational studies. It portrays knowledge work as an information-sending and information-receiving process through a transmission channel. Internet and intranet technologies have created an insatiable demand for and access to information. But how valuable is it? What use is to be made of it? What does it mean?

Knowledge work is not simply about combining, sharing, or making information commonly available. It is about social connections and interpretations. It happens through meaningful communication. Technologies alone cannot produce such meaning. Even with the emphasis in many organizations now beginning to shift away from a "database-centered" view of IT toward the communication potential of new technologies from ITs to ICTs (information and communications technologies), technologies alone cannot produce meaning. They can, however, serve as important enablers of communication, as discussed next.

Using Technology to Support Knowledge Work

A pipeline view of knowledge management focuses on the direct influence of information systems technologies as the primary drivers of knowledge creation, dissemination, and application. For example, it addresses how the intranet can directly influence access to knowledge sources and dissemination of knowledge in organizations (Doyle & du Toit, 1998). But evidence suggests that a focus on technology alone as the driver of knowledge work is likely to lead to disappointing results. The most important influence of technology on knowledge work may be much less direct—as an enabler of the processes that underlie it. For example, by enabling the decentralization of decision making and increasing the availability of information, the intranet may play an indirect role in supporting the social processes that make up knowledge work.

Information management systems are becoming more sophisticated every day. This probably means that they will play an ever larger role in supporting knowledge work in organizations. Technologies *do* have an enormous role to play, but they can play it meaningfully only to the extent that they respond to the social context. For example, several years ago Texaco's information technology group installed Lotus Notes, hoping it would lead to greater collaboration. They soon discovered that employees only used it for e-mail. Not until they had an urgent need to collaborate and change the way they worked together did they use the software in the way the IT group had envisioned. Information technology can support and reinforce an organization's norms about documenting, sharing information, and using the ideas of others, but it cannot itself create those norms (McDermott, 1999). Instead, the first step must be to understand how and why people interact.

ABB provides an example of a company that uses IT to support the emergence of working patterns that let people interact and communicate in new ways. The company employs a powerful corporate intranet technology to enhance meaningful communication on a real-time basis among far-flung global business activities. The strategic plans of various units are integrated and translated into action plans that are put on-line, available over the corporation's intranet to the company's relevant global managers. Managers are empowered to modify the action plans for which they are responsible, taking into account the local realities as unanticipated developments occur. Strategic planning staffs monitor these changes and inform the senior managers as new strategic issues emerge. Such a use of the intranet taps into the implicit mental models of its users, leading to the diffusion of tacit as well as explicit knowledge. It enhances sensitivity to diverse events, facilitates participation and integration of managers at various levels, and importantly, enables managers to arrive at realistic interpretations for better decisions (Senthilkumar & White, 2000).

Paris-based BDDP Advertising provides another example of IT systems that support meaningful communication. Employees use an internal communication Web site that is fast becoming a virtual watercooler for the organization. Courtesy of a Web browser, thousands of copywriters, graphic designers, account executives, and other advertising workers around the globe go into a virtual huddle, sending text, graphic files, video clips, and faxes (Fryer, 1998). The system not only supports but also actually enhances the work that gets done at BDDP. Employees rate the content of information that is posted on the Web. The most popular, useful information gets top billing on the Web site. The result is a culture shift. Instead of copywriters and designers hiding their best ideas in a file folder where no one else can see them, ideas are continually and even joyfully shared and improved.

How BDDP's system was designed offers an important lesson for those of us interested in improving knowledge work in organizations. Simply figuring out a way to distribute information on a corporate intranet was not how the company began the process. Instead, the leaders hired someone to do the "cultural anthropology" necessary to develop a schematic for the network. The IT anthropologist went to New York, Paris, London, and Singapore and listened to employees talk about how they worked and interacted, and from that he attempted to cull a conceptual design that actually reflected their work patterns. The new system was designed to appeal to the workers' sense of self-expression and even to their vanity (Fryer, 1998).

Systems like that one are based on social engineering that derives more from scripts in psychology and anthropology than from scripts in Java. A truly meaningful application of IT, such as BDDP's, demands careful observation of the way people work, an understanding of their motivations, and knowledge of what they are trying to do in their jobs. Unfortunately, BDDP appears to be an exceptional case. Most knowledge management efforts are technology- rather than people-driven (Fryer, 1998).

In sum, the information management efforts that effectively enable meaningful communication begin with and place their primary focus on individuals in interaction and communication rather than on the technology. As Noe and colleagues suggest in Chapter Eight, the barriers to effective knowledge creation and transfer tend to be social and cultural rather than technological. To break down these barriers, people need to make sense of and coordinate the ambiguous and complex meanings in their environment, rather than strip meaning from their work through simplified codification. This means supporting informal social interactions rather than isolating people on information islands.

Improved Structures for Effective Knowledge Management

According to a second line of research, the key to effective knowledge management is to focus on the organizational structures that influence the flow of information (Nass, 1994). Formal organizational structures show the intended configuration of positions, job duties, and the lines of authority among different parts of an organization. Structures have traditionally been important to how firms process knowledge because members interact not only as individuals but also as actors performing organizational roles (Lane & Lubatkin, 1998). Organizational structures are thus often viewed as a proxy for a firm's knowledge-processing system (Van den Bosch, Volberda, & De Boer, 1999).

A structural approach to knowledge management is once again based on a pipeline view of the process. A structure is something made up of a number of parts that are held or put together in a particular way (Berube, 1985). The belief is that structures can be put in place to organize and move knowledge as a thing that is out there, and to influence a firm's ability to synthesize and apply that knowledge—its absorptive capacity (Cohen & Levinthal, 1990). Like pipelines, physical structures can be measured, appraised, and evaluated (Bontis, Dragonetti, Jacobsen, & Roos, 1999), making them more accessible and manageable than the social processes of knowledge work.

Research suggests that organizational structures must be put in place to increase the speed with which managers receive information and to expand the range of information they receive (Kiesler & Sproull, 1982). The assumption is that developing structures that support greater speed and breadth of information leads to more highly differentiated knowledge structures and enhanced decision making. Following this general premise, Thomas and McDaniel (1990), for example, showed that the information-processing structure of the top management team accounted for some of the variance in how CEOs in different organizations interpreted information. They did not clearly specify how structural differences lead to differences in interpretation. However, they assumed—as have most researchers—that structural characteristics directly affect how knowledge is processed and applied.

The assumption in management research has long been that structures directly affect knowledge work. What has changed over time are beliefs about what types of organizational structures are most appropriate for the effective management of knowledge processes. The following sections briefly describe the shift from top-down to flatter organizational structures.

Top-Down Structures

Traditionally, three well-known organizational forms have been discussed in the management literature, each with a different configuration of a top-down structure: functional, divisional, and matrix. The three organizational forms can roughly be described by analyzing methods of grouping activities and by the number of hierarchical levels on the organization chart. Each form represents, in theory, trade-offs between efficiency and the flexibility and scope of knowledge absorption (Van den Bosch et al., 1999).

Functional structures group individuals by skill and specialized knowledge. They have a high potential for efficiency but a low potential for both scope and flexibility of knowledge absorption because the organization is carved into specialized, narrow knowledge domains. There also tends to be rigidity—that is, resistance to change—especially if change in one functional area is needed to help in others. *Divisional structures* group individuals by products, services, or clients. Though the scope of knowledge is broader, they tend to have a low potential for flexibility of knowledge absorption because of the focus on specific and defined targets. There tends to be difficulty in coordination across divisions. *Matrix structures* use both functional and divisional forms simultaneously. Workers in the middle of the matrix have two bosses—one functional and one product-, service-, or client-based. This structure is less efficient because of the multiple lines of authority, but in theory it has a higher potential for both scope and flexibility of knowledge absorption because it increases the lines of communication (Van den Bosch et al., 1999).

All three traditional structures rely on top-down direction, despite the different groupings of activities. They are based on what Mohrman (Chapter Four) refers to as industrial era assumptions of bureaucratic structures and hierarchical controls. They assume that the more complex an activity, the greater the number of locations in which that activity must be carried out, and the more stringent the performance specifications for the outcome of that activity, the greater must be the reliance on knowledge integration through top-down direction.

Flattened Structures

An alternative view is that hierarchies of capabilities do not correspond closely with their authority-based structures as depicted in organization charts, so top-down direction may not be the most effective way to manage an organization's capabilities. A further problem with top-down processes of collecting and distributing information is that they can be cumbersome and slow. Worse, the power to withhold or manipulate that information may be misused by a small central group at the top. Finally, and maybe most important, is the loss of knowledge that often occurs in top-down direction. Direction involves codifying tacit knowledge into explicit rules and instructions. For example, the implicit recognition, based on experience, that the market tends to respond well to price reductions before Christmas may be codified into an explicit rule of a 10 percent price cut at that time. This rule lacks the accompanying more implicit knowledge that the assumed market response occurs only if prices have been stable and generally higher than the competition, and based on other factors known from experience that are difficult to express in a single formula. Converting tacit knowledge into explicit knowledge in the form of rules and directives inevitably involves substantial knowledge loss. It is thus critical to preserve the tacit understanding and facilitate its dissemination through continuous informal social interactions.

For all of these reasons, companies are flattening their hierarchies and making them less bureaucratic by relying on teams to manage and recasting traditional managers as coordinators of cross-functional teams (Despres, 1996). New organizational forms are replacing structures that provide central control over activities. Three concepts that represent these new forms are the *shamrock organization, network organization,* and *virtual corporation.*

Charles Handy described the shamrock organization in his book *The Age of Unreason* (1989). A shamrock has three leaves on each stem. Each leaf represents a different group of people. The first represents full-time employees with critical core competencies. The second represents a group of outside operators who contract with the core group to perform a variety of jobs. The third represents a group of part-timers who can be hired temporarily by the core group, depending on the needs of the business.

A network organization relies on alliances and partnerships of various kinds between formerly independent organizations. The blurring of industry boundaries between, for instance, computers, consumer electronics, entertainment, banking, and telecommunications has spawned experimentation with new networked organizational forms (Van den Bosch et al., 1999). *Fortune* magazine, for example, reported that alliances were so central to Corning's strategy that the company defines itself as a network of organizations (Sherman, 1992).

An extreme version of the network organizational form is the virtual corporation (Davidow & Malone, 1993). This organization exists only as a temporary network of otherwise independent companies that are jointly pursuing a particular opportunity. Members of a virtual corporation may include suppliers, customers, and even competitors, which temporarily share such things as skills, costs, and access to global markets.

Besides describing shamrocks and virtual networks, management futurologists have conceptualized the new organizational landscape as a cellular organization (Miles, Snow, Mathews, Miles,

& Coleman, 1997), hypertext organization (Nonaka & Takeuchi, 1995), and platform organization (Ciborra, 1996). All of these conceptualizations have one thing in common: the flattening of organizational hierarchies.

The way organizational leaders describe their own structures reflects the same flattening. Eastman Kodak calls its organizational structure a pizza chart because it depicts all employees as equal (the pepperonis are randomly distributed), PepsiCo's pyramidal organization chart shows the apex at the bottom, and McKinsey & Company's organization chart shows a structure of three boxes floating above a set of multifunctional processes (Despres, 1996).

What are the implications of such flattened structures for knowledge work? In theory, flatter organizations draw on the core competencies of each member. This should increase access to the most valuable knowledge. Relationships are often temporary and focused on one opportunity, breaking up once the opportunity no longer exists. This should ensure the flexibility of new knowledge creation and the destruction of knowledge that is no longer needed. Finally, the boundaries around groups in organizations as well as around the organization itself are more permeable, in theory allowing a freer flow of knowledge.

Researchers and practitioners alike seem to have come to the conclusion that tall, top-down structures are bad and that flatter structures are good. I wonder if this is a pendulum swing that will soon swing back the other way. Pendulum swings are common historically as each new approach fails to meet expectations. One wonders if it is really an organization's structure that matters after all, or if it is the extent to which the structure supports the interactions of employees as members of a community that counts. Smart companies recognize that knowledge is transferred in informal, unstructured ways, mainly through conversations between employees (Sbarcea, 1999). To the extent that structures enable such conversations—even in top-down organizations—they will enhance knowledge work. To the extent that they suppress such conversations—even in flat organizations—they will not enhance knowledge work. Flatter structures would seem more likely to allow for unstructured and informal relationships than top-down structures, but the structures themselves do not produce the relationships.

We really have very little solid evidence for the claimed advantages of flat organizational structures. Though there are successful virtual companies, for example, there are even more failures that have not made the headlines, at least not yet (Chesbrough & Teece, 1996). The stated advantages of flattened structures of various kinds remain largely theoretical. Most studies of these forms are based on retrospective accounts of single-case examples of an organizational form at a single point in time—for example, Sun Microsystems' virtual organization, Dell Computer's dynamic network, Acer's cellular form, Sharp's hypertext form, Olivetti's platform organization. The theory underlying these ideas has not been developed (Lewin & Volberda, 1999), nor have the forms been around long enough to test their value.

Limitations of a Structural Approach

A structural approach to knowledge management is guided by the belief that organizations can be modeled as information-processing systems. Actual knowledge use in organizations, however, frequently differs from the information-processing framework (Meindl et al., 1996). As noted earlier, knowledge work happens all the time in unstructured and informal ways that may have little to do with an organization's formal structures.

Organizational structures often mirror the technical architecture of a firm (Morris & Ferguson, 1993). When this occurs, the problems of a technical focus noted earlier repeat themselves at the higher level of a firm's structural context. The same limitation holds: knowledge is treated as an object that can simply be moved across contexts, without an appreciation of its social, symbolic, and interpretive character (Boland et al., 1995).

Besides not being the primary driver of knowledge work, a structure may actually hinder effective use of knowledge. Overspecification of structures can encourage mindlessness in organizations (Weick, Sutcliffe, & Obstfeld, 1999), squelching meaningful communication. This has important implications for research that has argued that well-specified structures must be put in place to increase the breadth of information and the speed with which managers receive the information in order to improve knowledge work. Inaccurate information and old, useless knowledge may get codified into policies, procedures, and overspecified structures that have become inflexible. Overspecified structures may also narrow the focus of attention, ensuring that new sources of knowledge are not considered and that old irrelevant knowledge is not discarded.

I agree with Weick and his colleagues (1999), who proposed that overspecified structures tend to reduce mindful knowledge work in organizations. They were referring to high reliability organizations, like nuclear power plants, where mindfulness is the rule rather than the exception. How does their assertion relate to organizations that are not as mindful in their processing of information? If an organization is not highly mindful to begin with, underspecified structures will simply tend to support the lack of awareness or responsibility (Fiol & O'Connor, in press). Structures are not the primary drivers of knowledge work and cannot, in and of themselves, produce mindful and meaningful communication. They can, however, serve as important enablers for building communities of knowing in organizations, to which I turn next.

Using Structures to Support Knowledge Work

Van den Bosch and colleagues (1999) described an organization's capacity for knowledge work as depending on both its structures and its capabilities for synthesizing and applying the knowledge. They referred to organizational structures as the bones and the combinative capabilities as the flesh and the blood of an organization. Structural approaches to knowledge management focus on the bones. Capabilities for synthesizing and applying the acquired knowledge—the flesh and blood of organizations—derive from broad, tacitly understood norms for appropriate actions and interactions (Van den Bosch et al., 1999) rather than from physical structures. The creative and combinative capabilities that produce knowing are the flesh and the blood. Bones do not give life to a being, but they are needed to support the life. In order to determine how structural bones might support the life of knowledge work, one must first understand the system's living processes.

I once again draw on the analogy of pipelines and rivers to contrast a view of structures as primary drivers of knowledge work versus structures as enablers. Organizational designers as "pipeline engineers" seek to change the flow of water directly through structural means. From a river perspective, they cannot do this effectively without tapping into the currents and channeling them in ways that support their natural flow. The critical questions from a river perspective have to do with understanding the hidden currents, eddies, and dynamics of that river rather than formal structures.

A river perspective of supporting knowledge work through structures starts with an intimate understanding of the work that people do and the meanings they assign to that work, and then develops structures that allow the different meanings to be translated across the organization. Without some minimal level of shared meanings, meaningful communication between organizational members cannot happen. Purser, Pasmore, and Tenkasi (1992) did a comparative study of two knowledge-intensive product development projects of equal technical complexity in a high-technology firm. One project succeeded whereas the other failed. Two factors accounted for the differences: a higher incidence of barriers to knowledge sharing among the members on the failed project team, and a failure to understand the meanings of others on the team. Failure to achieve common understanding through exchanging representations of their unique worlds significantly reduced the possibilities for successful knowledge work (Boland et al., 1995).

Clearly, some structures enable and accommodate human interactions more effectively than others. To enable understanding among people most effectively, organizational structures must be made subordinate to social processes. The focus must be on building bridges that foster the sharing of ideas even when people assign different meanings to them. The bridges may be collective, as with the formation of overlapping work teams. More often than not, the bridges are personal, in the form of organizational translators. Translators are people who can frame the interests of one community in terms of another's perspective. The translator must be sufficiently knowledgeable about the work of both communities to be able to make such a translation. As noted in the next section, this requires trust on the part of everyone involved.

Figure 3.1 summarizes the differences I have described between primary drivers and secondary enablers of knowledge work in organizations. The drivers of the process are the interactions that happen in trusting communities of practice. Trusting relationships cannot be directly managed. They emerge from informal, social, and interpretive processes in organizations. In contrast, technologies and

Figure 3.1. Drivers and Enablers of Knowledge Work.

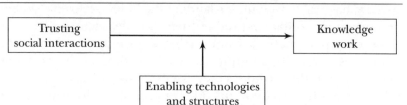

structures are formal, physical, and objective enablers of knowledge work, aimed at influencing knowledge flows (see Boudreau, Chapter Thirteen) rather than serving as the driving source of those flows.

The Role of Trust in Knowledge Work

The effectiveness of knowledge work in organizations does not depend on sharing the exact meaning of information. In fact, new knowledge creation is difficult in a social setting where meanings are completely shared. What must be shared, however, is a level of trust to coordinate use of the knowledge (Fiol, 1994). Organizations must thus promote knowledge sharing in a climate of trust and openness (Raitt et al., 1997), as Noe and colleagues discuss at length in Chapter Eight. At least in the strict sense of the words, technologies and structures do not operate strongly here. Instead, the fist step in achieving a competitive advantage through knowledge work is to embed it in a culture of valuing and trust (Lloyd, 1996).

Trust is confidence in the integrity, ability, character, and truth of a person or thing (Berube, 1985). It is an essential element of all social relations (Sitkin & Roth, 1993). Without trust in social relations, knowledge is withheld instead of disseminated, protected rather than enlarged upon. When the level of trust is low, people are gripped by worry and fear, and they use their energies to protect themselves and limit personal involvement.

The notion that trusting relations are needed for effective knowledge work builds on Nonaka's idea that connection, cooperation, and emotional attachment contribute to the creation and dissemination of new knowledge (Cohen, 1998). Know-how may be shared quite unexpectedly if there are trusting relations. Brown and Duguid (1998) reported an illustrative study conducted by Julian Orr at Xerox. Orr studied Xerox technicians who service machines on-site and therefore spend most of the time in relative isolation, alone at a customer's office, carrying with them extensive documentation about the machines they work with. Orr noted that they would seem to be the last people to have collective knowledge. Yet the study revealed that despite the individualistic character of their work and the large geographical areas they often had to cover, the technicians spent time with one another at lunch or over coffee. They continuously swapped "war stories" about malfunctioning machines that outstripped the documentation. In the process of telling and analyzing these stories, the reps both fed into and drew on the group's collective knowledge. The knowledge sharing did not directly have to do with structures or technologies and had everything to do with open and trusting relationships.

Advanced technologies may actually make trust harder to achieve in organizations. By making implicit understanding and thought processes more explicit, information technologies may make technology users vulnerable to a deeper, more repressive, embedded means of control, through electronic surveillance of their knowledge representations (Orlikowski, 1991). Moreover, one organizational group may take control of the IT system while others remain silent or mistrust it.

Organizational structures put in place to increase trust in organizations may also have the unintended effect of actually reducing it. Formal structures can represent barriers between people that foster an escalating and self-reinforcing spiral of formality and distance (Granovetter, 1985). Sitkin and Roth (1993) offered three reasons why the formality of legalistic structures is likely to erode rather than build trust in organizations. First, they can erode the interpersonal foundations of a relationship they are intended to strengthen by replacing reliance on individual goodwill with objective, formal requirements. Second, they are usually tailored to a specific context that does not cover the multifaceted nature of human relations. And third, they create a structural barrier that tends to increase the perceived distance between people, eroding the more stable and renewable foundation on which trust is built.

Even the newer flatter structures may inhibit the development of trusting relations. Studies of networks as new organizational forms generally have not addressed issues of domination and power that are often implicit in networks (Knights, Murray, & Willmott, 1993). They have largely neglected deeply embedded institutional power relations that may restrict knowledge work as much as old top-down structures. Efforts to create more open processes in organizations through flatter structures may also encounter opposing political efforts to gain power and dominance that may lead to the suppression or distortion of communication (Meindl et al., 1996). Many network organizations, for example, suffer from the tendency of partners to think that their own way of doing things is best, a lack of trust between partners, and the desire to control rather than collaborate (Sherman, 1992).

How can technologies and structures be used to help develop and maintain trusting relations? Ironically, they can be used by not attempting to do so directly but rather by building on already-existing human relationships. The examples of effective technologies and structures provided earlier in this chapter all point to their secondary and enabling role.

In sum, knowledge work in organizations happens through action and interaction. Like the currents of a river, knowledge is created, moved, and moved again in the flow. To enhance knowledge work in organizations, we must focus first and foremost on that flow of action and interaction among people. We must be anthropologists before technologists.

Implications for Future Research and Practice

There is no doubt that objective knowledge—a sort of disembodied thing—exists and is stored in an organization's libraries and computers. There is also no doubt that organizational memory exists in a firm's archives and routines. And there is no doubt that appropriate structures and technologies are essential for storing, retrieving, and disseminating this knowledge. But that cannot be the beginning of the story of knowledge work in organizations. If we begin there, we are likely to end up with a set of tools no one uses and a decision framework that promotes mindlessness.

I have argued that we must begin by understanding communities of practice. Only then can we meaningfully describe and prescribe how such knowledge becomes attached to and embedded in the meaning-making processes of an organization. Structures and technologies can only enable that embodiment. They cannot create it.

Embodied and meaning-filled knowledge work in organizations happens when people understand each other and are willing to interact. Understanding and willingness are socially motivated. They happen when people work in trusting relationships. They have less to do with people being in a particular place on the organizational chart and more to do with people feeling that they are members of a community.

Implications for Research

We can usefully view knowledge work from both a pipeline and a river perspective. The choice of starting point, however, will affect our research variables and our outcomes. As discussed, a pipeline viewpoint tends to assume that knowledge is a thing that can be transferred, whereas a river perspective leads to greater exploration of the process of knowing. Those beginning with a pipeline view tend to think about knowledge as it is passed between individuals; if one begins with a river view, one will tend to focus more on groups in interaction. A pipeline view begins by emphasizing formal incentives for knowledge creation and dissemination; a river approach gives more initial attention to nurturing connections between people. Each view is partial without the other, but I have argued that they are not equal as starting points in the process of managing knowledge work. If we begin from a pipeline perspective, we are not likely to see the processes underlying knowledge work. But if we begin by focusing on human interactions, then we are likely to understand better how to enable and support those processes.

Most of the current research has focused on the enablers or modifiers of the relationship between social interactions and knowledge work rather than on the social interactions that drive the creation and dissemination of knowledge in organizations. A river-type approach to research on knowledge work emphasizes:

(1) mechanisms for bringing about informal connections among people (the "linkages" that Maurer, Lee, & Mitchell refer to in Chapter Eleven of this volume); (2) ways to structure organizations around changing practice-based networks rather than around areas of internal expertise (see Noe et al., Chapter Eight); (3) processes for continually questioning the usefulness of current knowledge (for example, GE's Workout sessions, intended to challenge the status quo); and (4) compensation for people who actively use communication tools to enhance social interactions. As for the last point, Lawler (Chapter Ten) agrees that we need research that can help us assess what type of knowledge-based reward system will lead to greater willingness among people to engage in knowledge creation and sharing.

Unlike technologies and structures, social interactions are not easily measured. It is little wonder that our research has tended to focus on structures and technologies rather than on the trusting relationships that are the living source of knowledge work. If we are truly to understand and enhance knowledge work in organizations, however, we must undertake the hard work of understanding knowledge workers in relationships in their communities of practice.

Finally, as I already have noted, most research on knowledge management has focused narrowly on intellectual capital, ignoring the important links to organizational action. If our research on knowledge work begins to embrace the processes that link knowledge and action more fully, it can contribute to related fields, such as organizational learning. An organization's learning effectiveness is closely related to its ability to transfer and absorb knowledge inside and across its boundaries. Organizational learning is a concept that has been examined for decades without much coherence or useful widespread application. I believe the concept can only become useful when its component parts are understood and brought down to an operational level. That becomes possible through continued and more process-oriented research on knowledge work.

Implications for Practice

As noted in the first chapter of this volume, for individuals' knowledge to be useful as a competitive asset, it must be mobilized into focused collective action. Firms that are able to integrate various types of specialized new knowledge quickly and effectively into their operational routines and discard it when it is no longer useful can achieve superior returns.

The barriers that make knowledge work difficult for managers are likely to be social and cultural rather than technological or structural. There tend to be fights over who owns the knowledge; there tends to be too little space to connect and learn, limited discussion, or overemphasis on technology and structure. Specific projects that offer quick results, provide opportunities for safe learning, and foster trusting relationships will tend to lead to effective knowledge work. As this chapter emphasized, knowing in and across knowledge communities can be supported and nurtured but not precisely measured or managed.

History can get in the way. Most managers have grown up in an environment where structures and technologies are of the greatest importance. There has been a central concern with information—how it is stored, retrieved, and disseminated. The idea of a knowledge community suggests less emphasis on explicit information exchange and more on trust, personal connection, and commitment to shared success. This poses a huge practical challenge. Trust is not manageable in the traditional sense. The dimensions of trust are less tangible, less visible, and less explicitly codifiable than structures and technologies.

New knowledge in organizations often emerges out of chaos. A pipeline view of knowledge management overlooks this important point. It presupposes that designers are omniscient when it comes to what pieces of information mean and how they might be used. That works for routine and operational uses of data (for example, ERP systems), but it may hinder the novel recombination and interpretation of data into new configurations and meanings. From a river perspective, although designers can create rough directionality for the overall flows, the specific channels are emergent. Attempts to rechannel the flows can cause both intended and unintended consequences. The unintended ones often result in creative new knowledge. A safe and nonjudgmental climate enhances people's willingness to share those creative ideas with others (Oldham, Chapter Nine of this volume).

A final implication for knowledge work in organizations is that new knowledge is often created at the boundaries of the old, and that old, no longer useful knowledge is often uncovered at the boundaries of the new and different. So the processes described in this chapter extend beyond the formal boundaries of organizations. Most organizations still see knowledge management as the path to leveraging internal expertise. This must change, because the most important knowledge in the world is, by definition, found outside the boundaries of the company. Organizations must manage what may be termed the *boundary paradox*—organizational borders must be open to flows of information and knowledge from the networks and markets in which they operate while at the same time the organization must protect and nurture its own knowledge base.

References

Anders, G. (2001). John Chambers after the deluge. *Fast Company, 48,* 100–107.

Attewell, P. (1992). Technology diffusion and organizational learning: The case of business computing. *Organization Science, 3*(1), 1–19.

Berube, M. S. (Ed.). (1985). *American heritage dictionary.* Boston: Houghton Mifflin.

Blumentritt, R., & Johnston, R. (1999). Towards a strategy for knowledge management. *Technology Analysis & Strategic Management, 11,* 287–300.

Boland, R. J. Jr., Tenkasi, R. V., & Ramkrishnan, T. V. (1995). Perspective making and perspective taking in communities of knowing. *Organization Science, 6,* 350–372.

Bontis, N., Dragonetti, N. C., Jacobsen, K., & Roos, G. (1999). The knowledge toolbox: A review of the tools available to measure and manage intangible resources. *European Management Journal, 17,* 391–401.

Brown, J. S., & Duguid, P. (1998). Organizing knowledge. *California Management Review, 40,* 90–111.

Bryant, S. E. (2000, August). *The role of transformational and transactional leadership in cultivating knowledge.* Paper presented at the Academy of Management Meeting, Toronto, Canada.

Chesbrough, H. W., & Teece, D. J. (1996, January-February). When is virtual virtuous? Organizing for innovation. *Harvard Business Review,* pp. 65–73.

Choudhury, V., & Sampler, J. L. (1997). Information specificity and environmental scanning: An economic perspective. *MIS Quarterly, 21*(1), 25–53.

Ciborra, C. U. (1996). The platform organization: Recombining strategies, structures, and surprises. *Organization Studies, 7,* 103–118.

Cohen, D. (1998). Toward a knowledge context: Report on the first annual UC Berkeley forum on knowledge and the firm. *California Management Review, 29,* 22–39.

Cohen, W., & Levinthal, D. (1990). Absorptive capacity: A new perspective on learning and innovation. *Administrative Science Quarterly, 35,* 128–152.

Davidow, W. H., & Malone, M. S. (1993). *The virtual corporation: Structuring and revitalizing the corporation of the 21st century.* New York: HarperCollins.

Davis, M. C. (1998, Fall). Knowledge management. *Information Strategy: The Executive's Journal,* pp. 11–22.

Deloitte & Touche Consulting Group. (1998, December 16). Knowledge management. *Crossborder Monitor,* pp. 4–5.

Despres, C. J. (1996). Work, management, and the dynamics of knowledge. *Sasin Journal of Management, 2,* 1–13.

Doyle, D., & du Toit, A. (1998). Knowledge management in a law firm. *Aslib Proceedings, 50,* 3–8.

Fiol, C. M. (1994). Consensus, diversity, and learning in organizations. *Organization Science, 5,* 403–420.

Fiol, C. M., & O'Connor, E. J. (in press). Waking up! Mindfulness in the face of bandwagons. *Academy of Management Review.*

Fryer, B. (1998). Creative disruption. *Information Strategy, 3,* 34–36.

Goodwin, B. (1999, May 6). Cisco saves millions with staff intranet. *Computer Weekly,* p. 12.

Granovetter, M. (1985). Economic action and social structure: The problem of embeddedness. *American Journal of Sociology, 91,* 481–510.

Grant, R. M. (1996). Prospering in dynamically-competitive environments: Organizational capability as knowledge integration. *Organization Science, 7,* 375–387.

Hamel, G., & Prahalad, C. K. (1994). *Competing for the future.* Boston: Harvard Business School Press.

Handy, C. (1989). *The age of unreason.* Boston: Harvard Business School Press.

Jensen, B. (1998, June-July). Communication or knowledge management? *Communication World,* pp. 44–47.

Kiesler, S., & Sproull, L. (1982). Managerial response to changing environments: Perspectives on problem sensing from social cognition. *Administrative Science Quarterly, 27,* 548–570.

Knights, D., Murray, F., & Willmott, H. (1993). Networking as knowledge work: A study of strategic interorganizational development in the financial services industry. *Journal of Management Studies, 30,* 975–995.

Kogut, B., & Zander, U. (1992). Knowledge of the firm, combinative capabilities, and the replication of technology. *Organization Science, 3,* 383–397.

Lane, P. J., & Lubatkin, M. (1998). Relative absorptive capacity and interorganizational learning. *Srategic Management Journal, 19,* 461–477.

Leonard-Barton, D. (1992). Core capabilities and core rigidities: A paradox in managing new product development. *Strategic Management Journal, 13,* 111–125.

Lewin, A. Y., & Volberda, H. W. (1999). Prolegomena on coevolution: A framework for research and strategy and new organizational forms. *Organization Science, 10,* 519–534.

Lloyd, B. (1996). Knowledge management: The key to long-term organizational success. *Long-Range Planning, 29,* 576–580.

Lopres, A., & Babbitt, T. G. (2000, August). *Knowledge management: Differing ideals, differing IT implications.* Paper presented at the Academy of Management Annual Meeting, Toronto, Canada.

Lubit, R. (2001). Tacit knowledge and knowledge management: The keys to sustainable competitive advantage. *Organizational Dynamics, 29*(4), 164–178.

Lucier, C., & Torsilieri, J. D. (2000). Steal this idea. *Strategy + Business, 20,* 21–24.

Marshall, C., Prusak, L., & Shpilberg, D. (1996). Financial risk and the need for superior knowledge management. *California Management Review, 38,* 77–101.

McDermott, R. (1999). Why information technology inspired but cannot deliver knowledge management. *California Management Review, 41,* 103–117.

Meindl, J. R., Stubbart, C., & Porac, J. F. (Eds.). (1996). *Cognition within and between organizations.* Thousand Oaks, CA: Sage.

Miles, R. E., Snow, C. C., Mathews, J. A., Miles, G., & Coleman, H. J. Jr. (1997). Organizing in the knowledge age: Anticipating the cellular form. *Academy of Management Executive, 11,* 7–20.

Morris, C. R., & Ferguson, C. H. (1993, March-April). How architecture wins technology wars. *Harvard Business Review,* pp. 86–96.

Nass, C. (1994). Knowledge or skills: Which do administrators learn from experience? *Organization Science, 5,* 38–50.

Nonaka, I., & Takeuchi, H. (1995). *The knowledge-creating company.* New York: Oxford University Press.

Orlikowski, W. J. (1991). Integrated information environment or matrix of control? The contradictory implications of information technology. *Accounting, Management, and Information Technologies, 1,* 9–42.

Pinelli, T. E., & Barclay, R. O. (1998). Maximizing the results of federally-funded research and development through knowledge management: A strategic imperative for improving U.S. competitiveness. *Government Information Quarterly, 15,* 157–172.

Polanyi, M. (1966). *The tacit dimension.* New York: Routledge.

Purser, R. E., Pasmore, W. A., & Tenkasi, R. V. (1992). The influence of deliberations on learning in new product development teams. *Journal of Engineering and Technology Management, 9,* 1–28.

Raitt, D., Loekken, S., Scholz, J., Steiner, H., & Secchi, P. (1997). Corporate knowledge management and related initiatives at ESA. *ESA Bulletin, 92,* 112–118.

Sbarcea, K. (1999, February-March). Knowledge management: The new challenge. Part II. *Knowledge Management,* pp. 17–18.

Senthilkumar, M., & White, M. A. (2000, August). *Competitive advantage through cognitive leverage: A model of dynamic knowledge-based strategy process.* Paper presented at the Academy of Management Meeting, Toronto, Canada.

Sherman, S. (1992, September 21). Are strategic alliances working? *Fortune,* pp. 76–78.

Sitkin, S. B., & Roth, N. L. (1993). Explaining the limited effectiveness of legalistic "remedies" for trust/distrust. *Organization Science, 4,* 367–392.

Starbuck, W. H. (1992). Learning by knowledge-intensive firms. *Journal of Management Studies, 29,* 714–740.

Thomas, A. (2001). Corridor chatter: Information and knowledge management on a shoestring? *Computers and Law, 12*(1), 4–7.

Thomas, J. B., & McDaniel, R. R. Jr. (1990). Interpreting strategic issues: Effects of strategy and the information-processing structure of top management teams. *Academy of Management Journal, 33, 286*–306.

Van den Bosch, F. A., Volberda, H. W., & De Boer, M. (1999). Coevolution of firm absorptive capacity and knowledge environment: Organizational forms and combinative capabilities. *Organization Science, 10,* 551–568.

Volberda, H. W. (1996). Toward the flexible form: How to remain vital in hypercompetitive environments. *Organization Science, 7,* 359–374.

Walsh, J. P., & Ungson, G. R. (1991). Organizational memory. *Academy of Management Review, 16,* 57–91

Weick, K. E., Sutcliffe, K. M., & Obstfeld, D. (1999). Organizing for high reliability: Processes of collective mindfulness. In R. I. Sutton & B. M. Staw (Eds.), *Research in organizational behavior* (pp. 81–123). Greenwich, CT: JAI Press.

CHAPTER 4

Designing Work for Knowledge-Based Competition

Susan Albers Mohrman

There is broad agreement that we live in an era when knowledge-based resources have replaced financial capital, natural resources, and unskilled labor as the most important competitive resource for many companies (for example, Drucker, 1993). Today's dominant strategic framework is resource-based, with competencies and capabilities viewed as the most important assets (Prahalad & Hamel, 1990; Stalk, Evans, & Shulman, 1992) and the creation and sharing of knowledge a source of organizational advantage (Nahapiet & Ghoshal, 1998). As DeNisi, Hitt, and Jackson argue in the first chapter of this book, acquiring talented knowledge workers is not sufficient for deriving value from this human capital. Knowledge resides in the minds of employees, but it is also embedded in the processes and products of the organization (Leonard-Barton, 1995). Increasingly, strategic competencies lie in processes such as developing and delivering knowledge-based products that entail collaboration and complex interactions among many different disciplines and functions. Effective organization and management of knowledge workers is central to the success of the knowledge enterprise (Quinn, Anderson, & Finkelstein, 1996), which relies on these employees' initiative, their willingness to contribute knowledge, and also their collective work (Nonaka & Takeuchi, 1995; see Lepak & Snell, Chapter Five, this volume). Work design defines and organizes the activities of knowledge workers in relationship to the work processes of the organization, the activities of others in the organization, and external stakeholders.

This chapter examines the design of knowledge work. It argues that because of the dynamic and highly interdependent nature of knowledge work, the trend toward geographically dispersed work systems, the characteristics of knowledge workers, and the critical importance of learning in the knowledge system, changes in organizational forms and the design of work are required. Modifications and extensions to traditional work design theory are proposed, and research directions are suggested.

Historical Perspective on Work Design

The prevailing academic paradigm of work design evolved with the industrial economy. Early scientific management and bureaucratic theories emphasized simplified and specialized jobs, a clear division of labor, clear functional reporting lines, and reliance on rules and procedures and managerial control (Gilbreth, 1914; Taylor, 1911). Psychological expectancy–based job design theory (for example, Hackman & Lawler, 1971; Hackman & Oldham, 1975) combined a focus on employee outcomes and task effectiveness. Five task attributes—significance, variety, identity, autonomy, and feedback—were posited to lead to critical psychological states—meaningfulness, responsibility, and knowledge of results—which in turn would promote work motivation, performance, effectiveness, and satisfaction (Hackman, 1977). A number of job design approaches were suggested to enrich the job and increase the motivational potential of work: forming natural work groups, combining tasks, establishing relationships with clients, vertically loading the job with responsibilities such as planning and control, and opening feedback channels from the work itself (Dunnette, Campbell, & Hakel, 1967; Hackman, 1983; Hulin & Blood, 1968). Subsequent research introduced the notion that job design must fit with the nature of the workforce, the design of the organization, and the patterns of interdependence inherent in the work technology (Porter, Lawler, & Hackman, 1975; Rousseau, 1977). The basic task attributes approach has been expanded for work that is carried out by teams (for example, Hackman, 1983, 1990). However, with a few exceptions, work design has been largely overlooked as a research topic over the past decade, a time when organizational forms have been fundamentally transformed in the transition to the knowledge economy.

The early work design frameworks were fashioned uncritically of the prevailing organizational forms. These forms fit the bureaucratic principle that the job is the fundamental unit of work and the Parsonian notion that there is a clear differentiation of responsibilities between bureaucratic levels—that is, institutional and strategic responsibilities were viewed as executive work. Control of operations was managerial work, and execution was the responsibility of front-line employees (Parsons, 1960). Work design theory dealt largely with the work of front-line employees. Technology was accepted as a given, and work was defined to conform to it. These assumptions began to be challenged by the sociotechnical systems (STS) theory and related work on high-involvement systems (Lawler, 1986) and high-commitment organizations (Walton, 1985). These frameworks were based on a belief that work could be purposely designed to optimize the performance of both the technical and the social subsystems of the organization (Trist, 1981; Pasmore, 1988) and to involve front-line employees more fully in business success. They built on the motivational principles of the job design literature but generated explicit tenets that are in direct contradiction to the notion of bureaucratic control. Rather than minimize investment in people, for example, they advocated investing in people as a resource to be developed and equipping them with many broad skills so they can do more tasks and be deployed flexibly. Rather than simplifying and breaking down work into small chunks, they advocated creating optimal task groupings, designing work around processes that can be relatively self-contained and controlled or self-regulated by the employees, and building adaptive capabilities into work units.

In their willingness to challenge the bureaucratic form and their focus on work designed to fit with the technical and other lateral processes of the organization and to enhance the organization's ability to develop and benefit from employees' knowledge and skills, these approaches anticipated many work design issues of the knowledge economy. Although initially employed in industrial settings (for example, Trist & Bamforth, 1951; Walton, 1982), the sociotechnical framework has subsequently guided the design of knowledge work settings such as hospitals, banks, and technical organizations (for example, Pava, 1983, 1986; Taylor, 1986; Pasmore, Petee, & Bastian, 1987). Work design in contemporary knowledge work settings has often followed similar principles, with various kinds of process-defined lateral work structures such as teams set up for work that cannot easily be partitioned into individual jobs (for example, Mohrman, Cohen, & Mohrman, 1995). The next section will deal with the nature of knowledge work and the challenges of designing knowledge work.

Characteristics of Knowledge Work

Knowledge work involves applying knowledge, processing information, and generating new knowledge (Mohrman, Mohrman, & Cohen, 1995). Routine knowledge work involves applying existing and often codified knowledge to carry out recurring tasks and problems. Nonroutine knowledge work involves uncertainty, either because the problems are not fully analyzable or because there are many exceptions to routine approaches (Perrow, 1967). Such work involves making judgments (Thompson & Tuden, 1959), applying tacit knowledge, and often, generating new knowledge. The core competencies of the knowledge organization lie not only in the knowledge held by its employees but also in the knowledge embedded in its processes and systems. In the knowledge economy, a competitive advantage can be derived if a firm excels at generating and leveraging knowledge and developing social and intellectual capital.

By viewing the organization as a knowledge enterprise we can identify the characteristics of work in the knowledge economy and their implications for work design (see Table 4.1). These will be briefly discussed in the following paragraphs.

Strategic Competencies

Knowledge is growing geometrically. The knowledge economy is dynamic, with potential competitive threats coming from rapid technological advances that disrupt existing business models (Christiansen, 1997; Hitt, Keats, & DeMarie, 1998). Strategy guides the competencies that the organization must protect and enhance. It also guides the work activities, and consequently the work design, of the knowledge system. For example, consider the new competencies

**Table 4.1. Characteristics of Knowledge Work
and Implications for Work Design.**

Characteristics	Implications			
	Dynamic work structures	Cross-boundary collaboration	System focus and integration	Work includes learning
Strategic competencies	X	X	X	X
Saturated interdependency		X	X	X
Process orientation		X	X	X
Geographical linkages		X	X	
Improvement and encoding	X	X		X
Generating and leveraging knowledge	X	X	X	X

required when a large equipment maker changes its strategy to sell "hours of service" instead of just equipment. Product development work has to be designed to bring together technologists, financial experts, and marketers who have a deep understanding of usage patterns, failure modes, recovery times, and economic modeling of the customer's business situation. The selling process has to include the customization of equipment and the development of new economic and pricing models as new kinds of customers are secured. In this situation, the work design must ensure that the product development and selling processes are carried out in a coordinated manner by employees who understand their own company's business model and are knowledgeable about the customer's business model and needs. In a dynamic knowledge environment, work cannot be fully specified; much must be left to the employees' discretion and initiative as the organization charts a path through a turbulent competitive environment. Employees are required to focus on the purposes and strategy of the larger system in order to know how to focus their own work and with whom to coordinate and collaborate. As they collaborate to solve problems, develop new processes, products, and services, and find new ways to deliver value to customers, employees may create new knowledge that in a sense defines the future directions of the organization.

Saturated Interdependence

Knowledge work does not fit the reductionist organizing approaches of scientific management, such as partitioning and segmenting work, because it often does not involve linear work flows (Pava, 1983). It may consist of multiple, concurrent work flows that influence each other. For example, Dougherty (2001) found that new product development organizations have simultaneous, interacting processes for technical, market, business, and knowledge aspects of the work. Pava described the "saturated" interdependence in knowledge systems, where often "it seems as though everything totally depends on everything else" (1983, p. 52). Work designs must enable integration of the work of multiple specialists, all with their unique disciplinary perspectives (Dougherty, 1992).

Knowledge that is valuable competitively includes firm-specific process and product knowledge, and often tacit industry and market knowledge that comes from dealing with problems and processes in particular contexts (Leonard-Barton, 1995). Much knowledge creation occurs at the intersection of several disciplines and at the intersection of deep knowledge bases with the world of applications (Boland & Tenkasi, 1995). Collaboration across boundaries in problem solving and knowledge creation is core to creating value from knowledge. The importance of such collaboration has grown as customers demand integrated solutions. Working at knowledge intersections requires *T-shaped skills* (Iansiti, 1995), skill sets that include a deep technical knowledge base combined with broad knowledge so that individuals understand the systemic impact of their work and can collaborate with coworkers from other disciplines. Work designs include forums, such as cross-functional teams, for the integration of the work of several contributors with different knowledge bases. For example, chemists, analytical mathematicians, microbiologists, and physicians may work together in teams that collaborate to turn promising compounds into viable drug therapies. Tax and estate specialists and several different investment specialists may collaborate to manage a wealthy client's investment portfolio. In professional services firms, diversification into new service areas allows the configuration of diverse project teams to capture knowledge synergies (Hitt, Bierman, Shimizu, & Kochhar, 2001).

Process Orientation

The knowledge economy has emerged along with the recognition that value is delivered to the customer through work processes, not through a series of discrete tasks. This awareness was raised by proponents of the total quality management (TQM) movement (for example, Deming, 1986; Juran, 1989), who emphasized designing work processes to deliver value to internal and external customers. They argued that knowledge, information, and understanding are lost as work meanders through the organization. Increasing the value delivered to customers requires integrating the interdependent activities that constitute a process and the various streams of activity that come together to yield outcomes. Optimal performance requires awareness of the whole process.

Business process reengineering theorists (Hammer & Champy, 1993; Davenport, 1993) are explicit about the close relationship between knowledge and work processes. They stress the role that information technology can play in enabling value-delivering processes by ensuring that the necessary information is available to employees throughout the organization. IT is viewed as an integral part of the work design in the organization. Reengineering approaches include the automation of easily codified process steps that do not require human judgment, the elimination of steps that do not add value to the customer, and the combination of tasks in the roles of individuals or units that have IT-enabled access to information that was previously located in organizational pockets.

Geographical Linkages

Knowledge travels easily between locations, enabling virtual work designs. Even services as personalized as health care can be delivered through work processes that link contributors in several locations. Physicians send test data and electronic patient records to specialty labs in other cities and consult with experts in medical centers in different parts of the world in collaborative diagnostics.

Similarly, centralized technical support teams for a control systems company have electronic access to the specifications and real-time performance data for heating and cooling systems in a client corporation's global locations. They can detect and in many cases solve problems from great distances, often working with technicians on location.

Companies seek global markets in order to recoup their investments in new knowledge-based products, services, and processes. Increasingly, having a global strategy and global markets means doing work in many countries (Galbraith, 2000). Designing work to link knowledge across locations is a key strategic competency for many knowledge firms. Companies seek talent wherever they can find it, service global customers, and locate various aspects of their operations close to the cutting-edge technology, talent concentrations, and industry centers.

Improvement and Encoding

Continual improvement of work processes and work designs has become a competitive requirement. Process learning is now part of the core work of many firms. Employees are often expected to be part of a learning system by searching for the root causes of process quality problems and making process breakthroughs that improve performance. Companies such as British Petroleum and General Electric expect their managers to manage performance in their units and also participate in cross-unit learning processes. Process breakthroughs are frequently the product of cross-functional and cross-unit improvement teams that can look at work flows, intersections, and integration of the knowledge of different disciplines and functions. Process breakthroughs in one part of the organization can be encoded and shared with other parts of it, and thus become embedded in the organization's functioning (Nonaka & Takeuchi, 1995). Iterations of process learning yield dynamic work processes that may require ongoing changes in work design.

Generating and Applying Knowledge

Knowledge generation and application are inherent in knowledge work. Knowledge is contextual and relational—people construct social knowledge as they interact in a social context, and this knowledge in turn influences their behaviors, perceptions, and cognitions (Berger & Luckmann, 1966). Knowledge is "information combined with experience, context, interpretation, and reflection" (Davenport, De Long, & Beers, 1998, p. 43) that becomes "anchored in the beliefs and commitments of its holder" (Nonaka & Takeuchi, 1995, p. 58) through active involvement in its creation or through collective sense-making and local learning (Orlikowski & Robey, 1991). For example, units that implement a new information technology are not the passive recipients of knowledge that has been developed elsewhere. They engage in local experimentation and sense-making, and learn how to use the new technology to increase their effectiveness. The knowledge-creating firm is characterized by a cycle of learning through which individuals' often tacit knowledge is shared through collaborative work, becomes explicit through such means as building models and articulating analogies, and eventually is made available to the larger organization (Nonaka & Takeuchi, 1995; Liedtka, Haskins, Rosenblum, & Weber, 1997). Interdependence is inherent in using and creating knowledge, and collaborative work is the source of the relationships that grow intellectual and social capital.

The diverse activities of a firm are held together by its intent, or strategy (Nonaka & Takeuchi, 1995), but also by the shared meaning that develops as people work together toward desired outcomes for customers, the company, and one another (Liedtka et al., 1997). Learning is both a collective and an individual process. Knowledge is embedded in knowledge communities and develops as people participate together in the practices of a social community (Wenger, 1998). Knowing is deeply personal (Dixon, 2000), and willingness to share and learn from one another comes from connections between people, both in and across units and locations. Connection to these knowledge communities must be built into the work design of the organization. Creating knowledge connections and building geographically dispersed knowledge communities are key competencies for a global knowledge firm.

Implications for Knowledge Work Design

The six characteristics of knowledge work described in the previous section collectively point to several work design features that support a firm's ability to compete on knowledge. (See again Table 4.1.) These work design features may provide the basis for strategic flexibility—the ability to apply resources flexibly in support of a dynamic strategy (Hitt et al., 1998). Each feature is briefly described here.

Work Designs Are Dynamic

As strategies change and new knowledge is generated and built into processes and applications, the configuration of activity in the organization also changes to reflect new and evolving capabilities and competencies, and new ways of delivering value. Knowledge is developed and value is delivered through temporary work units with shifting membership.

Work Is Designed for Collaboration

The optimal application of knowledge resources requires lateral linkages across boundaries—between functions and disciplines, geographical locations, business units, and companies. Many of the core competencies of a knowledge firm involve interdependent contributions from multiple knowledge bases in carrying out and improving the processes of the organizational system, generating and leveraging new knowledge, and delivering value to customers. In the laterally linked organization, individuals may simultaneously belong to several organizational units or may work across them. Coordination and control are no longer the domain solely of hierarchical managers. Many front-line knowledge workers may have such formal roles as liaison, project leader, or expert consultant, or they may have dual membership roles.

As knowledge rather than capital becomes the currency of the organization and powerful IT tools allow for easy exchange of information and coordination from a distance, the location of work is no longer limited by the location of capital equipment. Work processes can be designed across geographies and time zones, taking advantage of expertise no matter where it is located. IT systems are no longer simply tools for doing work; the design of work and the design of IT systems are inextricably linked.

Work Designs Focus on the Larger System and Local Performance

Because of saturated interdependencies, interweaving processes that deliver value to customers, and the need to achieve competitive advantage by leveraging knowledge continually, the local mission and goals must be viewed in context—the context of the mission and goals of the larger system that is itself continually changing. In the knowledge economy, change occurs too quickly for organizational subsystems to be fully aligned from the top. Self-regulation is systemic, with individuals and units mutually adapting and re-forming with reference to one another and to the larger system's purposes and strategies (Mohrman, Mohrman, & Cohen, 1995).

Work Is Designed for Learning

Changes in strategy and the rapid growth of basic discipline knowledge and advanced analytical tools drive the need for new knowledge and competencies. A key competitive capability is leveraging the initially tacit knowledge that is gained by front-line workers dealing with concrete problems. Training and development activities are only one of the many ways in which learning is facilitated and intellectual capital is developed (see Chapter Eight). Organizational learning and knowledge leverage are everyone's concern, and much occurs on the job.

These work design principles have changed fundamentally from traditional work design principles. Yet little rigorous work has been done to ascertain their prevalence and their impact on employee and firm effectiveness.

Work Design and Motivation in the Knowledge Firm

Work design has so far been discussed with little consideration of the attributes of the knowledge worker. One of the most striking attributes of knowledge workers is that they are in short supply. Despite sharp economic fluctuations, demographic trends such as the retirement of the baby boom generation and its replacement by a much smaller cohort suggest that the labor market for knowledge workers is likely to remain tight for several decades (Russell, 1993). To a great extent, firms "rent" the knowledge of these scarce employees, but they also contribute to the development of their knowledge. This knowledge and the company's investment in it can easily walk out the door. Today's technical workers are mobile—willing to change firms for advancement opportunities and increased pay (Finegold, Mohrman, & Spreitzer, 2002)—making it imperative to find approaches to build their attachment to a company (Coff, 1997). Work design relates to performance motivation and to commitment and retention. It also provides the context for the effective employment of scarce and perhaps temporary talent (Quinn et al., 1996). This section examines work design, motivation, and the knowledge worker. It proposes testable refinements, reinterpretations, and additions to the traditional job characteristics model.

Attributes of Knowledge Workers

Knowledge workers enter the workforce with skills and knowledge that they have usually obtained through formal education. With experience, they develop deeper expertise and broad practice-based knowledge as they apply their knowledge in different contexts to solve diverse problems. Knowledge workers who perform nonroutine tasks may continually expand their competencies through experience and additional formal education and thus become increasingly valuable employees.

As already noted, there is no clear line between managerial and knowledge work. Managers are knowledge workers. However, nonmanagement knowledge workers perform functions, such as planning, integration, coordination, invention, and innovation, that used to be considered managerial in the industrial organization (Mohrman, Cohen, & Mohrman, 1995). Based on their expertise, they expect autonomy (Von Glinow, 1988)—to be able to carry out their work free from close supervision. In the industrial economy, front-line workers were viewed as having jobs and managers as having careers, but knowledge workers enter the workforce seeking careers. Their loyalty is to their careers and their professional identity rather than to a firm (Von Glinow, 1988).

They expect their work to allow for career growth and competency development. Given the flatter structures that have emerged as organizations increasingly work laterally (Galbraith, 1994), that career growth may occur through the technical or professional ranks rather than through a succession of managerial positions. Furthermore, an increasing number of knowledge workers operate as independent contractors, being hired by companies solely because of their ability to perform particular tasks in particular projects.

Knowledge workers operate through personal networks (Adler & Kwon, 2002). Networks are built through and facilitate work performance and collaborative learning in the highly interdependent and distributed knowledge firm. In addition, professional networks are essential to career building. It is through such networks that knowledge workers become aware of opportunities both inside and outside the firm. In fact, in technical firms young knowledge workers report being closely linked electronically to their professional networks and keep each other abreast of job opportunities, salary trends, and qualitative information about different firms (Mohrman & Finegold, 2000). They also use their networks to stay aware of emerging trends and competencies so that they can direct their personal growth and development and seek opportunities that will maintain their employability.

Many knowledge workers are highly dependent on advanced analysis, modeling, and communication tools. Tools that embody knowledge have become extensions of the knowledge worker and the knowledge work team. Knowledge workers, tools, and tasks are linked together to deliver value (Argote & Ingram, 2000). For example, insurance actuaries create powerful tools for modeling risk and determining net present value. Three-dimensional models and system simulation tools are designed with sophisticated engineering knowledge and serve as powerful productivity enhancers. Knowledge workers must be able to master up-to-date tools; doing so is critical to their professional identities and employability. They depend on their tools to tap into knowledge communities, work teams, and projects from remote locations, and to keep in contact with a shifting group of coworkers. These tools have also made it possible for them to be anywhere in the world and still work together with teammates elsewhere.

Job Design for Knowledge Work

Job characteristics theory and the expectancy theory of motivation stress designing work in a way that is psychologically rewarding to employees, enables effective performance, and yields desired employee outcomes as a consequence of good performance. Although there is no reason to believe that the fundamental psychological mechanisms of motivation have changed, the knowledge economy has changed the organizational and technical contexts. Increasingly, instead of holding clearly defined and stable jobs, individuals are flexibly deployed to a sequence of assignments and roles that require their competencies. In addition to being held accountable for how well they play their individual roles, they may be held accountable for how well they contribute to the larger knowledge system. Defining work design principles that fit this context and result in high motivation is a challenging research focus.

Earlier research found few individual differences in the receptiveness of employees to the five key task attributes of classic job design theory (Griffin, Moorhead, & Welsh, 1981). Given the high growth needs that can be expected to characterize knowledge workers, these job attributes are expected to be important to them as well. However, we may need new images of how to achieve these job attributes in systemic and interdependent knowledge work with its inherent learning requirements (see Exhibit 4.1). The remainder of this section describes how our understanding of these job characteristics may need to change to fit the knowledge enterprise. It is also argued that two new job attributes should be considered: growth and development and network-building opportunities are likely to contribute to employee motivation and outcomes and to performance in knowledge work settings. This discussion is intended to provide a rich menu of testable propositions.

Task Identity

Saturated interdependence and the collaborative nature of knowledge work make it difficult for individuals to perform "whole" tasks, as would be called for by the traditional job attributes framework. Products and services are often delivered through complex processes that involve the collective outputs of many different interacting

Exhibit 4.1. Knowledge Work Motivating Characteristics and Work Design Forms.

Motivating Work Design Characteristics	Proposed Knowledge Work Forms
Task identity	Sequence of assignments to well-defined tasks and projects
Task variety	Application of deep skills in multiple contexts over time; development of broad skills through diverse assignments and performing more aspects of the process or systems integrating tasks
Task significance	Knowledge of contribution to larger business context and success, to external customer, to knowledge community
Job feedback	Knowledge of performance of team, project, and larger units; individual feedback from job and from multiple sources
Autonomy	Collective or individual self-regulation with relationship to larger context
Growth and development*	Enhancing personal competency through work assignments
Network building*	Connections to knowledge community; task connections; customer connections

Note: Items with asterisk not included in original Hackman & Oldham (1980) task attributes framework.

teams. Members of teams established for such purposes as new product development or customer service may change over time as the required competencies change, making it difficult for any one member to feel responsible for the team's ultimate output. "Virtual" work involves individuals and teams in different locations coordinating electronically and working synchronously and asynchronously on the same problem or model, resulting in a product where it is difficult for members to see, let alone identify, personal contributions. Knowledge emerges through a juxtaposition of ideas from many sources, and ideas generated by individuals in one team may end up coming to fruition in another team.

We know little about how task identity is achieved in knowledge settings or whether it is important. It may exist primarily at the collective level—through the missions and objectives of different temporary teams and networks and through individuals' often shifting understanding of their roles and expected contribution in these work structures. Rather than having a clearly defined job in a stable work unit, many knowledge workers have a succession of assignments. In the short term, they may identify with clear individual assignments or being a member of one or more teams with well-defined outputs. But individuals may also have to link between teams or be part of coordinating teams, where success is measurable only at the higher system level. Perhaps over time a sense of identity comes from clarity about the knowledge and competencies a person contributes to the system and from developing a deeper understanding of how these contributions affect the larger system. It is proposed that task identity can be achieved if work is designed so that the tasks of all the performing elements—individuals, teams, and business units—have a clearly articulated relationship to the effectiveness of the larger knowledge system and to other performing units and so that the sequence of assignments allows individuals to develop a greater understanding of the overall system over time.

Task Variety

The traditional view was that task variety was achieved if a job included several horizontal and vertical tasks rather than being narrowly specialized. Designing work for the knowledge economy requires understanding how specialized knowledge and knowledge workers add value in particular organizational contexts, and what kinds of adjacent knowledge need to be coordinated to increase knowledge contribution (Quinn et al., 1996). In some situations, such as with neurosurgery, a specialist delivers the central value, and work designs that promote the ability of this critical specialist to perform effectively by aligning other knowledge specialists in supporting roles are most appropriate. Allowing neurosurgeons to concentrate on neurosurgery makes more sense than increasing the variety of their tasks by requiring them to prepare their own instruments, conduct their own CT scans, or do their own billing. Variety for the neurosurgeon may come from the individual differences of multiple cases; such variety contributes to the development of deeper and perhaps tacit expertise. Where several specialties come together to develop a system or systemic approach—such as when internists, dieticians, cardiologists, internists, and physical therapists collaborate to develop an overall treatment plan for a chronically ill patient—variety is introduced not only through the different individual cases but also through the range of considerations required of the members of the group. These specialists learn to work together and combine their knowledge to yield a plan, but they only minimally develop overlapping knowledge. When related specialists such as electrical engineers, software engineers, biologists, chemists, and medical doctors form a team to develop an electrochemical medical device, variety may come not only from the range of technical considerations but also from the overlap of tasks and collaborative work on the problem, often leading to a broadening and perhaps even redefining of knowledge that enables the specialists to contribute in more general ways. When it is understood that a new product development team contributes to a company's success not only by inventing the latest gadget but also by inventing one that can be economically and reliably manufactured and easily serviced, the variety of that team's considerations and responsibilities is greatly increased. T-shaped skills are developed in the new product development team whose members develop overlapping knowledge that enables them to combine specialized knowledge more effectively.

Thus, variety may best be defined in relationship to the knowledge structure inherent in the technical and business requirements of the organization. It may be achieved as workers apply deep skills in several contexts over time. Or it may be achieved when they develop broad skills through diverse assignments, perform more aspects of the process, or focus on the integration of the system. Research might fruitfully examine the impact of different kinds of variety on knowledge worker outcomes, on the enhancement of knowledge-based competitiveness, and on system performance.

Task Significance

Significance refers to the belief that one's work makes a difference or has an impact, such as for customers or for some larger mission. Just as task identity is problematic for knowledge workers, the complexity of processes may make it difficult for them to see how their personal work is significant. Clarity about the organizational processes that deliver value through the integrated activities of several contributors in a diffuse work system may come from an increased sense of significance of one's own individual contribution to the overall processes. Perceptions of significance can be enhanced if direct links to the customer are created so that all involved can understand the customer's needs and see how the customer perceives value. Some companies routinely find a time early in their employees' careers to give them at least one assignment where they have direct customer contact. Others may hold customer focus groups or celebrations to allow employees to see their impact on customers.

Feedback systems that enable knowledge workers to see the impact of their team's and unit's work on business performance can increase their perception of significance to the company. In today's economy, where knowledge work is often carried out in organizations with a strong strategic and financial orientation, balanced scorecards with measures that force a systemic focus and are broken down into appropriate submeasures for various teams and units may provide awareness of the overall significance of work. The same work design approaches that are required because of the interdependency of work—creating cross-functional teams to address more systemic problems, and building links across interdependent parts of the organization—may create an awareness of how one's contribution is significant for the larger system. Workers may also gain a greater feeling of significance if their work assignments are sequenced so that they get experience in various units and can see how the units depend on each another. Based on the extensive literature documenting the gap between the orientation of professional employees toward furthering their discipline and their employers' orientation toward successful business outcomes, it is critical to gain a better understanding of how to align these two concerns.

Job Feedback

Traditional job design theory emphasized intrinsic satisfaction and receiving feedback from doing a job rather than external feedback from management. Software programmers, for example, receive positive feedback if their piece of the code runs without error messages. A software program team gets positive feedback when the members combine their code and run their module successfully. Feedback about the systemic aspects of performance stems from collective work: How much does it cost to run the code? Does it fit with the larger software system or does it have to be modified? Are "bugs" discovered in the field? Does the application fit the customer's requirements? Ultimately, how much revenue does the company receive from this software package, and how much market share is gained or lost? Personally relevant feedback, like significance and identity, may operate at multiple systems levels.

If the tracking of team and project success is built into the work process itself, this may be a way to achieve meaningful work-based feedback in a highly interdependent knowledge work system. Because knowledge workers tend to work in a variety of networks and teams and collaborate across boundaries, feedback from multiple sources is relevant. Peer and customer project reviews that are integrated with milestones and process flows maintain the principle that feedback comes from the work itself. Such approaches are consistent with the integral relationship of learning as part of knowledge work. Through multiple source project reviews, knowledge workers individually and collectively learn how other knowledge workers experience their contribution and get feedback about how to improve it. For example, software companies such as Microsoft build regular "time-outs" into the software development process. Code may be temporarily frozen as different teams examine each other's products and codes for integrity, reliability, and system compatibility. This provides periodic feedback from the work, and it enhances the likelihood of project success by facilitating learning and enabling midcourse corrections to prevent errors. Again, we know little about the characteristics of work-related feedback systems in complex knowledge work or how to create personal lines of sight.

Autonomy

It may be especially important to understand the role of autonomy in dynamic and highly interdependent knowledge systems that cannot be fully "programmed" from the top. Autonomy has been found to be a key issue for professional knowledge workers. Traditionally it has meant that individuals or teams have the responsibility and authority to carry out their work without close supervision. Professional autonomy has been viewed as independence in applying sound professional knowledge using accepted standards and methodologies. Self-regulating work teams have been viewed as autonomous in determining how they organize their resources and the strategies they apply to accomplish the outputs required by the organization. These traditional views depend on the ability to segment work so that people "own" a piece of it and can manage their own activities.

But in the dynamic and highly interdependent knowledge system, autonomy may be best understood as individual or collective self-regulation in continual interaction with the other elements of the system and the shifting purposes of the larger context. Self-regulation occurs both in response to top-down direction, and through awareness, connection, and accountability to the other elements of the system. Mutual adjustment is a fundamental process enabling autonomy; it depends on shared understandings and norms in the system. When organizational designs include common processes and systems and when talent strategies facilitate the movement of knowledge resources from one project to another without having to rebuild understandings from scratch, this allows resources to be reconfigured for a dynamic strategy (Galbraith, 1997). To achieve value from knowledge and learning, what is learned must quickly become accessible to other parts of the organization and embedded in processes. The autonomy of various elements of the knowledge system—such as individuals and teams—is limited by the need to adjust to a changing context, where collaboration and flexibility are enabled by adhering to shared principles of interaction. At the same time, each element is responsible for figuring out how to carry out its role to support the larger system and operate in synergy with the others. The organization changes too quickly for control from the top, yet it needs to adjust itself continually in response to systemwide direction. We need to understand better the nature of autonomy that enables optimum application of and advancement of knowledge while facilitating system self-regulation.

Growth and Development

Although it has been found that performance is highest if tasks are accomplished by the most qualified individuals (Argote & Ingram, 2000), designing work to take advantage of current competencies may not be the best approach in fast-paced knowledge settings. There are both social and technical reasons why growth and development should be considered a work design characteristic in the knowledge economy. Personal growth and development are of key importance to knowledge workers, and organizations that compete on knowledge have demanding requirements for organizational learning and improvement. The growth and development activities of a firm are building blocks for the establishment of the shared understanding and system awareness that enable employees to work effectively in a dynamic, interdependent system and the firm to derive value from knowledge (Mohrman, Finegold, & Mohrman, 2002). We can therefore hypothesize that building growth and development into work will contribute to employee satisfaction and commitment as well as to performance.

As with variety, growth and development work must be designed in the framework of the various competencies required by the system and their implications for the needed mix of deep and broad knowledge. Designing for growth and development is not solely or even primarily a matter of planning training activities. Experience is critical to the development of explicit and tacit knowledge (see Chapters One and Eight, this volume). Job assignments are a way not only to use talent but also to develop it. Careful composition of work groups and design of work processes allow members to learn from each other and to transfer practice from one part of the organization to another. Cross-functional process-oriented teams offer an opportunity to develop broader knowledge; communities of practice offer opportunities to develop deeper knowledge. Research is needed to discover the mix of learning approaches suitable in different knowledge contexts and for different knowledge bases.

It is likely to be highly motivating to knowledge workers if the overlap of learning and doing is increased because growth and development are embedded in the work design and in the sequence of assignments and roles assumed. Tying the broadening and deepening of skills not only to the company's need for competencies but also to the individual's personal needs for career growth strengthens the motivational expectancy cycle. Competency-based human resource practices enable this alignment (Finegold, Lawler, & Ledford, 1998). Development plans can be set up for individuals and teams, and their work can be defined to include the learning required to carry out the organization's strategy and meet its competency requirements. Other human resource practices such as assessments, career paths, and rewards can also include a focus on learning. Because learning is part of the work of knowledge firms, carrying out these development plans can be included in the system's metrics. Process improvement, dissemination, and adoption of innovation can be built into the objectives and plans for each element of the system: individuals, teams, projects, and business units. Although human resource competency-based systems have been described and studied, these studies have usually not included a focus on the design of individual and collective work or on their performance impact in enabling knowledge-based competition.

Network Building

There are both social and technical reasons why network building should be an explicit work design characteristic in the knowledge firm. Networks are the basis for increasing social capital through the resources derived from relationships in the organization (see Chapter Eight, this volume). In order to benefit from the knowledge of the many specialists in the organization, people need to be aware of who knows what (Argote & Ingram, 2000). The organization relies on its dispersed elements to collaborate with and adjust to one another. For such behavior to occur, interpersonal networks must be built on a foundation of trust, familiarity, and shared understandings (see Chapter Three, this volume). Knowledge workers rely on their personal networks for many purposes—to develop their competencies, to become personally visible in the organization and aware of opportunities, and to be able to operate effectively in the interdependent knowledge system. They derive a sense of professional identity and peer support from their knowledge communities.

Networks can be formally established, built into the work design of the organization. Technical councils and communities of practice can be established as formal work units. Networks may also be built into the core work units of the organization. When people serve on the same temporary and possibly emergent teams or take on liaison roles with other parts of the organization, they remain part of each other's personal networks long after a project has been completed and the team disbanded. If they have a sequence of assignments and team memberships, they develop a network of contacts based on their experience working with each other and becoming aware of each other's competencies. More informally, IT systems such as expert lists and readily accessible project and knowledge files can extend the reach of all employees to each other's knowledge and experience and enable connections throughout the organization. Organizations can plan development activities such as training sessions, business processes such as planning meetings, and collective work activities such as peer project reviews and customer visits to expose people to one another and build networks.

By attending to the network-building aspects of work design, an organization can create a web of formal and informal connectivity that matches the saturated interdependency of the system. This approach also meets the needs of professional workers to have networks for various career and work effectiveness purposes. Although much research has described how networks are formed and maintained, there are many unanswered questions. What kinds and density of networks contribute to work effectiveness and employee outcomes in different kinds of knowledge settings? How many active links can employees maintain before they become less productive?

Conclusion: A Framework for Knowledge Work Design

To design work for the knowledge organization, we must understand the nature of the knowledge system and follow new principles of work design that address its dynamic and interdependent nature. Because knowledge work takes a variety of forms, each enterprise needs to be individually designed. Although we do not expect the basic underlying psychological mechanisms of motivation to change because people are knowledge workers, technical, contextual, and environmental forces dictate a change in the assumptions underlying work design and the mechanisms for motivating employees. Based on the framework that has been presented in this chapter, the following principles are proposed to guide knowledge work design.

Design for Systemic Performance

Knowledge work designs both connect the elements of a system to each other and differentiate and clarify accountability and responsibility of the parts. Employees will be asked to wear two hats: to focus on local objectives and performance and to focus on the contribution of the local unit to the system as a whole. The latter requires making adjustments so that the whole system performs optimally.

Create Dynamic Designs

Work designs are not intended to be, nor portrayed as, permanent. Rather, work design is a strategic and operational tool that changes as the system's strategy and mix of activities change.

Focus on Sequences of Assignments, Not Jobs

The organization cannot be conceptualized as a group of individuals with stable jobs. It is composed of dynamic knowledge processes and tasks to which people with various skills and knowledge are deployed. The sequence of assignments determines the experiential learning of the employees and the knowledge they bring to subsequent tasks.

Blur Distinctions Between Managerial and Knowledge Work

Managerial leadership work is simply one form of knowledge work, often best carried out within and across performing units. Self-regulation and mutual adaptation are the responsibilities of all elements of the organization. Many employees are expected to link up with other parts of the organization and elements external to it for interdependent task performance and for learning.

Design Work to Allow Processes to Cut Across Boundaries

Dynamic knowledge work processes cut across disciplines and functions, geographies, product and service groupings, and customer sets. No matter what the core structural units of the organization, if it is to leverage and generate knowledge and apply it for diverse purposes it must assemble and connect dispersed resources (virtually or physically) so that they focus on common outcomes. The work design is independent of a person's "home base" in the organization.

Design Work to Develop Talent

Development can no longer be seen as something external to work. Learning is now part of the work itself. Employees develop through sequences of job assignments, tasks, and experiences as much as through formal training and learning networks.

Focus on the Employment Relationship

Motivation to perform and commitment to contribute are the result of the expectations built into the system, including the organization's expectations for employee performance and contributions and employees' expected outcomes. Work design is integrally related to these expectations and underpins the employment relationship. Clarifying how this relationship changes in the knowledge economy and ensuring a viable set of mutual expectations is critical to the ability to attract, effectively employ, and retain talent. To align work designs with the knowledge requirements of the system, it may be necessary also to redefine human resource practices such as career progression, rewards, development, and performance management so that they fit with the knowledge and competency needs of the system, its work design approaches, and employee expectations.

Taken in full, these principles reflect some very fundamental changes from the literature. Although much has been written about changing organizational forms, little is known about the more micro work-design approaches that are effective and sustainable in the new organizational forms. Furthermore, little is known about how employees respond to these new forms and to the new work relationships and structures that they imply. In the evolution of the knowledge economy, practice has preceded research. It is critical that academics catch up with these new directions and generate theory and empirical evidence to underpin new ways of organizing work.

References

Adler, P. S., & Kwon, S. W. (2002). Social capital: Prospect for a new concept. *Academy of Management Review, 27*(1), 17–41.

Argote, L., & Ingram, P. (2000). Knowledge transfer: A basis for competitive advantage in firms. *Organizational Behavior and Human Decision Processes, 82*(1), 150–169.

Berger, P. L., & Luckmann, P. (1966). *The social construction of reality.* New York: Doubleday.

Boland, R. J., & Tenkasi, R. V. (1995). Perspective making and perspective taking in communities of knowing. *Organization Science, 6*(4), 350–373.

Christensen, C. M. (1997). *The innovator's dilemma: When new technologies cause great firms to fail.* Boston: Harvard Business School Press.

Coff, R. W. (1997). Human assets and management dilemmas: Coping with hazards on the road to resource-based theory. *Academy of Management Review, 22*(2), 374–403.

Davenport, T. H. (1993). *Process innovation: Re-engineering work through information technology.* Boston: Harvard Business School Press.

Davenport, T. H., De Long, D. W., & Beers, M. C. (1998). Successful knowledge management projects. *Sloan Management Review, 39*(2), 43–59.

Deming, W. E. (1986). *Out of the crisis.* Cambridge: Massachusetts Institute of Technology, Center for Advanced Engineering Study.

Dixon, N. (2000). *Common knowledge: How companies thrive by sharing what they know.* Boston: Harvard Business School Press.

Dougherty, D. (1992). Interpretive barriers to successful product innovation in large firms. *Organizational Science, 3*(2), 179–202.

Dougherty, D. (2001). Re-imagining the differentiation and integration of work for sustained product innovation. *Organization Science, 12*(5), 621–631.

Drucker, P. (1993). *Post-capitalist society.* Oxford, England: Butterworth Heinemann.

Dunnette, M. D., Campbell, J. P., & Hakel, M. D. (1967). Factors contributing to job satisfaction and dissatisfaction in six occupational groups. *Organizational Behavior and Human Performance, 2,* 143–174.

Finegold, D., Lawler, E. E. III, & Ledford, G. E. Jr. (1998). Organizing for competencies and capabilities: Bridging from strategy to effectiveness. In S. A. Mohrman, J. R. Galbraith, & E. E. Lawler III (Eds.), *Tomorrow's organizations: Crafting winning capabilities in a dynamic world.* San Francisco: Jossey-Bass.

Finegold, D., Mohrman, S. A., & Spreitzer, G. M. (2002). Age effects on the predictors of technical workers' commitment and willingness to turnover. *Journal of Occupational Behavior, 23*(2), 1–20.

Galbraith, J. R. (1994). *Designing organizations: An executive briefing on strategy, structure, and process.* San Francisco: Jossey-Bass.

Galbraith, J. R. (1997). Managing the new complexity (Publication IMD 97–5). Lausanne, Switzerland: IMD.

Galbraith, J. R. (2000). *Designing the global corporation.* San Francisco: Jossey-Bass.

Gilbreth, F. B. (1914). *Primer of scientific management.* New York: Van Nostrand Reinhold.

Griffin, R., Moorhead, B., & Welsh, A. (1981). Perceived task characteristics and employee performance: A literature review. *Academy of Management Review, 6*(4), 655–664.

Hackman, J. R. (1977). Work design. In J. R. Hackman & J. L. Suttle (Eds.), *Improving life at work: Behavioral science approaches to organizational change.* Santa Monica, CA: Goodyear Press.

Hackman, J. R. (1983). Designing work for individuals and groups. In J. R. Hackman, E. E. Lawler III, & L. W. Porter (Eds.), *Perspectives on behavior in organizations* (2nd ed.; pp. 242–257). New York: McGraw-Hill.

Hackman, J. R. (Ed.). (1990). *Groups that work (and those that don't): Creating the conditions for effective teamwork.* San Francisco: Jossey-Bass.

Hackman, J. R., & Lawler, E. E. III. (1971). Employee reactions to job characteristics. *Journal of Applied Psychology Monograph, 55,* 259–286.

Hackman, J. R., & Oldham, G. R. (1975). Development of the job diagnostic survey. *Journal of Applied Psychology, 60,* 159–170.

Hackman, J. R. & Oldham, G. R. (1980). *Work redesign.* Reading, MA: Addison-Wesley.

Hammer, M., & Champy, J. (1993). *Re-engineering the corporation.* New York: HarperCollins.

Hitt, M. A., Bierman, L., Shimizu, K., & Kochhar, R. (2001). Direct and moderating effects of human capital on strategy and performance in professional service firms: A resource-based perspective. *Academy of Management Journal, 44*(1), 13–28.

Hitt, M. A., Keats, B. A., & DeMarie, S. M. (1998). Navigating in the new competitive landscape: Building strategic flexibility and competitive advantage in the 21st century. *Academy of Management Executive, 12,* 22–42.

Hulin, C. L., & Blood, M. R. (1968). Job enlargement, individual differences, and worker responses. *Psychological Bulletin, 69,* 41–55.

Iansiti, M. (1995, Fall). Shooting the rapids: Managing product development in turbulent environments. *California Management Review, 38,* 37–58.

Juran, J. M. (1989). *Juran on leadership for quality.* New York: Free Press.

Lawler, E. E. III. (1986). *High involvement management.* San Francisco: Jossey-Bass.

Leonard-Barton, D. (1995). *Wellsprings of knowledge: Building and sustaining the sources of innovation.* Boston: Harvard Business School Press.

Liedtka, J. M., Haskins, M. E., Rosenblum, J. W., & Weber, J. (1997). The generative cycle: Linking knowledge and relationships. *Sloan Management Review, 39*(1), 47–58.

Mohrman, S. A., Cohen, S. G., & Mohrman, A. M. (1995). *Designing team-based organizations: New forms for knowledge work.* San Francisco: Jossey-Bass.

Mohrman, S. A., & Finegold, D. (2000, February). *Strategies for the knowledge economy: From rhetoric to reality.* Monograph presented at the World Economic Forum, Davos, Switzerland.

Mohrman, S. A., Finegold, D., & Mohrman, A. M. Jr. (2002). *An empirical model of the organization knowledge system in new product development firms.* Working paper, Center for Effective Organizations, University of Southern California.

Mohrman, S. A., Mohrman, A. M. Jr., & Cohen, S. G. (1995). Organizing knowledge work systems. In M. M. Beyerlein, D. A. Johnson, S. T. Beyerlein (Eds.), *Advances in interdisciplinary study of work teams* (pp. 61–92). Greenwich, CT: JAI Press.

Nahapiet, J., & Ghoshal, S. (1998). Social capital, intellectual capital, and the organizational advantage. *Academy of Management Review, 23*(2), 242–266.

Nonaka, I., & Takeuchi, H. (1995). *The knowledge-creating company.* New York: Oxford University Press.

Orlikowski, W. J., & Robey, D. (1991). Information technology and the structuring of organizations. *Information Systems Research, 2*(2), 143–169.

Parsons, T. (1960). *Structure and process in modern societies.* New York: Wiley.

Pasmore, W. A. (1988). *Designing effective organizations: The sociotechnical systems perspective.* New York: Wiley.

Pasmore, W. A., Petee, Jr., & Bastian, R. (1987). Sociotechnical systems in health care: A field experiment. *Journal of Applied Behavioral Science, 22*(3), 329–340.

Pava, C. (1983). *Managing new office technology: An organizational strategy.* New York: Free Press.

Pava, C. (1986). Redesigning sociotechnical systems design: Concepts and methods for the 1990s. *Journal of Applied Behavioral Science, 22*(3), 201–222.

Perrow, C. (1967). A framework for the comparative analysis of organizations. *American Sociological Review, 32,* 194–208.

Porter, L. W., Lawler, E. E. III, & Hackman, J. R. (1975). *Behavior in organizations.* New York: McGraw-Hill.

Prahalad, C. K., & Hamel, G. (1990, May-June 3). The core competence of the corporation. *Harvard Business Review, 68,* 79–88.

Quinn, J. B., Anderson, P., & Finkelstein, S. (1996, March-April). Managing professional intellect: Making the most of the best. *Harvard Business Review,* pp. 71–80.

Rousseau, D. M. (1977). Technological differences in job characteristics, employee satisfaction, and motivation: A synthesis of job design research and sociotechnical systems theory. *Organizational Behavior and Human Performance, 19,* 18–42.

Russell, C. (1993). *The master trend: How the baby boom generation is remaking America.* New York: Plenum Press.

Stalk, G., Evans, P., & Shulman, L. E. (1992, March-April). Competing on capabilities: The new rules of corporate strategy. *Harvard Business Review,* pp. 57–69.

Taylor, F. W. (1911). *The principles of scientific management.* New York: HarperCollins.

Taylor, J. (1986). Long-term sociotechnical systems change in a computer operations department. *Journal of Applied Behavioral Science, 22*(3), 303–314.

Thompson, J. D., & Tuden, A. (1959). Strategies, structures and processes of organizational decision. In J. D. Thompson, P. B. Hawkes, B. H. Junker, & A. Tuden (Eds.), *Comparative studies in administration* (pp. 195–216). Pittsburgh: University of Pittsburgh Press.

Trist, E. L. (1981). The sociotechnical perspective: The evolution of sociotechnical systems (Paper No. 2). Toronto: Quality of Working Life Center.

Trist, E., & Bamforth, K. (1951). Some social and psychological consequences of the longwall method of coal getting. *Human Relations, 1,* 3–38.

Von Glinow, M. A. (1988). *The new professionals: Managing today's high tech employees.* New York: Ballinger.

Walton, R. (1982). The Topeka work system: Optimistic visions, pessimistic hypotheses, and reality. In R. Zaeger & M. Rosow (Eds.), *The innovative organization.* New York: Pergamon.

Walton, R. (1985). From control to commitment in the workplace. *Harvard Business Review, 63*(2), 76–84.

Wenger, E. (1998). *Communities of practice: Learning, meaning, and identity.* New York: Cambridge University Press.

PART 3

Staffing Organizations for Knowledge-Based Competition

CHAPTER 5

Managing the Human Resource Architecture for Knowledge-Based Competition

David P. Lepak
Scott A. Snell

The notion of knowledge-based competition has gained significant attention in recent years (Grant, 1996; Liebeskind, 1996), with scholars focusing on how firms create, transfer, and leverage knowledge for competitive advantage. And although there are many reasons for the success of firms competing on knowledge, human capital is at least in part a foundation for core competencies and an underlying source of competitive success (DeNisi, Hitt, & Jackson, Chapter One, this volume; Hitt, Bierman, Shimizu, & Kochhar, 2001; Wright, Dunford, & Snell, 2001). Yet whereas all people contribute knowledge, innovation, creativity, and the like, not all employees are equal in their knowledge-based contributions.

Virtually all work performed in firms requires employees to use some knowledge and skill. Organizations must manage a wide assortment of employees; some contribute based on the knowledge they possess whereas others contribute based on the jobs they do (see, for example, Drucker, 1999). The challenge that organizations face is this: there are important distinctions between managing traditional work and managing knowledge work. Identifying these differences, and perhaps more importantly, understanding how to manage them, may be crucial for building competitive capability.

In some ways, the new focus on managing the knowledge of a firm's workforce represents a departure for human resource management. Traditionally, the field has viewed the job, rather than knowledge, as the fundamental unit of analysis. We believe that shifting our emphasis from job management to knowledge management—that is, to what people know and how they use that knowledge—may have significant implications for HRM research and practice. One possible way to address these issues is to view a firm as a portfolio of multiple types of human capital that range in the kinds and levels of knowledge used to perform jobs. Once this distinction is made, we can address issues fundamental to the management of knowledge workers as well as to the management of other types of workers.

This chapter focuses on understanding how organizations make decisions to acquire, allocate, and manage the human capital they need to be successful, paying particular attention to the management of human capital in those organizations that compete based on knowledge. First, we review the notion of knowledge-based competition and discuss the implications that a shift toward knowledge management has on managing human capital. We then examine the human resource architecture presented by Lepak and Snell (1999), which provides a conceptual map for examining the decisions that firms make about the allocation of human capital to alternative modes of employment and the design of HRM systems to manage different groups of employees. To address issues related to managing human capital for knowledge-based competition, we use this architectural perspective to view three different levels of analysis: individual, cohort, and organizational. Throughout the chapter, we discuss implications for both research and practice.

An Architectural Perspective on Human Capital Management

To understand the importance that the traditional job-based approach has had for HRM, we need to look back at its history. In the past, and still in the present, jobs represent a microstructural artifact of a firm's operational imperatives. Put more simply, jobs are created as components of production and service processes. Once the jobs are created, individuals are sought to perform them efficiently. The logic of this approach is grounded in the principles of Weber's bureaucratic organization and Taylor's scientific management. By studying the tasks that workers performed, analyzing the necessary components of performing those tasks, and eliminating the unnecessary components, jobs could be designed so people could execute the needed tasks in the simplest way (Drucker, 1999; Mohrman, Chapter Four, this volume). This is not to say that knowledge and experience were not important, but the knowledge of any one individual was deemphasized.

Adopting a job-based approach has proven to be effective for organizations, particularly when the environment is stable, change is slow, and jobs do not evolve quickly. As this became the fundamental job design strategy during the early part of the last century, HRM developed around these ideas. Indeed, most HRM textbooks acknowledge job analysis as the bedrock of the field (for example, Bohlander, Snell, & Sherman, 2001; Gomez-Mejia, Balkin, & Cardy, 2001). Without it, observers might ask, how would we know what tasks employees would perform? Without a clear understanding of the requisite tasks, how would we know what knowledge, skills, and abilities to emphasize in recruitment and selection? Similarly, how would we know the criteria for evaluating employee performance, rewarding pay, designing incentive systems, and so forth?

Perhaps the greatest difference between knowledge management and a traditional HRM approach is managing how employees contribute to a firm's core competencies rather than focusing solely on what jobs they do (Snell, Lepak, & Youndt, 1999; Drucker, 1999; DeNisi et al., Chapter One). As noted by Drucker (1999), "In manual work, the task is always given. . . . [I]n knowledge work the key question is: What is the task? One reason for this is that knowledge work, unlike manual work, does not program the worker" (pp. 84–85). This is not to say that certain jobs do not correlate with certain types of knowledge. But the main emphasis is on leveraging the knowledge base of employees rather than making their job performance more efficient. In many cases, there may be no job to manage per se.

To extend traditional approaches to managing human capital so that they focus on contributions to core competencies in knowledge-based competition, we take an architectural perspective. As noted by Lepak and Snell (1999), an *architectural perspective* views a firm as a portfolio of human capital. This perspective is based on several assumptions. The first assumption is that a firm must often simultaneously rely on employees who contribute in different ways to its competitive advantage. Some contribute based on the knowledge they possess, some contribute primarily based on the jobs they perform, and many contribute based on a combination of the two. Therefore, it would be misleading to suggest that all employees are likely to be knowledge workers. Rather, knowledge workers are likely to make up a portion of the workforce, and the size of that portion depends on the firm.

An architectural perspective also assumes that organizations may draw on the knowledge of employees who are not necessarily a part of their permanent workforce but rather are part of the contingent labor pool (Davis-Blake & Hui, Chapter Seven, this volume; Lepak & Snell, 1999). Relying on external labor may enable firms to gain access to skills that would be too costly or difficult to develop internally (Matusik & Hill, 1998). Rather than constantly hiring and firing workers, firms use contingent workers to increase quickly both the number of workers at their disposal and the types of knowledge skills they possess (Davis-Blake & Hui, Chapter Seven, this volume; Tsui, Pearce, Porter, & Hite, 1995; Pfeffer & Baron, 1988).

Finally, an architectural perspective assumes that as the relative contribution of employees to a firm's core competencies differ, so too will the way they are managed. Whether the employees are internal or external or contribute based on their knowledge or on their job performance, a firm is likely to adapt its HRM system in an attempt to maximize their potential contribution. The challenge is to design an HRM system that facilitates the management of jobs and knowledge for both internal and external employees.

Applying the Architectural Perspective to Knowledge-Based Competition

For firms to apply the architectural perspective to human capital for knowledge-based competition, they must address two primary issues. First, they must ensure that their workforce possesses the needed competencies to contribute to their competitiveness, growth, and performance. Building the knowledge and skill base, however, is not sufficient. In order for human capital to contribute to an organization's competitive ability on knowledge, a firm must also manage contribution and knowledge exchanges (DeNisi et al., Chapter One; Quinn, Anderson, & Finklestein, 1996). In an HR architecture, these exchanges occur between organizational members as well as with knowledge contributors who reside outside a firm's boundaries.

For a firm to adopt an architectural perspective, it also needs to view its entire portfolio of human capital. We recognize here that knowledge management issues exist at the individual, employee group, and organizational levels. Knowledge, at its root, is an individual-level phenomenon (Argyris & Schon, 1978; Grant, 1996; Quinn et al., 1996). As already noted, individual employees have differing types and degrees of knowledge, skills, and capabilities, and firms must understand their knowledge base and establish mechanisms for them to share it. And they rely on a variety of employee groups who contribute in different ways: some based on their knowledge, others on how they perform a job. Firms may also use different types of employees, such as contract workers, full-time employees, and consultants, to contribute to their competitiveness. Finally, a firm's portfolio of human capital and its respective knowledge base may be viewed also as an organizational asset that must be managed and leveraged. Figure 5.1 highlights the main issues that emerge when we consider how firms manage human capital competencies and knowledge contributions from multiple levels of analysis. We address these issues in the remainder of the chapter.

Individual Level of Analysis

At the individual level of analysis, it is first important to recognize that there are several fundamentally different forms of knowledge (Becker, 1964; Matusik & Hill, 1998; Schultz, 1961). Most individuals possess a degree of general or public knowledge, what economists refer to as *generic human capital*. As noted by Matusik and Hill (1998), public knowledge "resides in the public domain" (p. 683). As a result, it is applicable in firms in a variety of industries.

Employees also may possess occupation-specific human capital—that is, a common body of knowledge that is relatively codified

**Figure 5.1. Multilevel Perspective of the
HR Architecture in Knowledge-Based Competition.**

	Competencies	Contributions
Organizational level	• Managing the portfolio of human capital	• Knowledge sharing between internal and external employee cohorts • Appropriating knowledge across employee cohorts for competitive advantage
Employee group level	• Internalizing versus outsourcing employee competencies • Managing employment relationships of employee groups	• Enhancing employee group contribution
Individual level	• Understanding the profile of human capital • Mobility and retention	• Incentives to share knowledge

throughout a broader professional or institutionalized group. For example, although the talent of individuals may differ, doctors and lawyers draw primarily from a body of knowledge that is accessible to all in those communities.

Individuals are also likely to possess a certain degree of knowledge about a particular industry—that is, industry-specific human capital—such as biotechnology, retail, or utilities. Although still in the public domain, occupation- and industry-specific knowledge should be viewed differently from purely generic human capital. These knowledge domains are often well established and consist of a body of knowledge that must be obtained in order for practitioners to be certified or gain legitimacy in the field. Unlike generic human capital, not all employees are likely to attain a significant level of these types of knowledge. Moreover, acquiring employees whose jobs involve primarily generic knowledge (that is, basic math, reading, writing, interpersonal skills, and so on) will likely be easier than acquiring employees whose contribution is based on industrial or occupational knowledge.

Finally, firm-specific knowledge is by definition limited in its application to a particular firm. As noted in transaction cost economics (Williamson, 1975), firm-specific knowledge and assets are only applicable or valuable in a particular firm. Matusik and Hill (1998) refer to this as private knowledge that is based on "such items as a firm's unique routines, processes, documentation, or trade secrets" (p. 583).

Although there are clearly different forms of knowledge, the reality is that employees do not possess only one but contribute to a company based on certain amounts of all four types. However, they differ substantially in their respective individual knowledge profiles. As Figure 5.2 shows, we can map the knowledge profile of human capital by considering the relative degree of each form of knowledge that people use in their contribution. For instance, a recent college graduate (Employee A in Figure 5.2) with an engineering degree might contribute to a firm based on a high amount of general knowledge and a modest amount of occupational knowledge but rely very little on industrial- or firm-specific knowledge. Another employee (Employee B) might use a great deal of occupational knowledge but rely to a lesser degree on general, industrial, and firm-specific knowledge. A third employee (Employee C) might contribute based on her extensive firm-specific and in-depth industry knowledge and rely very little on occupational or generic knowledge. The potential combinations of knowledge are unlimited, but the specific profile will likely have two main implications for the management of employees.

Mobility and Retention of Competencies

The first implication for the management of human capital for knowledge-based competition at the individual level is employee mobility (Teece, Pisano, & Shuen, 1997). The threat of mobility is a direct function of how transferable an employee's knowledge and skills are in different contexts. In general, the threat of mobility increases as an individual's knowledge becomes less firm-specific and

Figure 5.2. The Knowledge Profile of Human Capital.

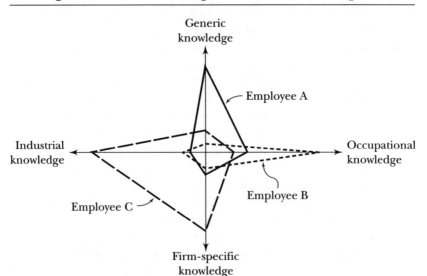

more generic (Galunic & Anderson, 2000; Williamson, 1975). Human capital theory (Becker, 1964) and transaction cost economics (Williamson, 1975) suggest that a firm invests in employees and provides employment security to the extent that these investments will translate into knowledge, skills, and abilities that are specific to that firm. In other words, firms provide security and rewards to employees in exchange for their diminished mobility.

Furthermore, employees are likely to have diminished mobility as their knowledge profile shifts from mostly generic knowledge to industry- or occupation-specific knowledge to firm-specific knowledge. Looking again at Figure 5.2, increased mobility would likely be reflected in a greater proportion of an employee's knowledge profile in the top half of their profile. Similarly, decreased mobility would be reflected if a greater proportion of an employee's knowledge appeared in the bottom half of the profile. Thus, for the three hypothetical employees, Employees A and B likely have greater mobility than Employee C.

Contribution and Knowledge Exchange

Although mobility issues are not likely to be as critical for employees whose contributions are based on firm-specific knowledge, issues related to the sharing of their knowledge are. Horibe (1999) noted that "intellectual capital can only be invited" (p. 154). Compared with traditional assets such as property and machinery, competing on knowledge-based assets is somewhat paradoxical: firms base their success on something they do not technically own. Employees, not firms, own their knowledge (Becker, 1964; Drucker, 1999). This is a human capital dilemma: knowledge is a *corporate* asset that resides primarily in the minds of individuals who are free to do what they wish with it. Organizations may only secure and leverage knowledge if their employees cooperate (Coff, 1997).

As employees are able to command value in their own firm for what they uniquely know, there is an inherent dilemma in trying to encourage them to share their knowledge (Coff, 1997; Hansen, Nohria, & Tierney, 2000). From the employee's perspective, this may be the equivalent of a company sharing proprietary information with its industry. Doing so might diminish its proprietary value. Because information is power in a knowledge-based context, employees may not be willing to share (Davis-Blake & Hui, Chapter Seven). Unless there are adequate incentives to do so, employees with firm-specific knowledge might hold the firm hostage in an effort to leverage their valued asset (Davenport & Prusak, 1998; Quinn et al., 1996).

As shown in Figure 5.3, these two fundamental problems associated with managing individual knowledge are inversely related. Problems of mobility increase when an individual's knowledge is proportionately more generic, and problems with knowledge sharing increase as an individual's knowledge becomes proportionately more firm-specific.

Looking at Figure 5.3, the greatest challenge may be to manage employees who contribute based on occupational or industry-specific knowledge, those whose knowledge profile tends to fall to the left or right sides of the human capital profile. Compared with efforts to recruit, retain, and replace workers who contribute based on general knowledge, efforts involving those who contribute

**Figure 5.3. HR Challenges Associated
with Knowledge Management.**

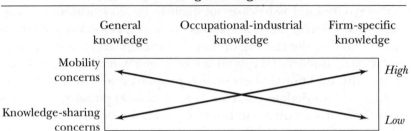

based on these knowledge domains is often considerably more difficult. Employees with common knowledge may be more mobile, but the importance (or costs) of the mobility may be greater with employees who contribute based on occupational or industrial knowledge. Furthermore, the ability of these individuals to perform their roles effectively does not depend on specific firm context, even though it is limited to a specific task or industry domain.

These tensions may be particularly pronounced when the labor supply for these types of knowledge workers is tight. Interestingly, most professional service and consulting organizations are structured around industry (for example, utilities, biotechnology, and so on) or occupational knowledge domains (accounting, tax, strategic management, and so on). These firms are able to capitalize on their client organizations' concerns about mobility and retention while retaining an ability to apply their occupational or industrial knowledge to serve a variety of different companies.

Research Implications

Perhaps the key research issue in managing knowledge at the individual level is to understand the implications of using different HRM practices for employees with different knowledge profiles. Researchers examining psychological contracts (Rousseau, 1995), social exchange theories (Tsui, Pearce, Porter, & Tripoli, 1997), and perceived organizational support (Eisenberger, Fasolo, & Davis-LaMastro, 1990) provide convincing evidence that employees display different attitudes and behaviors based on their perceptions of how they are managed by their firm. Do differences in employees' knowledge profiles influence how they view and respond to organizational investments?

Although employees may not use their full repertoire of knowledge in a particular organization, other forms of knowledge that they possess might be valued in other organizations. Thus the following dilemma: if employees are less mobile when they develop firm-specific knowledge what is their incentive to do so? Similarly, how do firms encourage employees with firm-specific knowledge to stay and share their knowledge with others when they possess a high degree of occupational or industrial knowledge that might be valued by competitors? Which combinations of HRM practices are most effective for encouraging knowledge sharing? Do these differ from practices that enhance employee retention? Are there trade-offs that must be made in focusing on retention rather than knowledge sharing? Although there is no clear answer to these questions, these research issues are likely to become more important when we focus on managing knowledge at an individual level of analysis rather than solely on managing jobs.

Employee Cohort Level of Analysis

Rather than focusing on understanding the knowledge profile of employees, at the cohort level we examine how firms deploy groups of employees who have similar forms of human capital in order to maximize their strategic contribution. It should be noted that we are not necessarily referring to individuals with the same knowledge content per se. Cohorts are individuals who have similar *profiles* or *combinations* of generic, industry, occupation, and firm-specific human capital. The particular content—that is, *what they know*—may differ substantially. This point will become clearer later on.

Managing the Competencies of Employee Cohorts

Building on the resource-based view of the firm (for example, Barney, 1991), transaction cost economics (for example, Coase, 1937; Williamson, 1975), and human capital theory (for example, Becker, 1964), as well as the theoretical arguments of Snell, Youndt, and Wright (1996) and Ulrich and Lake (1991), an architectural perspective begins by focusing on the strategic value and uniqueness of human capital in order to understand its potential contribution (Lepak & Snell, 1999).

The *strategic value* of human capital can be ascertained by analyzing the benefits that employees provide to customers, shareholders, and other relevant stakeholders in comparison with the costs they incur in providing those benefits. What is valuable is likely to be distinct to each particular firm because each firm's goals and objectives differ. Theorists such as Barney (1991) and Quinn (1992) suggest that as the strategic value of human capital increases, so too does the likelihood that firms will employ it internally rather than outsource it or purchase it from outside. According to Bettis, Bradley, and Hamel (1992), outsourcing this kind of human capital is likely to jeopardize the competitive advantage of the firm by eroding its stock of core skills.

The contribution of human capital also depends on its *uniqueness*—the degree to which needed knowledge or skills are firm-specific or need to be applied in an idiosyncratic fashion (Lepak & Snell, 1999). We have previously discussed the idea that human capital ranges from completely generic to occupation-, industry-, and ultimately firm-specific. A fundamental tenet of the resource-based view of firms is that they are more likely to gain a competitive advantage when valued resources are firm-specific and not available to competitors (Barney, 1991). As noted in transaction cost economics (Williamson, 1975), firms have an economic incentive to sustain internal relationships with employees possessing firm-specific skills in order to overcome problems with information asymmetries and ensure a return on investment. Human capital theory (for example, Becker, 1964) posits that firms are more likely to invest in human capital when it is not transferable. Accordingly, individuals are expected to make their own investments in generic (transferable) skills, whereupon firms simply acquire these skills at a market rate (Schultz, 1961; Wallace & Fay, 1988).

Strategic value and uniqueness serve as contingency factors in determining how firms might balance both internal and external employment decisions. As employees are increasingly able to contribute directly to organizational outcomes such as efficiency, innovation, customer responsiveness, and the like, organizations have an incentive to internalize their employment relationship to capitalize on these productive capabilities. Uniqueness has its most direct effect on employment in its influence over a firm's commitment to development over time (ranging from task-focused to relationship-focused). And though this "make versus buy" decision is often made in the context of internal employment, Matusik and Hill (1998) suggest that firms might invest more in relationships with contingent workers when their partnership focuses on creating and transferring private knowledge.

Figure 5.4 provides a conceptual map for how a firm might allocate human capital to different employee groups to optimize their relative contributions to its core competencies (Lepak & Snell, 1999; Snell, Lepak, & Youndt, 1999).

Human capital that is unique and has high strategic value is most likely to contribute directly to a firm's core competencies on

**Figure 5.4. Human Capital Characteristics
and Employment Modes.**

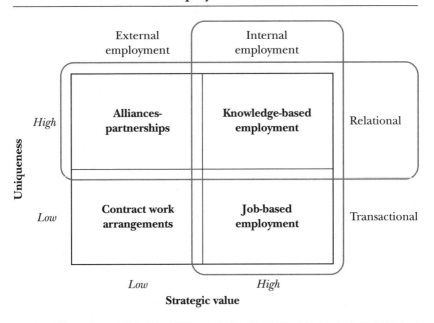

Note: Adapted from Lepak & Snell, 1999, and Snell, Lepak, & Youndt, 1999.

the basis of the employees' knowledge—that is, what they know and how they do something with it (Snell et al., 1999; Purcell, 1999). Given uniqueness, managers are encouraged to focus on establishing a long-term relationship with these employees to enable them to develop firm-specific talents and contribution (Lepak & Snell, 1999). Given strategic value, firms have an incentive to internalize their employment and focus on developing and cultivating their knowledge, skills, and abilities to enhance their value-creating potential (Snell et al., 1999). Because core knowledge workers are both valuable and unique, they have the greatest potential to contribute to the competitive success of a firm that competes on knowledge.

Employee cohorts with knowledge that is valuable but not unique are likely to be managed for the job they do more than for their firm-specific use of knowledge. For example, sales clerks and production workers are often called upon to perform jobs that might require considerable knowledge, skill, and training. Yet when these employees are expected to contribute immediately to a firm by performing a specific set of tasks or activities based on a standardized knowledge domain, they are likely to be seen differently than core employees (Lepak & Snell, 1999). This is not to imply that these are simple jobs. In fact, they may be quite complex and require considerable knowledge and skills. However, although jobs that are valuable but of limited uniqueness are required for organizational effectiveness, often they do not differentiate any one firm from another, as is the case with a firm's core knowledge workers (Snell et al., 1999).

Lepak and Snell (1999) suggested that firms are most likely to outsource work for tasks that are limited in scope, purpose, or duration. An organization's unskilled or semi-skilled positions often fall into this domain. Given their low uniqueness and high transferability, the capabilities of these workers are likely to be widely available. And given their limited value, organizations have little incentive to internalize their employment relationship. As the strategic value of these employees diminishes and the requisite skills approach that of a commodity, outsourcing may be more efficient and effective than internalization (Stewart, 1997; Leonard-Barton, 1995; Snell et al., 1999).

In the top left quadrant of Figure 5.4 we find employees with knowledge and skills that are of limited strategic value but unique to a firm. Some forms of unique human capital (for example, lawyers, consultants) may be employed so infrequently that they do not justify the cost of internal employment. Or a firm may desire these employees for their potential contribution but cannot hire them into the firm. In these scenarios, Lepak and Snell (1999) suggested that firms might establish ongoing alliances or partnerships with these external parties to perform some tasks or projects jointly. Consultants are perhaps the most direct example of this phenomenon, but the same can be true for legal aid, tax advising, enterprise resource planning solutions, and the like. Although both contract workers and alliance partners are external to a firm, alliance partners are expected to apply their skills in some unique capacity, usually over a longer time frame, whereas contract workers are expected to use their existing skills to perform a preset task or activity.

One of the key points of an architectural perspective is that although the employment options may be similar across firms, where employees or jobs actually fall in the matrix is likely to differ (Lepak & Snell, in press). For instance, lawyers might be found in any of the four quadrants. In a law firm, staff attorneys may be viewed as an important element of the business operations. But although their knowledge would contribute to the core competence of the organization, it would not be an element that, on its own, substantially differentiates the firm from competitors. In those same firms, other (perhaps more senior) attorneys may develop specific knowledge that establishes a unique position with clients and customers. In other firms attorneys may serve as an external source of expertise and ongoing advice. Some organizations may establish continuing partnerships with a cadre of lawyers that facilitates the development of firm-specific knowledge that is necessary for them to function effectively. Lawyers who work with the same clients for a number of years may have idiosyncratic knowledge of the clients' history, operations, strategy, and so on that other lawyers do not possess. Yet other firms might view external relationships with lawyers in more transactional terms, using the lawyers' standardized occupational knowledge on a one-off basis to address more limited issues or only once or over a short period of time.

This example highlights an important component of this framework: decisions about employment are not fixed for a particular job but by the strategic value and uniqueness of how the human capital is used in firms. Though the title of the job may be the same, the role of the individual vis-à-vis the firm's competitive position may differ widely. As a result, some firms may internalize certain types of jobs whereas others may use external labor for them. And just as understanding the nature of employee contributions to a firm—their strategic value and uniqueness—is important for understanding how the firm employs its human capital, there are likely to be significant implications for HRM as well.

Managing Employee Cohort Contributions

As we already suggested, an architectural perspective focuses on managing the contributions of multiple cohorts of workers. From an HR architectural perspective, a key issue is that HRM systems that are in place are likely to be different for each distinct employee group. Several researchers have examined variations in how firms manage different groups of employees. For instance, Jackson, Schuler, and Rivero (1989) found that "within organizations, different personnel practices are in effect for employees at different levels. Furthermore, the *relationships* between organizational characteristics and personnel policies are different for hourly and managerial employees" (p. 773).

Similarly, Tsui et al. (1997) found that the HRM practices used to manage permanent employees tend to fall into one of four coherent patterns that characterize the nature of the employee-organizational relationship: a long-term balanced approach, a short-term balanced approach, an underinvestment approach, or an overinvestment approach. Osterman (1987) suggested that firms might rely on salaried, wage, craft, or industrial employment subsystems in their management of different groups. Bamberger and Meshoulam (2000) suggested that firms might adopt a commitment, paternalistic, free agent, or secondary strategy for the management of their human capital. Though the focus of these authors varies, they converge on one point: there are different personnel practices for employees not only in different organizations but also *within* organizations. Although a discussion of the specific HRM practices that make up each system is beyond the scope of this chapter, we briefly review the nature of the HRM systems for different groups of employees in an architectural perspective.

Because of the value-creating potential of core knowledge workers, firms must have mechanisms in place to ensure their investment in and retention of these workers (Quinn et al., 1996). Lepak and Snell (1999) suggest that a commitment-based HRM system (Arthur, 1992, Huselid, 1995) is likely to be most effective in encouraging knowledge workers to assume the risk of developing firm-specific knowledge and adopt a long-term perspective for organizational success. For instance, firms might structure knowledge work to allow for change and adaptation and provide empowerment and participation in decision making to ensure these workers make their best contribution to company competitiveness.

In contrast, a productivity-based HRM system that emphasizes immediate contribution is consistent with the underlying expectations of job-based employees. This system most closely resembles traditional approaches to managing employees—that is, hiring employees to contribute immediately, paying them an equitable wage, and focusing on their job performance (Lepak & Snell, 1999). The job these people perform is the focus, not the idiosyncratic knowledge, skills, and abilities that they possess. Thus, the primary focus for these workers is likely to ensure that they immediately contribute to a firm's competitiveness. This represents the crux of the "make or buy" distinction for human capital.

Because contract workers are often solicited to apply a very standardized knowledge base to well-defined tasks, the main challenge for firms is to ensure that these workers comply with the necessary protocol and perform efficiently. And given the limited nature of the tasks these workers perform, a HRM system that focuses on ensuring compliance is likely to be most effective (Lepak & Snell, 1999; Tsui et al., 1995). Finally, a collaborative-based HRM system might be particularly effective in managing strategic partners with limited value but great uniqueness. As noted by Snell et al. (1999), this type of idiosyncratic knowledge might be best leveraged if it is linked with other employee groups with more demonstrative value. This is likely to require a significant degree of knowledge sharing and information exchange.

Research Implications

Researchers have long noted that differences exist based on exempt versus nonexempt status (Huselid, 1995), departmental differences (Snell & Dean, 1992, 1994), and the like. Although within-firm variations in the use of HRM systems is not new to HRM research, researchers have tended to focus primarily on full-time employees who contribute based on the jobs that they do. Research is needed on the potential trade-offs firms make in how they design their HRM systems to manage different employee groups.

Researchers including Rousseau (1995), Robinson (1996), Wayne, Shore, and Liden (1997), Tsui et al. (1997), and Shore and Berksdale (2000) have focused on understanding the employee outcomes from a firm's management of the social exchange. Though that research tends to focus on permanent employees, the logic of social exchange theories might extend to employees in other employment modes. For example, contract workers may expect limited investments in their development but organizations may "overinvest" in these employees or expect greater contributions. Similarly, core workers may expect extensive investments and support from organizations but be given investments that do not meet their expectations. The relative balance in this inducements-contribution exchange (March & Simon, 1958) is likely to influence the attitudes, behaviors, and productivity of employee groups significantly. As firms increasingly differentiate how they allocate their human capital, this is one research domain that would benefit from greater attention.

Although not all employees may have equal strategic importance (Stewart, 1997), all have the potential to affect a firm's bottom line. Although it clearly is important to understand how to manage core employees optimally, we would be remiss to assume that other workers in a firm, and the way they are managed, are not important as well (Davis-Blake & Hui, Chapter Seven). From an architectural perspective, several research questions need to be addressed. Which dimensions of employee contribution are most desirable for different employee groups? How should HRM practices be combined to enhance employee contributions across employee groups? It is imperative that HRM researchers clearly establish the relationships among different HRM practices and the logic for their inclusion or exclusion into HRM systems.

Organizational Level of Analysis

While managing the contributions of human capital in knowledge-based companies is gaining significant attention, it is important to remember that knowledge workers likely make up only a portion of any firm's workforce. They will likely be deployed alongside other employees, some contributing their manual skills, some the jobs they perform regardless of their knowledge or skills, some their industry or occupational knowledge, and some who are externalized. Figure 5.5 illustrates how a firm's HR architecture might look for a hypothetical company with regard to the strategic value and uniqueness of its employees. Each symbol represents the relative strategic value and uniqueness of the contributions of a particular employee across several job domains. We believe that

Figure 5.5. Example of Human Capital in a HR Architecture.

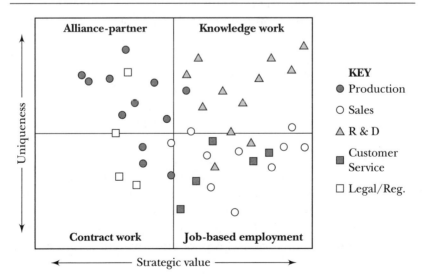

viewing a firm's human capital in this fashion highlights several key issues for managing human capital in organizations.

Managing the Portfolio of Human Capital Competencies

At the organizational level of analysis, an architectural perspective suggests that firms must balance the use of multiple employment modes to optimize access to and use of knowledge. Decisions about which tasks and activities should be carried out internally and which should be outsourced are particularly important, and their complexity should not be understated. For instance, a firm with a high reliance on knowledge workers may run a considerable risk because firm-specific investments take time to materialize, often involve extensive costs, and may be inefficient if the firm overinvests in employees who would not otherwise be deemed core. However, a firm that does not do so runs the risk of competing based on talent that competitors may already have or talent that they could lure away. At the same time, a firm that relies extensively on outsourcing runs the risk of failing to develop the core competencies it may need to compete in the future (Bettis et al., 1992; Davis-Blake & Hui, Chapter Seven). However, for a firm that decides to deploy its human capital competencies, managing human capital moves beyond managing individual employees to focusing on coordinating and integrating the contributions of various employee groups.

It is also important to realize that the overall design of a firm's architecture, or its overarching framework for allocation and deployment of human capital and HRM systems, will likely be unique to its particular circumstances. Becker, Huselid, Pickus, and Spratt (1997, p. 41) note that at the firm level HRM systems "are highly idiosyncratic and must be tailored carefully to each firm's individual situation to achieve optimum results. . . . The appropriate design and alignment of the HRM systems with business priorities is highly firm-specific." Because firms differ in what they do and how they compete, the relative contributions of different groups of human capital will differ for them as well. The challenge for each firm is to identify the optimal mix of employment arrangements for its unique circumstances and to design HRM systems that maximize their relevant contribution to the firm's success.

A final issue needs to be addressed. A firm's portfolio of human capital should not be viewed as static but rather as dynamic, because the relative strategic value and uniqueness of human capital are likely to shift over time. For instance, when a firm alters its technology or strategic objectives, there are likely to be implications for the contributions of its human capital. As the core competencies of a firm change, the requisite human capital knowledge and skills will change as well. This point is underscored by Barney (1995) when he notes, "Although a firm's resources and capabilities have added value in the past, changes in customer tastes, industry structure, or technology can render them less valuable in the future" (p. 51).

Leveraging Knowledge Across the HR Architecture

The notion of knowledge-based competition presupposes that organizations can leverage their employees' knowledge. At first glance, the logic of the HR architecture implies that only employees with high value and uniqueness contribute to a firm's core competencies. But that perspective may be simplistic. Although core competencies are certainly a function of people, they are also a function of processes and systems (DeNisi et al., Chapter One; Fiol, Chapter Three; Prahalad & Hamel, 1990; Wright et al., 2001). Competencies are capabilities made up of aggregated knowledge, processes, technologies, and the like—not just human capital. And although not all workers are necessarily in the knowledge-worker category, some employees who themselves are not knowledge workers may perform activities or be involved in key processes that are instrumental to a firm's core competencies; they may have a link to a firm's competitiveness. For example, although the skills of aircraft maintenance employees at Southwest Airlines are not likely to be viewed as core competencies in themselves, they are instrumental in contributing to an operations system that allows Southwest to maintain one of the top rankings for on-time delivery. The challenge for organizations is to understand how employees in different employment cohorts—not just knowledge workers—contribute to core competencies and then enhance their potential contribution.

Although firms may want and need employees to possess a certain type or degree of knowledge, they may be unable to hire such employees full-time. Relying on external sources for human capital may enable greater flexibility and access to the types of knowledge a firm needs. As noted by Matusik and Hill (1998), "The use of contingent work also may stimulate the accumulation and creation of valuable knowledge within firms" (p. 686). Competing on knowledge likely requires organizations to establish mechanisms to exchange knowledge across employee groups to engender learning and innovation. This may be especially true in organizations that base their competitiveness on organizational learning and innovation.

In addition, firms must plan to manage how they can leverage their workers' contributions over time. They may be able to alter the strategic value and uniqueness of groups of human capital and change the nature of their contribution through firm-specific investments (uniqueness) and increased strategic value (Lepak & Snell, 1999). To increase firm specificity, firms may try to customize the uniqueness of an individual's contribution through on-the-job experiences that develop tacit knowledge that is not transferable to competing firms. Though employees may not currently be of particular value for a firm's competencies, they may be a source for future products or services (see, for example, Prahalad & Hamel, 1990; Leonard-Barton, 1995). The challenge is to design management systems that link the current knowledge of the employees with the firm's future growth. Though it certainly takes time to make the necessary human capital investments, firms that do so may enhance their ability to leverage the knowledge of their human capital.

Research Implications

We believe that these issues point to several areas of research in how firms balance their portfolio of human capital. As firms increasingly rely on different types of human capital for the knowledge and skills they need, research is needed on how to manage the entire system—rather than just one group of employees—effectively. In addition, research is needed on different combinations in a firm's portfolio of human capital. For instance, do firms that rely more extensively on internal labor for knowledge generation outperform firms that rely more on external workers? Considering the potential costs related to investing in core knowledge workers, is there a point of diminishing returns in trying to shift noncore employees into this group? There are no clear answers to these questions, but their importance is likely to increase as firms continue to differentiate the nature of their employees' contributions.

When assessing effectiveness, it is also important to consider multiple performance outcomes. In the strategic HRM research, there is a tendency to focus primarily on accounting or market-based measures of firm performance (Rogers & Wright, 1998). Yet many possible outcomes are relevant. For example, Dyer and Reeves (1995) suggested several types of effectiveness measures: HRM outcomes (absenteeism, turnover), organizational outcomes (quality, service), financial-accounting outcomes (return on assets), and capital market outcomes (stock price). The key issue is to identify which outcome is most appropriate based on the context of the study (Becker & Gerhart, 1996). We would argue that performance measures should be more proximal to the actual outcomes required from employee groups. In some companies, job-based employees may be held primarily to efficiency criteria whereas knowledge workers might be evaluated primarily on innovation and new ideas. Looking only at a firm-level performance measure such as return on assets or return on equity would not likely reflect how well (or poorly) a firm is managing these different groups of workers. Instead, it would capture an aggregated average across the groups.

In addition, there may be potential performance effects related to how firms manage the overall architecture that might exceed the management of any single group of employees. It may be the case that firms that effectively balance the concerns of multiple groups simultaneously are able to enhance the effectiveness of all their employees. It is possible that a firm that adequately manages all of its employees outperforms a firm that effectively manages its knowledge workers but is ineffective in managing other groups. As firms increasingly differentiate among their workforces, how well they can balance the demands of all of their employees will likely be a determinant of their performance.

Conclusion

The purpose of this chapter was to discuss how organizations that compete based on knowledge make decisions to acquire, allocate, and manage the human capital they need to be successful. To address this issue we took an architectural perspective and examined organizations as a portfolio of human capital from individual, cohort, and organizational levels of analysis. We believe that insights into the management of human capital for knowledge-based competition requires consideration of both micro and macro perspectives.

To enhance employee contributions, we need to understand how individual employees and employee cohorts or groups contribute to a firm's success. This is most directly a function of a firm's core competencies and is reflected in their strategic value and uniqueness. At the same time, we also need to understand how different HRM practices and systems affect individuals and employee groups. Each employee group is likely to have a unique perception of obligations or a unique psychological contract with an organization. For example, job-based employees may have different expectations than knowledge workers, even though both groups are internal full-time employees (Tsui et al., 1995). The extent to which firms can attend to these concerns while adhering to their own strategic demands and developing their core competencies should be positively related to their overall performance.

Clearly, many avenues for future research emerge when we view knowledge management from an architectural perspective. These two areas of the field are complementary; each ultimately depends on the other. The architectural perspective provides focus and clarity to the practice of knowledge management; knowledge management establishes a strategic context for activities designed in the architecture. We hope that this chapter has provided some interesting ideas to stimulate future work in this area.

References

Argyris, C., & Schon, D. A. (1978). *Organizational learning: A theory of action perspective.* Reading, MA: Addison-Wesley.

Arthur, J. B. (1992). The link between business strategy and industrial relations systems in American steel minimills. *Industrial and Labor Relations Review, 45,* 488–506.

Bamberger, P., & Meshoulam, I. (2000). *Human resource strategy: Formulation, implementation, and impact.* Thousand Oaks, CA: Sage.

Barney, J. (1991). Firm resources and sustained competitive advantage. *Journal of Management, 17,* 99–129.

Barney, J. (1995). Firm resources and sustained competitive advantage. *Academy of Management Executive, 9*(4), 49–61.

Becker, B. E., & Gerhart, B. (1996). The impact of human resource management on organizational performance: Progress and prospects. *Academy of Management Journal, 39,* 779–801.

Becker, B. E., Huselid, M. A., Pickus, P. S., & Spratt, M. (1997). HR as a source of shareholder value: Research and recommendations. *Human Resource Management, 36,* 39–47.

Becker, G. S. (1964). *Human capital.* New York: Columbia University Press.

Bettis, R. A., Bradley, S. P., & Hamel, G. (1992). Outsourcing and industrial decline. *Academy of Management Executive, 6,* 7–22.

Bohlander, G., Snell, S., & Sherman, A. (2001). *Managing human resources.* Cincinnati, OH: South-Western.

Coase, R. H. (1937). The nature of the firm. *Economica, 4,* 386–405.

Coff, R. W. (1997). Human assets and management dilemmas: Coping with hazards on the road to resource-based theory. *Academy of Management Review, 22,* 374–402.

Davenport, T. H., & Prusak, L. (1998). *Working knowledge: How organizations manage what they know.* Boston: Harvard Business School Press.

Drucker, P. F. (1999). Knowledge-worker productivity: The biggest challenge. *California Management Review, 41,* 79–94.

Dyer, L., & Reeves, T. (1995). Human resource strategies and firm performance: What do we know and where do we need to go? *International Journal of Human Resource Management, 6,* 656–670.

Eisenberger, R., Fasolo, P., & Davis-LaMastro, V. (1990). Perceived organizational support and employee diligence, commitment, and innovation. *Journal of Applied Psychology, 75,* 51–59.

Galunic, D. C., & Anderson, E. (2000). From security to mobility: Generalized investments in human capital and agent commitment. *Organization Science, 11,* 1–20.

Gomez-Mejia, L. R., Balkin, D. B., & Cardy, R. L. (2001). *Managing human resources.* Englewood Cliffs, NJ: Prentice Hall.

Grant, R. M. (1996). Toward a knowledge-based theory of the firm. *Strategic Management Journal, 17,* 109–122.

Hansen, M. T., Nohria, N., & Tierney, T. (2000, March-April). What's your strategy for managing knowledge? *Harvard Business Review,* pp. 106–116.

Hitt, M. A., Bierman, L., Shimizu, K., & Kochhar, R. (2001). Direct and moderating effects of human capital on strategy and performance in professional service firms: A resource-based perspective. *Academy of Management Journal, 44,* 13–26.

Horibe, F. (1999). *Managing knowledge workers: New skills and attitudes to unlock the intellectual capital in your organization.* New York: Wiley.

Huselid, M. A. (1995). The impact of human resource management practices on turnover, productivity, and corporate financial performance. *Academy of Management Journal, 38,* 635–672.

Jackson, S. E., Schuler, R. S., & Rivero, J. C. (1989). Organizational characteristics as predictors of personnel practices. *Personnel Psychology, 42,* 727–786.

Leonard-Barton, D. (1995). *Wellsprings of knowledge: Building and sustaining the sources of innovation.* Boston: Harvard Business School Press.

Lepak, D. P., & Snell, S. A. (1999). The human resource architecture: Toward a theory of human capital allocation and development. *Academy of Management Review, 24,* 31–48.

Lepak, D. P., & Snell, S. A. (in press). Examining the human resource architecture: The relationships among human capital, employment, and human resource configurations. *Journal of Management.*

Liebeskind, J. P. (1996). Knowledge, strategy, and the theory of the firm [Winter special issue]. *Strategic Management Journal, 17,* 93–107.

March, J. G., & Simon, H. A. (1958). *Organizations.* New York: Wiley.

Matusik, S. F., & Hill, C.W.L. (1998). The utilization of contingent work, knowledge creation, and competitive advantage. *Academy of Management Review, 23,* 680–697.

Osterman, P. (1987). Choice of employment systems in internal labor markets. *Industrial Relations, 26,* 46–67.

Pfeffer, J., & Baron, J. (1988). Taking the workers back out: Recent trends in the structuring of employment. In L. L. Cummings & B. M. Staw (Eds.), *Research in organizational behavior* (pp. 257–303). Greenwich, CT: JAI Press.

Prahalad, C. K., & Hamel, G. (1990). The core competence of the corporation. *Harvard Business Review, 68,* 79–91.

Purcell, J. (1999). High commitment management and the link with contingent workers: Implications for strategic human resource management. In P. M. Wright, L. D. Dyer, J. W. Boudreau, & G. T Milkovich (Eds.), *Research in personnel and human resource management* (pp. 239–257). Greenwich, CT: JAI Press.

Quinn, J. B. (1992). *Intelligent enterprise.* New York: Free Press.

Quinn, J. B., Anderson, P., & Finkelstein, S. (1996, March-April). Managing professional intellect: Making the most of the best. *Harvard Business Review,* pp. 71–80.

Robinson, S. L. (1996). Trust and breach of the psychological contract. *Administrative Science Quarterly, 41,* 574–599.

Rogers, E. W., & Wright, P. M. (1998). Measuring organizational performance in strategic human resource management: Problems, prospects, and performance information markets, *Human Resource Management Review, 8,* 311–331.

Rousseau, D. M. (1995). *Psychological contracts in organizations: Understanding written and unwritten agreements.* Thousand Oaks, CA: Sage.

Schultz, T. W. (1961, March). Investments in human capital. *American Economic Review, 52,* 1–17.

Shore, L. M., & Berksdale, K. (2000). Examining degree of balance and level of obligation in the employment relationship: A social exchange approach. *Journal of Organizational Behavior, 19,* 731–744.

Snell, S. A., & Dean, J. W. Jr. (1992). Integrated manufacturing and human resource management: A human capital perspective. *Academy of Management Journal, 35,* 467–504.

Snell, S. A., & Dean, J. W. Jr. (1994). Strategic compensation for integrated manufacturing: The moderating effects of job and organizational inertia. *Academy of Management Journal, 37,* 1109–1140.

Snell, S. A., Lepak, D. P., & Youndt, M. A. (1999). Managing the architecture of intellectual capital: Implications for strategic human resource management. In P. M. Wright, L. D. Dyer, J. W. Boudreau, & G. T. Milkovich (Eds.), *Research in personnel and human resource management* (pp. 175–193). Greenwich, CT: JAI Press.

Snell, S. A., Youndt, M. A., & Wright, P. M. (1996). Establishing a framework for research in strategic human resource management: Merging resource theory and organizational learning. In G. R. Ferris (Ed.), *Research in personnel and human resource management* (pp. 61–90). Greenwich, CT: JAI Press.

Stewart, T. (1997). *Intellectual capital.* New York: Doubleday-Currency.

Teece, D. J., Pisano, G., & Shuen, A. (1997). Dynamic capabilities and strategic management. *Strategic Management Journal, 18,* 509–533.

Tsui, A. S., Pearce, J. L., Porter, L. W., & Hite, J. P. (1995). Choice of employee-organization relationship: Influence of external and internal organizational factors. In G. R. Ferris (Ed.), *Research in personnel and human resource management* (pp. 117–151). Greenwich, CT: JAI Press.

Tsui, A. S., Pearce, J. L., Porter, L. W., & Tripoli, A. M. (1997). Alternative approaches to the employee-organization relationship: Does investment in employees pay off? *Academy of Management Journal, 40,* 1089–1121.

Ulrich, D., & Lake, D. (1991). Organizational capability. Creating competitive advantage. *Academy of Management Executive, 7,* 77–92.

Wallace, M. J., & Fay, C. H. (1988). *Compensation theory and practice.* Boston: PWS-Kent.

Wayne, S. J., Shore, L. M., & Liden, R. C. (1997). Perceived organizational support and leader-member exchange: A social exchange perspective. *Academy of Management Journal, 40,* 82–111.

Williamson, O. E. (1975). *Markets and hierarchies: Analysis and antitrust implications.* New York: Free Press.

Wright, P. M., Dunford, B. B., & Snell, S. A. (2001). Human resources and the resource-based view of the firm. *Journal of Management, 27,* 701–721.

CHAPTER 6

Hiring for Knowledge-Based Competition

Elaine D. Pulakos
David W. Dorsey
Walter C. Borman

Over the last century, the core of wealth creation shifted from capital-based industries like the automotive industry to knowledge-based industries such as information technology, biotechnology, and communications, where innovation, flexibility, responsiveness, and the creative redefinition of markets and opportunities became the new sources of competitive advantage (Dess & Picken, 2000). As the strategic emphasis continues to shift from effective management of mass markets and tangible assets to the effective use of knowledge and information, significant changes are also required in the development and management of human capital. To compete successfully in today's world, firms must increasingly rely on the knowledge, skills, and experience of their human assets to create and assimilate new knowledge, innovate, and learn to compete in fast-moving business environments.

Effective management of human capital involves a variety of different aspects, from providing organizational environments and leaders that encourage and support innovation to creating continuous learning cultures in organizations and establishing mechanisms that enable effective knowledge sharing and dissemination. Another critical element of success is identifying the individuals for hire—and convincing them to take the job—who have the requisite skills, knowledge, and disposition to perform effectively in today's competitive environments. In this chapter, we explore the recruitment and selection of knowledge workers in organizations that are characterized by knowledge-based competition because it is these individuals who are responsible for executing the organization's knowledge-based strategy. Although the recruiting strategies and staffing models we discuss are targeted to organizations that compete on the basis of knowledge, aspects of them are also likely to be applicable to knowledge workers in other types of organizations.

Recruiting and Competing for Star Performers

Organizations that are characterized by knowledge-based competition are the largest growing segment of organizations in the U.S. economy. Accordingly, there is significant competition for high-performing knowledge workers to fill their jobs. At the same time, there is a shift from employers having clear control over the employment process to individual job holders and job seekers having considerable ability to create employment opportunities for themselves. For example, Internet recruiting firms such as Monster.com have emerged as an important force in our economy. As characterized by Pink (1998), employees are declaring "free agency" and selling their talents to the highest bidder; they may even hire an agency to manage their careers, much like movie stars or sports celebrities. This state of affairs has significant implications for the design and implementation of recruiting strategies that are targeted to attracting knowledge workers for knowledge-based competition. We turn to that subject next.

Recruitment Strategies

The recruitment issues and strategies that are relevant to organizations characterized by knowledge-based competition are not significantly different from those for other types of organizations. However, the specific ways in which recruitment strategies are designed, targeted, and implemented do have some unique elements for knowledge-based jobs. Thus, although we will discuss recruiting approaches that may apply essentially to any organization that hires, we will note what is unique about implementing them in organizations characterized by knowledge-based competition.

In developing any recruitment strategy, an important initial step is to consider the key motivators for individuals in the target industry, so that these can be used as much as possible in realistic job previews and other recruitment efforts. The motivators for knowledge workers are often different than for workers in other types of industries. For instance, many knowledge workers seek opportunities to be involved with innovative and creative endeavors; they enjoy working with the latest technologies and are attracted to organizations that do "cool things" (Choi & Varney, 1995). Organizations engaged in knowledge-based competition may thus achieve great benefits by advertising and capitalizing on such factors when they develop materials and communications to recruit knowledge workers. Besides what is presented in these materials, the organization's image and reputation can be a key factor in recruiting for knowledge-based competition. For example, if an organization has a well-known reputation for being an innovation leader or offering a culture that is congruent with the personalities and preferences of the knowledge workers it seeks, these workers will more likely be attracted to it than to other organizations. This suggests that organizations involved in the recruitment of workers for knowledge-based competition could increase their competitive edge by working to create images and reputations that attract these workers. Of course, systematic research should be conducted to investigate both the role of the organization's image and the impact of incorporating key motivators in recruiting materials on recruitment success.

Note that in the preceding discussion, we recommended focusing on what the *organization* has to offer, not the specific job. This is because we believe that recruiting strategies that emphasize person-organization (P-O) fit are highly desirable for knowledge-based competition. P-O fit focuses on organizational attributes, including values and beliefs, as the target criteria (Chatman, 1991). The applicant's personality, values, or needs tend to be the predictors (Kristof-Brown, 2000). In the case of organizations characterized by knowledge-based competition, P-O fit is likely to be relevant because of the fluidity of jobs and the high probability of continual movement from team to team or project to project. There may not even be an actual "job" for which knowledge workers are being recruited; instead there may be a series of projects or assignments that draw workers from various units and bodies inside and possibly even outside of the organization.

The role of P-O fit in the context of knowledge-based competition is another interesting area for research. For example, it may be that P-O fit is more relevant to the degree that knowledge worker skills are more broadly applicable across positions in an organization. Also, as mentioned earlier, knowledge workers are likely to have professional identities, values, and interests oriented toward involvement with creative endeavors and "cool" technologies. Does such an orientation necessitate attention to P-O fit as opposed to the immediate job context alone? These two research questions address both the *demands-abilities* and *needs-supplies* perspectives of P-O fit (Kristof, 1996), suggesting that such distinctions may be useful for framing research on these issues. Specifically, demands-abilities refers to an individual providing abilities required to meet organizational demands, whereas needs-supplies refers to an organization satisfying an individual's needs.

A key strategy in successfully recruiting knowledge workers, like all highly desirable workers, is offering attractive compensation packages. The increased competition for knowledge workers has led to the design of very creative compensation packages that offer nontraditional perks to potential employees—for example, luxury cars, club memberships, day-care services at the work setting, and so on. Today's job candidates may be offered signing bonuses, stock options, and salaries, sometimes even exceeding those of current employees with the same levels of responsibility who are performing very effectively. Such actions, of course, have an impact on internal equity concerns and retention of current employees, but they are sometimes deemed necessary to attract workers that organizations view as vital to their future success.

Another consequence of the competitive landscape for recruiting knowledge workers is that organizations must be mindful of the impression their recruitment and selection practices make on job candidates. In the fast-paced environment of knowledge-based competition, organizations are unwise to use time-consuming processes or make potential employees jump through hoops, because they may find themselves losing candidates to competitors who move more quickly and have friendlier recruitment and selection practices. In the following section on staffing practices, we discuss specific types of selection procedures that are likely to work well in situations characterized by knowledge-based competition.

In general, a natural strategy for recruiting workers is to go after the most highly qualified candidates—the best and the brightest. But in some instances this approach may be shortsighted. If the most qualified candidates are also the most difficult to retain because of high demand for them in the market *and* if the target jobs can be adequately staffed with somewhat less qualified people who are less in demand, it may be wiser to recruit from the latter group. For example, a computer-aided design company providing technical support for architects began recruiting from junior colleges instead of from elite four-year universities and found that its turnover was significantly reduced while performance remained about the same (Cappelli, 2000). One implication is that those who are developing the recruiting strategy should first determine where it is most critical to attract "stars" and where competent knowledge workers will suffice. Such an analysis will not only help organizations determine their recruiting priorities but also allow them to spend their resources accordingly.

In the example of the computer-aided design company, it was possible to manage turnover and also enhance performance by recruiting less qualified workers. Yet in many situations involving knowledge workers in knowledge-based organizations, trade-offs between these two outcomes may need to be considered. For instance, if a particular but rare skill is deemed to be essential for an organization to meet its current competitive challenges, then maximizing performance in the short run may be more important than worrying about turnover in the future. Research is needed to assess the relative costs and benefits of recruiting strategies for turnover rather than for performance, and the circumstances under which these different strategies may be more advantageous to organizations engaged in knowledge-based competition.

Based on our discussion thus far, it may be tempting to think that there is significant competition for knowledge workers in all jobs that involve knowledge-based competition. This may or may not be the case. Certainly, if competition for workers is high, organizations will need to design their recruitment, staffing, and compensation practices to address this reality effectively. But it is important that organizations carefully assess the actual amount of competition for their target workforce before implementing human resources practices that assume an incorrect level of competition.

Recruitment Sources

We now turn to another important issue in the recruitment process: determining the most effective avenues for reaching potential employees. Knowledge workers are generally professionals who have ties and loyalties to their occupations. Thus, effective sources for reaching job candidates are likely to be through such channels as professional associations and societies, conferences, and publications. Also, because workers in knowledge-based industries tend to be more technologically savvy than the average worker, Internet resources may be more effective in reaching them than more conventional sources.

Another recruitment source is an organization's own employees, with both research (for example, Rynes, 1991) and recent practice (Joyce, 1999) suggesting that referrals by present employees result in successful recruiting. Joyce recounts the experience of a mortgage financing company that provides $1,000 bonuses for referring a successful job candidate, $2,000 if the new hire is a high-tech person. Fully 30 percent of recent new employees in this company were referrals, and at least anecdotal evidence suggests that the best employees came from this source. In addition, it is estimated that, even with these incentive costs, the organization saved $5,000 in recruiting and advertising expenses per employee hired (Joyce, 1999). Similarly, informal sources can play a large role in job search and choice (Kilduff, 1990). For example, friends tend to interview with the same organizations.

Yet a third recruitment source that has been adopted by many of today's knowledge organizations is "poaching" from competitors' workforces. In fact, the traditional "no-raid" agreements between competitors have often been put aside, leaving corporate recruiters to act as external search firms and freely raid other organizations' employees (for example, Useem, 1999). This movement, combined with the previously discussed practice of employees' constantly shopping for more attractive job opportunities, has created a seller's market in favor of skilled workers, especially high-tech and other knowledge workers. One reason why organizations "poach" is that outside hiring has strategic value as well as near-term benefits. Specifically, hiring experienced workers from competitor organizations can allow for expansion into new areas and markets where these individuals have already established expertise (Cappelli, 2000). Of course, a consequence of this recruiting strategy is that competitor organizations may be more inclined to poach from organizations that have poached from them.

Summary

In sum, we have discussed some alternative ways of thinking about recruitment in the context of knowledge-based competition. It is clear that job candidates and employees, especially those in organizations characterized by knowledge-based competition, have much more leverage and many more opportunities than workers used to have. These factors have significant implications for the development of effective recruiting strategies. We proposed that successful recruitment of knowledge workers could be facilitated by incorporating the motivations of these workers into recruiting communications and strategies, highlighting person-organization fit, developing competitive compensation packages, and using recruitment and staffing practices that attract rather than turn off desired workers. We also suggested the need in today's highly competitive environment to establish recruitment priorities and apply recruiting resources accordingly. To find sources of workers for knowledge-based competition, we suggested going through professional associations, offering referral incentives to current employees, and examining other organizations for talent. Although we have suggested several potential strategies and sources that may be fruitful for recruiting valued knowledge workers, future research is needed to examine their costs, benefits, and efficacy. In the next section, we turn our attention to staffing issues.

Selecting Workers for Knowledge-Based Competition

To select workers who will perform effectively in situations characterized by knowledge-based competition, we first must understand what *performance* we are trying to predict. Accordingly, this section begins with the development of a taxonomy of performance for knowledge workers engaged in knowledge-based competition. Once we have a better understanding of what constitutes effective performance in such environments, we will examine what individual attributes underlie this performance and discuss the types of selection procedures that appear most promising for predicting it. It is important to point out that individuals involved in knowledge-based competition often work in teams. Also, a variety of organizational factors can inhibit or enhance the creation and exploitation of knowledge. Although such team and organizational factors have a profound impact on what products are produced and what outcomes are realized, our focus in this chapter is on describing individual performance and identifying individual attributes for purposes of developing a staffing model.

A Proposed Taxonomy of Performance for Knowledge-Based Competition

As noted, in order to hire workers who will perform effectively, we must first understand what performance we are trying to predict. We thus begin with the development of a taxonomy of job performance for knowledge-based competition, along the lines of the job performance model developed by Campbell, McCloy, Oppler, and Sager (1993). These authors proposed and tested alternative models for the substantive content and latent structure of job performance. In their theory, job performance is defined as synonymous with behavior; it is what people do that can be observed and measured in terms of each individual's proficiency or level of contribution.

An important contribution of the Campbell et al. (1993) theory of performance was the specification of a taxonomy of eight major performance components, some subset of which can describe the highest-order latent variables for every job in the occupational domain. These are the performance components: job-specific task proficiency, non-job-specific task proficiency, written and oral communication, demonstrating effort, maintaining personal discipline, maintaining peer and team performance, supervision-leadership, and management-administration. Since the development of the initial performance taxonomy, additional substantive specifications for performance have been offered by several authors, including Borman and Motowidlo (1993), Ilgen and Hollenbeck (1991),

Murphy (1989), and Organ (1997), among others. Campbell (1999) points out that the performance factors suggested by these authors can be easily integrated as subfactors into the eight-component taxonomy to form a hierarchical description of the latent structure of performance.

Campbell (1999) also noted that an important performance component not included in the original model that would be a genuine addition is how well individuals adapt to new conditions or job requirements. Accordingly, Pulakos, Arad, Donovan, and Plamondon (2000) developed and tested a model of adaptive job performance consisting of the following eight subfactors: solving problems creatively; handling work stress; dealing with uncertain and unpredictable work situations; learning new tasks, technologies, and procedures; demonstrating interpersonal adaptability; demonstrating cultural adaptability; handling emergency and crisis situations; and demonstrating physical adaptability. We would expect adaptive performance to be particularly important for knowledge workers engaged in knowledge-based competition because of the importance of several of its facets in creating and applying knowledge—such as innovation, creative problem solving, and learning new knowledge areas and technologies. The Campbell et al. (1993) and Pulakos et al. (2000) job performance models will thus be used as reference points as we discuss the performance requirements of knowledge workers engaged in knowledge-based competition.

Defining Performance for Knowledge-Based Competition

As Campbell et al. (1993) argued with respect to performance in general, to identify what is important and to enable researchers to define their variables clearly there needs to be understanding and consensus about what performance for knowledge-based competition means in various job, occupational, or role assessment situations. To this end, we reviewed the literature on knowledge-based competition to develop a definition and a preliminary model that could be used as a starting point for understanding relevant aspects of performance. Several authors have discussed performance requirements associated with knowledge-based competition (see, in addition to this volume, Kelley & Caplan, 1993; Hargadon & Sutton,

2000). Besides technical competence in the relevant content specialty, several consistent themes have emerged from these discussions; we label them here *building and applying knowledge, sharing knowledge,* and *maintaining knowledge.* It is around these three main themes that we will develop a proposed model of performance for knowledge-based competition and relate it to the previous performance models in the literature (Campbell et al., 1993; Pulakos et al., 2000). We should note that in specifying these three areas, our intent is to focus on performance aspects of knowledge worker jobs that are most relevant to knowledge-based competition rather than discuss elements of performance that may apply to any job—such as demonstrating initiative and work effort. In the following sections, we provide our rationale for proposing these three dimensions as the most critical performance factors for knowledge-based competition.

Building and Applying Knowledge

A critical aspect of performance for knowledge-based competition is being able to build new knowledge (create and innovate), apply knowledge to solving problems, and translate these efforts into new products and services that will be competitive and attractive in the marketplace. In fact, several authors have argued that enhancing the creative and innovative performance of their human capital is critical if organizations are to achieve competitive advantage (Amabile, 1988; Devanna & Tichy, 1990; Shalley, 1995). The process by which employees create and innovate involves developing new and useful products, ideas, and procedures, often by spotting how old ideas can be used in new places and new combinations (Hargadon & Sutton, 2000; Cradwell, 1995). If successful, it is the initiation, follow-through, and implementation of these innovations that enable organizations to respond to opportunities and thus adapt, grow, and compete successfully. In addition to generating creative ideas and innovating, another key aspect of this performance factor is understanding customer needs and how to position new products or services in the marketplace.

The concept of building and applying knowledge as it relates to knowledge-based competition is defined behaviorally in Exhibit 6.1. The definition of this performance factor shares content with dimensions from both the Campbell et al. (1993) and Pulakos et

Exhibit 6.1. Definitions of Three Performance Dimensions for Knowledge-Based Competition.

- *Building and applying knowledge:* Gather information and sift through it to identify key issues and gain an accurate understanding of a situation or content area; analyze data, integrate data, and think "outside the box" to create new knowledge, enhance a knowledge base, or develop solutions; develop new and innovative strategies, approaches, tools, and products that increase competitive advantage; anticipate changes in competitive and market demands and proactively address these; exploit technology to enhance productivity and performance.

- *Sharing knowledge:* Share knowledge and expertise freely in written or oral form to help others accomplish goals; collaborate effectively with others to arrive at solutions, innovate, or implement; develop effective networks with other experts to facilitate information and knowledge exchange; document, organize, and capture knowledge for reuse by others; package and present information in a meaningful manner (style, tone, level of detail) that is on-point, persuasive, and effectively addresses the receiver's needs and expectations.

- *Maintaining knowledge:* Demonstrate enthusiasm and curiosity for learning and advancing knowledge; develop and maintain specialized knowledge, skills, and expertise that enable significant contributions to work outcomes; stay abreast of new methods or content areas.

---

al. (2000) performance models. Specifically, this dimension consists of elements relevant to Campbell et al.'s job-specific task proficiency as well as Pulakos et al.'s creative problem solving and dealing with uncertain and unpredictable work situations. In the context of knowledge-based competition these dimensions are likely to be inextricably linked; this is not necessarily the case in other types of jobs and environments. In essence, then, we believe it is the combination of these dimensions as defined in Exhibit 6.1 that uniquely describes a subset of the performance domain for knowledge-based competition.

Sharing Knowledge

Our second proposed dimension of performance for knowledge-based competition is sharing knowledge. Many discussions of knowledge-based competition and innovation stress the importance of sharing or disseminating knowledge to others (for example, Roberts & Fusfeld, 1982; Hargadon & Sutton, 2000). In one study of creative professionals (Kelley & Caplan, 1993), for example, networking was described as one of the most critical aspects of getting the job done. Networking was described as a kind of barter system, where individuals needed to establish their areas of expertise and demonstrate their value by sharing their knowledge with others. Once they showed their value in this way, they were permitted access to the knowledge network. To stay in the network they had to maintain a kind of balance of trade, with individuals providing help and information to others in return for being able to take advantage of others' knowledge and expertise.

Establishing and maintaining networks obviously does not have to work in this precise way, but the key point is that it is important to develop relationships with others for the purpose of sharing and gaining access to knowledge. In situations characterized by knowledge-based competition, where the scope of the work is usually too great for one person and requires a team of individuals and possibly even outside sources to accomplish, this aspect of performance is critical. In line with these ideas, researchers have begun analyzing what is likely a reciprocal relationship between intellectual and social capital (Nahapiet & Ghosal, 1998). The concept of social capital, in fact, centers on networks of relationships as a valuable resource. Therefore, more research is needed to help us understand better the relationships between social capital, intellectual capital, and knowledge-based competition. A related aspect of sharing knowledge that follows logically from this is organizing, packaging, and presenting information in a manner that is persuasive, meaningful to others, and meets their needs.

Exhibit 6.1 presents a behavioral definition of sharing knowledge. This performance factor combines content from two of Campbell et al.'s (1993) performance dimensions: written and oral communication and maintaining peer and team performance. Although facilitative team and collaborative behaviors are generally separate from performance involving written and oral communication, we again believe that these performance aspects are inextricably linked in environments characterized by knowledge-based competition. This is because the types of interpersonal and team behaviors that often predominate in these situations involve relating to others for the purpose of exchanging needed information and knowledge.

Maintaining Knowledge

A third aspect of performance that is highly relevant to knowledge-based competition is continuous learning and upgrading of knowledge to remain competitive (Dess & Picken, 2000; Hitt, 2000; Noe & Ford, 1992; Thach & Woodman, 1994). This aspect of performance is important because of the rapid pace of technological advancement and change in today's organizations (Hesketh & Neal, 1999; London & Mone, 1999). Effective performers anticipate future needs and adapt to changing requirements by continually learning new tasks, technologies, procedures, and roles to maintain their competitive edge. Exhibit 6.1 presents a behavioral definition of maintaining knowledge, which was derived from Pulakos et al's. (2000) adaptive performance taxonomy.

Summary

A few comments are warranted to summarize the distinctions we are proposing between the dimensions of knowledge-based competition presented here and the Campbell et al. (1993) and Pulakos et al. (2000) performance models. First, we are not suggesting that performance in situations characterized by knowledge-based competition is outside the content already covered in these existing performance models. But we are suggesting that there is more emphasis on certain aspects of these performance models for situations characterized by knowledge-based competition. We also believe that performance for knowledge-based competition inextricably integrates several key aspects of Pulakos et al's. (2000) adaptive performance dimensions and several of Campbell's performance factors. We now turn to a discussion of cognitive and noncognitive attributes that underlie the proposed performance dimensions.

Individual Attributes That Underlie Performance for Knowledge-Based Competition

Although we could find no empirical research on the validity of predictor measures for knowledge-based competition per se, several studies have examined measures that are relevant. For example, a large body of literature has focused on determining personality characteristics and individual attributes associated with creativity (Barron & Harrington, 1981; Davis, 1989; Martindale, 1989). This research has examined personal characteristics ranging from biographical data to assessments of cognitive styles and intelligence (for example, Barron & Harrington, 1981; Davis, 1989; Woodman & Schoenfeldt, 1989). In aggregate, such studies have found a fairly stable and core set of personality traits that relate positively to measures of creative performance in a variety of contexts. The traits include broad interests, attraction to complexity, intuition, aesthetic sensitivity, tolerance of ambiguity, and self-confidence. Other research on predictors of adaptive performance in organizations also suggests a number of constructs that may be relevant to predicting performance for knowledge-based competition, such as cooperativeness, willingness to learn, initiative, achievement motivation, situational flexibility, interpersonal flexibility, openness, tolerance for ambiguity, and emotional stability (Judge, Thoresen, Pucik, & Welbourne, 1999; Kobasa, 1979; Pulakos & Dorsey, 2000; Whitbourne, 1986). Yet other research has suggested and examined a number of cognitively oriented variables as potential predictors of adaptability, innovation, and general performance (Fleishman, 1992; Hunter & Hunter, 1984; Owens, 1969; Pulakos & Dorsey, 2000; Wagner, 1986). Constructs such as reasoning ability, critical thinking, fluency of ideas, and oral and written communication skills may all be relevant to the prediction of knowledge-based performance as defined here.

To hypothesize more specific relationships between potential predictors and the present target performance domain, we identified candidate predictor constructs that appeared to be the most conceptually and empirically relevant based on the literature and our proposed performance model. Fifteen experienced selection experts were then asked to judge the relevance of each predictor construct for each of the three proposed performance dimensions.

Schmidt, Hunter, Croll, and McKenzie (1983) have shown that expert judgments of test validities approximate actual validities quite well. Exhibit 6.2 defines the most relevant predictor constructs— that is, those rated of high or very high relevance—for each of the proposed performance dimensions. Based on the expert judgments, different predictor constructs appear to underlie each of the three different performance dimensions. However, there appears to be a relatively strong cognitive component to all three dimensions. For example, reasoning ability, critical thinking, and problem solving are relevant for building and applying knowledge, writing is relevant for sharing knowledge, and reading and learning are relevant for maintaining knowledge. Thus, measures of general intelligence would likely be good candidates for predicting performance for knowledge-based competition. Of course, the hypothesized predictor-criterion relationships shown in the exhibit will need to be tested in future empirical research to assess the true relevance of these constructs for predicting performance in jobs characterized by knowledge-based competition. In addition, other measures such as memory may prove to be fruitful predictors.

Most of the individual difference variables we suggest as being potentially useful predictors of performance for knowledge-based competition are well-defined and well-researched constructs from the cognitive and noncognitive domains. However, two of our proposed predictor measures—content-relevant experience and domain-specific knowledge—have not been as well specified or as extensively studied as the others. Thus, building from the work of researchers such as Schmidt and Hunter (1993), we believe that an important direction for future research is further exploration and understanding of the fundamental constructs of job knowledge and job experience. As these authors suggested, the construct of job knowledge is broad and potentially includes concepts such as tacit knowledge and practical intelligence. Moreover, it is likely that many measures of job knowledge incorporate the effects of variables such as job experience and intelligence. Thus, it is somewhat surprising that much of the literature on knowledge work, knowledge workers, intellectual capital, and human capital makes little or no reference to the literature on job knowledge.

Given what we know and do not know about job knowledge as a construct, we believe that much could be gained through further

**Exhibit 6.2. Most Relevant Predictor Constructs
by Performance Dimension.**

- Building and applying knowledge
  Reasoning ability: Draw conclusions from a set of facts, recognize
      patterns or trends, determine the consequences of actions.
  Critical thinking: Use logic and analysis to identify strengths and
      weaknesses of different approaches; weigh the costs and benefits
      of a potential action or decision.
  Fluency of ideas: Come up with a number of ideas about a given
      topic; apply old ideas to new situations or in new combinations.
  Creativity: Develop innovate ideas and creative solutions to problems.
  Information gathering: Identify, locate, and obtain essential
      information efficiently and effectively.
  Information integration: Synthesize and integrate pieces of
      information into meaningful concepts and ideas.
  Problem solving: Identify and define problems and develop effective
      solutions for problems.
  Initiative: Identify opportunities, show initiative, take action to
      bring about meaningful change.
  Content-relevant experience: Have previous work and training
      experiences relevant to a content domain.
  Domain-specific knowledge: Have knowledge of a specific content
      domain.
- Sharing knowledge
  Active listening: Listen to what other people say and ask questions as
      appropriate.
  Writing: Communicate effectively in writing based on the needs of
      the audience.
  Speaking: Orally convey information effectively.
  Interpersonal flexibility: Adapt own behavior to the interpersonal
      demands of a wide range of situations and people.
  Cooperativeness: Work effectively with others toward a common
      purpose, giving and taking in an effort to achieve group goals.
- Maintaining knowledge
  Reading comprehension: Understand written paragraphs in work
      documents.
  Willingness to learn: Demonstrate enthusiasm and curiosity for
      learning new things.

exploration and explication. For example, what is the right level of specificity in defining and measuring knowledge requirements? Many useful measures of job knowledge have been developed and applied, but these measures are developed idiosyncratically at varying levels of specificity in knowledge domains. Thus a question for further consideration is this: Would a more taxonomic approach to describing knowledge requirements, as exists in an area such as human abilities, prove to be practically useful? In domains such as mathematics, statistics, and computing, researchers have suggested that critical qualitative changes in how individuals organize knowledge (for example, using higher-order concepts) occur as a function of experience (Dorsey, Campbell, Foster, & Miles, 1999; Hong & O'Neil, 1992). If we extend our understanding of such issues, it may suggest improvements in how knowledge requirements are defined and assessed for knowledge-based work.

Other important research questions relate to the relationships among assessments of past experience, as mentioned earlier, and various measures of job knowledge. Specifically, what are the implications of various conceptualizations of experience and knowledge? For example, Lance and Bennett (2000) suggest that different conceptualizations of experience play somewhat different causal roles in the determination of job knowledge, proficiency, and supervisory ratings of performance. As they pointed out, considering job versus task experience may reflect a difference in underlying experience constructs, with both constructs potentially affecting the acquisition of job knowledge and job proficiency. Also, given the performance dimensions proposed here, are hiring decisions better informed through assessments focusing on knowledge specifically or on predictor constructs related to the skills and abilities by which individuals build, apply, share, and maintain knowledge? Moreover, research should be conducted to investigate the validity gains that are achieved by considering the variety of individual difference measures discussed here.

Selection Measures

When it comes to developing actual selection measures, paper-and-pencil measures of any of the proposed constructs could be developed, and in fact some already exist (for example, measures of cognitive abilities and personality constructs). However, assessments of past experience relevant to the performance dimensions themselves (such as biodata measures), as well as high-fidelity assessments of relevant predictor constructs, may hold more promise when selecting knowledge workers for knowledge-based competition than general cognitive and personality measures alone. The higher-fidelity assessments may include, for example, job or computer-based simulations. In fact, previous research has suggested that there are subtleties differentiating star performers from more average performers in knowledge-based competition that may not be readily identified through general predictor construct measures.

Kelley and Caplan (1993) reported that tests ranging from standard IQ tests to personality inventories showed little meaningful differences between star performers and solid workers at Bell Labs. Instead, the differences at this high end of the distribution related to the strategic ways in which the actual top performers did their jobs. Behaviors similar to those included in our performance model—such as developing new ideas and following through, planning for the future, and developing networks—were some of the key behaviors that effectively differentiated the truly exceptional from the solid but unexceptional performers in their study. Thus, an experience-based structured interview (Motowidlo et al., 1992; Pulakos & Schmitt, 1995) targeted at key behavioral dimensions may improve the prediction of performance beyond that observed with more general cognitive and personality measures for knowledge-based competition. This hypothesis, of course, needs to be investigated further. Also, although we have not focused on assessing specific types of knowledge per se—because this will vary considerably based on the nature of the particular job in question—assessment of both tacit and explicit knowledge relevant for a given organization and job would also be important in selecting workers for knowledge-based competition, especially for predicting performance in building and applying knowledge.

One final consideration in developing selection measures: it is important to be mindful of applicant reactions to the entire selection process (for example, Ployhart, Ryan, & Bennett, 1999). As we discussed in the section on recruiting knowledge workers, competition for the best and brightest can be stiff. Thus, although organizations want to hire top performers, this desire must be balanced against the speed with which other organizations are moving to hire the exact same workers as well as candidate perceptions of the relative ease or hassle of joining one organization rather than another. Especially in highly competitive situations, more streamlined selection processes and a very efficient assessment of skills may be necessary. The structured interview option discussed earlier could be implemented with relative ease and efficiency and might be the most practical and effective option when concerns about speed or applicant reaction to extensive testing are great. Future research is needed, however, to assess applicant response to such an interview format as well as other measures that may be used to select workers for situations characterized by knowledge-based competition.

Conclusion

In this chapter we have addressed the increasingly important questions of how companies can attract, recruit, and hire the talent they need to engage in knowledge-based competition. We offered several recruiting strategy ideas and sources that we felt would be effective given the nature of knowledge-based competition and the attributes of the individuals who seek such work. However, virtually no systematic research has addressed the issues of recruiting strategies or sources for knowledge-based competition directly, and thus the proposals and hypotheses suggested here need to be evaluated by future research.

As for staffing issues, underlying our discussion was the belief that developing human capital for knowledge-based competition can be informed by further defining and understanding the fundamental nature of knowledge work. We endeavored to lay a foundation for the development of robust staffing models for knowledge work by proposing a basic taxonomy of performance targeted to knowledge-based competition. This taxonomy included three key dimensions of knowledge work. We also specified individual differences that were likely to underlie effective performance in these dimensions. We believe that further work designed to answer such questions will significantly add to the knowledge base on how organizations hire for, and effectively engage in, knowledge-based competition. In addition, more work is needed to specify further content-relevant experience, domain-specific knowledge, and their interrelationships, as well as the incremental validity of the various types of predictor measures suggested here.

References

Amabile, T. M. (1988). A model of creativity and innovation in organizations. In B. M. Staw & L. L. Cummings (Eds.), *Research in organizational behavior* (Vol. 10; pp. 123–167). Greenwich, CT: JAI Press.

Barron, F. B., & Harrington, D. M. (1981). Creativity, intelligence, and personality. *Annual Review of Psychology, 32,* 439–476.

Borman, W. C., & Motowidlo, S. J. (1993). Expanding the criterion domain to include elements of contextual performance. In N. Schmitt & W. C. Borman (Eds.), *Personnel selection in organizations* (pp. 35–70). San Francisco: Jossey-Bass.

Campbell, J. P. (1999). The definition and measurement of performance in the new age. In D. R. Ilgen & E. D. Pulakos (Eds.), *The changing nature of performance: Implications for staffing, motivation, and development.* San Francisco: Jossey-Bass.

Campbell, J. P., McCloy, R. A., Oppler, S. H., & Sager, C. E. (1993). A theory of performance. In N. Schmitt & W. C. Borman (Eds.), *Personnel selection in organizations* (pp. 35–70). San Francisco: Jossey-Bass.

Cappelli, P. (2000). A market-driven approach to retaining talent. *Harvard Business Review, 78,* 103–111.

Chatman, J. A. (1991). Matching people and organizations: Selection and socialization in public accounting firms. *Administrative Science Quarterly, 36,* 459–484.

Choi, T. Y., & Varney, G. H. (1995). Rethinking the knowledge workers: Where have all the workers gone? *Organization Development Journal, 13,* 41–50.

Cradwell, D. (1995). *The Norton history of technology.* New York: Norton.

Davis, G. A. (1989). Testing for creative potential. *Contemporary Educational Psychology, 14,* 257–274.

Dess, G. G., & Picken, J. C. (2000). Changing roles: Leadership in the 21st century. *Organizational Dynamics, 29*(4), 18–34.

Devanna, M. A., & Tichy, N. (1990). Creating the competitive organization of the 21st century: The boundaryless corporation. *Human Resource Management, 29,* 445–471.

Dorsey, D. W., Campbell, G. E., Foster, L. L., & Miles, D. E. (1999). Assessing knowledge structures: Relations with experience and post-training performance. *Human Performance, 12*(1), 31–57.

Fleishman, J. A. (1992). *Fleishman-Job Analysis Survey (F-JAS).* Palo Alto, CA: Consulting Psychologists Press.

Hargadon, A., & Sutton, R. I. (2000). Building an innovation factory. *Harvard Business Review, 78,* 157–166.

Hesketh, B., & Neal, A. (1999). Technology and performance. In D. R. Ilgen & E. D. Pulakos (Eds.), *The changing nature of performance:*

Implications for staffing, motivation, and development. San Francisco: Jossey-Bass.

Hitt, M. A. (2000). The new frontier: Transformation of management for the new millennium. *Organizational Dynamics, 29*(4), 7–17.

Hong, E., & O'Neil, H. F. (1992). Instructional strategies to help learners build relevant mental models in inferential statistics. *Journal of Educational Psychology, 84*(2), 150–159.

Hunter, J. E., & Hunter, R. F. (1984). Validity and utility of alternative predictors of job performance. *Psychological Bulletin, 96,* 72–98.

Ilgen, D. R., & Hollenbeck, J. R. (1991). The structure of work: Jobs and roles. In M. D. Dunnette & L. M. Hough (Eds.), *Handbook of industrial and organizational psychology* (Vol. 2; 2nd ed.; pp. 165–208). Palo Alto, CA: Consulting Psychologists Press.

Joyce, A. (1999, June 7). Coaxing staffers to aim hire. *Washington Post.*

Judge, T. A., Thoresen, C. J., Pucik, V., & Welbourne, T. M. (1999). Managerial coping with organizational change: A dispositional perspective. *Journal of Applied Psychology, 84,* 107–122.

Kelley, R., & Caplan, J. (1993). How Bell Labs creates star performers. *Harvard Business Review, 71,* 128–139.

Kilduff, M. (1990). The interpersonal structure of decision making: A social comparison approach to organizational choice. *Organizational Behavior and Human Decision Processes, 47,* 270–288.

Kobasa, S. C. (1979). Stressful life events, personality, and health: An inquiry into hardiness. *Journal of Personality and Social Psychology, 37,* 1–11.

Kristof, A. L. (1996). Person-organization fit: An integrative review of its conceptualizations, measurement, and implications. *Personnel Psychology, 49,* 1–50.

Kristof-Brown, A. L. (2000). Perceived applicant fit: Distinguishing between recruiters' perceptions of person-job and person-organization fit. *Personnel Psychology, 53,* 643–672.

Lance, C. E., & Bennett, W. (2000). Replication and extension of models of supervisory job performance. *Human Performance, 13*(2), 139–158.

London, M., & Mone, E. M. (1999). Continuous learning. In D. R. Ilgen & E. D. Pulakos (Eds.), *The changing nature of performance: Implications for staffing, motivation, and development.* San Francisco: Jossey-Bass.

Martindale, C. (1989). Personality, situation, and creativity. In J. A. Glover & C. R. Reynolds (Eds.), *Handbook of creativity* (pp. 211–232). New York: Plenum.

Motowidlo, S. J., Carter, G. W., Dunnette, M. D., Tippins, N., Werner, S., Burnett, J. R., & Vaughn, M. J. (1992). Studies of the structured behavioral interview. *Journal of Applied Psychology, 77,* 571–587.

Murphy, K. (1989). Dimensions of job performance. In R. Dillon & J. Pelligrino (Eds.), *Testing: Applied and theoretical perspectives* (pp. 218–247). New York: Praeger.

Nahapiet, J., & Ghoshal, S. (1998). Social capital, intellectual capital, and the organizational advantage. *Academy of Management Review, 23*(2), 242–266.

Noe, R., & Ford, K. J. (1992). Emerging issues and new directions for training research. *Research in Personnel and Human Resource Management, 10,* 345–384.

Organ, D. W. (1997). Organizational citizenship behavior: It's construct clean-up time. *Human Performance, 10,* 85–97.

Owens, W. A. (1969). Cognitive, noncognitive, and environmental correlates of mechanical ingenuity. *Journal of Applied Psychology, 53,* 199–208.

Pink, D. H. (1998, August). The talent market. *Fast Company, 16,* 87–116.

Ployhart, R. E., Ryan, A., & Bennett, M. (1999). Explanations for selection decisions: Applicants' reactions to informational and sensitivity features of explanations. *Journal of Applied Psychology, 84*(1), 87–106.

Pulakos, E. D., Arad, S., Donovan, M. A., & Plamondon, K. E. (2000). Adaptability in the workplace: Development of a taxonomy of adaptive performance. *Journal of Applied Psychology, 85,* 612–624.

Pulakos, E. D., & Dorsey, D. W. (Eds.). (2000). *The development and validation of measures to predict adaptive job performance* (Technical Report No. 347). Minneapolis: Personnel Decisions Research Institutes.

Pulakos, E. D., & Schmitt, N. (1995). Experience-based and situational interview questions: Studies of validity. *Personnel Psychology, 48,* 289–308.

Roberts, E. B., & Fusfeld, A. R. (1982). Critical functions: Needed roles in the innovation process. In B. Katz (Ed.), *Career issues in human resource management* (pp. 182–207). Englewood Cliffs, NJ: Prentice Hall.

Rynes, S. L. (1991). Recruitment, job choice, and post-hire consequences: A call for new research directions. In M. D. Dunnette & L. M. Hough (Eds.), *Handbook of industrial and organizational psychology* (Vol. 2; 2nd ed.; pp. 399–444). Palo Alto, CA: Consulting Psychologists Press.

Schmidt, F. L., & Hunter, J. E. (1993, February). Tacit knowledge, practical intelligence, general mental ability, and job knowledge. *Current Directions in Psychological Science, 2*(1), 8–9.

Schmidt, F. L., Hunter, J. E., Croll, P. R., & McKenzie, R. C. (1983). Estimation of employment test validities by expert judgment. *Journal of Applied Psychology, 68*(4), 590–601.

Shalley, C. E. (1995). Effects of coaction, expected evaluation, and goal setting on creativity and productivity. *Academy of Management Journal, 38,* 483–503.

Thach, L., & Woodman, R. W. (1994). Organizational change and information technology: Managing on the edge of cyberspace. *Organizational Dynamics, 23*(1), 30–46.

Useem, J. (1999, July 5). For sale online: You. *Fortune, 140*(1), 66–78.

Wagner, R. K. (1986). The search for intraterrestrial intelligence. In R. J. Sternberg & R. K. Wagner (Eds.), *Practical intelligence: Nature and origins of competence in the everyday world.* Cambridge: Cambridge University Press.

Whitbourne, S. K. (1986). Openness to experience, identity flexibility, and life changes in adults. *Journal of Personality and Social Psychology, 50,* 163–168.

Woodman, R. W., & Schoenfeldt, L. F. (1989). Individual differences in creativity: An interactionist perspective. In J. A. Glover & C. R. Reynolds (Eds.), *Handbook of creativity* (pp. 77–92). New York: Plenum.

CHAPTER 7

Contracting Talent for Knowledge-Based Competition

Alison Davis-Blake
Pamsy P. Hui

During the 1990s, employment in nonstandard work arrangements increased much more rapidly than standard employment (see Kalleberg, 2000, for a review). Standard employment arrangements are characterized by "work done on a fixed schedule—usually full-time—at the employer's place of business, under the employer's control, and with the mutual expectation of continued employment" (Kalleberg, Reskin, & Hudson, 2000, p. 258). All other employment arrangements, including contract work, temporary work, part-time work, and self-employment, are considered nonstandard. Contract work is one of the most prevalent types of nonstandard work. Kalleberg et al. (1997) found that in 1995, 7.7 percent of all U.S. workers were employed as contractors and more than a quarter of all individuals in nonstandard work arrangements were contractors. The prevalence of contract work is due in part to the popularity of outsourcing a variety of functions that are not part of an organization's core competence. The American Management

Note: Many of the ideas in this chapter are drawn from research funded by the Alfred P. Sloan Foundation and the Center for Construction Industry Studies at the University of Texas at Austin. We thank them for their generous support of our research.

Association (1997) reported that between 1994 and 1997 contracting for knowledge-intensive activities grew at a particularly rapid rate: financial services contracting increased by 50 percent, information technology (IT) contracting increased by 40 percent, and contracting for marketing services increased by 35 percent. In contrast, manufacturing contracting increased by only 27 percent, and contracting for transportation and distribution services increased by only 18 percent.

This rapid expansion in the use of contractors has not been accompanied by an equally rapid increase in knowledge about how to manage contract workers and the standard employees with whom contractors work (Davis-Blake, Broschak, Gibson, Rodriguez, & Graham, 1999; Gibson, Davis-Blake, Broschak, & Rodriguez, 1998). The purpose of this chapter is to address this gap in our knowledge by describing the factors that determine the effectiveness of contracting for talent when competition is knowledge-based. The chapter is organized into five sections. First, we describe the scope of the chapter and present a few key definitions. Second, we discuss the assessment of contracting feasibility. Third, we explore how human resource management systems and organizational knowledge management systems can be used to increase contracting effectiveness. In our discussion of contracting feasibility and effectiveness we focus on the attributes of the project and the focal firm; attributes of the intermediary are beyond the scope of this chapter. Fourth, we discuss key issues for future research on contracting. Finally, we end with some brief prescriptions for managers.

Scope of the Chapter and Key Definitions

A brief word on the scope of the chapter and some definitions are in order here.

Scope of the Chapter

Contracting for talent is an extremely heterogeneous phenomenon that encompasses everything from long-term subcontracting of entire functions (for example, product design, benefits administration) to short-term employment of a single independent contractor. We focus on contracting situations that involve both individuals providing contract services *and* at least one intermediary organization. Thus, we discuss only two types of contracting situations: an organization hires individuals on a contract basis through a labor market intermediary (such as a professional employer organization), or an organization subcontracts a discrete set of activities to another firm. We focus on those situations involving intermediaries because they are the most common but also the most complex contracting situations (Kalleberg et al., 2000). We do not discuss direct hires of individual contractors, although some of the principles described in this chapter could be simplified to apply to them.

In keeping with the theme of this volume, we also focus only on contracting situations where knowledge-based resources, as defined in Chapter One, are critical to the success of the project. We focus on situations where the core project activities involve the application of tacit knowledge, explicit knowledge, or both, rather than on situations where the core project activities are physical. For example, when constructing capital facilities, it is common to outsource both the planning and design of the facility and the construction of the facility; we focus on the former activities rather than the latter. We consider two specific types of situations where knowledge-based resources are critical to project success.

First, we consider situations in which an organization's main source of competitive advantage is knowledge and the organization contracts for talent to develop or deliver that knowledge (as described in Barney, 1999, and Matusik & Hill, 1998). For example, SAP, a firm that develops and delivers enterprise management software, derives its competitiveness from its ability to apply explicit and tacit knowledge about software development to the general problem of enterprise management and specific client situations. SAP's decision to partner with third-party consultants to implement its system at client sites is an example of contracting for the delivery of knowledge that is a key source of competitive advantage (Parker & Anderson, in press).

Second, we discuss situations in which an organization contracts for knowledge that is not a direct source of competitive advantage but is part of the "architecture" on which its competitive advantage is built. Such architectural features include IT and physical facilities (Ross, Beath, & Goodhue, 1996). For example, the accounting firm Ernst & Young has developed a knowledge repository that is accessible to all of its knowledge workers. This required the creation of a centralized database and the standardization of IT hardware and software throughout the firm (Ernst & Young, 2001). Similarly, although patents are a key source of competitive advantage in the pharmaceutical industry, companies often cannot realize the value of their patents unless they complete new manufacturing facilities quickly enough to allow them to produce a drug for the entire time that it is under patent (Gibson et al., 1998).

Key Definitions

Throughout this chapter, we will refer to the organization contracting for talent as the *focal firm* or the *focal organization* and to the organization providing the talent as the *contractor* or *intermediary*. We use the term *project* to refer to the set of activities for which talent is contracted; by project we mean a discrete set of interrelated activities with measurable goals or objectives. Examples of knowledge-based projects include designing a new facility, developing and implementing a new inventory control system, or recruiting all the staff required to open a manufacturing plant. *Contracting feasibility* refers to the likelihood that the focal firm *can* contract for talent, and *contracting effectiveness* refers to the extent to which the project meets its objectives. Thus, we take an outcome perspective on effectiveness rather than a process or resource view of it (Cameron, 1978, 1986; Tsui, 1990; Yuchtman & Seashore, 1967).

Establishing Contracting Feasibility

In this section, we briefly describe the types of projects for which contracting is feasible but not necessarily optimal. Thus, we identify a broader range of projects than those discussed by Lepak and Snell (see Chapter Five of this volume), who focus on situations where contracting for talent is optimal. We believe that it is important to identify this broader range of options because, as illustrated by several of the following examples, many organizations contract for talent when doing so is not the best option based on Lepak and Snell's typology.

Three key factors affect the feasibility of contracting talent for knowledge-based projects: the firm-specificity of required knowledge, the nature of project interdependencies, and the type of flexibility desired from contracting. In cases where the factor that affects contracting feasibility also influences contracting effectiveness, we briefly comment on effectiveness. Exhibit 7.1 summarizes our arguments about contracting feasibility.

Exhibit 7.1. Determinants of the Feasibility of Contracting for Talent.

Determinant	Contracting for Talent Most Feasible When:
Firm-specificity of required knowledge	• Knowledge is public and not private (firm-specific). • The risk of transferring private knowledge to contractors is minimal.
Nature of interdependencies in project	• Key project tasks are not highly interdependent. • Key project tasks are not heterogeneous with respect to the level of required interdependence. • Contracting for talent is unlikely to create significant violations of the psychological contract.
Desired type of flexibility	• The goal is functional flexibility. • The goal is numerical flexibility *and* adequate contractor responsiveness to organizational changes and concerns can be ensured. • The goal is financial flexibility *and* the costs of contracting are not extremely high and the firm is unlikely to incur high switching costs in the future.

Firm-Specificity of Required Knowledge

Many authors have argued that firm specificity (or "privateness") of knowledge is an important determinant of the feasibility of contracting for talent. If knowledge is truly firm-specific, then by definition it is not available in the external labor market and a firm cannot contract for it. In fact, several authors have suggested that when knowledge is firm-specific, organizations need to ensure that private knowledge will not leave the firm. For example, Williamson (1975, p. 72) argued that organizations should embed individuals with firm-specific knowledge in "protective governance structures" such as internal labor markets in order to discourage turnover and prevent the loss of private knowledge.

Using contractors for a project that relies on public knowledge, however, may improve project effectiveness. Matusik and Hill (1998) argued that the public knowledge of contractors may be superior to the public knowledge of standard workers because of their frequent exposure to the labor market and their use of public knowledge in many different organizations. Thus, firms could leverage the public knowledge of contractors to increase project effectiveness.

Although contracting for private knowledge is usually infeasible, it may be possible for firms to contract for private knowledge by hiring back as contractors their own recently laid-off or retired employees. For example, both Hewlett-Packard and AT&T have experimented with creating pools of former employees to fill specific, short-term assignments inside the firm (Nollen & Axel, 1996). However, these arrangements are very difficult to manage and sustain. Firms often cannot provide continuous employment for contract workers, so these workers move to competitors once their contracts expire. Even when firms attempt to create a pool of long-term contractors, differences between the needs of specific projects and the skills of available contractors often mean that the pools are not economically viable (Nollen & Axel, 1996). Also, because competitors may want access to firm-specific knowledge, competition for the skills of contract workers who have firm-specific knowledge can drive up their rates of pay. Cascio (1993) reported that it is common for laid-off employees rehired as contractors to earn substantially more as contractors than they did as employees. This increased compensation may make it economically infeasible to rehire employees as contractors.

In many projects the public knowledge of contract employees is combined with the private knowledge of the focal firm. For example, in order to design a facility to manufacture drugs developed through biotechnology, engineers must combine public knowledge about matters such as the design of fluid handling and electrical systems with private knowledge about the specific steps required to manufacture the drug. In cases like this, contracting for talent is feasible because some of the project work is based on public knowledge. However, Matusik and Hill (1998) argued that using contractors to combine public and private knowledge creates a risk that they will learn and disseminate firm-specific knowledge. Also, as we discuss in the following section, it is difficult to combine contracted public knowledge with internal private knowledge because organizational structures and processes that effectively integrate public and private knowledge are absent or underdeveloped in many firms that contract for talent.

Interdependencies of the Project

Two types of interdependencies must be examined when evaluating the feasibility of contracting for talent: task interdependencies and governance interdependencies.

Task Interdependencies

According to Thompson (1967), the greater the interdependencies between tasks, the closer the tasks should be located physically, structurally, and temporally. Contracting can increase the physical, structural, or temporal distance between tasks, and firms often use tactics such as colocation of contract and standard employees to reduce this distance. Even when contracting does not increase distance, it introduces the need to coordinate with an intermediary and thus to communicate across organizational boundaries. Therefore, contracting usually increases the intensity of communication and coordination required to manage the interdependencies inherent in the task (Davis-Blake et al., 1999). When tasks are tightly coupled, the additional communication and coordination costs associated with contracting may overwhelm the potential gains. Sometimes these costs are so prohibitive that knowledge transfer is infeasible. For example, in order to be effective IT planning must match an organization's business strategy (Ross, Beath, & Goodhue, 1996). If IT planning is outsourced, the contractor must learn about focal firm's business and the focal firm must learn about the contractor's work style and technological expertise. Such mutual learning may be more costly than keeping IT planning in-house.

Even if knowledge transfer is feasible, contracting for talent may not be effective if key project tasks are heterogeneous with respect to the level of interdependence between people performing the tasks. When interdependencies are heterogeneous, managers are likely to shift the most interdependent (and the most complex) tasks to employees of the focal firm (Ho & Ang, 1998; Pearce, 1993). In their study of standard and contract workers developing software, Ang and Slaughter (1998) found that standard workers reported lower levels of perceived organizational support than contract workers. They argued that because contract workers engaged in few citizenship behaviors and were perceived by their managers as less trustworthy than standard workers, managers gave tasks requiring planning, coordination, and interaction with others to the standard rather than the contract workers, even when the latter were technically able to perform the tasks. This off-loading of tasks in turn reduced the standard workers' perception of organizational support. Smith (1994) reported that, because they distrusted contract workers, standard employees sometimes made this shift in tasks themselves. This shift in tasks increases the difficulty of the standard employees' jobs, usually without any increased compensation, which can lead to feelings of inequity and attendant consequences among standard workers, such as increased turnover, decreased performance, and decreased extra-role behavior.

Governance Interdependencies

In addition to interdependencies between tasks in the project, interdependencies between the project tasks and other organizational commitments can affect the feasibility of contracting. In particular, the psychological contract between the organization and its standard employees can be an important limitation on the feasibility of contracting for talent (Rousseau, 1995). Robinson, Kraatz, and Rousseau (1994) reported that the expectation of job security was a part of many employees' psychological contracts. When a firm contracts for talent it also often lays off standard workers and sometimes transfers staff to the intermediary; both of these phenomena may be perceived by standard employees as violations of the psychological contract. George (1996) reported that the use of contractors increased the frequency of reported violations of the psychological contract. Research has linked psychological contract violations associated with the use of contract workers to lower commitment, decreased trust in the organization, poorer relations with management, and increased turnover among standard employees (Davis-Blake, George, & Broschak, in press; George, 1996; Pearce, 1993). These consequences of violating the psychological contract may make contracting infeasible.

Desired Type of Flexibility

Increasing organizational flexibility is perhaps the most common reason for contracting. Harrison and Kelley (1993) identified three types of flexibility that organizations desire from contracting: functional, numerical, and financial. In the following paragraphs we discuss these three types of flexibility and their implications for contracting feasibility and effectiveness. We argue that it is most feasible to gain functional flexibility through contracting, whereas gaining financial flexibility can be extremely difficult. Gaining numerical flexibility is an intermediate case.

Functional flexibility refers to redesigning work so that the organization does not maintain on its staff employees for whom it has "insufficient and irrelevant demand to warrant the development of an internal capacity to do that work" (Harrison & Kelley, 1993, p. 126). For example, firms do not require the constant services of management consultants, so contracting is a useful way to obtain their advice as issues arise. In general, the desire for functional flexibility often derives from the specific needs of a project and is compatible with project effectiveness.

Numerical flexibility refers to efforts to redesign work so that workforce size can be adjusted easily to match the volume of work (Harrison & Kelley, 1993). Work is redesigned so that at least some job incumbents can be terminated with minimal economic and psychic costs and other individuals can be rehired on a short-term basis as the volume of work increases. Contracting and other nonstandard work arrangements (for example, temporary employment) can be important sources of numerical flexibility (Davis-Blake & Uzzi, 1993; Uzzi & Barsness, 1998). However, Pearce (1998) argued that the use of contract workers for numerical flexibility may impede project effectiveness. Because they lack job security, contract workers are less likely than standard workers to invest in acquiring new project-specific knowledge and in adapting to changes in project design and structure. For example, studies of contract labor in the petrochemical industry have found that contracting for services was associated with lower levels of firm-specific training and led to more workplace accidents (Kochan, Smith, Wells, & Rebitzer, 1994).

Financial flexibility refers to "efforts by managers to reintroduce greater competition among individual workers," thus reducing the expense of performing specific organizational functions (Harrison & Kelley, 1993, p. 216). One way to introduce competition is to contract out all or part of specific projects. Several recent labor disputes illustrate how employees may perceive contractors as a threat to their income and job security. The use of contract employees was a key issue in the dispute between Verizon Communications (created by the merger of Bell Atlantic and GTE) and its telecommunication workers. Those formerly employed by Bell Atlantic feared that expanding GTE's practice of using contract workers beyond the GTE wireless division would mean less job security and more limited benefits (Young, 2000).

The feasibility of contracting to achieve financial flexibility is highly dependent on costs. Although there are certainly cases where contracting has been financially successful (Abraham & Taylor, 1993), Hui, Davis-Blake, and Broschak (2000) found that the financial impact of contracting for engineering design was contingent on the level of contracting. Contracting for *some* design services on a project was associated with worse financial outcomes than either not contracting or contracting for all of the services. The authors argued that at either high or low levels of outsourcing, most of the daily communication and coordination related to the outsourced work takes place inside the boundaries of a single firm. However, moderate levels of outsourcing require higher levels of interoganizational coordination and can lead to conflict over control of specific activities. In turn, this increased conflict can interfere with outsourcing effectiveness.

Moreover, when contracting to achieve financial flexibility, the focal firm also needs to consider whether it will grow too dependent on the contractor. High dependence on a contractor can lead to prohibitive costs if the firm switches to a different, more desirable contractor in the future. As Lei and Hitt (1995, p. 850) noted, "Excessive reliance on a partner or supplier introduces a dependency on an external entity for sources of new skills and capabilities." For example, many organizations contract out the bulk of their IT work. Once the work is contracted out, the focal firm must make huge investments in the installation of contractor-specific IT and training. If the focal firm then decides to switch contractors, it has to abandon these investments and bear additional costs. The likelihood of incurring prohibitively high switching costs can make contracting to achieve financial flexibility infeasible.

Enhancing Contracting Effectiveness

Once the feasibility of contracting talent for a knowledge-based project has been established, the focal firm must then staff the project—with some mix of contractors and its own employees—and manage the productivity of the personnel. The focal firm's human resource management systems are important determinants of how effectively it will be able to staff and manage the project. Once a project is operating, the focal firm's knowledge management systems will determine how effectively both contract and standard staff combine and use their knowledge. Exhibit 7.2 summarizes our key arguments about contracting effectiveness.

Designing Human Resource Management Systems

In the following paragraphs we discuss the impact of the focal firm's human resource management systems on both its employees and the contract workers. We explore how key aspects of the focal firm's selection, training, compensation, and retention systems influence the effectiveness of contracting for talent.

**Exhibit 7.2. Determinants of the Effectiveness
of Contracting for Talent.**

Determinant	Contracting for Talent Most Effective When:
Human resource management systems	• Selection systems are based on a clear specification of tasks for standard and contract employees; identify new skills required when contracting for talent; ensure screening of both contract and standard employees.
	• Training systems provide formal training in required new skills; compensate for reduced opportunities for on-the-job training.
	• Compensation systems provide incentives for knowledge sharing between contract and standard employees.
	• Retention systems encourage appropriate continuity of contract employees; prevent leakage of standard employees into the contract workforce.
Knowledge management systems	• The focal firm has the following boundary management capabilities: *relationship management* (adequate resource devoted to managing the interface with contractors); *contractor evaluation* (retention of adequate capability to evaluate contractor's technical and relationship performance).
	• The focal firm invests in knowledge dissemination and retention capabilities.

Selecting Project Employees

Individuals working with contract talent (as peers or supervisors) require additional skills that are often unnecessary when contractors are not present. When some project personnel are contractors, individuals in the focal firm have to work across organizational boundaries and adapt to the cultures of both the focal firm *and* the intermediary. Many contracting arrangements with intermediaries resemble what Williamson (1991) called the *hybrid organizational form,* a form intermediate between markets and hierarchies. He argued that hybrids require more complex forms of cooperation and adaptation than either markets or hierarchies. Davis-Blake et al. (1999) reported that engineers working with contract designers required several types of skills they usually did not need when design teams included standard workers alone. For example, they needed business skills because they were often in the position of explaining the business purpose of a facility to contractors who lacked firm or industry knowledge. They also needed exceptional communication and influence skills because they had to resolve many issues through negotiation. It is possible for the focal firm to develop these skills over the course of an individual's career. But as discussed in the section on training, contracting often limits training opportunities and thus selecting individuals with these skills is critical. It is also important to note that individuals with this enhanced skill set may command higher salaries than individuals with a more limited skill set. The cost of hiring for these skills may limit the economic viability of contracting.

In adjusting its selection systems to make contracting more effective, the focal firm must address three issues. First, to select the most appropriate individuals for the project, it must clearly identify the tasks to be performed by standard employees and by contractors. Williamson (1991, p. 271) argued that hybrid organizational arrangements are governed by "neoclassical contract law," in which agreements between the parties are incomplete and substantial future adaptation and adjustments are expected. If this incompleteness extends to the descriptions of basic tasks, then selecting individuals with the skills required to perform those tasks becomes very difficult. For example, Anderson, Patil, and Gibson (2000) reported that contracts for the design of capital facilities did not adequately specify the tasks to be performed by contractors and by standard workers, causing delays and duplication of effort. Lack of specificity is also a common problem in IT outsourcing. For example, the installation of SAP's enterprise software at American pharmaceutical wholesaler FoxMeyer failed largely because Fox-Meyer did not communicate to the IT implementation consultants exactly how SAP would need to be customized to fit the firm's complex, rapidly changing, high-volume pricing environment (Jesitus, 1997).

Second, the focal firm's job analysis and description systems must account for changes that occur in the skill requirements of jobs in the focal firm when contracting for talent. Third, the focal firm needs to develop a mechanism for monitoring the selection systems of intermediaries. When contracting for talent, the focal firm usually turns over selection of project personnel entirely to the intermediary with limited specification of the skills contractors will require, little or no description of contractor working conditions, and no additional screening by the focal firm (Davis-Blake & Broschak, 2000). These conditions make it difficult for the intermediary to understand the focal firm's selection requirements and to select contractors who fit those requirements. Monitoring intermediary screening systems is particularly important when the focal organization is contracting for talent in a tight labor market. Monitoring may discourage intermediaries from selecting contractors with marginal talent, thus enhancing project effectiveness.

Training Project Employees

Although it is possible for standard employees to learn the new skills they need to work with contractors while on the job, opportunities for on-the-job training in these skills are not likely to occur. When a firm contracts for talent it often has eliminated some jobs, thus shortening career paths that previously served to develop individual skills (Cascio, 1993). In particular, the use of contractors tends to eliminate positions that served as training grounds for the jobs now done outside of the organization (Barnett & Miner, 1992; Doeringer & Piore, 1971). The elimination of these positions makes it difficult for employees of the focal firm to understand the work of contractors and thus to communicate and negotiate effectively with them (Anderson & Anderson, 2000). The lack of on-the-job training opportunities for learning the new skills required when contracting suggests that, to ensure project effectiveness, the focal firm needs to provide formal training in these skills.

Compensating Project Employees

Lawler (Chapter Ten, this volume) argues that knowledge-based competition requires firms to offer incentives for their employees to develop, transmit, and use knowledge. Moreover, Williamson (1991) stated that hybrid organizational forms, such as those created by contracting, require stronger incentives than hierarchies. In sum, these arguments suggest that strong incentives for sharing knowledge between standard and contract employees are particularly important when contracting for talent. Effective use of contract employees' knowledge often requires contract employees to share that knowledge with standard workers who understand the specific application of the knowledge in the focal firm. However, Matusik and Hill (1998) noted that contract employees may be reluctant to share their knowledge because doing so could reduce their value to the focal firm. Matusik and Hill suggested that offering contractors the incentive of permanent employment may encourage them to share their knowledge, but providing permanent employment may not be feasible if the goal of contracting is numerical or functional flexibility. In these cases, more traditional monetary incentives, such as bonuses for meeting budget, schedule, or quality goals, may be more appropriate.

It is important to note that reluctance to share knowledge is not limited to contract workers. Standard workers may also prefer not to share their knowledge with contract workers because it would reduce their own power, influence, and potential value to the focal firm (Pfeffer, 1981). Because the use of contract workers may be seen as a violation of the psychological contract and make standard workers feel more insecure about their jobs, enhancing their sense of job security may be an effective incentive for them to share knowledge.

Retaining Project Employees

As standard and contract employees work together over time, they develop mutual trust and specific routines and relationships that are critical to project performance. There is some evidence that managers of contract talent take steps to integrate these individuals into ongoing work groups and increase their identification with the focal firm (Smith, 1998). Mutual trust, effective ways of working together, and some feelings of identification with the focal firm are important assets that can enhance the performance of future projects (Kern, 1997). As Noe, Colquitt, Simmering, and Alvarez note (see Chapter Eight of this volume), some level of membership stability is required for teams to develop intellectual capital. Thus, it is common for the focal firm to try to use the same group of contract workers on multiple projects (Davis-Blake et al., 1999). However, the focal firm's desire for continuity of contract workers across projects usually conflicts with the desire of the intermediary to keep its staff fully employed. For instance, many IT contracting arrangements involve staff transfers from the focal firm to the intermediary (Huber, 1993; Seger & McFarlan, 1993). Because of the intermediary's concerns about cost and flexibility, many transferred staff members may eventually be laid off or assigned to projects other than those at the focal firm.

The issue of retaining contractor personnel is perhaps one of the most difficult yet also one of the most important in contracting for talent. The inability of intermediaries to provide continuity of personnel in situations where continuity is desirable can limit project effectiveness. However, existing methods of retaining contractor personnel, such as paying to cover downtime between projects, can be prohibitively expensive and conflict with flexibility goals (Davis-Blake et al., 1999). Finding retention methods that allow firms some continuous flexibility in contract staffing is a great challenge for firms that contract for talent.

To benefit from relationship-specific assets, the focal firm needs to do more than ensure continuity of contractor personnel; it also needs to retain its own key employees. Increasingly fluid labor markets, coupled with strong economic incentives to perform contract work, can lead to leakage of the focal firm's workforce into the contract workforce. Also, as Pfeffer (2001) has noted, the current trend toward perceiving individuals outside the firm as more valuable than the firm's own employees could also fuel the departure of key employees. This leakage is likely to be greatest when the focal firm employs many contract workers and thus standard employees gain substantial knowledge about contract employment. Because contracting for talent can put key employees at greater risk for turnover, contracting is an occasion for the focal firm to strengthen its retention systems for standard employees.

Designing Knowledge Management Systems

Two aspects of the focal firm's knowledge management systems are critical to contracting effectiveness: its boundary management capabilities and its knowledge dissemination and retention capabilities.

Boundary Management Capabilities

When contracting for talent, it is not uncommon for organizations to give the task of managing the day-to-day relationship with the intermediary to overburdened line managers (Davis-Blake & Broschak, 2000). Thus, line managers are in the position of managing both the contract talent and the relationship with the intermediary. The relationship between the focal firm and the intermediary is a valuable asset that needs to be managed. Research has found that while well-managed relationships with intermediaries bring substantial knowledge gains (Dyer & Nobeoka, 2000), poorly managed relationships often lead to unmet expectations and disappointment (DiRomualdo & Gurbaxani, 1998). In complex contracting situations requiring knowledge integration, it may be useful to develop specialist positions devoted to integration. In a case study of Hewlett-Packard (HP), Parker and Anderson (2000) found that as HP contracted out the design and manufacture of an increasing number of components, highly skilled supply chain integrators (often former middle-level line managers) who had the capability to translate and mediate knowledge among various contractors to fit HP's overall product vision became essential to project performance.

In some cases, especially when firms envision a long-term relationship with a specific intermediary, they create "relationship managers" or "alliance managers" whose job is to manage the relationship. Although these managers can be useful, they are often in relatively high-level positions at each firm and thus the agreements they forge do not address the specifics of what needs to happen in each organization for contracting to work effectively. For example, relationship managers often assume free information flow between firms but do little to remove barriers to information flow created by their own organization's IT. Similarly, alliance agreements specify that the intermediary will have responsibility for and control over key aspects of projects, but incentive systems for project managers in the focal firm hold those managers responsible for project outcomes, thus creating a contest for control between middle managers in both firms (Broschak & Davis-Blake, 1998).

In order to know whether to continue the relationship with a specific intermediary, the focal firm must assess the intermediary's performance. In some cases, particularly when functional flexibility is the goal, managers in the focal firm have little experience with the tasks performed by the contract talent. Inability to assess the performance of contract talent or intermediaries makes it difficult for focal firms to ensure that they have the right talent for the project and that these people are performing effectively. In some cases, contracting for talent reduces or even eliminates the ability of the focal firm to evaluate intermediaries. Parker and Anderson (in press, p. 10) report that a top PC manufacturer reversed its decision to contract out its manufacturing because, "after three years, the technology had changed sufficiently that internal people no longer knew enough about the product to determine whether a contract bid was sufficiently competitive. . . . [T]he firm could no longer make the product themselves and they had even lost the ability to determine the cost of products they were buying."

The ability to evaluate an intermediary goes beyond assessing specific project outcomes. When contracting for talent, the focal firm often has objectives for the type of working relationship it wants (desired level of cooperation or responsiveness to changes, for example). Davis-Blake et al. (1999) reported that managers in all the firms they studied were able to articulate their expectations for the relationship they desired with contractors and felt that meeting these expectations was critical to project performance. Yet none of the firms in the sample evaluated whether those expectations were met. Thus, contracting relationships are more likely to be effective if the focal firm is able to evaluate *both* specific project outcomes and the quality of the relationship that generated those outcomes.

Knowledge Dissemination and Retention Capabilities

Matusik and Hill (1998) argued that contracting for talent can be an important source of knowledge generation. However, unless the focal firm has mechanisms to capture and retain the knowledge that is generated, it will be of no benefit in the long run. Even when organizations invest resources in knowledge retention, they often have difficulty retaining internally generated knowledge (Argote, Beckman, & Epple, 1990); retaining knowledge generated jointly with contractors is even harder. Firms may not be motivated to invest in retaining knowledge that is externally generated because it may be seen as readily available in the marketplace. In fact, there is some evidence that, when contracting for talent, firms invest relatively few resources in capturing and retaining knowledge generated with and by contract talent (Davis-Blake et al., 1999). This lack of investment in knowledge retention means that some knowledge may need to be "re-created" for each new project, limiting project effectiveness.

Even if a firm is motivated to retain knowledge, it may not be able to do so if it does not have the capacity to absorb the knowledge. Cohen and Levinthal (1990) argued that a firm's absorptive capacity—its ability to recognize, assimilate, and apply new information—for externally generated knowledge is a function of the relationship between it and the external environment. The importance of this interface is demonstrated by Cockburn and Henderson's (1998) finding that "connectedness" between pharmaceutical company scientists and publicly funded researchers improved firms' performance in drug discovery. Their finding about connectedness is consistent with Noe et al.'s contention (see Chapter Eight) that communities of learning and practice are essential for knowledge creation. As previously discussed, the interface between the focal firm and intermediaries is often quite poor when contracting for talent.

Conceptually, it is possible to use contracting as a way to increase a firm's absorptive capacity. However, Cohen and Levinthal (1990, p. 135) have argued that "the effectiveness of such options is somewhat limited when the absorptive capacity in question is to be integrated with the firm's other activities. A critical component of the requisite absorptive capacity for certain types of information, such as those associated with product or process innovation, is often firm-specific and therefore cannot be bought and quickly integrated into the firm."

Future Research on Contracting for Talent

Because the empirical research on contracting for talent is so limited, there are numerous important directions for future research on this topic. We focus on two: documenting the use of contracting and organizational design for contracting effectiveness.

Documenting the Use of Contracting

Although there have been theoretical discussions of where contracting for talent is likely to be most beneficial (Lepak & Snell, 1999; Matusik & Hill, 1998), we know relatively little about the situations in which it is actually used. The demographic characteristics, attitudes, behaviors, occupations, and industrial settings of individual contractors have been given a great deal of attention (for example, Cohany, 1996, 1998; Hipple, 1998; Kalleberg et al., 1997; Kalleberg et al., 2000), but similar attention has not been paid to the use of contracting. Given the variety of tasks to which contracting is being applied and the rapid rate at which contracting is increasing (American Management Association, 1997), we need to understand the actual, rather than the theoretical, boundaries of its use.

In identifying where contracting occurs, it is important to keep in mind an issue we raised early in this chapter: contracting itself is a very heterogeneous phenomenon. Thus, researchers interested in the boundaries of contracting should identify the *nature* as well as the *location* of contracting. In particular, they should explore the role of intermediaries in contracting for talent. Both Abraham (1988) and Kalleberg and Schmidt (1996) have noted that the demand for all types of market-mediated employment, including contract employment, is partly driven by growth in the number of labor market intermediaries. Thus, it would be useful to understand more about the nature and frequency of intermediary involvement in contracting for talent.

Organizational Design for Contracting Effectiveness

Much of the research on contracting for talent has focused on differences in the attitudes and behaviors of contract and standard workers (for example, Pearce, 1993; Porter, 1995; Van Dyne & Ang, 1998). Authors have then attempted to make predictions about contracting effectiveness based on differences between the two classes of workers. However, Tilly's (1992, 1996) work on part-time employment highlights an important limitation in trying to link differences in job attitudes and behaviors to job status (standard or nonstandard, for example). Tilly reported that part-time employees could be separated into two groups. *Retention part-timers* were individuals to whom employers had granted part-time status to recruit or retain them; they usually had relatively high compensation and interesting tasks. *Secondary part-timers* were used solely to provide flexibility for the employer and usually had relatively low compensation and no prospects for advancement. Retention part-timers worked in conditions comparable to standard workers and had similar attitudes and behaviors, but secondary part-timers worked in inferior conditions and had less desirable attitudes and behaviors. Tilly's work demonstrates that the organizational context for a particular work status may be the critical determinant of the attitudes and behaviors of the individuals involved.

This chapter has identified two important areas of organizational design for the management of contract talent: human resource management systems and knowledge management systems. In the area of human resource management systems, we argued that selection and training systems in the contracting environment need to focus on additional skills although the basic systems may not need to change substantially. However, future research should examine whether selecting and training key employees of the focal firm for broader skill sets that include communication, negotiation, and problem solving is actually associated with increased contracting effectiveness. Pulakos, Dorsey, and Borman (Chapter Six of this volume) argued that because trust and communication are so important for generating and using knowledge, employee referrals are a good recruitment source when competition is knowledge-based. Their argument could be extended to contracting for talent. Contracting tends to create dense networks of interpersonal relationships as contractors and employees move from project to project and firm to firm. Thus, future research should examine whether recruitment and selection practices that tap into these networks increase contracting effectiveness.

The issues of incentives and retention take on a unique and potentially troublesome character in a contracting environment because organizations that contract for talent have conflicting goals in these domains. In the area of incentives, the focal firm wants to promote cooperation across work statuses while preventing leakage of people or ideas. In retention, the focal firm usually desires both continuity and flexibility. Thus, a critical question for future research becomes how firms can design human resource systems that strike an appropriate balance between these goals. One intriguing possibility in the area of compensation is that contracting functions work better not only when standard and contract worker are compensated for the same goals but also when they are compensated through the same mechanisms (for example, the same proportions of incentive pay). Future research should examine this possibility (see Lane & Lubatkin, 1998, for one example). Future research should also examine the impact of continuity on contracting effectiveness. It would be particularly useful to understand the boundary conditions of contractor continuity effects—for what kind of projects or project phases is contractor continuity particularly important?

In the area of knowledge management, an important question is how to manage the interface between the focal firm and the intermediary, particularly at lower levels. An especially important topic for future research is the integrator role. It would be useful to know if the presence of middle-level integrators who play an active role in daily interface management is associated with increased contracting effectiveness. Future research should also examine which integrator skills are particularly important. Integrators usually deal with issues of coordination and control as well as the transfer and retention of knowledge from contractors to the focal firm. Because knowledge cannot be transferred effectively if there is insufficient absorptive capacity on the receiver's part (Szulanski, 1996), it seems likely that integrators will function best when they have some relevant technical knowledge in addition to communication and coordination skills.

Other aspects of interface management also deserve attention. Although many firms assume that colocation of contract and standard workers increases contracting effectiveness, there is no empirical evidence for this. Similarly, it is unclear to what extent IT can substitute for physical colocation or whether it only complements colocation effects. Dyer and Nobeoka (2000) have found that organizations that have successfully leveraged knowledge to create competitive advantage usually have developed knowledge-sharing routines with partners. Advanced information technologies often allow real-time communication to take place even if project partners are not physically close.

Some of the tensions that affect the design of human resource systems also affect knowledge management systems. In particular, the focal firm's ability to increase flexibility by contracting for talent depends on the focal firm retaining the capacity to evaluate contract talent. Yet contracting for talent threatens the firm's evaluation capabilities. Identifying contracting mechanisms that preserve the focal firm's evaluation capabilities is an important issue for future research. Future research should examine how the design of the focal firm and the firm-intermediary interface affects both the capacity of the focal firm to absorb knowledge generated by contractors and the motivation of individuals inside the focal firm to absorb it. As Bassi, Lev, Low, McMurrer, and Siesfeld (2000) have noted, the greatest barriers to knowledge sharing between organizations are cultural and organizational, not technological. Lane and Lubatkin's (1998) finding that similarity in organizational design enhances absorptive capacity suggests that aligning the human resource systems of the two firms could have the unintended positive consequence of easing knowledge transfer between the firms. However, this possibility should be explored empirically.

A final area for future research is the quality of the relationship between the focal firm and intermediaries. As discussed earlier, the quality of this relationship is an important determinant of contracting effectiveness. However, we know relatively little about the factors that lead to a high-quality relationship. To date, research on interorganizational relationships suggests that the length of a relationship is an important determinant of its quality (for example, Baker, Faulkner, & Fisher, 1998; Levinthal & Fichman, 1988). However, maintaining long-term relationships with intermediaries may conflict with flexibility goals. Future research should address whether factors other than relationship length are important.

Implications for Managers

We believe that managers who contract for talent should take three key issues into consideration. First, although they often contract for talent in an attempt to reduce demands on the firm (for example, the demands of retaining a staff of intermittently used specialists), contracting places new demands on a firm and its employees. It introduces new boundaries that need to be managed and requires changes in organizational design, particularly the design of human resource and knowledge management systems. Managers interested in contracting for talent should balance the cost of managing these demands against the benefits of contracting.

Second, contracting for talent for "noncore" activities can have strategic implications. For example, Toyota recently reversed its forty-year-old decision to contract for the design and manufacture of electronics components because during that time period those components became critical to advancing car safety, comfort, and performance (Parker & Anderson, in press). Because it is difficult to transfer knowledge about the strategic implications of architectural activities, contracting for architectural activities can reduce the compatibility of these activities with the firm's core activities. And the inability to integrate architectural and core activities easily can harm firm performance. Thus, managers should carefully consider the potential strategic implications of outsourcing architectural activities.

Third, contracting for strategically critical activities may reduce a firm's ability to control and perform those activities. Contracting knowledge-based talent involves the transfer of some knowledge outside the firm. It is very difficult if not impossible to regain control of knowledge lost in this way. When IBM developed its personal computer in the 1980s, it contracted for the development of its operating system with Microsoft and for production of its microprocessor with Intel. These events allowed competitors such as Dell and Compaq to emerge because they could then purchase on the open market the two components of PCs that are most difficult to duplicate (Anderson & Anderson, 2000). Although contracting for talent has many potential benefits, much more experience with and research on this phenomenon is required in order to clarify its benefits and limitations.

References

Abraham, K. G. (1988). *Flexible staffing arrangements and employers' short-term adjustment strategies.* Working paper, National Bureau of Economic Research, Cambridge, MA.

Abraham, K. G., & Taylor, S. K. (1993). *Firms' use of outside contractors: Theory and evidence.* Working paper, National Bureau of Economic Research, Washington, DC.

American Management Association. (1997). *Outsourcing: The AMA survey.* New York: American Management Association.

Anderson, E. G. Jr., & Anderson, M. A. (2000). Are your decisions today creating your future competitors? Avoiding the outsourcing trap. *Systems Thinker, 11*, 1–5.

Anderson, S. D., Patil, S. S., & Gibson, G. E., Jr. (2000). *Developing optimal owner-contractor work structures: Case studies.* Austin: University of Texas.

Ang, S., & Slaughter, S. A. (1998). *Do I/S contractors help or hinder? Multiple informants' perspectives.* Working paper, Carnegie-Mellon University, Pittsburgh, PA.

Argote, L., Beckman, S. L., & Epple, D. (1990). The persistence and transfer of learning in industrial settings. *Management Science, 36*, 140–154.

Baker, W. E., Faulkner, R. R., & Fisher, G. A. (1998). Theory of market relationships. *American Sociological Review, 63*, 147–177.

Barnett, W. P., & Miner, A. S. (1992). Standing on the shoulders of others: Career interdependence in job mobility. *Administrative Science Quarterly, 37*, 262–281.

Barney, J. (1999). How a firm's capabilities affect boundary decisions. *Sloan Management Review, 40*, 137–145.

Bassi, L. J., Lev, B., Low, J., McMurrer, D. P., & Siesfeld, G. A. (2000). Measuring corporate investments in human capital. In M. Blair & T. Kochan (Eds.), *The new relationship: Human capital in the American corporation* (pp. 334–382). Washington, DC: Brookings Institution Press.

Broschak, J. P., & Davis-Blake, A. (1998, August). *The divergence of macro-structures and micro-dynamics: The effects of contingent work and outsourcing on workplace dynamics.* Paper presented at the annual meeting of the Academy of Management, San Diego.

Cameron, K. S. (1978). Measuring organizational effectiveness in institutions of higher education. *Administrative Science Quarterly, 23*, 604–632.

Cameron, K. S. (1986). Effectiveness as paradox: Conflict and consensus in conceptions of organizational effectiveness. *Management Science, 32*, 539–553.

Cascio, W. F. (1993). Downsizing: What do we know? What have we learned? *Academy of Management Executives, 7*(1), 95–104.

Cockburn, I. M., & Henderson, R. M. (1998). Absorptive capacity, coauthoring behavior, and the organization of research in drug discovery. *Journal of Industrial Economics, 46*(2), 157–182.

Cohany, S. R. (1996). Workers in alternative employment arrangements. *Monthly Labor Review, 119*(10), 31–45.

Cohany, S. R. (1998). Workers in alternative employment arrangements: A second look. *Monthly Labor Review, 121*(11), 3–21.

Cohen, W. M., & Levinthal, D. A. (1990). Absorptive capacity: A new perspective on learning and innovation. *Administrative Science Quarterly, 35*(1), 128–152.

Davis-Blake, A., & Broschak, J. P. (2000). Speed bumps or stepping-stones: The effects of labor market intermediaries on relational wealth. In D. Rousseau & C. Leana (Eds.), *Relational wealth: A new model for employment in the 21st century.* New York: Oxford University Press.

Davis-Blake, A., Broschak, J. P., Gibson, G. E., Rodriguez, F., & Graham, T. (1999). *Owner/contractor organizational changes: Phase II report.* Austin: University of Texas.

Davis-Blake, A., George, E., & Broschak, J. P. (in press). Happy together? How using nonstandard workers affects exit, voice, and loyalty among standard employees. *Academy of Management Journal.*

Davis-Blake, A., & Uzzi, B. (1993). Determinants of employment externalization: A study of temporary workers and independent contractors. *Administrative Science Quarterly, 38,* 195–223.

DiRomualdo, A., & Gurbaxani, V. (1998). Strategic intent for IT outsourcing. *Sloan Management Review, 39,* 67–80.

Doeringer, P. B., & Piore, M. J. (1971). *Standard labor markets and manpower analysis.* Lexington, MA: Heath.

Dyer, J. H., & Nobeoka, K. (2000). Creating and managing a high-performance knowledge-sharing network: The Toyota case. *Strategic Management Journal, 21*(3), 345–367.

Ernst & Young LLP. (2001). *Center for business knowledge.* [http://www.ey.com/global/gcr.nsf/US/Welcome_-_Center_for_Business_Knowledge_-_Ernst_&_Young_LLP].

George, E. (1996). *The effects of internal workers on external workers' organizational commitment.* Unpublished doctoral dissertation, Department of Management, University of Texas at Austin.

Gibson, G. E. Jr., Davis-Blake, A., Broschak, J. P., & Rodriguez, F. J. (1998). *Owner/contractor organizational changes Phase I report.* Austin: University of Texas.

Harrison, B., & Kelley, M. R. (1993). Outsourcing and the search for flexibility. *Work, Employment, and Society, 7,* 213–235.

Hipple, S. (1998). Contingent work: Results from the second survey. *Monthly Labor Review, 121,* 22–35.

Ho, V. T., & Ang, S. (1998, August). *Spillover of psychological contract: When employees become contract labor in an outsourcing context.* Paper presented at the annual meeting of the Academy of Management, San Diego.

Huber, R. L. (1993). How Continental Bank outsourced its "crown jewels." *Harvard Business Review, 71,* 121–129.

Hui, P., Davis-Blake, A., & Broschak, J. P. (2000). *Owner/contractor organizational changes: How outsourcing knowledge work affects project performance.* Austin: University of Texas.

Jesitus, J. (1997, November 3). Broken promises? *Industry Week,* pp. 5–6.

Kalleberg, A. L. (2000). Nonstandard employment relations: Part-time, temporary, and contract work. *Annual Review of Sociology, 26,* 341–365.

Kalleberg, A. L., Rasell, E., Cassirer, N., Reskin, B. F., Hudson, K., Webster, D., & Appelbaum, E. (1997). *Nonstandard work, substandard jobs: Flexible work arrangements in the U.S.* Washington, DC: Economic Policy Institute and Women's Research and Education Institute.

Kalleberg, A. L., Reskin, B., & Hudson, K. (2000). Bad jobs in America: Standard and nonstandard employment relations and job quality in the United States. *American Sociological Review, 65,* 256–278.

Kalleberg, A. L., & Schmidt, K. (1996). Contingent employment in organizations: Part-time, temporary, and subcontracting relations. In A. L. Kalleberg, D. Knoke, P. V. Marsden, & J. L. Spaeth (Eds.), *Organizations in America: Analyzing their structures and human resource practices.* Thousand Oaks, CA: Sage.

Kern, T. (1997, December). *The gestalt of an information technology outsourcing relationship: An exploratory analysis.* Paper presented at the International Conference on Information Systems, Atlanta.

Kochan, T. A., Smith, M., Wells, J. C., & Rebitzer, J. B. (1994). Human resource strategies and contingent workers: The case of safety and health in the petrochemical industry. *Human Resource Management, 33,* 55–77.

Lane, P. J., & Lubatkin, M. (1998). Relative absorptive capacity and interorganizational learning. *Strategic Management Journal, 19,* 461–477.

Lei, D., & Hitt, M. A. (1995). Strategic restructuring and outsourcing: The effect of mergers and acquisitions and LBOs on building firm skills and capabilities. *Journal of Management, 21*(5), 835–859.

Lepak, D. P., & Snell, S. A. (1999). The human resource architecture: Toward a theory of human capital allocation and development. *Academy of Management Review, 24,* 31–48.

Levinthal, D. A., & Fichman, M. (1988). Dynamics of interorganizational attachments: Auditor-client relationships. *Administrative Science Quarterly, 33,* 345–369.

Matusik, S. F., & Hill, C.W.L. (1998). The utilization of contingent work, knowledge creation, and competitive advantage. *Academy of Management Review, 23,* 680–697.

Nollen, S. D., & Axel, H. A. (1996). *Managing contingent workers: How to reap the benefits and reduce the risks.* New York: AMACOM.

Parker, G. G., & Anderson, E. G. Jr. (2000). *From buyer to integrator: The transformation of the supply-chain manager in the vertically disintegrating firm.* Working paper, University of Texas at Austin.

Parker, G. G., & Anderson, E. G. Jr. (in press). Supply-chain integration: Putting Humpty-Dumpty back together again. In T. Boone & R. Ganeshan (Eds.), *Future directions in supply chain & technology management.* New York: AMACOM.

Pearce, J. L. (1993). Toward an organizational behavior of contract laborers: Their psychological involvement and effects on employee coworkers. *Academy of Management Journal, 36,* 1082–1096.

Pearce, J. L. (1998). Job insecurity is important, but not for the reasons you might think: The example of contingent workers. *Trends in Organizational Behavior, 5,* 31–46.

Pfeffer, J. (1981). *Power in organizations.* Boston: Pitman.

Pfeffer, J. (2001). Fighting the war for talent is hazardous to your organization's health. *Organizational Dynamics, 29*(4), 248–259.

Porter, G. (1995, August). *Attitude differences between regular and contract employees of nursing departments.* Paper presented at the annual meeting of the Academy of Management, Vancouver, BC.

Robinson, S. L., Kraatz, M. S., & Rousseau, D. M. (1994). Changing obligations and the psychological contract: A longitudinal study. *Academy of Management Journal, 37,* 137–152.

Ross, J. W., Beath, C. M., & Goodhue, D. L. (1996). Develop long-term competitiveness through IT assets. *Sloan Management Review, 38,* 31–42.

Rousseau, D. M. (1995). *Psychological contracts in organizations.* Thousand Oaks, CA: Sage.

Seger, K. N., & McFarlan, E. W. (1993). *General Dynamics and Computer Sciences Corporation: Outsourcing the IS function (A).* Boston: Harvard Business School.

Smith, V. (1994). Braverman's legacy: The labor process tradition at 20. *Work and Occupations, 21,* 403–421.

Smith, V. (1998). Teamwork versus tempwork: Managers and dualisms of workplace restructuring. In K. Campbell, D. Cornfield, & H. McCammon (Eds.), *Working in restructured workplaces: New directions for the sociology of work.* Thousand Oaks, CA: Sage.

Szulanski, G. (1996, Winter). Exploring internal stickiness: Impediments to the transfer of best practice within the firm. *Strategic Management Journal, 17,* 27–43.

Thompson, J. D. (1967). *Organizations in action.* New York: McGraw-Hill.

Tilly, C. (1992). Dualism in part-time employment. *Industrial Relations, 31,* 330–347.

Tilly, C. (1996). *Half a job: Bad and good part-time jobs in a changing labor market.* Philadelphia: Temple University Press.

Tsui, A. S. (1990). A multiple-constituency model of effectiveness: An empirical examination at the human resource subunit level. *Administrative Science Quarterly, 35,* 458–483.

Uzzi, B., & Barsness, Z. (1998). Contingent employment in British firms: Organizational determinants of the use of fixed-term hires and part-time workers. *Social Forces, 76,* 967–1007.

Van Dyne, L., & Ang, S. (1998). Organizational citizenship behavior of contingent workers in Singapore. *Academy of Management Journal, 41,* 692–703.

Williamson, O. E. (1975). *Market and hierarchies: Analysis and antitrust implications.* New York: Free Press.

Williamson, O. E. (1991). Comparative economic organization: The analysis of discrete structural alternatives. *Administrative Science Quarterly, 36,* 269–296.

Young, S. (2000, August 4). Verizon faces East Coast strike if contract negotiations falter. *USA Today,* pp. 20–21.

Yuchtman, E., & Seashore, S. E. (1967). A system resource approach to organizational effectiveness. *American Sociological Review, 32,* 891–893.

PART 4

Developing and Motivating Employees for Knowledge-Based Competition

CHAPTER 8

Knowledge Management
Developing Intellectual and Social Capital

Raymond A. Noe
Jason A. Colquitt
Marcia J. Simmering
Sharon A. Alvarez

Traditionally, psychologists interested in training and learning have focused on how the characteristics of a specific instructional event, such as a course or program, lead to learning and transfer of training to the job. However, recently the interest has broadened beyond discrete learning outcomes to a better understanding of knowledge itself. Reasons for this trend include the recognition that human resources can be a sustainable competitive advantage for organizations, an economy in which employee knowledge is critical for developing and providing high-quality products and services, and studies showing a positive relationship between the management of human capital and company financial performance (Hitt, Bierman, Shimizu, & Kochhar, 2001).

A Few Definitions

Knowledge may be defined as information that is relevant, actionable, and at least partially based on experience (Leonard & Sensiper, 1998). Knowledge can be considered to be tacit or explicit (Nonaka & Takeuchi, 1995; Polanyi, 1962; DeNisi, Hitt, & Jackson,

Chapter One, this volume). *Tacit knowledge* refers to personal knowledge based on individual experience, influenced by perceptions and values. The communication of tacit knowledge is often difficult (or even impossible) and requires personal discussion and demonstrations. *Explicit knowledge* refers to more easily codified knowledge that can be presented in manuals, formulas, and specifications. Tacit knowledge is most critical for organizational success because it is based on the knowledge and skills that an organization accumulates over time through the experiences of its employees (King, Fowler, & Zeithaml, 2001).

Important tacit and explicit knowledge includes knowledge about the company, customers, and the company's business processes (Tobin, 1998). For example, employees need to understand the company's business, strategy, financial statements, and organization. This helps them have some idea of where to go with new ideas, when to seek help with problems, and how to create opportunities for cross-functional businesses.

For knowledge to contribute to a sustainable competitive advantage it must be transferred to divisions, teams, and employees, where it can be useful for developing products and providing services. *Knowledge transfer* is the process through which an individual, team, department, or division is affected by the experience of another (Argote, Ingram, Levine, & Moreland, 2000). Knowledge transfer has been studied at the individual and team level by cognitive and industrial/organizational psychologists and at the organizational level by strategic management and organization theory researchers. For example, research in cognitive psychology has investigated how experience in one task relates to performance on another (Singley & Anderson, 1989). Industrial/organizational psychologists have studied the phenomenon of transfer of training (for example, Baldwin & Ford, 1988) and sharing and helping in teams (for example, Janz, Colquitt, & Noe, 1997). Strategic management research has focused on how knowledge management influences outcomes at the organizational level of analysis, such as in productivity and profitability.

The purpose of this chapter is to explore the process of developing intellectual and social capital in organizations. The development, management, and transfer of knowledge is critical for creating intellectual and social capital. We discuss the development of intellectual and social capital from the individual, group, and firm-level perspectives. A multilevel perspective is important because intellectual and social capital development and transfer occur at several levels. At the individual level, two formal organizational systems—knowledge management systems and training and development systems—influence the development and transfer of intellectual and social capital. The group-level perspective considers how team processes and design characteristics contribute to the development of intellectual capital. The firm-level perspective focuses on entrepreneurship activities; such activities inside firms require investing in innovation to create new knowledge. We discuss how firms should protect knowledge to benefit from the rent-generating capabilities created through innovation. The chapter concludes with a discussion of future research questions related to the development of intellectual and social capital.

What Are Social Capital and Intellectual Capital?

Nahapiet and Ghoshal (1998) define *social capital* as the sum of the actual and potential resources available that derive from the relationships possessed by an individual or in a social unit (for example, team, community). *Intellectual capital* is created through two key mechanisms: the combination and exchange of existing intellectual resources, including tacit and explicit knowledge. *Combination* refers to the connection of elements previously unconnected or the development of novel ways of combining elements that previously were associated. *Exchange* refers to social interaction between parties though teamwork, collaboration, and sharing. For combination and exchange to occur the parties must have the opportunities to make the combination or exchange as a result of aspects of their work environment or technology; believe that interaction, exchange, and involvement will create value; feel that interaction, exchange, and involvement will be valuable to them personally; and have the capability to engage in combination or exchange because they have relevant prior knowledge.

Figure 8.1 shows Nahapiet and Ghoshal's (1998) model for the creation of intellectual capital. They propose that structural, cognitive, and relational dimensions of social capital influence the combination and exchange of intellectual capital, which then directly

**Figure 8.1. How Social and Intellectual Capital
Influence the Creation of Intellectual Capital.**

SOCIAL CAPITAL

Structural Dimension
Network ties
Network configuration
Appropriable organization

Cognitive Dimension
Shared codes
  and language   Combination   Creation of
Shared narratives   and exchange   new capital
                        of intellectual capital

Relational Dimension
Trust
Norms
Obligation
Identification

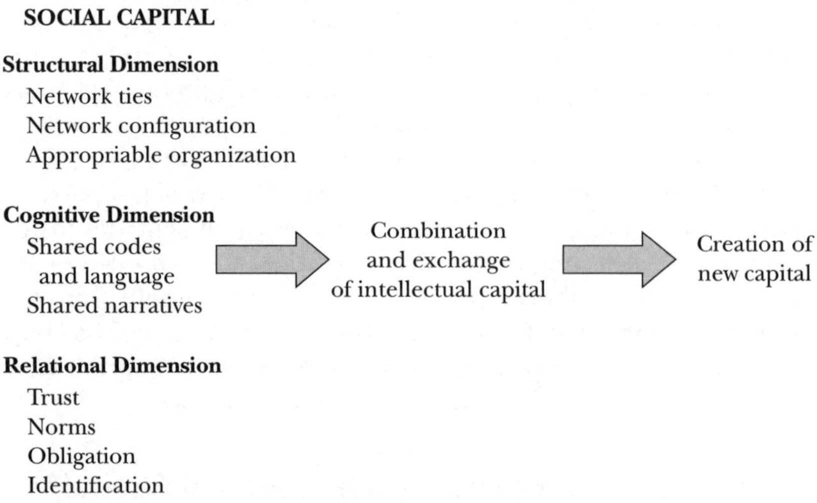

Source: Based on Nahapiet & Ghoshal, 1998, pp. 242–266.

affects intellectual capital creation. For example, the structural dimension "network ties" refers to the access persons have for combining and exchanging knowledge and anticipating the value of such an exchange, the ability of personal contacts to provide information sooner than it becomes available to persons without such contacts, and processes providing information on available opportunities to persons. Network ties may influence the access to parties for combining and exchanging intellectual capital and the value of doing so.

In contrast, the cognitive dimension in Nahapiet and Ghoshal's (1998) model suggests that the availability of shared narratives, myths, and stories enables the creation and transfer of new interpretations of events between persons. Shared language and communication codes are important because they are the means through which persons discuss and exchange information, ask questions, and conduct business.

Finally, the relational dimension of the model suggests that trust, norms, obligations, expectations, and identification are dimensions of social capital that influence combination and exchange by affecting the access to other parties and the motivation of those parties. Trust, or willingness to be vulnerable to another party, is needed for persons to be open to the exchange of information. Similarly, norms of openness and teamwork, cooperation, and experimentation facilitate the exchange and value of information (De Long & Fahey, 2000).

Knowledge Management

To create, share, and transfer knowledge, firms must have systems in place for both the physical and social support of such activity. The technology used is primarily the Internet or intranets, which commonly make use of traditional training principles while allowing for more self-directed learning and easier sharing of knowledge. Social facilitation through action learning and communities of practice are intended to provide people with a forum for sharing knowledge with others.

What Is Knowledge Management?

Knowledge management involves recognizing, generating, documenting and distributing, and transferring between persons explicit and tacit knowledge to increase organizational effectiveness (Davenport & Prusak, 1998; Rossett, 1999). It involves developing a system for collecting and maintaining data, information, experiences, and lessons, as well as understanding how to facilitate social interaction so that both explicit and tacit knowledge are developed and exchanged. The former involves information technology or hardware development; the latter involves training and development activities, the physical arrangement of the work environment, and effective processes for work teams.

Most knowledge management efforts emphasize technology—the capture, storage and transfer of codified information such as statistics, presentations, and reports using an intranet or other type of computer network (for example, Pfeffer & Sutton, 1999). This emphasis on technology misses a key ingredient of knowledge management: facilitating workplace learning and generating knowledge. Most firm priorities are directed to developing knowledge management technology (for example, creating an intranet, knowledge repositories, decision support tools) and not to creating a social system to support knowledge development and sharing (Bassi, Lev, Low, McMurrer, & Siesfeld, 2000; Ruggles, 1998). This is unfortunate, for the greatest impediments to knowledge sharing are cultural barriers, lack of support from top management, lack of a shared understanding of the business strategy or model, and lack of an appropriate organizational structure.

Considering the importance of social conditions, a key question is this: "How might different types of knowledge be shared?" According to Nonaka and Takeuchi (1995), there are multiple modes of knowledge sharing, including socialization (sharing tacit knowledge by sharing experiences), externalization (translating tacit knowledge into explicit knowledge using metaphors, models, and rules), combination (systematizing explicit concepts into a knowledge system by analyzing, categorizing, and repurposing information), and internalization (converting explicit knowledge into tacit knowledge through simulations, action learning, and on-the-job experiences).

The development, socialization, and knowledge management literatures all support the idea that most knowledge—both explicit and tacit—is shared informally, through job experiences and relationships with peers, customers, managers, and mentors, when questions are asked and experiences, stories, or narratives are shared (for example, Brown & Duguid, 1991; McCauley, Ruderman, Ohlott, & Morrow, 1994; Morrison & Brantner, 1992). In practice, companies manage knowledge through information systems (networks and software) that allow employees to store information and share it with others, electronic catalogues that identify each employee's expertise, informational maps that identify where different types of knowledge are available in a company, on-line libraries of resources such as journals, manuals, training and development opportunities, and work areas that facilitate employees' exchange of ideas (see Tobin, 1998; also see the Buckman Labs Web site—www.buckmanlabs.com). For example, British Petroleum business unit managers have a two-part job description (Hansen & von Oetinger, 2001). First, they are expected to manage the business unit effectively with profit-and-loss, balance sheet, capital expenditures, and other responsibilities. Second, they are also expected to engage in a variety of cross-unit knowledge-sharing activities in face-to-face meetings, teleconferences, and e-mails. These activities include collaborating in a peer group made up of people from the business unit as well as interacting with people from different parts of the company who are focused on the same responsibility (for example, increasing gas production).

Internet and Intranet Tools

The training and development components of the information technology infrastructure may include distance learning, Web-based training, e-libraries, and simulations (Beckman, 1999). These technologically based forms of knowledge management can be highly effective in communicating embedded knowledge, through many types of interactive sessions, to other employees (Wiig, 1999). Also, the structured environment provided by Internet- or intranet-based knowledge management technology helps employees to coordinate their activities (Baek, Liebowitz, Prasad, & Granger, 1999). Furthermore, much knowledge work involves self-directed learning (such as finding information to complete a project), and learning technologies provide an organized structure that supports such learning (Romiszowski, 1997).

Distance Learning

Distance learning is a powerful tool for knowledge organizations because employees who are physically separated or work at different organizational sites may more efficiently gain competencies and share knowledge (Foy, 1999; Wiig, 1999). Distance learning is characterized by having an instructor who is physically and technologically remote from the learner (Belanger & Jordan, 2000; Willis & Dickinson, 1997), and it can make use of several media, including radio, television, and computers. Increased use of the Web has made distance learning over the Internet without an instructor present in "real time" a common, effective tool (Hill, 1997).

The absence of personalized attention from an instructor who is not physically present limits the types of knowledge that can be shared. But if tacit knowledge exists in one part of an organization, it is more easily shared with geographically remote parts of the organization with distance learning.

Web-Based Training and E-Learning

As intranets and the Internet are becoming more popular in organizations, they are increasingly being used for sharing and transferring knowledge. Web-based training refers to instructional programs that use the attributes and resources of the World Wide Web to create a learning environment (Khan, 1997). All instruction is delivered over the Web—trainers may be electronically linked to the students to serve as resource persons but they do not deliver instruction. Its low cost over time and the increased availability of information make Web-based instruction a vehicle for efficient knowledge sharing.

Knowledge has often been disseminated during traditional classroom training, but this can be expensive and inefficient (Wiig, 1999). Web-based training provides an alternative by offering primarily self-directed learning that can support just-in-time training, or training that must be updated frequently. Unlike traditional training media, which require reprinting and redistribution of updated materials, Web-based training allows for changes to be made to materials in one time and place for all learners. A positive learning environment can be developed into the system to include assessment of learning, feedback, multiple practice exercises, and learner control. In addition, Web-based training gives learners an opportunity to link to additional resources, including Web sites and trainers, fellow trainees, chat rooms, and bulletin boards that may enhance the learning experience, facilitate sharing of explicit and tacit knowledge, and increase its meaningfulness. However, anecdotal evidence suggests that employees are resistant to "pure" e-learning or Web-based training approaches even if they allow for electronic communications with other people. This is because employees prefer face-to-face contact with instructors and other learners (for example, Zielinski, 2000). As a result, organizations are blending Web-based training and face-to-face instruction as part of their learning strategies.

Simulations

Traditional classroom training environments do not facilitate the transfer and sharing of tacit knowledge. Simulations are emerging as a method for distributing tacit knowledge across organizations (Bostock, 1997). Web-based simulations can offer a high level of fidelity to the actual physical or interpersonal work environment with few logistical constraints. In a simulation, the learner responds to a wide range of stimuli that may include tactile and cognitive information, as well as interpersonal communications. In real time learners see how the environment (for example, equipment, people) reacts to their behavior.

Simulations can be helpful for teaching "soft skills" or transmitting tacit knowledge. The stimuli and responses used in simulations should be based on veteran employees' experiences. Simulations are particularly important for knowledge work because they can promote learning tacit skills with low risk. For example, IBM's "Basic Blue for Managers" program includes interactive simulations on people and task management (Lewis & Orton, 2000). New managers learn by viewing videos, interacting with models and problem employees, making decisions about how to deal with problems, issues, or requests, and receiving feedback on their decisions. The simulations are one part of IBM's blended learning model, which also includes Web training, collaborative learning, and learning labs.

Social Facilitation

Knowledge management is a social activity; whether it is mediated by technology or not, sharing knowledge involves people working together. Creation of intellectual capital can be facilitated through action learning and use of communities of learning or practice. It is important to note that there has been little empirical research on the effectiveness of action learning and communities of practice, although case studies suggest they are effective in developing intellectual capital.

Action Learning

Action learning involves giving teams a real business problem or issue to work on, having them work on solving it and commit to an action plan, and then holding them accountable for carrying out the plan (Dotlich & Noel, 1998). The issues or problems vary but usually relate to changing the culture, raising revenue, or reducing costs. The teams often have to do research and visit plants or customers to understand the problem and come up with solutions. Action learning is a good method for generating intellectual capital and sharing tacit knowledge because employees are required to work together, share their perspectives and expertise, seek out resources, and report back to the team what they have learned.

Communities of Learning and Practice

Learning in organizations is increasingly being recognized as a social activity, and many work tasks are performed collectively. Communities of learning and practice, in which groups of employees who work together learn from each other and develop a common understanding of how to get work accomplished, provide a context for dealing with workplace problems and tasks involving real relationships in real time. They often include formal information that can be found in typical classroom instruction as well as the social interactions that make that information useful in the work environment (Beer, 2000). Examples of communities of learning and practice include Internet- or intranet-based discussion boards, listservs, and other forms of computer-mediated communication through which people exchange messages.

Intellectual capital is created in communities of learning and practice because the knowledge of individual employees can be quickly shared with others to develop innovative and creative solutions to work problems and tasks. Communities of learning and practice also help speed up solutions to routine work problems, particularly for less experienced employees. Employees can share information and experiences in a way that benefits those who might otherwise not communicate because of functional or geographic barriers. One unique benefit of communities of learning and practice is that they are often built around practice- or person-based networks and not geography or organizational function (Sena & Shani, 1999). This facilitates a broader distribution of knowledge.

Teams as Mechanisms for the Creation of Intellectual Capital

Intellectual capital often resides in (and is created by) collectives. As noted earlier, Nahapiet and Ghoshal (1998) review two primary means of creating intellectual capital: combination and exchange. Combination represents, in part, the incremental change and development of existing knowledge to create new knowledge; this is primarily the purview of training and knowledge management systems. In contrast, exchange represents the emergence of new knowledge as a result of collaboration or communication between several individuals. Thus, it is the primary mechanism by which social capital results in intellectual capital. In fact, the potential power of exchange is one reason for the dramatic increase in team-based work over the past few decades (Mohrman, Mohrman, & Cohen, 1995). Indeed, Mohrman et al. note that "teams are advocated as the agents of organizational learning" (p. 75).

In the following paragraphs we discuss how teams are a mechanism for the creation of intellectual capital. We explore three primary questions: How does intellectual capital manifest itself in teams? What team process behaviors can be leveraged to increase intellectual capital? What team design characteristics can be leveraged to increase intellectual capital?

Intellectual Capital in Teams

In describing the intellectual capital of firms, Nahapiet and Ghoshal (1998) describe four types of knowledge: individual explicit knowledge, individual tacit knowledge, social explicit knowledge, and social tacit knowledge. The explicit versus tacit distinction conveys whether the knowledge can be codified and formalized or whether it is incommunicable (see Polanyi, 1962). The individual versus shared distinction conveys whether the knowledge is in individual or aggregate form.

Although this depiction of intellectual capital is comprehensive, more discussion of social knowledge is needed to understand truly how intellectual capital is created in team contexts. Assume for a moment that we are interested in the relationship between team experience and team performance. We could operationalize team experience as the sum of all the experience of all the team's members. So, for example, a team with five members who possess one, two, three, five, and seven years of experience, respectively, have a total team experience of eighteen years. Unfortunately, operationalizing social knowledge or team intellectual capital is much more complex. To understand why we must first describe the distinction between *composition* and *compilation*.

According to Kozlowski and Klein (2000), "A phenomenon is emergent when it originates in the cognition, affect, behaviors, or other characteristics of individuals, is amplified by their interactions, and manifests as a higher-level, collective phenomenon" (p. 55). Because it originates in individual member knowledge, team intellectual capital is an emergent phenomenon. The authors further argue that emergent phenomena can be created through two different processes: composition and compilation. Composition describes phenomena that remain essentially identical as they emerge from a lower level to a higher level. Team experience would be an example of such a phenomenon. Compilation describes phenomena that remain in the same domain of content but become distinctly different concepts as they emerge from a lower level to a higher level. Team performance is an example of compilation. Although it is functionally equivalent to individual member performance, it is not merely an average of that lower-level variable because some member contributions are weighted more or less depending on role assignments and task characteristics.

We would argue that intellectual capital in teams is an example of an emergent phenomenon created by a compilation process. The knowledge of individual members, whether tacit or explicit, contributes differently to the team's social knowledge and intellectual capital depending on factors like role demands, knowledge redundancy, communication skills, social loafing, and production blocking. Moreover, the team's social knowledge further depends on the compatibility or synergy of the members' knowledge. Consider, for example, a three-person team where one member knows how to use Microsoft Powerpoint software, one member knows how to structure the text of a presentation, and one member knows how to deliver an oral presentation stylistically. The compatibilities or synergies among these different forms of knowledge increase the intellectual capital of the team compared with another in which all three members know Powerpoint. In this instance, we can accurately say that the team "knows" how to make effective presentations, even though no individual member does. The team provides a mechanism for bundling complementary pieces of individual knowledge, thereby creating intellectual capital.

In considering intellectual capital in teams it is important to distinguish between potential capital creation and actual capital creation. As noted, team intellectual capital emerges through a compilation process that depends in large part on between-member synergies in communication and knowledge. But what if the team's work is characterized more by "process loss" than by synergy? That is, what if poor communication, member redundancy, infrequent interaction, and frequent production blocking prevents the whole of intellectual capital from becoming more than the sum of its individual parts? Nahapiet and Ghoshal define social capital as the actual and potential resources accessible through social networks. Unfortunately, in teams characterized by process loss actual resources fall short of potential resources. Therefore, it becomes important to find ways to manage and design teams to avoid process loss in order to improve intellectual capital creation.

Team Processes and Intellectual Capital

Input-process-output approaches to team effectiveness focus on the team design characteristics (inputs) and team behaviors (processes) that can be used to improve team effectiveness (output). In the current discussion, the output is the creation of team intellectual capital, and the team processes are behaviors that enhance synergistic knowledge sharing and coupling. Although almost any process behavior is relevant to this issue, some behaviors are particularly critical to team intellectual capital creation. We review three such behaviors: constructive controversy, creativity behaviors, and adaptation.

Constructive Controversy

Tjosvold and Tjosvold (1995, p. 12) define constructive controversy as "open discussion of opposing views" and maintain that it is critical to the success of teams performing knowledge work. The constructive controversy construct is similar to Jehn's (1995) notion of task-based (rather than relationship-based) conflict. She found that task-based conflict had negative effects for teams doing routine work but could actually be beneficial for teams performing nonroutine tasks. This offers some support for the beneficial effects of constructive controversy in knowledge work contexts.

Constructive controversy should improve the creation of intellectual capital in teams in a number of ways. Most simply, the more discussion that occurs in teams, the greater the chance that new knowledge will be shared and disseminated among the members. More importantly, the discussion of opposing viewpoints should enhance the voicing of compatible or synergistic views and opinions. As noted earlier, intellectual capital should be hindered to the extent that the knowledge voiced by individual members is redundant. Constructive controversy should enhance the extent to which the team captures the full set of its members' information, thereby promoting the building of intellectual capital.

Creativity Behaviors

Teams have long been viewed as a means of enhancing the creation of new ideas (see Oldham, Chapter Nine, this volume), though empirical evidence for this view has been found lacking (Paulus, Larey, & Dzindolet, 2001; see also Sutton & Hargadon, 1996). Too often process loss, in the form of social loafing and production blocking, prevents team members from producing more new ideas than they would have had they worked alone. Paulus et al. (2001) describe certain process behaviors that can be used to improve creativity in teams, thereby bringing their actual performance closer to their potential performance. These behaviors include brainstorming behaviors, such as discouraging evaluation of ideas and building on each other's ideas, and process management behaviors, such as setting goals, taking breaks, and scheduling iterative team and individual idea sessions.

Like constructive controversy, these types of creativity-enhancing behaviors should enhance intellectual capital creation in a number of ways. If evaluation of others' ideas is discouraged, that should prevent self-censoring of views that could help build the team's intellectual capital. The practice of idea building should lead to the complementary, synergistic knowledge that emerges from the member interaction. It is these instances of knowledge that are truly possessed by the team, as opposed to any individual member. Finally, process management behaviors like goal setting should discourage the types of process losses that can dampen the creation of intellectual capital.

Adaptation

We define *adaptation* as a beneficial change in task behaviors that comes in response to shifting task demands (Kozlowski, Gully, Nason, & Smith, 2000; LePine, Colquitt, & Erez, 2000). It is a reactive set of behaviors that allow the individual or team to remain successful even in unstable task environments. Such behaviors include noticing the shift in task demands, formulating a new approach, and successfully implementing the new approach. Thus individuals or teams who fail to adapt may not have noticed the need for it, or they may have implemented an ineffective response to the change in task demands.

Adaptation behaviors are critical to the creation of intellectual capital because they act to replace outdated or outmoded capital. Unless a team adapts, its intellectual capital will—at best—remain stagnant. At worst, it will actually decrease as the current repertoire of information goes from knowledge to misconception. Thus, whereas constructive controversy and creativity behaviors create intellectual capital, adaptation replaces, replenishes, and builds on existing intellectual capital.

Team Design Characteristics and Intellectual Capital

We believe three characteristics are uniquely relevant to the creation of intellectual capital in teams: membership stability, diversity, and personality. These design characteristics may promote constructive controversy, creativity behavior, and adaptation (process behaviors) that are necessary for building intellectual capital in teams.

Membership Stability

Although some types of teams remain stable over long periods of time (for example, project teams, semiautonomous work groups), most teams in knowledge work settings have relatively unstable memberships. Members are constantly added or subtracted, or they merely fail to take part in the team's functioning for an extended period of time. In their discussion of membership dynamics in work groups, Arrow and McGrath (1995) make a distinction between *standing groups* and *acting groups* (see also McGrath, 1984). Standing group members are formal members of a given team; acting group members actually participate in the team's work. Membership stability can be reflected in standing groups, as when members are formally added or subtracted, or in acting groups, as when members are merely absent from meetings or sessions for a given period. The former reflects instability in the basic composition of the team; the latter reflects instability in the team's current configuration (Arrow & McGrath, 1995).

The relationship between membership stability and intellectual capital creation is likely to be complex. Periodic changes in the basic composition of the team can introduce new sources of individual intellectual capital, but they may also remove intellectual capital, particularly if the member who leaves possessed tacit knowledge. A moderate degree of instability should aid constructive controversy, creativity, and adaptability. New members (or merely new configurations of existing members) should prevent the group from "getting stale" and falling back on routines that stagnate intellectual capital. This should be particularly true for teams who formalize explicit member knowledge, in effect creating a kind of team memory that can outlast individual members. However, there is certainly a point at which membership instability will become counterproductive. Too much variation in either the standing or acting group will result in a situation where intellectual capital must repeatedly reemerge in the new collective, as members must first decide what they know before worrying about improving on that knowledge.

Task Interdependence

Wageman (2001) defines task interdependence as the "features of inputs into the work itself that require multiple individuals to complete the work" (p. 198). Team tasks vary in the degree to which one member's actions elicits and constrains another's (means interdependence) and the degree to which different members must share common resources (resource interdependence). Moreover, two teams can work on identical tasks but have different levels of task interdependence. Such differences are a function of what Wageman calls *behavioral interdependence* as team members react to task requirements by either neutralizing or enhancing natural levels of task interdependence.

Task interdependence should increase intellectual capital in teams. This should be particularly true in cross-functional teams, where the interdependency exists between members with different knowledge and skill sets (Tjosvold & Tjosvold, 1995). High levels of task interdependence should increase the process behaviors needed to create intellectual capital in teams. Janz et al. (1997) linked task interdependence to knowledge sharing and innovation in teams of knowledge workers, suggesting positive effects for constructive controversy. The interaction created by task interdependence should also foster many creativity-enhancing behaviors, such as idea building. Finally, Kozlowski et al.'s (2000) discussion of adaptive teams argues that task interdependence creates the kind of performance demands that prompt adaptation.

Personality

A key question is this (Mohrman & Cohen, 1995): What team member personalities will foster the creation of intellectual capital in teams? One personality dimension that may be particularly relevant is openness to experience, a Big Five factor composed of the following six facets: ideas (for example, having intellectual curiosity), actions (for example, valuing experimentation and learning), fantasy (having an active imagination), aesthetics (being intrigued by art), feelings (experiencing strong emotions), and values (believing that moral issues and social policies should constantly change) (Costa & McCrae, 1992).

Open individuals are likely to have amassed a wider variety of experiences than less open individuals. This suggests that teams composed of open individuals will already begin with an intellectual capital advantage. Moreover, recent empirical work on openness to experience suggests a beneficial relationship with some of the process behaviors discussed earlier. For example, LePine et al. (2000) showed that open individuals were more likely to adapt to changing task demands by positively altering their approach to their task. Similar results were found by Colquitt, Hollenbeck,

Ilgen, LePine, and Sheppard (2002), who showed that open teams responded more favorably to new communication technologies. Other work has linked openness to creativity and learning proficiency (Barrick & Mount, 1991; George & Zhou, 2001; McCrae, 1987; Oldham, Chapter Nine).

Firm-Level Knowledge Creation and the Appropriation of Rents

We have emphasized that through knowledge management, training and development systems, and facilitating specific team processes, firms can stimulate creation and sharing of intellectual capital. From a more macro perspective, firms can try to acquire intellectual capital through new organizational forms such as mergers, licensing, alliances, and joint ventures (see Deeds, Chapter Two, this volume). They can also develop intellectual capital through entrepreneurial activities that stimulate investment in innovation. For the returns on this investment to be realized, firms need to appropriate the "rents" created from their knowledge. A "rent" refers to the difference between a venture's ex post value and the ex ante cost of the resources combined to form a venture (Alvarez & Barney, 2000). For example, if a venture is making $5 on a widget that can recover all profits at $3, the difference of $2 is the entrepreneurial rent. The incentive to invest in the creation of new knowledge through innovation depends on the firm's ability to appropriate the rent from this knowledge creation. Although entrepreneurial firms have usually created knowledge through innovation, they have not usually been able to appropriate the rents from that knowledge (Alvarez & Barney, 2001).

Entrepreneurs can use either market forms of governance (contracts) to coordinate the knowledge necessary to realize an economic opportunity or they can use a firm, as a form of hierarchical governance, to realize opportunities generated through knowledge. When there is a need to coordinate knowledge and appropriate the rent generated by this knowledge, the firm is the governance structure of choice. The question then becomes why the entrepreneurial firm is a superior choice over the market form of governance when there is a need to coordinate knowledge. Under what conditions can entrepreneurial knowledge be most efficiently realized?

In the following paragraphs we discuss how choosing the right governance structure to protect the knowledge created and appropriate the rents from this knowledge is important to realize benefits from entrepreneurial knowledge.

Knowledge Assets and Economic Rents

It is unusual for a single entrepreneur to possess all the intangible and tangible knowledge necessary to exploit a market opportunity (Conner & Prahalad, 1996). In the case of tacit knowledge it can be assumed that no two individuals possess identical stocks of knowledge because of cognitive limitations. Individual entrepreneurs possess experience, insights, or skills that are different from other actors. Because of cognitive limitations, individuals must specialize in their acquisition of knowledge (Grant & Baden-Fuller, 1995). This individual knowledge is specialized knowledge. The creation of rents through the recognition and exploitation of market opportunities usually requires numerous different types of specialized knowledge to be applied.

However, knowledge by itself does not directly convert to rents. If each individual specializes in a specific type of knowledge but attempts to use it without relying on others, then the rent achieved would be less than if everyone had some knowledge about everything, or generalized knowledge. Knowledge is best learned as specialized knowledge, but its use to achieve rents requires that the knowledge specialist use the knowledge of other specialists. This cannot be done by learning what others know or by purchasing information in the form of facts; both of these means undermine the gains from specialized knowledge.

Both explicit and tacit knowledge can be used to create economic rents. Explicit knowledge can be used to create economic rents when it describes how a market opportunity can be exploited and when only a small number of entrepreneurs possess this knowledge. However, absent external constraints on information sharing, explicit knowledge about market opportunities is likely to diffuse quickly. This is because, absent these constraints, explicit knowledge is not costly for others to understand. Thus, any economic rents that are created by exploiting explicit knowledge are often difficult to appropriate.

As the number of entrepreneurs who possess explicit knowledge about a market opportunity increases, competition to appropriate the rent created by this knowledge will also increase (Schumpeter, 1934). Indeed, profit-seeking entrepreneurs will continue to increase their investment in appropriating a rent created by explicit knowledge until the cost of investing in this opportunity rises to equal the economic value it creates (Barney, 1986). In other words, although explicit knowledge can be valuable, it is usually not costly to imitate or to communicate and thus cannot be a source of sustained economic rents. If the value of the knowledge is publicly known, and if several entrepreneurs can obtain this knowledge, then entrepreneurs competing for this knowledge will at best earn only a normal economic return from this knowledge. If the value of the knowledge is known only by one or a few entrepreneurs and if only one or a few of them can obtain this knowledge, then economic rents can be obtained in the short term but they will not be sustainable.

Like explicit knowledge, tacit knowledge can also be used to create economic rents when it describes how a market opportunity can be exploited and when only a small number of entrepreneurs possess this knowledge. However, unlike explicit knowledge, tacit knowledge is very costly for others to understand. Because of that, any rents created by exploiting tacit knowledge can often be appropriated by those who create them. The slow diffusion of tacit knowledge ensures that competition for the resources necessary to exploit a market opportunity will not increase, and the cost of investing to realize this opportunity for those who possess the tacit knowledge will remain below the value created (Barney, 1986). In this way, using tacit knowledge to exploit a market opportunity can be a source of sustained rent creation.

Entrepreneurial Knowledge and the Knowledge Expert

In distinguishing between entrepreneurial knowledge and the knowledge expert, Kirzner (1979) argues that knowledge experts do not fully recognize the value of their knowledge or how to turn it into a profit or else they would be entrepreneurs. The entrepreneur may not have the specific knowledge of the expert (such as technological expertise), but the entrepreneur does recognize the value and the opportunity of that knowledge. Although the entrepreneur may have specialized knowledge, it is usually the tacit generalized knowledge about how to organize specialized knowledge that is the entrepreneur's critical intangible skill.

Both Kirzner (1979) and Schumpeter (1934) describe the entrepreneurial role as the decision to direct inputs (in this case, knowledge) into certain processes rather than into other processes. Entrepreneurship involves what Schumpeter termed *new combinations* of resources such as knowledge. He further maintained that innovation was driven by the entrepreneur (who is at the heart of the firm). Schumpeter suggested five situations where the phenomenon of bundling knowledge by entrepreneurs to produce new resources occurs. The entrepreneur "reforms or revolutionizes the pattern of production by (1) exploiting an invention or an untried technology for producing a new commodity or (2) producing an old one in a new way, (3) by opening up a new source of supply of materials (4) or a new outlet for products, or (5) by reorganizing an industry" (Schumpeter, 1934, p. 132). Thus, entrepreneurial knowledge is defined as the ability to take conceptual, abstract information on where and how to obtain undervalued resources—explicit and tacit—and to deploy and exploit these resources (Alvarez & Busenitz, 2001).

Tangible Knowledge and Rents

Decisions about organizing the creation of economic rents cannot be separated from decisions about organizing their appropriation. In particular, when the knowledge needed to create an economic rent is explicit, the decision to coordinate all the knowledge resources needed to create an economic rent through market contracting is likely to increase the competitiveness of the market. This increased competition reduces the ability of the entrepreneurs attempting to create a rent to appropriate it.

For example, suppose someone—based on explicit knowledge—recognizes an opportunity to create economic rents but concludes that others will have to become involved for him to realize the opportunity fully. Because explicit knowledge is easy to understand, once discussions about the use of market contracts to coordinate these multiple resources begins, other parties will be able to recognize the value of this opportunity. Once other parties understand the value, they will seek to appropriate any rents it might generate— for example, by trying to exploit the opportunity through contacting other parties who possess the requisite knowledge. They will be at no competitive disadvantage compared with the individual who first spotted the opportunity. In this case, the act of using market contracts to try to coordinate the knowledge resources needed to exploit an opportunity will increase competition for that opportunity. The increased competition reduces the amount of the rent that any one of these individuals can appropriate.

Resource-based theorists recognize that the hierarchical organization has important advantages over the market organization in slowing the diffusion of explicit knowledge across multiple entrepreneurs. Because explicit knowledge is often codifiable and thus observable, it can be easily copied and difficult to protect. Explicit knowledge is easily expropriated or imitated and becomes increasingly vulnerable to diffusion when multiple entrepreneurs are needed to commercialize it.

For example, when a biotechnology firm has a technology that it cannot commercialize on its own, it will often seek a larger pharmaceutical partner to help bring it to market. The biotechnology firm must reveal its research findings to the larger firm, giving the larger firm an opportunity to expropriate the knowledge for its own benefit (Alvarez & Barney, 2001). This is consistent with the work of Mansfield, Schwartz, and Wagner (1981), who found that imitators can duplicate first movers' patent-based advantages very quickly—60 percent of all patents are imitated within four years of being granted without the patent rights obtained by the first movers being legally violated. Whether the form of protection is a patent, trade secret, copyright, or contract, all of these methods are costly to write and costly and difficult to enforce, and they can usually be invented around within a few short years (Mansfield, 1985; Lieberman, 1982, 1987).

Because intellectual property and trade secret protections are costly and difficult to enforce, it may be more effective and more efficient to conduct explicit knowledge transactions inside firms rather than across markets. Firms can prevent expropriation of knowledge and reduce its observability, thereby protecting against imitation. They can create possession rights to knowledge that are just as valuable as, if not more valuable than, the limited property rights to knowledge accorded under the law (Liebeskind, 1996). The implication of the firm as a protector of knowledge for entrepreneurship is that entrepreneurship is about innovation, and in order to make the investment in innovation worthwhile, the knowledge created must be protected so that the rents may be appropriated by the entrepreneur.

Intangible Knowledge and Rents

When the knowledge that needs to be coordinated in order to create and appropriate an economic rent opportunity is tacit, hierarchical organizations or firms will be preferred over market organizations. Communicating tacit knowledge from one economic actor to another required to create a rent will usually require one or perhaps both of these actors to make specific investments in order to understand the knowledge (Williamson, 1975). These specific investments put parties to this exchange at risk of opportunism. Because the risk is high, hierarchical governance will be preferred over market governance when the knowledge that must be coordinated to create the rents associated with a market opportunity is tacit.

According to resource-based theory, firms will be preferred when the knowledge that must be organized to realize a market opportunity is tacit. Firms play a critical role in protecting knowledge. Because property rights to intangible knowledge are weak and costly to enforce, the firm is the preferred choice of organization because it can employ organizational arrangements that are not available in markets to protect the value of knowledge (Liebeskind, 1996). Through the firm, tacit knowledge can be protected from expropriation and against imitation by reducing the observability of the knowledge.

Entrepreneurial Firms and Knowledge

New knowledge is generated by investment in innovation. Schumpeter (1934) distinguished between invention and innovation, with invention being the discovery of an opportunity and innovation being the exploitation of a profitable opportunity. The importance of the distinction is that it focuses on the firm as the protector of new knowledge, thus enabling innovation. It does this in two ways:

first, because innovation is costly and inherently an uncertain process, through the protection of new knowledge more of it will be generated, and second, by protecting new knowledge the creators of knowledge can appropriate the rents earned by the knowledge (Liebeskind, 1996). The more a firm succeeds in protecting its knowledge and appropriating the rents from it, the more that firm will have the incentive to produce new knowledge through investment in innovation.

Entrepreneurship involves what Schumpeter termed *new combinations* and Coase (1937) described as *coordinating disparate knowledge*. Schumpeter (1934) maintained that innovation was driven by the entrepreneur (who is at the heart of the firm) and not consumer driven markets. Schumpeter suggested that the entrepreneur "reforms or revolutionizes the pattern of production by exploiting an invention or an untried technology" (Schumpeter, 1934, p. 132). Thus, the process of creating knowledge through innovation is entrepreneurial, and the process of organizing in a firm to protect this knowledge so that the rents generated can be appropriated is an entrepreneurial act.

In particular, since the coordination of explicit knowledge is most efficiently organized through the use of a hierarchical organization (to increase the probability that any rents that are created by the actions of an economic actor will be appropriated by that economic actor), and since the coordination of tacit knowledge is most efficiently coordinated by a hierarchical organization (to reduce the threats of specific investments and because hierarchical organization facilitates shared understanding about the nature of tacit knowledge), it follows that when the knowledge that must be coordinated to exploit a market opportunity has both tangible and intangible elements, hierarchical organization will be preferred over market forms of organization. A firm will be formed by an entrepreneur economic actor to protect the knowledge generated by innovation and appropriate the rents.

Toward an Entrepreneurial Theory of the Firm

This discussion suggests that one reason for entrepreneurs to organize a firm is to coordinate the knowledge assets they need to create and appropriate economic rents. A second reason is to protect the knowledge that is created through innovation so that the creator of the knowledge can appropriate the rents from it and continue to reinvest in new knowledge creation. The incorporation of knowledge coordination and protection through the firm begins to bring us closer to an entrepreneurial theory of the firm. The entrepreneurial theory of the firm would suggest that rents come from the coordination of knowledge and the protection of new knowledge through the use of the firm.

Conclusion and Future Research Directions

In this chapter we discussed how social and intellectual capital can be developed through knowledge management, teams, and entrepreneurial firms. We introduced Nahapiet and Ghoshal's (1998) model of how intellectual capital is created to help explain the concepts of social and intellectual capital and the factors that influence their development. In exploring these issues, we discussed the role of knowledge management (technology and social facilitation) in developing intellectual capital at the individual level. Next, we suggested that fostering behaviors such as constructive controversy, creativity, and adaptation can create team process gains that create intellectual capital. Designing teams to have moderate stability, high task interdependence, and high member openness may increase these behaviors in teams. At the firm level, we focused on knowledge created by entrepreneurial activities and the role of economic rents in realizing the benefits of this knowledge. From our discussion, several important areas for research on developing intellectual and social capital emerge.

First, research is needed to test the proposed relationships in the Nahapiet and Ghosal (1998) model. The training literature provides some support for the relationships between social capital and intellectual capital displayed in their model. For example, research on transfer of training and continuous learning has found a positive relationship between various dimensions of the culture and climate (including social support, organizational promotion of innovation and learning, and reinforcement and reward consequences) and transfer of learned behavior to the job (Rouiller & Goldstein, 1993; Tracey, Tannenbaum, & Kavanaugh, 1995). Culture and climate contain many of the social capital dimensions shown in the authors' model, from network ties and shared language to norms and obligations.

An important concern in conducting research on social capital, intellectual capital, and knowledge transfer is to ensure that the criterion used is construct-valid and collected at the appropriate level of analysis for the research question being addressed. There are several different approaches to measuring intellectual capital. For example, a dynamic approach suggests that knowledge is found in three basic elements of organizations—employees, tasks, and tools—and the interaction between these elements (McGrath & Argote, 2001). A static approach to identifying intellectual capital is to focus on identifying the relevant criterion space. Van Buren (1999) suggests that intellectual capital includes human capital (the knowledge, skills, and competencies of employees), innovation capital (capability of an organization to develop new products and services), process capital (the organization's processes, systems, and tools related to information technology), and customer capital (the value of the organization's relationship with its customers). Walsh and Ungson (1991) emphasize that generation of intellectual capital requires measuring changes in knowledge repositories, including employees, roles and structures, the organization's standard operating procedure and practices, organizational culture, and the physical structure of the workplace. Reinhardt, Bornemann, Pawlowsky, and Schneider (2001) argue that intellectual capital should be broadened from measures of tangible assets alone to include characteristics such as tacitness.

Knowledge transfer in organizations involves transfer at the individual level but also includes other levels of analysis such as the team, product line, department, or division (Argote & Ingram, 2000). For example, in a study of how organizational learning affected outflow of knowledge to other units, three different types of organizational knowledge were measured: knowledge about technologies, knowledge about sales and marketing, and knowledge about government agencies. The relevance of these types of knowledge to the companies included in the study was determined through interviews with a small sample of top-level managers before the study began. Similar attention should be paid to identifying the appropriateness of measures of knowledge in future studies of knowledge management and transfer.

A variety of individual factors may either directly affect intellectual capital or moderate the relationship between intellectual capital and social capital. In particular, training research suggests that there are many individual characteristics (such as attitudes, personality variables) that affect motivation to learn and learning (see Colquitt, LePine, & Noe, 2000). These individual characteristics, which are not aspects of social capital, may directly affect the four conditions for combination and exchange. For example, individuals who lack self-confidence or are low in self-efficacy may be less likely to participate in exchange because of concerns about their capability. There may also be a relationship between participation in knowledge sharing or exchange and organizational commitment or collectivism. Individuals with high organizational commitment, or individuals who believe that the interests and well-being of the collective take precedence over personal interests, may participate more frequently in information exchange because of a stronger sense of personal value.

Researchers have just begun to examine which employees learn best in Web-based training environments and the conditions under which they learn best. Goal orientation theory, which describes differences among learners in preferences for task difficulty, reasons for learning, and beliefs about success (Dweck, 1986) may be particularly useful for helping us understand which employees are likely to share and transfer knowledge. It is possible that employees with a mastery orientation may be more likely to use technology to share knowledge with others than employees with a performance orientation. In a study of computer-delivered training, Brown (2001) found that employees' performance orientation interacted with learning self-efficacy to affect practice so that the relationship between learning self-efficacy and practice was negative for those with below-average performance orientation and positive for those with above-average performance orientation. Unexpectedly, mastery orientation had a negative relationship with the number of practice activities trainees performed. Clearly, more research is needed as technology gives employees responsibility for and control over learning and managing knowledge. Studies are also needed to examine if blended learning—that is, learning including both face-to-face and Web-based instruction—is superior to electronic learning alone in cost, time to master content, and transfer of training.

Future research also needs to address the conditions in which knowledge is shared and transferred. Some barriers to sharing knowledge might include perceptions of inequality in status among employees, physical distance, time, evaluation apprehension, thinking or learning style preferences, and experts' perceived loss of financial and social status (Leonard & Sensiper, 1998; Starbuck, 1992). These barriers are especially important to identify as sharing knowledge becomes more prevalent in employees' performance domain (see Pulakos, Dorsey, & Borman, Chapter Six, this volume). Communities of practice are a growing method for knowledge transfer, but little is known about their effectiveness, and there may be sizable barriers to their successful implementation. For instance, participation is often voluntary in communities of practice and therefore some individuals may not share their knowledge (Williams & Cothrel, 2000). If knowledge sharing is viewed as an extra-role behavior, the literature on organizational citizenship behavior may serve as a theoretical basis for studies on development of intellectual capital and knowledge exchange. Another potential drawback of these communities is information overload; employees receive so much information that they fail to process it effectively. This may cause them to withdraw from the community and fail to learn more or to contribute to others' knowledge.

Several research questions about teams and development of social and intellectual capital also need to be addressed. First, do constructive controversy, creative behaviors, and adaptation relate to the development of team intellectual capital? Using shared team experience as a proxy for the value of stock of tacit knowledge, Berman, Down, and Hill (2002) found that a positive relationship between shared team experience and team performance declined and eventually became negative as shared experience grew. Constructive controversy, creative behaviors, and adaptation may moderate the relationship between shared team experience and team performance or attenuate the negative relationship between shared team experience and performance that occurs over time. Second, what is the relationship between membership stability and creation of intellectual capital? Third, do high levels of task interdependence create a positive condition for constructive controversy, creativity, and adaptability in teams? Finally, do team members' personality characteristics, such as openness to experience, foster the creation of intellectual capital in teams?

Although a significant portion of this chapter addressed issues of knowledge dissemination, in the section on entrepreneurial knowledge we discussed the importance of knowledge protection to enable the appropriation of rents. Knowledge in this context comes from innovation; if the rents created by the knowledge are not appropriated, then investment in innovation will cease. Our suggestion that the firm is a superior choice of organization because the exploitation of knowledge often requires both a knowledge specialist and a knowledge generalist needs to be empirically validated.

References

Alvarez, S. A., & Barney, J. B. (2000). Entrepreneurial capabilities: A resource-based view. In Meyer and Heppard (Eds.), *Entrepreneurship as strategy: Competing on the entrepreneurial edge*. Thousand Oaks, CA: Sage.

Alvarez, S. A., & Barney, J. B. (2001). How can entrepreneurial firms really benefit from alliances with large firms? *Academy of Management Executive, 15,* 139–148.

Alvarez, S. A., & Busenitz, L. W. (2001). The entrepreneurship of resource-based theory. *Journal of Management, 27,* 755–775.

Argote, L., & Ingram, P. (2000). Knowledge transfer: A basis for competitive advantage in firms. *Organizational Behavior and Human Decision Processes, 82,* 150–169.

Argote, L., Ingram, P., Levine, J. M., & Moreland, R. L. (2000). Knowledge transfer in organizations: Learning from the experience of others. *Organizational Behavior and Human Decision Processes, 82,* 1–8.

Arrow, H., & McGrath, J. E. (1995). Membership dynamics in groups at work: A theoretical framework. In L. L. Cummings & B. M. Staw (Eds.), *Research in organizational behavior* (Vol. 17; pp. 373–411). Greenwich, CT: JAI Press.

Baek, S., Liebowitz, J., Prasad, S. Y., & Granger, M. (1999). Intelligent agents for knowledge management: Toward intelligent Web-based collaboration within virtual teams. In J. Liebowitz (Ed.), *Knowledge management handbook* (pp. 11-1–11-23). Boca Raton: FL: CRC Press.

Baldwin, T. T., & Ford, J. K. (1988). Transfer of training: A review and directions for future research. *Personnel Psychology, 41,* 63–105.

Barney, J. B. (1986). Strategic factor markets: Expectations, luck, and business strategy. *Management Science, 42,* 1231–1241.

Barrick, M. R., & Mount, M. K. (1991). The Big Five personality dimensions and job performance: A meta-analysis. *Personnel Psychology, 44,* 1–26.

Bassi, L. J., Lev, B., Low, J., McMurrer, D. P, & Siesfeld, G. A. (2000). Measuring corporate investments in human capital. In M. Blair &

T. Kochan (Eds.), *The new relationship: Human capital in the American corporation* (pp. 334–382). Washington, DC: Brookings Institution Press.

Beckman, T. J. (1999). The current state of knowledge management. In J. Liebowitz (Ed.), *Knowledge management handbook* (pp. 1-1–1-22). Boca Raton, FL: CRC Press.

Beer, V. (2000). *The Web learning fieldbook: Using the World Wide Web to build workplace learning environments.* San Francisco: Jossey-Bass.

Belanger, F., & Jordan, D. H. (2000). *Evaluation and implementation of distance learning: Technologies, tools, and techniques.* Hershey, PA: Idea Group Publishing.

Berman, S. L., Down, J., & Hill, C.W.L. (2002). Tacit knowledge as a source of competitive advantage in the national basketball association. *Academy of Management Journal, 45,* 13–31.

Bostock, S. J. (1997). Designing web-based instruction for active learning. In B. H. Khan (Ed.), *Web-based instruction* (pp. 225–230). Englewood Cliffs, NJ: Educational Technology Publications.

Brown, K. G. (2001). Using computers to deliver training: Which employees learn and why? *Personnel Psychology, 54*(2), 271–296.

Brown, J. S., & Duguid, P. (1991). Organizational learning and communities of practice: Toward a unified view of working, learning, and innovation [Special issue: Organizational learning: Papers in honor of James G. March]. *Organizational Science, 2*(1), 40–57.

Coase, R. H. (1937). The nature of the firm. *Economica, 4,* 386–405.

Colquitt, J. A., Hollenbeck, J. R., Ilgen, D. R., LePine, J. A., & Sheppard, L. (2002). Computer-assisted communication and team decision making performance: The moderating role of openness to experience. *Journal of Applied Psychology, 87,* 402–410.

Colquitt, J. A., LePine, J., & Noe, R. A. (2000). Toward an integrative theory of training motivation: A meta-analytic path analysis of 20 years of research. *Journal of Applied Psychology, 85,* 678–700.

Conner, K. R., & Prahalad, C. K. (1996). A resource-based theory of the firm: Knowledge versus opportunism. *Organization Science, 7*(5), 477–501.

Costa, P. T. Jr., & McCrae, R. R. (1992). *Revised NEO Personality Inventory manual.* Odessa, FL: Psychological Assessment Resources.

Davenport, T. H., & Prusak, L. (1998). *Working knowledge.* Boston: Harvard Business School Press.

De Long, D. W., & Fahey, L. (2000). Diagnosing cultural barriers to knowledge management. *Academy of Management Executive, 14*(4), 113–127.

Dotlich, D. L., & Noel, J. L. (1998). *Action learning.* San Francisco: Jossey-Bass.

Duffy, J. (1999). *Harvesting experience: Reaping the benefits of knowledge.* Prairie Village, KS: ARMA International.

Dweck, C. S. (1986). Motivational processes affecting learning. *American Psychologist, 41,* 1040–1048.

Foy, P. S. (1999). Knowledge management in industry. In J. Liebowitz (Ed.), *Knowledge management handbook* (pp. 15-1–15-10). Boca Raton, FL: CRC Press.

George, J. M., & Zhou, J. (2001). When openness to experience and conscientiousness are related to creative behavior: An interactional approach. *Journal of Applied Psychology, 86,* 513–524.

Grant, R. M., & Baden-Fuller, C. (1995). A knowledge-based theory of interfirm collaboration. *Academy of Management, Best Papers Proceedings,* pp. 17–21.

Hansen, M. T., & von Oetinger, B. (2001, March). Introducing T-shaped managers: Knowledge management's next generation. *Harvard Business Review,* pp. 106–117.

Hill, J. R. (1997). Distance learning environments via the World Wide Web. In B. H. Khan (Ed.), *Web-based instruction* (pp. 75–80). Englewood Cliffs, NJ: Educational Technology Publications.

Hitt, M. A., Bierman, L., Shimizu, K., & Kochhar, R. (2001). Direct and moderating effects of human capital on strategy and performance in professional service firms: A resource-based perspective. *Academy of Management Journal, 44,* 13–26.

Janz, B. D., Colquitt, J. A., & Noe, R. A. (1997). Knowledge worker team effectiveness: The role of autonomy, interdependence, team development, and contextual support variables. *Personnel Psychology, 50,* 877–904.

Jehn, K. A. (1995). A multimethod examination of the benefits and detriments of intragroup conflict. *Administrative Science Quarterly, 40,* 256–282.

Khan, B. H. (1997). Web-based instruction (WBI): What is it and why is it? In B. H. Khan (Ed.), *Web-based instruction* (pp. 5–18). Englewood Cliffs, NJ: Educational Technology Publications.

King, A. W., Fowler, S. W., & Zeithaml, C. P. (2001). Managing organizational competencies for competitive advantage: The middle management edge. *Academy of Management Executive, 15*(2), 95–106.

Kirzner, I. (1979). *Perception, opportunity, and profit.* Chicago: University of Chicago Press.

Kozlowski, S.W.J., Gully, S. M., Nason, E. R., & Smith, E. M. (2000). Developing adaptive teams: A theory of compilation and performance across levels and time. In K. J. Klein & S.W.J. Kozlowski (Eds.), *Multilevel theory, research, and methods in organizations* (pp. 240–292). San Francisco: Jossey-Bass.

Kozlowski, S.W.J., & Klein, K. J. (2000). A multilevel approach to theory and research in organizations: Contextual, temporal, and emergent processes. In K. J. Klein & S.W.J. Kozlowski (Eds.), *Multilevel theory, research, and methods in organizations* (pp. 3–91). San Francisco: Jossey-Bass.

Leonard, D., & Sensiper, S. (1998). The role of tacit knowledge in group innovation. *California Management Review, 40*(3), 112–132.

LePine, J. A., Colquitt, J. A., & Erez, A. (2000). Adaptability to changing task contexts: Effects of general cognitive ability, conscientiousness, and openness to experience. *Personnel Psychology, 53,* 563–594.

Lewis, N., & Orton, P. (2000, June). The five attributes of innovative e-learning. *Training & Development,* 47–51.

Lieberman, M. B. (1982). *The learning curve and pricing in the chemical processing industries.* Unpublished doctoral thesis, Harvard University, Cambridge, MA.

Lieberman, M. B. (1987). The learning curve, diffusion, competitive strategy. *Strategic Management Journal, 9,* 41–58.

Liebeskind, J. P. (1996). Knowledge, strategy, and the theory of the firm [Winter special issue]. *Strategic Management Journal, 17,* 93–107.

Mansfield, E. (1985). How rapidly does new industrial technology leak out? *Journal of Industrial Economics, 35,* 217–223.

Mansfield, E., Schwartz, M., & Wagner, S. (1981). Imitation costs and patents: An empirical study. *Economic Journal, 91,* 907–918.

McCauley, C. D., Ruderman, M. N., Ohlott, P. J., & Morrow, J. E. (1994). Assessing the developmental components of managerial jobs. *Journal of Applied Psychology, 79,* 544–560.

McCrae, R. R. (1987). Creativity, divergent thinking, and openness to experience. *Journal of Personality and Social Psychology, 52,* 1258–1265.

McGrath, J. E. (1984). *Groups: Interaction and performance.* Englewood Cliffs, NJ: Prentice-Hall.

McGrath, J. E., & Argote, L. (2001). Group processes in organizational contexts. In M. A. Hogg & R. S. Tindale (Eds.), *Blackwell handbook of social psychology. Group processes* (Vol. 3). Oxford, England: Blackwell.

Mohrman, S. A., & Cohen, S. G. (1995). When people get out of the box: New relationships, new systems. In A. Howard (Ed.), *The changing nature of work* (pp. 365–410). San Francisco: Jossey-Bass.

Mohrman, S. A., Mohrman, A. M. Jr., & Cohen, S. G. (1995). Organizing knowledge work systems. In M. M. Beyerlein, D. A. Johnson, & S. T. Beyerlein (Eds.), *Advances in interdisciplinary studies of work teams* (Vol. 2; pp. 61–92). Greenwich, CT: JAI Press.

Morrison, R. F., & Brantner, T. M. (1992). What enhances or inhibits learning a new job? A basic career issue. *Journal of Applied Psychology, 77,* 926–940.

Nahapiet, J., & Ghoshal, S. (1998). Social capital, intellectual capital, and the organizational advantage. *Academy of Management Review, 23*(2), 242–266.

Nonaka, I., & Takeuchi, H. (1995). *The knowledge-creating company: How Japanese companies create the dynamics of innovation.* New York: Oxford University Press.

Paulus, P. B., Larey, T. S., & Dzindolet, M. T. (2001). Creativity in groups and teams. In M. E. Turner (Ed.), *Groups at work: Theory and research* (pp. 319–338). Hillsdale, NJ: Erlbaum.

Pfeffer, J., & Sutton, R. I. (1999). Knowing "what" to do is not enough: Turning knowledge into action. *California Management Review, 42*(1), 83–91.

Polanyi, M. (1962). *Personal knowledge: Towards a post-critical philosophy.* New York: Routledge.

Reinhardt, R., Bornemann, M., Pawlowsky, P., & Schneider, U. (2001). Intellectual capital and knowledge management: Perspectives on measuring knowledge. In M. Dierkes, A. B. Anthal, J. Child, & I. Nonaka (Eds.), *Handbook of organizational learning and knowledge* (pp. 774–820). Oxford, England: Oxford University Press.

Romiszowski, A. J. (1997). Web-based distance learning and teaching: Revolutionary invention or reaction to necessity? In B. H. Khan (Ed.), *Web-based instruction* (pp. 25–37). Englewood Cliffs, NJ: Educational Technology Publications.

Rossett, A. (1999, May). Knowledge management meets analysis. *Training & Development,* pp. 63–68.

Rouiller, J. Z., & Goldstein, I. L. (1993). The relationship between organizational transfer climate and positive transfer of training. *Human Resource Development Quarterly, 4,* 377–390.

Ruggles, R. (1998). The state of the notion: Knowledge management in practice. *California Management Review, 40*(3), 80–88.

Schumpeter, J. (1934). *The theory of economic development.* Cambridge, MA: Harvard University Press.

Sena, J. A., & Shani, A. B. (1999). Intellectual capital and knowledge creation: Toward an alternative framework. In J. Liebowitz (Ed.), *Knowledge management handbook* (pp. 8-1–8-16). Boca Raton, FL: CRC Press.

Singley, M. K., & Anderson, J. R. (1989). *The transfer of cognitive skills.* Cambridge, MA: Harvard University Press.

Starbuck, W. H. (1992). Learning by knowledge-intensive firms. *Journal of Management Studies, 29,* 713–740.

Sutton, R. I., & Hargadon, A. (1996). Brainstorming groups in context: Effectiveness in a product design firm. *Administrative Science Quarterly, 41,* 685–718.

Tobin, D. R. (1998). *The knowledge-enabled organization*. New York: AMACOM.

Tjosvold, D., & Tjosvold, M. M. (1995). Cross-functional teamwork: The challenge of involving professionals. In M. M. Beyerlein, D. A. Johnson, & S. T. Beyerlein (Eds.), *Advances in interdisciplinary studies of work teams* (Vol. 2; pp. 1–34). Greenwich, CT: JAI Press.

Tracey, J. B., Tannenbaum, S. I., & Kavanagh, M. J. (1995). Applying trained skills on the job: The importance of the work environment. *Journal of Applied Psychology, 80*(2), 239–252.

Van Buren, M. E. (1999, May). A yardstick for knowledge management. *Training & Development*, pp. 71–78.

Wageman, R. (2001). The meaning of interdependence. In M. E. Turner (Ed.), *Groups at work: Theory and research* (pp. 197–217). Hillsdale, NJ: Erlbaum.

Walsh, J. P., & Ungson, G. R. (1991). Organizational memory. *Academy of Management Review, 16*, 57–91.

Wiig, K. M. (1999). Introducing knowledge management into the enterprise. In J. Liebowitz (Ed.), *Knowledge management handbook* (pp. 3-1–3-41). Boca Raton, FL: CRC Press.

Williams, R. L., & Cothrel, J. (2000, Summer). Four smart ways to run online communities. *Sloan Management Review*, pp. 81–91.

Williamson, O. E. (1975). *Markets and hierarchies: Analysis and antitrust implications*. New York: Free Press.

Willis, B., & Dickinson, J. (1997). Distance education and the World Wide Web. In B. H. Khan (Ed.), *Web-based instruction* (pp. 81–84). Englewood Cliffs, NJ: Educational Technology Publications.

Zielinski, D. (2000, March). Can you keep learners on-line? *Training*, pp. 65–75.

CHAPTER 9

Stimulating and Supporting Creativity in Organizations

Greg R. Oldham

There is now considerable evidence to suggest that human resources are a critical source of sustainable competitive advantage in contemporary organizations (DeNisi, Hitt, & Jackson, Chapter One, this volume; Lawler, Chapter Ten). Individual employees are often seen as significant resources because they possess knowledge that may be exploited to address organizational problems and changing circumstances (Nonaka, 1991). But earlier theory and research suggest that achieving competitive advantage involves more than applying existing knowledge—it also involves the continuous creation of *new* knowledge and the dissemination of this knowledge to others throughout the organization (Fiol, Chapter Three, this volume; Nonaka & Takeuchi, 1995; Pulakos, Dorsey, & Borman, Chapter Six). When new knowledge is created and transferred to others, there is a greater likelihood that the others will use it and apply it in their own work, further develop it, and then transfer it to other individuals in the organization for their own use and development. In sum, the use and development of new

Note: I thank Angelo DeNisi, Susan Jackson, and Jing Zhou for their helpful comments on an earlier draft of this chapter and Diana Jimeno-Ingrum for her help with the literature review. I also thank Howard Weiss for his suggestions concerning the effects of mood on creativity.

knowledge should ultimately allow the organization to adjust better to shifting market conditions, respond to opportunities, and thus adapt, grow, and compete (Nonaka, 1991).

This chapter examines the development and dissemination of new knowledge in the workplace. In particular, it focuses on employees' creative ideas and the ways that organizations might be populated, structured, and managed in order to stimulate the development of these ideas and to encourage their sharing and dissemination in the organization. Creative ideas are novel, potentially useful ideas about organizational products, practices, or procedures (Amabile, 1996; Oldham & Cummings, 1996). The significance of generating and sharing ideas has long been acknowledged in the strategy literature (Boudreau, Chapter Thirteen, this volume; Jackson & Schuler, 2001)—the concepts of knowledge "stocks" and "flows" are similar to the concepts of idea generation and sharing, respectively. By generating creative ideas and making them accessible to others, employees essentially provide the organization with new knowledge that can be used, applied, and implemented. And as suggested earlier, it is the application and development of these new ideas that should have substantial, lasting benefits for the organization (Nonaka, 1991).

This chapter explores a variety of personal and contextual conditions that may affect employee creativity and provides a theoretical perspective that explains these effects. The emphasis is on both the formulation of creative ideas and the sharing of these ideas with relevant others in the organization. With few exceptions (see Frese, Teng, & Wijnen, 1999), earlier research has focused exclusively on the determinants of creative idea generation (Amabile, 1996; Oldham & Cummings, 1996). Yet it is clear that creative ideas must be made available to the organization if they are to be used and developed (Noe, Colquitt, Simmering, & Alvarez, Chapter Eight, this volume). Hence, this chapter examines "enabling" contextual conditions (Boudreau, Chapter Thirteen), conditions that encourage creative idea generation and affect creative idea sharing. The contextual conditions examined include those both inside *and* outside the organizational boundaries. There is considerable evidence that individuals' behavior in organizations is affected by "nonwork" conditions (Ray & Miller, 1994), but most earlier research on creativity in organizations has focused on conditions inside the organization, ignoring potentially relevant nonwork variables (see Amabile, 1996; Woodman, Sawyer, & Griffin, 1993). This chapter takes a more balanced perspective and addresses both types of variables.

In the pages that follow, I provide a detailed definition of creative ideas and discuss several possible mechanisms for sharing these ideas inside the organization. I present a theoretical framework that addresses how personal and contextual conditions might influence creative idea formulation and sharing, and then review the relevant literature and integrate it into this framework. In many instances, relatively few investigations have focused on the conditions suggested; I propose new research that might contribute to this literature. I conclude the chapter with a general discussion of possible future research directions.

Formulating and Sharing Creative Ideas

As already suggested, if creative ideas are to become candidates for future use and development they must be formulated and then shared with others in the organization. This section considers separately these two processes. I begin with an analysis of creative ideas and follow that with a discussion of idea sharing. Following earlier work (such as Shalley, 1991; Sternberg & Lubart, 1996; Zhou & George, 2001), ideas are considered creative if they satisfy two basic conditions: they are novel or original, and they are potentially relevant for or useful to the organization that employs the individual. An idea is considered novel if it is unique compared with other ideas currently available in the organization. That is, if an idea has been neither made available to others in the organization nor transformed into organizational practice or policy, it will be considered novel. Thus, if an employee comes up with an idea that has not been made public in her employing organization but that is readily available in a competitor's organization, that idea would still be considered novel according to this definition. Note that the concept of novelty is not synonymous with the scope or magnitude of an idea. A novel idea may be radical or frame-breaking (such as an idea for an entirely new product line) or incremental or adaptive (such as an idea for changing the order of steps in a work process). Again, all that is required for an idea to be considered novel is that it is not currently available to others in the target organization.

The concept of potential usefulness is perhaps more ambiguous. An idea is considered useful if it has the potential for direct or indirect value to the organization in either the short or the long term. Thus, if an employee's idea has implications for the development of a new product line that might be launched by the organization in the near future, this idea would be considered potentially useful. Similarly, if an employee's idea might be applied by a coworker in his job, the idea would be useful. Or if an employee had an idea that could change the culture of the organization and make it a more attractive place to work for future employees, this too would be considered a potentially useful idea. Finally, if an individual's idea might stimulate the generation of ideas by other employees, and if their ideas had some potential practical value to the organization, then the initial idea would be considered potentially useful. All that is necessary for an idea to be useful, then, is that it have the potential to make some contribution to the organization's short-term or long-term growth or effectiveness.

Based on this discussion, it is clear that an employee could generate novel and potentially useful ideas in any location— whether inside or outside the boundaries of the organization. For example, an employee could come up with an idea for a new product line while at her workstation, in the company cafeteria, at home, at the grocery store, or even on the golf course. But if the ideas are to be applied in the organization and contribute to its growth and development, they must be made available to others there (Axtell et al., 2000; DeNisi et. al, Chapter One, this volume; Frese et al., 1999). If employees were to keep their creative ideas private, or perhaps share them only with people outside the organization, there is little reason to expect these ideas to be of substantial benefit to the organization. The literature suggests many possible mechanisms that employees might use in making public their creative ideas (Frese et al., 1999). For example, they might make them public through a formal suggestion program or they might prepare a formal written report, make a personal demonstration, speak with or write (a memo) to a manager, or have an informal discussion with a coworker (Oldham & Cummings, 1998).

The mechanism that is actually used to make an idea available to the organization may be a function of the nature of the idea itself. Although systematic research has yet to test this possibility, it may be that different mechanisms are used to share different kinds of ideas. For example, if an idea is highly abstract, or what Nonaka (1991) refers to as tacit knowledge, it might be difficult for an individual to express it in writing. With such an idea it might be necessary for an employee to make a personal demonstration in order to share it with others (Nonaka & Takeuchi, 1995). In contrast, a completely different mechanism might be used if the idea is relatively concrete—explicit knowledge, according to Nonaka (1991). In this case, it might be most efficient for an employee to use some form of oral or written communication to make the idea available to others. Regardless of the methods employed, however, this perspective suggests that ideas must be made public and available to others in the organization if they are to contribute substantially to its knowledge and success.

Like earlier authors (such as Grant, 1996; Madjar, Oldham, & Pratt, 2002; Nonaka, 1991; Oldham & Cummings, 1996), I consider the individual employee to be the source of creative ideas—regardless of his or her level, position, or title in the organization. Of course, it is possible that the nature or scope of the creative ideas will vary depending on the individual's position in the organization. For example, individuals working in R&D are likely to generate more ideas (or more radical ideas) than employees working on the shop floor. Yet there is good reason to believe that employees in all positions have the potential to generate creative ideas (Nonaka, 1991) and that these ideas can be valuable to the organization. Therefore, in this chapter I focus on the enabling conditions that might enhance the generation and sharing of creative ideas by all employees.

A Model of Creative Idea Formulation and Sharing

Previous research suggests that different personal and contextual variables affect individuals' formulation of creative ideas and their willingness to make these ideas available to others in an organization (see Axtell et al., 2000; Frese et al., 1999). Therefore, I suggest a number of personal and contextual conditions that may separately affect the idea formulation and sharing constructs. The expected relations among personal and contextual conditions and the generation and sharing of creative ideas are described in Figure 9.1.

Figure 9.1. A Model of Creative Idea Formulation and Sharing.

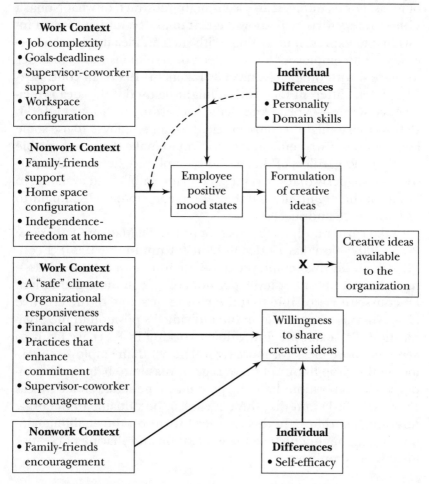

Contextual Conditions and Formulation of Creative Ideas

I have argued that creative ideas may be generated in either work or nonwork settings, and that contextual conditions in these settings have the potential to influence the nature of the ideas that individuals formulate. Therefore, the following paragraphs examine both the work and the nonwork conditions that may influence employees' creative ideas. It should be noted that most of the research reviewed includes measures of the creative ideas that employees have generated *and* made available to the organization, not the entire set of ideas that they may come up with but not make public. Thus, in my discussion of the literature I argue that the contextual conditions identified influence idea generation, and this is based on evidence about ideas that have been made public. In the concluding section, I suggest a research strategy that will allow a direct test of the argument that certain contextual conditions influence the generation of creative ideas.

Employee Mood States

As shown in Figure 9.1, employee mood states are expected to influence the generation of creative ideas directly. All of the work and nonwork contextual conditions are posited to affect employee idea generation through their effects on moods. Thus, conditions in the work (such as supervisory behavior) and nonwork (such as spousal support) contexts are expected to enhance or restrict relevant mood states, which, in turn affect the generation of ideas (George & Brief, 1992; Isen, 1999).

Moods refer to pervasive generalized affective states that are not necessarily directed at any particular object or behavior (Isen, 1999). Moods are transient states that are experienced over the short run and fluctuate over time (George & Brief, 1992). Previous work suggests that moods consist of two independent dimensions: positive (characterized by emotions ranging from high to low levels of excitation and elatedness) and negative (characterized by feelings of distress and fear) (Isen, 1999).

Early theoretical work suggests that when individuals experience *positive moods* their cognitive or motivational processes are enhanced so that they produce more creative ideas (Vosburg, 1998). For example, Isen (1999) argues that when individuals experience positive moods, they make more connections between divergent stimulus materials, use broader categories, and see more interrelatedness among stimuli. As a result, they may be more likely to recognize a problem and to integrate a variety of resources, resulting in ideas that are more creative. Other theorists argue that *negative moods* facilitate creativity (Kaufmann & Vosburg, 1997; Zhou & George, 2001). According to this position, creativity requires individuals to experience tension and dissatisfaction—conditions that are associated with negative moods.

Previous research provides strong support for the argument that positive moods encourage the generation of creative ideas (see Isen, 1999). For example, Isen, Johnson, Mertz, and Robinson (1985) showed that when individuals experienced positive mood via receiving refreshments or viewing a positive film, they generated more unusual and diverse first word associations to neutral stimulus words than individuals in control conditions. In contrast, few studies support the proposed connection between negative moods and creativity. Specifically, research suggests that negative moods have statistically nonsignificant relations to measures of creativity (Kaufmann & Vosburg, 1997; Madjar et al., 2002).

Overall, then, the research reviewed suggests that positive mood enhances creativity, but that negative mood has little consistent relation to it. Based on these findings, any contextual condition that raises or lowers individuals' positive moods should affect their creative idea generation (George & Brief, 1992). Therefore, I now turn to a discussion of several potentially relevant contextual characteristics.

Job Complexity

As shown in Figure 9.1, the context of employees' jobs is expected to have an impact on their positive mood states and on the creativity of their ideas (Amabile, Conti, Coon, Lazenby, & Herron, 1996; Hatcher, Ross, & Collins, 1989; Saavedra & Kwun, 2000). When employees have complex, challenging jobs—that is, jobs characterized by high levels of autonomy, feedback, variety, identity, and significance (Hackman & Oldham, 1980)—they are likely to feel excited and enthusiastic and respond to these feelings by having ideas that are both novel and potentially useful to the organization.

Previous research provides some support for these arguments. For example, Saavedra and Kwun (2000) demonstrated that a measure of employee job complexity correlated positively and significantly with a measure of positive mood. Hatcher et al. (1989) found a positive, significant relation between a job complexity index and the number of new ideas employees submitted to a suggestion program. And Oldham and Cummings (1996) demonstrated that a measure of job complexity correlated positively with supervisory ratings of employee creativity.

These earlier studies did not directly examine the entire causal sequence suggested here (job complexity–positive mood–creative ideas), and such research is needed if the framework presented in Figure 9.1 is to receive support. Such research may be especially valuable if other explanations for the effects of job complexity are examined at the same time. For example, it might be useful to contrast the mood state perspective described here with the perspective that it is simply the discretionary time associated with autonomous, complex jobs that allows individuals to generate creative ideas while they are at work.

Performance Goals and Deadlines

The presence of specific production goals and deadlines may also have an impact on the generation of creative ideas (Amabile et al., 1996; Shalley, 1991). When individuals have been assigned performance targets or given specific deadlines for the completion of a project or product, they are likely to focus their energies and attentions on achieving those goals or deadlines, not on the generation of creative ideas (Shalley, 1991). These negative effects might be further amplified if the goals or deadlines are perceived as difficult or unrealistic. In these circumstances, not only are individuals' energies likely to be directed toward reaching the goals or deadlines but their positive moods should also be lowered because of the pressure and expectations.

A few previous studies support these arguments. For example, Amabile and her colleagues (1996) demonstrated that individuals who experienced extreme time pressures in work groups exhibited lower creativity than those who experienced fewer pressures. Shalley (1991) showed that individuals exhibited lower creativity when assigned difficult performance goals than if they were assigned either no goals or easy goals. Interestingly, the adverse effects of the difficult performance goal were reduced when individuals were simultaneously assigned a goal to produce creative work. These latter results suggest that the presence of creativity goals can counteract the negative effects of difficult performance goals on creative idea generation. It may be that creativity goals have these effects because they cause individuals to direct their attentions away from the production goal and toward the development of creative ideas. Alternatively, it may be that individuals become excited and enthusiastic in anticipation of achieving creativity goals, and it is these positive feelings that enhance the creativity of ideas generated. Future research is now needed to examine these explanations.

Support from Supervisors and Coworkers

Figure 9.1 suggests that the behavior supervisors and coworkers exhibit in the workplace may have an impact on employees' mood states and the creative ideas they generate. In particular, when supervisors and coworkers are supportive—that is, provide employees with time, resources, information, and encouragement (West, 1990)—the employees' positive mood states may be boosted, resulting in more creative ideas.

Previous research offers substantial support for such general arguments (Ramus, 2001; Scott & Bruce, 1994; Sosik, Kahai, & Avolio, 1998; Tierney, Farmer, & Graen, 1999; Zhou & George, 2001). For example, Oldham and Cummings (1996) demonstrated that a measure of supportive supervision made a significant contribution to the number of patent disclosures employees wrote over a two-year period. Amabile et al. (1996) showed that individuals in work teams were more creative when their coworkers were supportive and encouraging. Finally, Madjar et al. (2002) demonstrated that support from supervisors and coworkers contributed to employees' positive moods and creativity, and that these moods effectively explained the support-creativity relations. In total, then, results of previous studies suggest that support from supervisors and coworkers enhances employee mood states, which in turn boosts their creative ideas. Work is now needed to tease apart the support construct and investigate the relative effects of the various elements of support (time, information, resources, and encouragement) on employee moods and creativity.

Physical Configuration of the Workspace

The configuration of the area in which an employee works may have an impact on his mood states and creative ideas. Key here is the extent to which the workspace limits or permits intrusions. Specifically, work areas that are configured to reduce the number of unwanted intrusions and interruptions (that is, low spatial density—few people per unit of space—many physical boundaries, and large distances between workstations) enhance positive mood states and the generation of creative ideas. In contrast, spaces that encourage uncontrolled intrusions (high density) may result in less positive moods and fewer creative ideas.

Only a few investigations have examined the effects of the configuration of work areas on moods and creativity, but this research is consistent with these arguments. For example, Nagar and Pandey (1987) found that individuals in low-density areas experienced more positive mood states than those in crowded, high-density areas. Aiello, DeRisi, Epstein, and Karlin (1977) showed that individuals in low spatial density conditions exhibited higher performance on a creativity task than individuals in high-density conditions. An interview study by Soriano de Alencar and Bruno-Faria (1997) found that employees mentioned "inadequate physical environment" (lack of space and presence of noise) as a factor that inhibited their creativity. And a laboratory study by Shalley and Oldham (1997) showed that when competitors were present, individuals who worked in a room with physical boundaries exhibited higher creativity than those who worked in a room with no boundaries.

All of this suggests that unwanted interpersonal intrusions may reduce the formulation of creative ideas. Individuals are likely to find such intrusions distracting and disturbing, which, in turn, should lower their mood states and creativity. Research is now needed to test this entire causal sequence and to investigate the elements of the spatial configuration that have the strongest effects on moods and creativity. Research is also needed to determine if these effects generalize to all positions or if individuals in certain jobs might find uncontrolled interruptions less disturbing or even stimulating and exhilarating.

Support from Family Members and Friends

I suggested earlier that supportive behavior on the part of supervisors and coworkers could make a substantial contribution to positive mood states at work and to the creative ideas generated in the work setting. It is also possible that support from others outside the organization—namely, family members and friends—could also make a contribution to individuals' moods and creative ideas. Support from nonwork others might affect creative idea generation in several ways. First, support from these people might have direct effects on positive moods at work, which then influence the creativity of ideas generated in that setting. Or such support might affect nonwork mood states, which then affect moods and creativity at work. Finally, support from nonwork others could affect moods in nonwork settings and the creative work-related ideas individuals generate in those settings.

Earlier research offers general support for these arguments. For example, Ray and Miller (1994) showed that support from family members reduced the level of emotional exhaustion employees experienced at work. Fusilier, Ganster, and Mayes (1986) showed that support from family members and friends lowered employees' depression and anxiety levels and increased their general life satisfaction. And Chan and Margolin (1994) demonstrated that individuals' moods at home often "spilled over" to their moods at work.

A few studies have also shown that support from family members can have an impact on individuals' creativity. Harrington, Block, and Block (1987) assessed parenting practices when children were three to five years old and obtained judgments of their creativity when they were eleven to fourteen years old. They found that children scored high on the creativity measures when parents had been supportive. Walberg, Rasher, and Parkerson (1980) showed that individuals who were highly creative as adults usually, as children, had received support from their parents. Finally, Madjar et al. (2002) examined the effects of support from the families and friends of adult employees on the mood states and creativity of those employees. Consistent with the relations posited in Figure 9.1, their results showed that support from family members and friends boosted employees' positive moods, which then enhanced their creativity. Research is now needed on the extent to which nonwork support influences the creative ideas employees generate at work through effects on their nonwork mood states, and if support from others at work influences ideas generated at home through effects on nonwork moods. In addition, work is needed to determine which nonwork others (spouse, sibling, friend) have the strongest effects on an individual's moods and creativity.

Physical Configuration of Space in the Home

Research reviewed earlier suggests that the configuration of employees' workspaces can have a substantial impact on their mood states and creativity. But as shown in Figure 9.1, the spatial configuration of the home environment may also have an impact on individuals' mood states, which then has implications for the generation of creative ideas. Specifically, it is possible that home environments that provide little control over unwanted intrusions (such as dense environments or homes without a place to which an individual might retreat to be alone) influence nonwork moods, and in turn, extend to moods at work (Chan & Margolin, 1994), influencing creative idea generation there. Alternatively, individuals may come up with novel and useful ideas in the home environment, and the moods that are created by the home configuration may have a direct impact on these ideas.

No study has directly examined these proposed associations. However, numerous studies have demonstrated that the spatial configuration of nonwork areas can have a significant impact on an individual's attitudes and mood states (Baum & Valins, 1977; Bruins & Barber, 2000; Nogami, 1976). For example, Paulus (1988) demonstrated that individuals housed in dense, crowded prison cells experienced lower positive moods than those in less crowded conditions. Bruins and Barber (2000) showed that supermarket shoppers felt more comfortable in uncrowded stores than in crowded ones.

Research is now needed to examine directly the effects of several characteristics of home configurations (such as number of rooms and availability of private areas) on the creativity of ideas generated in both the work and the home environments. This work would be especially relevant if it also assessed individuals' mood states and determined if they explained any effects of home spatial configurations on creative ideas.

Independence and Personal Freedom at Home

The framework shown in Figure 9.1 suggests that individuals who have substantial freedom and independence in their nonwork lives are likely to experience positive mood states and to produce creative ideas. When individuals are independent and have control over their lives outside of work, they are likely to feel excited and exhilarated. As discussed earlier, these mood states may have positive effects on the creativity of ideas they generate outside of work or spill over to their work moods and affect the ideas they generate in organizations.

A number of studies provide indirect support for these arguments. For example, considerable research suggests that individuals who experienced freedom and autonomy in their childhood homes exhibit high levels of creativity later in life (Halpin, Payne, & Ellett, 1973; MacKinnon, 1962). Another stream of research shows that adults' experiences of personal control and freedom in the nonwork domain contribute to their positive affective states (see Haidt & Rodin, 1999). For example, Rodin and Langer (1977) showed that an intervention designed to increase nursing home residents' opportunities for personal control over ongoing daily events resulted in significant increases in their positive mood states.

Research is now needed to test the contribution of independence and freedom to moods and to the generation of creative ideas inside and outside the organization. In addition, studies are needed to determine if there are cumulative effects of personal freedom—that is, if the freedom people have outside of work contributes to creativity above and beyond the freedom they have at work.

Individual Differences and Formulation of Creative Ideas

The model shown in Figure 9.1 includes individual characteristics and suggests that different characteristics are likely to affect the stages of creative idea generation and willingness to share. This section focuses on two general categories of individual differences expected to affect idea generation.

Personality

The model suggests that individuals' personalities have a direct effect on the creativity of ideas they generate. Numerous investigations have examined the effects of personality on individuals' creativity in a variety of settings (Feist, 1999). Much of this earlier work included one of two measures of personality. The first of these is the Creative Personality Scale (CPS; Gough, 1979). Individuals who score high on this measure can be characterized as having creative personalities, and therefore, are expected to approach problems with broad interests that enable them to recognize divergent information and opinions (Barron & Harrington,

1981). In addition, these individuals are thought to possess the self-confidence and tolerance for ambiguity to be patient with competing views and to persist in developing their own original ideas.

Results of previous investigations provide strong support for the argument that creative personality has a positive impact on the generation of creative ideas (see Feist, 1999, for a review). For example, Gough (1979) examined correlations between the CPS and creativity ratings for twelve groups of individuals (such as architects and scientists). Positive, significant correlations were obtained in ten of the twelve groups. Moreover, in two cross-validation samples, Gough reported significant relations between the CPS and creativity.

The second measure of personality used in previous research, openness to experience, has also been shown to predict creativity consistently in a variety of samples (Feist, 1998). People who are high in openness have greater access to a variety of feelings, perspectives, and ideas; may be more adaptable to changing circumstances; and tend to be able to come up with new ideas that challenge the status quo. Those who are low in openness are more conservative and demonstrate more of a liking for ideas that are familiar and conventional, rather than novel (McCrae, 1996). Measures of openness and creative personality (the CPS) have been shown to be moderately correlated with one another (McCrae, 1987).

In addition to showing main effects on individuals' creative responses, a few studies suggest that CPS and openness moderate relations between work and nonwork contextual conditions and creativity (George & Zhou, 2001; Oldham & Cummings, 1996; Zhou & Oldham, 2001). This research suggests that individuals who score high in openness or creative personality value highly conditions in the workplace that tend to support creative idea generation (that is, complex jobs and supportive supervision) and respond to these conditions by exhibiting relatively high levels of creativity. In contrast, those who score lower in openness or CPS tend to devalue these conditions and respond less positively to them.

However, the study by Madjar et al. (2002) suggests that individuals with *less* creative personalities respond most positively to support from family and friends. Apparently, supportive nonwork conditions compensate for the absence of creative potential among low CPS employees, whereas those with more creative personalities find support from these nonwork others redundant.

Because few studies have examined the moderating effects of personality on relations between contextual characteristics and creativity, caution should be used when interpreting these results. This is the reason why a dotted arrow, rather than one drawn with a continuous line, is used in Figure 9.1 to characterize these possible moderating effects. More studies are needed to determine if openness (or CPS) moderates the effects of all contextual conditions shown in the figure, and whether the direction of these effects differs by contextual characteristic.

Domain-Relevant Skills

Figure 9.1 suggests that individuals' domain-relevant skills have a direct impact on their creative ideas. Many commentators have argued that individuals must have factual knowledge, technical skills, and talents that are relevant in the domain if they are to generate creative ideas there (Amabile, 1996; Woodman et al., 1993). More broadly described, these skills could include facts, principles, attitudes toward various issues in the domain, knowledge of paradigms, performance scripts for solving problems in the domain, and aesthetic criteria (Amabile, 1996).

It is difficult to imagine that individuals could generate creative ideas unless they had an appropriate level of relevant skills and talents. Yet very few studies have directly examined the role of domain-relevant skills in the production of creative work (Amabile, 1996). One study that provides some support for the importance of such skills was conducted by Amabile and Gyrskiewicz (1987). In this interview study, 120 scientists indicated that several skills (such as talent and expertise in a subject area, broad general knowledge, and experience in many fields) enabled them to produce creative work.

More research is now needed to sort out the particular skills and talents that contribute to creativity across a variety of domains. In addition, work is needed to determine if there is a linear relation between such skills and creative idea generation or if there is simply a skill threshold that must be achieved in order for individuals to generate creative ideas. Research is also needed to understand if domain-relevant skills moderate the effects of several of the contextual conditions described earlier.

Contextual Conditions and Willingness to Make Ideas Available to the Organization

Up to this point, the chapter has focused on the personal and contextual conditions that may influence the formulation of creative ideas. But if these ideas are to be converted into new practices or procedures that are of use to the organization, they must be made available to others inside the organization's boundaries (DeNisi et al., Chapter One; Pulakos et al., Chapter Six). Which circumstances and conditions, then, are likely to prompt individuals to share their ideas? A few studies suggest that willingness to share may be a function of both the characteristics of the employee and the context in which he or she works (Axtell et al., 2000; Frese et al., 1999). These characteristics, which differ from those expected to stimulate ideas, are described in this section of the chapter. Because few studies have directly examined the construct of willingness to share and its immediate antecedents, no mediating mechanisms between the personal-contextual conditions and willingness are included in the figure. However, I speculate on possible mediating conditions in the concluding section of the chapter.

A "Safe," Nonjudgmental Climate

Figure 9.1 suggests that a safe, nonjudgmental organizational climate should enhance employees' willingness to share their creative ideas with others there. When individuals consider the possibility of making their ideas public, they are essentially considering taking a risk and putting their ideas forward for possible evaluation (Albrecht & Hall, 1991). If the organizational climate feels safe and individuals expect that their ideas will *not* be subject to ridicule or censure, then they are more likely to make them public (Axtell et al., 2000; West, 1990). In contrast, the anticipation of a critical, judgmental evaluation could constitute a threat to an employee's self-image and result in his sharing fewer ideas with the organization (see Edmondson, 1999; Kahn, 1990).

A number of studies provide results consistent with these arguments. For example, studies on brainstorming indicate that individuals suggest relatively few ideas in brainstorming groups when they expect a critical evaluation of their ideas by other group members

(Brown & Paulus, 1996). In addition, a study by Axtell et al. (2000) showed that individuals made more suggestions about aspects of their work when they experienced the organizational climate as nonjudgmental. Other research suggests that creativity is lower when individuals expect their work to be judged compared with circumstances when no critical evaluation is anticipated (Amabile, 1996; Shalley & Perry-Smith, 2001). For example, Amabile (1979) examined the effects of external evaluation on the creativity of artwork that students produced. Results showed that individuals who expected their work to be critically evaluated by expert judges submitted less creative artwork than individuals in no-evaluation conditions.

According to this research, removing the threat of critical, judgmental evaluations might enhance the number of creative ideas individuals suggest to an organization. Other research indicates that the anticipation of receiving "developmental" evaluations of creative ideas could further boost the number of ideas people make public (Shalley & Perry-Smith, 2001). Developmental evaluations are intended to provide noncritical assessments of ideas that may help individuals improve their creativity (Zhou & Oldham, 2001). For example, participants receiving such evaluations in the Shalley and Perry-Smith (2001) study were told that reviews of their work would be provided to them along with suggestions for alternative approaches they might consider in the future. Results of this study and others (such as Zhou & Oldham, 2001) suggest that individuals who anticipate developmental evaluations exhibit higher creativity than those who receive either no evaluations or critical evaluations of their work.

This discussion suggests that a safe climate should enhance the number of creative ideas employees make available to an organization. In such a climate, the threat of critical evaluation has been removed and the opportunity for developmental assessment may be provided. Research is now needed to examine whether the effects of such climates vary according to the scope of the creative idea. For example, it may be that safe climates are especially helpful in boosting the submission of radical ideas, because these ideas may be considered riskier and potentially threatening to an individual's self-concept.

Organizational Responsiveness to Creative Ideas

The extent to which the organization is responsive to the ideas employees make available may have an impact on the number of ideas they make public in the future. Should the organization recognize the individual employee as the source of an idea and either seriously consider the implementation of that idea or actually implement it, the employee may be encouraged to make other ideas available later on. But if their ideas are regularly dismissed or rejected, the number of ideas employees make public should decrease.

A few studies support these arguments. For example, Frese and his associates (1999) showed that fewer ideas were submitted to a suggestion program when individuals expected them to be rejected than when they expected acceptance. Research on quality circles and project teams suggests that individuals are more likely to submit ideas for organizational improvements if they believe these ideas will be implemented, and they may become disillusioned if their ideas are consistently rejected (see Lawler, 1986).

Research is now needed to investigate the degree of responsiveness that is most likely to prompt the submission of creative ideas. For example, research is needed on the frequency with which ideas must actually be implemented in order to enhance the number of new ideas submitted in the future. Studies might also examine if there are circumstances in which public recognition of an individual as the source of an idea compensates for the actual implementation of the idea and results in more idea sharing.

Financial Rewards for Idea Sharing

It may be possible to use financial rewards to encourage individuals to submit their ideas to the organization (Frese et al., 1999; Tesluk, Farr, & Klein, 1997). Based on the earlier discussion of the value of a nonjudgmental climate, care would have to be taken to ensure that rewards were provided for making ideas public rather than on the basis of an evaluation of quality. Some research suggests that evaluating creative ideas and making financial rewards contingent on the evaluations can adversely affect the creativity of ideas submitted (Amabile, 1996). It may be that financial rewards used in this way are perceived as an attempt to control an individual's behavior (Deci & Ryan, 1985), which reinforces the effects of the critical evaluation and makes individuals reluctant to submit ideas.

Therefore, if individuals are to be encouraged to share novel and potentially useful ideas with the organization, rewards should be offered that convey the message that all ideas are valued and that the organization is not interested in evaluating or controlling creativity. One way to accomplish this might be to offer financial rewards for sharing ideas that are relatively low in salience (Eisenberger & Selbst, 1994). For example, it may be that offering relatively small rewards, or offering rewards well after the submission of the idea, decreases their salience but demonstrates the organization's interest in creativity. Another possibility might be to offer nonfinancial rewards (such as plaques and improved parking conditions) instead of financial rewards. Again, employees may perceive such rewards as less salient but supportive of idea sharing.

Unfortunately, research has yet to examine the effects of a variety of reward programs and strategies on employees' willingness to share creative ideas with the organization. Research is now needed to test the possibilities discussed here and to determine if there are particular reward systems that encourage idea sharing without diminishing the creativity of the ideas that are ultimately shared.

Encouragement from Others for Idea Sharing

I discussed earlier the possibility that individuals both inside and outside the organization's boundaries might enhance the development of ideas by providing support and resources to the employee. In addition to assisting in the generation of ideas, work and nonwork others (supervisors, coworkers, family and friends) might also facilitate the actual sharing of these ideas with others in the organization. Specifically, individuals may be more likely to share their ideas if work and nonwork others (a) articulate the expectation that ideas formulated will be shared and (b) explicitly encourage individuals to take risks by making their ideas public (West & Anderson, 1996).

Only a few studies have directly tested these arguments. Frese and his colleagues (1999) showed that the more supervisors encouraged employees to share ideas, the more ideas they actually submitted to the organization's suggestion program. Axtell et al.

(2000) found that the more team members supported the sharing of new ideas, the more employees suggested changes to various aspects of work.

More research is needed to examine the effects of encouragement from work and nonwork others on idea sharing. This research might carefully address the role of the language that others use in encouraging ideas. A study by Zhou (1998) demonstrated that individuals showed lower creativity when they were given feedback about their work that included "controlling" language (you "should" or "must" behave in a certain way) versus language that was more neutral in character ("might" or "could"). This suggests that to encourage the sharing of new ideas effectively, others both inside and outside the organization might refrain from using controlling language (for example, "You should mention that idea to your manager") and instead employ language that is noncontrolling ("You might consider mentioning that idea to your manager"). Empirical research is now needed to examine the direct effects of language on idea sharing.

Practices and Characteristics That Enhance
Organizational Commitment

Figure 9.1 suggests that individuals are more likely to share their creative ideas with others in an organization when they are committed to, and intend to remain with, the organization. By making public their creative ideas, individuals are potentially helping the organization succeed and gain competitive advantage. Such behavior may be in an employee's interest if he is committed to the organization. However, obviously, if this commitment is absent and the individual intends to leave, there is little reason for him to make creative ideas available for possible use and application. This would seem the case especially if the individual intended to move to a new organization in the near future, and if that organization was a competitor of the current organization. In this situation, the individual would be giving the current organization access to ideas that could damage the other's competitiveness, and in the process, damage his own status in the new organization.

All of this suggests that practices and characteristics that have been shown to affect an individual's organizational commitment (see Meyer & Allen, 1997) should influence his or her willingness to make creative ideas available to others in the organization. For example, characteristics that have been shown to enhance commitment (such as supportive supervision and procedural justice) should have a positive effect on individuals' willingness to share ideas, whereas those that have been shown to lower commitment (such as simple jobs and organizational centralization) should reduce the likelihood of idea sharing.

Individual Differences and Willingness to Make Ideas Available to the Organization

The discussion thus far has focused on contextual conditions that are likely to influence individuals' willingness to share their ideas with the organization. It is also possible that individuals with certain personal characteristics are prone to making ideas available for assessment and possible use. One characteristic suggested by the earlier literature is self-efficacy (Axtell et al., 2000; Redmond, Mumford, & Teach, 1993; Tesluk et al., 1997). *Self-efficacy* refers to individuals' judgments of their capabilities to organize and execute courses of action required to attain certain types of performance (Bandura, 1986). With regard to idea sharing, self-efficacy involves an individual's belief in his or her ability to generate ideas that warrant implementation. Thus, if individuals have high self-efficacy, they are likely to have the confidence necessary to bring forward an idea (Frese et al., 1999).

Previous research provides some support for these arguments. Axtell and associates (2000) showed that a measure of self-efficacy correlated positively and significantly with the number of proposed changes individuals suggested for various aspects of their work. And Frese et al. (1999) demonstrated that a measure of self-efficacy was positively significantly related to the number of ideas an individual submitted to an organization's suggestion program. Interestingly, this same efficacy measure was also positively related to a self-report measure of ideas, suggesting that individuals with high efficacy are also likely to generate more work-related ideas.

Research is now needed to determine if there is a connection between efficacy and the personality dimensions described earlier that are expected to influence the creativity of ideas (creative personality and openness to experience), and whether these latter dimensions contribute to idea sharing.

Conclusion and Future Research Directions

This chapter focused on the personal and contextual conditions expected to affect employees' formulation of creative ideas and their willingness to make these ideas available to others in the organization. I argued that when employees formulate ideas and then disseminate them to others in the organization they are, in essence, providing the organization with new knowledge that can be used, applied, and developed. It is the application and subsequent development of these creative ideas that should enable the organization to respond to changing circumstances and conditions and thereby achieve competitive advantage.

If the arguments offered in this chapter, summarized in Figure 9.1, are accurate, it would suggest that several managerial strategies might be followed to boost the number of creative ideas made available in an organization. For example, it would suggest that managers consider staffing the organization with employees who are likely to generate and share creative ideas (such as those with high self-efficacy and openness to experience). Moreover, managers might consider designing the organizational context to support idea generation and sharing, perhaps by enriching jobs and creating a nonjudgmental climate. Although it may be difficult to modify nonwork contextual conditions that affect employee creativity (such as the spatial configuration of the home and explicit encouragement from family members), it may be possible for managers to suggest that employees seek out supportive contexts or even redesign nonwork contexts so that they become more supportive.

Research is now needed to test all of the direct, mediated, and interactive effects suggested by Figure 9.1. Specifically, work is needed to determine if the contextual conditions proposed to affect the formulation of creative ideas and the willingness to share these ideas actually operate as specified or if they affect different processes than expected. It would be necessary to develop separate measures of idea formulation and willingness to share, and include both in research investigations. As noted earlier, few studies have actually assessed these constructs, instead measuring only the ideas employees have actually made available to the organization (such as ideas forwarded to supervisors or suggestion programs, and ideas included in technical reports). Future studies that include direct measures of employees' willingness to share their ideas with others in the organization could make a real contribution to the literature. To ensure a comprehensive assessment of ideas, future studies might ask individuals to record all of their work-related ideas, perhaps by using a diary. They might record their ideas during both work and nonwork hours; this would enable the researcher to ascertain the location where the ideas were produced and the times when most creative ideas were formulated. This information could have important implications for the management of creativity.

Research is also needed to determine which characteristics and practices, other than those proposed, affect employees' mood states, idea generation, and willingness to share ideas. For example, workplace characteristics such as competition (Cummings & Oldham, 1997), interpersonal conflict (James, 1995), and organizational form (Williams & Yang, 1999) might affect the ideas individuals generate and share at work. In addition to research on these contextual factors, work is needed that directly examines the effects of various human resource practices and strategies (such as performance appraisal programs, training programs, reward practices) on idea generation and sharing. Many organizations now employ multiple source, 360-degree feedback programs (Tornow & London, 1998), but there has been little research on the effects of such systems on employees' creativity. It may be that performance feedback from multiple sources stimulates mood states and enhances creative idea generation. Or such feedback programs may be perceived by employees as controlling and thus restrict the number of creative ideas they share with others. Research is also needed on the effects of contemporary pay systems, such as skill-based pay (Lawler, Chapter Ten). Such systems essentially reward employees for acquiring new skills and competencies. But it is not clear if the acquisition of these skills will boost the number of creative ideas individuals develop and share or if skill-based pay will be deemed controlling and ultimately lower creativity. Finally, research is needed on the nature and design of training programs that are effective in encouraging the sharing of creative ideas with others as well as boosting the number of creative ideas employees generate at work (Basadur, Graen, & Scandura, 1986).

Much of the discussion in this chapter focused on the possibility that positive mood mediates the effects of contextual conditions on creative idea generation. Again, only a few studies have directly examined the mediating effects of moods (Madjar & Oldham, 2002; Madjar et al., 2002), and these studies looked at only creative ideas that had been made public and included few measures of contextual characteristics. Research is now needed that directly examines the mediating effects of work and nonwork moods on actual idea generation. In addition, work is needed to understand the psychological processes that explain the effects of contextual conditions on idea sharing. One intriguing possibility is suggested by the literature on risk taking (Isen & Geva, 1987; Isen & Patrick, 1983). If one assumes that making one's ideas public constitutes a risk, then conditions that explain risk taking also might explain employees' willingness to share ideas with others in the organization. Previous research suggests that positive mood states may increase the tendency for people to take risks, as long as the level of risk is relatively low, but may decrease risk taking when the risk itself is relatively high (Isen & Geva, 1987). If making ideas available to others in the organization is considered a relatively low-risk activity, this suggests that positive mood may explain the effects of the contextual conditions expected to prompt idea sharing as well as those expected to influence idea generation. Or it may be that level of risk associated with sharing an idea is partially a function of the magnitude of the idea to be shared. That is, sharing incremental ideas may be considered a low-risk activity whereas sharing radical or frame-breaking ideas may be considered very risky. If this is the case, the presence of positive mood may enhance the sharing of incremental ideas but restrict the sharing of ideas that are more radical. Research is now needed to investigate this possibility directly.

Research is also needed to examine whether the creative idea formulation and willingness to share variables interact as predicted to affect the ideas that are actually made available to the organization. This interaction would suggest that creative ideas are available for the organization's use only when employees both formulate the ideas and are ready to share them with others in the organization. Moreover, Figure 9.1 would suggest that the conditions expected to prompt idea formulation and willingness to share also should interact to affect idea availability. For example, creative ideas should be presented to the organization when conditions expected to prompt idea development (such as well-designed jobs) are present simultaneously with conditions that prompt sharing (such as a safe climate). Currently, there is little empirical evidence to support these arguments, and research is needed to test all of the relevant interactions suggested by the model.

The chapter has suggested that creative ideas formulated by employees and made available to others in an organization provide the organization with new knowledge that can be applied and further developed. Work is now needed to examine the connection between the nature and scope of these creative ideas and their contributions to the organization's success and competitiveness. For example, are radical or incremental ideas most likely to be transferred to others and help the organization achieve sustained competitive advantage? Research is also needed on the circumstances in which ideas that are public and available to the organization are actually used and applied in the workplace. What are the managerial practices and systems that must be in place if the employees' creative ideas are to be implemented? Finally, I argued throughout this chapter that the new ideas might be beneficial to all organizations in all types of circumstances. But it may be that creative ideas are more critical to the success of some organizations than to others. For example, it may be that organizations in rapidly changing markets would benefit more from employees' creative ideas than organizations in more stable markets. Research is now needed to test this possibility as well.

References
Aiello, J. R., DeRisi, D. T., Epstein, Y. M., & Karlin, R. A. (1977). Crowding and the role of interpersonal distance preference. *Sociometry, 40,* 271–282.

Albrecht, T. L., & Hall, B. J. (1991). Facilitating talk about new ideas: The role of personal relationships in organizational innovation. *Communication Monographs, 58,* 273–288.

Amabile, T. M. (1979). Effects of external evaluation on artistic creativity. *Journal of Personality and Social Psychology, 37,* 221–233.

Amabile, T. M. (1996). *Creativity in context.* Boulder, CO: Westview Press.

Amabile, T. M., Conti, R., Coon, H., Lazenby, J., & Herron, M. (1996). Assessing the work environment for creativity. *Academy of Management Journal, 39,* 1154–1184.

Amabile, T. M., & Gyrskiewicz, S. S. (1987). *Creativity in the R&D laboratory* (Technical Report No. 30). Greensboro, NC: Center for Creative Leadership.

Axtell, C. M., Holman, D. J., Unsworth, K. L., Wall, T. D., Waterson, P. E., & Harrington, E. (2000). Shopfloor innovation: Facilitating the suggestion and implementation of ideas. *Journal of Occupation and Organizational Psychology, 73,* 265–285.

Bandura, A. (1986). *Social foundations of thought and action.* Englewood Cliffs, NJ: Prentice Hall.

Barron, F. B., & Harrington, D. M. (1981). Creativity, intelligence, and personality. *Annual Review of Psychology, 32,* 439–476.

Basadur, M., Graen, G., & Scandura, T. (1986). Training effects on attitudes toward divergent thinking among manufacturing engineers. *Journal of Applied Psychology, 71,* 612–617.

Baum, A., & Valins, S. (1977). *Architecture and social behavior: Psychological studies of social density.* Hillsdale, NJ: Erlbaum.

Brown, V., & Paulus, P. B. (1996). A simple dynamic model of social factors in group brainstorming. *Small Group Research, 27,* 91–114.

Bruins, J., & Barber, A. (2000). Crowding, performance, and affect: A field experiment investigating mediational processes. *Journal of Applied Social Psychology, 30,* 1268–1280.

Chan, C.-J., & Margolin, G. (1994). The relationship between dual-earner couples' daily work mood and home affect. *Journal of Social and Personal Relationships, 11,* 573–586.

Cummings, A., & Oldham, G. R. (1997). Enhancing creativity: Managing work contexts for the high potential employee. *California Management Review, 40,* 22–38.

Deci, E. L., & Ryan, R. M. (1985). *Intrinsic motivation and self-determination in human behavior.* New York: Plenum.

Edmondson, A. (1999). Psychological safety and learning behavior in work teams. *Administrative Science Quarterly, 44,* 350–383.

Eisenberger, R., & Selbst, M. (1994). Does reward increase or decrease creativity? *Journal of Personality and Social Psychology, 66,* 1116–1127.

Feist, G. J. (1998). A meta-analysis of personality in scientific and artistic creativity. *Personality and Social Psychology Review, 2,* 290–309.

Feist, G. J. (1999). The influence of personality on artistic and scientific creativity. In R. Sternberg (Ed.), *Handbook of creativity* (pp. 273–296). New York: Cambridge University Press.

Frese, M., Teng, E., & Wijnen, C.J.D. (1999). Helping to improve suggestion systems: Predictors of making suggestions in companies. *Journal of Organizational Behavior, 20,* 1139–1155.

Fusilier, M. R, Ganster, D. C., & Mayes, B. T. (1986). The social support and health relationship: Is there a gender difference? *Journal of Occupational Psychology, 59,* 145–153.

George, J. M., & Brief, A. P. (1992). Feeling good, doing good: A conceptual analysis of the mood at work-organizational spontaneity relationship. *Psychological Bulletin, 112,* 310–329.

George, J. M., & Zhou, J. (2001). When openness to experience and conscientiousness are related to creative behavior: An interactional approach. *Journal of Applied Psychology, 86,* 513–524.

Gough, H. G. (1979). A creative personality scale for the Adjective Check List. *Journal of Personality and Social Psychology, 37,* 1398–1405.

Grant, R. M. (1996). Toward a knowledge-based theory of the firm. *Strategic Management Journal, 17,* 109–122.

Hackman, J. R., & Oldham, G. R. (1980). *Work redesign.* Reading, MA: Addison-Wesley.

Haidt, J., & Rodin, J. (1999). Control and efficacy as interdisciplinary bridges. *Review of General Psychology, 3,* 317–337.

Halpin, G., Payne, D. A., & Ellett, C. D. (1973). Biographical correlates of the creative personality: Gifted adolescents. *Exceptional Children, 39,* 652–653.

Harrington, D. M., Block, J. H., & Block, J. (1987). Testing aspects of Carl Rogers' theory of creative environments: Child-rearing antecedents of creative potential in young adolescents. *Journal of Personality and Social Psychology, 52,* 851–856.

Hatcher, L., Ross, T. L., & Collins, D. (1989). Prosocial behavior, job complexity, and suggestion contribution under gainsharing plans. *Journal of Applied Behavioral Science, 25,* 231–248.

Isen, A. M. (1999). On the relationship between affect and creative problem solving. In S. Russ (Ed.), *Affect, creative experience, and psychological adjustment.* New York: Brunner/Mazel.

Isen, A. M., & Geva, N. (1987). The influence of positive affect on acceptable level of risk: The person with a large canoe has a large worry. *Organizational Behavior and Human Decision Processes, 39,* 145–154.

Isen, A. M., Johnson, M.M.S., Mertz, E., & Robinson, G. F. (1985). The influence of positive affect on the unusualness of word associations. *Journal of Personality and Social Psychology, 48,* 1413–1426.

Isen, A. M., & Patrick, R. (1983). The effect of positive feelings on risk taking: When the chips are down. *Organizational Behavior and Human Decision Processes, 31,* 194–202.

Jackson, S. E., & Schuler, R. S. (2001). Managing individual performance: A strategic perspective. In S. Sonnentag (Ed.), *Psychological manage-*

ment of individual performance: A handbook in the psychology of management in organizations. New York: Wiley.

James, K. (1995). Goal conflict and originality of thinking. *Creativity Research Journal, 8,* 285–290.

Kahn, W. A. (1990). Psychological conditions of personal engagement and disengagement at work. *Academy of Management Journal, 33,* 692–724.

Kaufmann, G., & Vosburg, S. K. (1997). "Paradoxical" mood effects on creative problem-solving. *Cognition and Emotion, 11,* 151–170.

Lawler, E. E. (1986). *High-involvement management.* San Francisco: Jossey-Bass.

MacKinnon, D. W. (1962). The nature and nurture of creative talent. *American Psychologist, 17,* 484–495.

Madjar, N., & Oldham, G. R. (2002). Preliminary tasks and creative performance on a subsequent task: Effects of time on preliminary tasks and amount of information about the subsequent task. *Creativity Research Journal, 14,* 239–251.

Madjar, N., Oldham, G. R., & Pratt, M. G. (2002). There's no place like home? The contributions of work and non-work sources of creativity support to employees' creative performance. *Academy of Management Journal, 45,* 757–767.

McCrae, R. R. (1987). Creativity, divergent thinking, and openness to experience. *Journal of Personality and Social Psychology, 52,* 1258–1265.

McCrae, R. R. (1996). Social consequences of experiential openness. *Psychological Bulletin, 120,* 323–337.

Meyer, J., & Allen, N. (1997). *Commitment in the workplace.* Thousand Oaks, CA: Sage.

Nagar, D., & Pandey, J. (1987). Affect and performance on cognitive task as a function of crowding and noise. *Journal of Applied Social Psychology, 17,* 147–157.

Nogami, G. Y. (1976). Crowding: Effects of group size, room size, or density? *Journal of Applied Social Psychology, 6,* 105–125.

Nonaka, I. (1991). The knowledge-creating company. *Harvard Business Review, 69,* 96–104.

Nonaka, I., & Takeuchi, H. (1995). *The knowledge-creating company.* New York: Oxford University Press.

Oldham, G. R., & Cummings, A. (1996). Employee creativity: Personal and contextual factors at work. *Academy of Management Journal, 39,* 607–634.

Oldham, G. R., & Cummings, A. (1998). Creativity in the organizational context. *Productivity, 39,* 187–194.

Paulus, P. B. (1988). *Prison crowding: A psychological perspective.* New York: Springer-Verlag.

Ramus, C. A. (2001). Organizational support for employees: Encouraging creative ideas for environmental sustainability. *California Management Review, 43,* 85–105.

Ray, E. B., & Miller, K. I. (1994). Social support, home/work stress, and burnout: Who can help? *Journal of Applied Behavioral Science, 30,* 357–373.

Redmond, M. R., Mumford, M. D., & Teach, R. (1993). Putting creativity to work: Effects of leader behavior on subordinate creativity. *Organizational Behavior and Human Decision Processes, 55,* 120–151.

Rodin, J., & Langer, E. J. (1977). Long-term effects of a control-relevant intervention with the institutionalized aged. *Journal of Personality and Social Psychology, 35,* 897–902.

Saavedra, R., & Kwun, S. K. (2000). Affective states in job characteristics theory. *Journal of Organizational Behavior, 21,* 131–146.

Scott, S. G., & Bruce, R. A. (1994). Determinants of innovative behavior: A path model of individual innovation in the workplace. *Academy of Management Journal, 37,* 580–607.

Shalley, C. E. (1991). Effects of productivity goals, creativity goals, and personal discretion on individual creativity. *Journal of Applied Psychology, 76,* 179–185.

Shalley, C. E., & Oldham, G. R. (1997). Competition and creative performance: Effects of competitor presence and visibility. *Creativity Research Journal, 10,* 337–345.

Shalley, C. E., & Perry-Smith, J. P. (2001). Effects of social-psychological factors on creative performance: The role of information and controlling expected evaluation and modeling experience. *Organizational Behavior and Human Decision Processes, 84,* 1–22.

Soriano de Alencar, E. M., & Bruno-Faria, M. F. (1997). Characteristics of an organizational environment which stimulate and inhibit creativity. *Journal of Creative Behavior, 31,* 271–281.

Sosik, J., Kahai, S., & Avolio, B. (1998). Transformational leadership and dimensions of creativity: Motivating idea generation in computer-mediated groups. *Creativity Research Journal, 11,* 111–121.

Sternberg, R. J., & Lubart, T. (1996). Investing in creativity. *American Psychologist, 51,* 677–688.

Tesluk, P. E., Farr, J. L., & Klein, S. R. (1997). Influences of organizational culture and climate on individual creativity. *Journal of Creative Behavior, 31,* 27–41.

Tierney, P., Farmer, S., & Graen, G. (1999). An examination of leadership and employee creativity: The relevance of traits and relationships. *Personnel Psychology, 52,* 591–620.

Tornow, W., & London, M. (1998). *Maximizing the value of 360-degree feedback*. San Francisco: Jossey-Bass.

Vosburg, S. K. (1998). The effects of positive and negative mood on divergent-thinking performance. *Creativity Research Journal, 11,* 165–172.

Walberg, H. J., Rasher, S. P., & Parkerson, J. (1980). Childhood and eminence. *Journal of Creative Behavior, 13,* 225–231.

West, M. A. (1990). The social psychology of innovation in groups. In M. West & J. Farr (Eds.), *Innovation and creativity at work* (pp. 309–333). New York: Wiley.

West, M. A., & Anderson, N. R. (1996). Innovation in top management teams. *Journal of Applied Psychology, 81,* 680–693.

Williams, W. M., & Yang, L. T. (1999). Organizational creativity. In R. Sternberg (Ed.), *Handbook of creativity* (pp. 373–391). New York: Cambridge University Press.

Woodman, R. W., Sawyer, J. E., & Griffin, R. W. (1993). Toward a theory of organizational creativity. *Academy of Management Review, 18,* 293–321.

Zhou, J. (1998). Feedback valence, feedback style, task autonomy, and achievement orientation: Interactive effects on creative performance. *Journal of Applied Psychology, 83,* 261–276.

Zhou, J., & George, J. M. (2001). When job dissatisfaction leads to creativity: Encouraging the expression of voice. *Academy of Management Journal, 44,* 682–696.

Zhou, J., & Oldham, G. R. (2001). Enhancing creative performance: Effects of expected developmental assessment strategies and creative personality. *Journal of Creative Behavior, 35,* 151–167.

CHAPTER 10

Reward Systems in Knowledge-Based Organizations

Edward E. Lawler III

A number of forces have converged to create a world in which many of the traditional sources of competitive advantage no longer are effective. Physical location, natural resources, financial capital, and plant and equipment have faded as sources of sustainable competitive advantage. More and more, competitive advantage is about knowledge and the ability to use it to develop and improve products and services (Hitt, Keats, & DeMarie, 1998). Many traditional sources of competitive advantage have become relatively easy to obtain, and management systems have been developed that allow many of them—for example, financial capital—to be managed effectively. As a result, they are not difference-makers. The same cannot be said of knowledge. How to acquire it, manage it, move it, and use it remain important areas for learning, improvement, and potential advantage (Barney, 1991, 2001).

Traditional organizations were not designed with an eye to knowledge management. They were designed to be effective bureaucracies that controlled and managed products and services through hierarchical systems and structures. The reward systems in these organizations were designed and structured to support this organizational logic. They rewarded employees for the size of their job, the length of their service, and their individual performance. In the case of many hierarchically structured organizations today, this approach is quite appropriate. Because individuals have carefully defined and designed permanent jobs, seniority helps them to become experts in what they do. Since work is designed so that they perform discrete individual tasks, rewarding them for job size and individual performance is consistent with the design and structure of the organization. Usually, this type of reward system produces relatively little risk-taking behavior and little support for experimentation, knowledge development, and knowledge sharing (Lawler, 2000). When knowledge is not a critical source of competitive advantage, this may not be a negative, and indeed may contribute to organizational effectiveness (Gerhart, 2000). In a relatively stable hardwired world, predictability and little risk taking often provide a competitive advantage, not a disadvantage.

Knowledge-based approaches to competitive advantage require organizational behavior that is very different. They need behavior that develops new knowledge, transmits knowledge, and uses knowledge to develop and improve products and services. Creating a knowledge-based organization inevitably means increasing the focus on human capital. Other chapters in this book look at various dimensions of human capital in knowledge-based approaches to organizing. They make the point that it is important to attract and retain the best human capital. Indeed, elsewhere I have argued that we now are in the "era of human capital" and that in knowledge-based organizations human capital has a tremendous impact on organizational performance (Lawler, 2001). Often a truly outstanding individual can make an enormous difference in the financial performance of an organization because he or she is able to develop a breakthrough product or get a product to market faster (Davenport & Prusak, 1998; Lawler, 2000).

In knowledge-based organizations, human capital management systems can have a very strong impact on organizational performance. They must attract and retain the right human capital and motivate employees to develop their skills and knowledge and perform in ways that contribute to organizational effectiveness. This is where the reward system comes into play. In knowledge-based organizations the reward system needs to attract and retain individuals with the right knowledge, motivate them to learn what is critical to their organization's competitive position, and motivate them to develop and use knowledge in ways that create competitive advantage.

Motivation, satisfaction, attraction, and retention have been researched by psychologists for over a century. This research has produced a number of findings that suggest how workers are affected by rewards (Lawler & Jenkins, 1992). Although knowledge workers may be different in degree when it comes to the causes of their behavior, there is no reason to believe they are different in kind from other workers. They may, for example, value personal growth and development more than production workers do. However, the motivation principles concerning the relationship between amount of reward and satisfaction are still valid, as are those concerned with how motivation is affected by the relationship between rewards and performance. Thus, in discussing reward systems for knowledge work organizations I will draw on the extensive literature of how rewards affect organizational behavior.

I will first consider the issues of base pay and market pricing. Here the focus will be on the issues involved in paying the job versus paying individuals for their knowledge and skills. I will then consider issues that arise in paying for performance in knowledge-based organizations.

Paying the Job or the Person

The distribution of financial and status rewards in most organizations is largely based on the types of jobs people do. Indeed, with the exception of bonuses and merit salary increases, the standard policy in most organizations is to evaluate the job rather than the person and then set the reward level (Milkovich & Newman, 1996). This policy is based on the assumption that job worth can be determined and that the person doing the job is worth only as much to the organization as the job itself. This assumption is valid at least in part in many situations because, with the use of techniques such as job evaluation, it is possible to determine what other organizations are paying people in the same or similar jobs. But it is not clear that the worth of all or even most individuals can be equated to the worth of their jobs, particularly when they are doing knowledge work (Lawler, 2000).

The dangers of focusing on jobs as the basic building blocks of an organization's management systems are particularly apparent when the issue is determining how much to pay individuals (Lawler,

1994). People have a market value, jobs do not. Jobs are simply microstructures in a bureaucratic framework that can be used to estimate the market value of individuals. One reason why individuals leave organizations is because with their skills, knowledge, and human capital, they can earn higher pay elsewhere. Therefore, the key compensation issue in knowledge work organizations concerns what an individual is worth, not what a job is worth. More research is needed to determine conclusively how to price individuals in the market, but at this point it appears that this is done best by focusing on their skills and competencies (Lawler, 2000). Competency systems, in particular, are becoming more popular, and as a result organizations may be able to utilize survey data on competency-based salaries.

Job-based compensation programs often have the wrong impact on development. It is precisely because organizations pay individuals based on job size that they try to move up into bigger and bigger jobs. Virtually every job-based pay system rewards moving to a higher-level job but does not reward lateral moves and other experiences that lead to cross-functional learning or how to do one's present job better. Thus, job-based reward systems often result in individuals developing in ways that are optimal for organizational effectiveness if the organization needs more managers and hierarchy. But they do not lead to optimal development if the organization is flat, wants to operate with lateral teams, does not need more managers, or needs to develop technical experts.

Hierarchical reward systems can also work against individuals sharing their knowledge with others and using the good ideas of others. Because these systems foster a competitive culture, developing others and sharing knowledge is often seen as helping out a competitor. Similarly, using someone else's idea is seen as admitting that a competitor had a good idea.

An alternative to job-based pay that has been adopted by a number of organizations is to pay people based on their skills and competencies (Gerhart, 2000; Lawler, Mohrman, & Benson, 2001). This does not necessarily produce pay rates that are dramatically different from those produced by paying for the nature of the job. The skills people have usually match reasonably well with the jobs they are doing. Skill-based pay can, however, result in some employees being paid more than they would have been under a job-based system, or the reverse. Sometimes employees do not have the skills they need to do their job and therefore do not deserve the kind of pay that goes with it; in such instances they are paid less than they would be under a job-based system.

In many respects the skill-based approach fits better with the assumption that an organization's capabilities and competencies rest in its human capital. When individuals are the basic value-added component, they are key to organizational effectiveness, and so it makes sense to focus the reward system on them. Focusing on jobs rather than on individuals may sacrifice effectiveness for efficiency. Precisely because there are important individual differences, a system that tries to deal with a large number of people in a similar way simply because they are doing similar work cannot be the most effective. Most people will end up being treated suboptimally in the area of pay, skill development, or retention. This has to have negative repercussions for an organization that depends heavily on its human capital.

Perhaps the most important effect of person-based pay occurs in the kind of culture and motivation the system produces. Instead of being rewarded for moving up the hierarchy, people are rewarded for increasing their skills and developing themselves. Competition is reduced because individuals can increase their pay level without being promoted. Little research is available on the cultural impact of person-based pay, but it seems likely it will create a culture of concern for personal growth and development and a highly talented workforce—critical ingredients in establishing competitive advantage in knowledge-based organizations.

Skill-based pay has been used frequently in new plant start-ups and in plants that are moving toward high-involvement, team-based management (Lawler, 1996). In factories where skill-based pay has been used, it usually means that most employees can perform multiple tasks, that the workforce is knowledgeable and flexible (Jenkins, Ledford, Gupta, & Doty, 1992). Flexibility often means that less staff is needed. Absenteeism and turnover are reduced as well because people like having the opportunity to develop, use, and be paid for a wide range of skills. Skill-based pay can be challenging to administer, however, because often it is not clear how to assess the pay marketplace and determine how much a skill is worth. Skill assessment also can be difficult to do well. Consequently, the potential exists for internal equity problems and for adverse impact claims.

In knowledge work organizations where individuals are constantly assigned and reassigned to projects and tasks, skill-based plans that reward individuals for developing multiple skills are likely to be particularly effective. This is especially true if knowledge workers are asked to do a considerable amount of lateral process integration and self-management in order for the organization to operate effectively without extensive overhead and management costs.

A key management task in project-based organizations—professional service firms, for example—is to match individuals to the projects that need to be performed at a particular time. These organizations must operate like a giant matrix of individuals and tasks, with skills being matched to a constantly changing mix of work. Given the dynamic nature of projects, making this match often requires that a number of individuals have multiple skills because it is impossible to predict exactly what mix of skills will be needed at any given time.

In multiple-skill situations some employees may not directly use all of their skills all the time, but having them remains a critical asset for the organization. Such employees are flexible and so can be assigned to a variety of different projects; in addition, often they are better at managing and doing a particular project because they have skills that allow them to put the task they are performing into a larger perspective (Mohrman, Cohen, & Mohrman, 1995). This may increase their ability to self-manage, develop new knowledge, and solve problems, but there is little research evidence on just how much it improves their performance. In addition, individuals may not have all their time assigned to any one project. If they have multiple skills, they can work on several projects at once, projects that use the same or somewhat different skills.

Increasingly, organizations are choosing to use competency models to determine how much to pay their employees (Lawler et al., 2001). Doing this requires converting competencies into measurable characteristics that allow for the reliable and valid determination of pay rates. This is where many of the competency models fall short. A number of organizations use poorly defined, generic competencies (Zingheim, Ledford, & Schuster, 1996).

According to Spencer and Spencer (1993), the authors of an influential book on competencies, a competency is an underlying characteristic that makes an individual's performance effective and superior. They add that *underlying characteristic* means that the competency is a fairly deep and enduring part of a person's personality. They provide a dictionary of competencies that includes leadership, adaptability, innovation, team orientation, communication, customer focus, achievement orientation, and flexibility. For each of these competencies, they provide scales that describe their different levels. They also present an iceberg model that shows competencies as below the water line, and consequently hard to see and measure. Knowledge and skills are depicted as above the surface and therefore more easily measured.

Spencer and Spencer mention that individuals should be rewarded for the development of competencies. This raises obvious questions. If organizational effectiveness is about task performance, why try to measure and reward competencies that are below the surface and therefore difficult to measure and relate to the organization's core competencies and organizational capabilities? Is it not more effective for pay purposes to focus on what is most easily measurable and directly related to organizational effectiveness—knowledge, skills, and task performance?

Skill-based pay plans work best when they are linked to an individual's ability to perform a particular task and when good measures are available of how well that individual can perform a task (Jenkins et al., 1992). Once a person has performed a job, his or her task-related skills and knowledge can be determined and measured. Knowledge and skills, not underlying competencies, are the most useful basis for setting pay because they most directly determine what work individuals can do and will do well, and this, of course, is the key determinant of their value to their organization and their market value. This point is particularly true in the case of knowledge work organizations and knowledge workers.

Most person-based pay systems for managers and professionals start with the premise that there are tremendous gains to be had from paying the person rather than the job. Gains are said to include a better strategic focus and competitive advantages that come from superior organizational capabilities and competencies. It is hard to disagree with this argument, but there is little research to support it. We need research to determine which characteristics of individuals should be focused on to determine their market value and their organizational value. We also need research that looks at the impact that paying the person has on creating new knowledge and insights into how organizational effectiveness can be increased. One guess is that such pay systems may lead to both more explicit and more implicit knowledge. Finally, research is needed on the pay equity issues involved in paying the person.

Rewarding Performance

The potential benefits to organizations of rewarding performance are many. They include motivating employees to perform better, increasing the retention of effective employees and decreasing the retention of ineffective employees, and creating a culture that values performance. These are clearly outcomes that any knowledge-based organization would like to achieve and indeed may need to achieve in order to be competitive.

Unfortunately, it is one thing to state the potential advantages of effectively rewarding performance and quite another to achieve those advantages by doing so (Lawler, 1990). This is true whether the work to be done is knowledge work or more traditional production and service work. It is also true that it is somewhat more difficult to reward performance in knowledge work settings. In order to reward performance, organizations need to be able to measure it in a reliable, valid, and credible manner (Lawler, 1971). In simple assembly and production jobs this is not easy to do, but it is easier than in most knowledge work situations. In many knowledge work situations, it is difficult to specify what the product is and which individuals are responsible for producing it. Further, in knowledge work situations many behaviors that are important to creating knowledge, using intellectual capital, and transferring both explicit and implicit knowledge are difficult to measure and therefore to reward.

Because of the variety of types of knowledge work, it is likely that no single performance reward system will be universally appropriate or effective. In some cases it may make sense to reward individuals for their performance, whereas in others measuring individual performance may be so difficult that it is impossible to single out and specially reward particular individuals. A brief review of the main approaches to measuring and rewarding performance follows. It will focus on the strengths and weaknesses of the different approaches, and of course, on their applicability to knowledge work.

Rewarding Individual Performance

The key to using rewards as motivators is the perceived connection between the behavior of individuals and their receiving rewards they value. With individual pay for performance it often is possible to establish a clear connection, or line of sight, between performance and rewards (Bartol & Locke, 2000; Lawler, 1971). At least in theory, how well people are rewarded can be put completely under their control. Thus, with an effective individual pay-for-performance system, it is possible to create a highly motivated workforce because employees see a close relationship between how well they perform and how much they are paid (Jenkins, Mitra, Gupta, & Shaw, 1998). It is also possible to tailor the rewards offered to the preferences and motives of individuals. If one person is particularly motivated by large cash payments, they can be offered; if another is particularly motivated by a vacation to Hawaii, that can be offered. Admittedly, tailoring rewards to individual preferences can get complicated, but it can also ensure that the rewards offered are powerful incentives for those who receive them.

Individual pay for performance can have an extremely positive effect on the retention of excellent employees. Paying outstanding performers well enough to retain them requires either paying everybody a high wage—hardly a financially wise thing to do—or identifying the best performers and being sure they are well compensated (Lawler & Jenkins, 1992). Individual pay-for-performance programs can take the latter approach. They can create the possibility of giving significantly higher rewards to good performers; this in turn can ensure that high performers are at or above market, whereas poor performers are at or below market. Thus, an effective individual pay-for-performance system can also help to remove poor performers from an organization. When pay is effectively tied to performance, the result can be a reduction in the pay of poor performers until they cannot afford to remain as employees. The key is having enough pay dependent on performance so that poor performers end up under the market. Just this frequently happens in commissioned sales work.

The thousands of different ways to pay for individual performance can be divided into two general types: merit pay increases based on individual performance, and onetime payments or bonuses for accomplishing a particular objective or reaching a particular performance level. These two approaches have been extensively studied and have very different effects, so it is important to consider them separately and to reach some conclusions about how applicable each one is to knowledge work.

Requirements for an Effective System

The research literature clearly indicates what it takes for individual pay-for-performance systems to be effective (Lawler, 1990). Essentially, comprehensive measures of individual performance need to be developed, standard levels of performance established, and a pay system developed that clearly ties pay to how the performance of individuals compares with performance standards. Stated this way it sounds simple to do, but often it is not.

Basic to the measurement of individual performance is the existence of identifiable, regularly assigned work activities. In other words, an employee needs to have a well-defined job. As noted earlier, this is often the situation in a traditionally managed and designed organization. Elaborate job descriptions can be developed that describe in great detail the activities that individuals are supposed to perform; indeed, when they are well done, they often specify what the outcomes of these activities should be and how they can be measured.

In pay-for-performance programs it is particularly critical that all key elements of performance be measured. Things that get measured and rewarded get attention; those that do not get ignored (Kerr, 1975). This point is particularly appropriate when knowledge work is involved because things like sharing knowledge are often hard to measure, yet research indicates that whether or not it is rewarded has a significant influence on how much of it occurs (Lawler et al., 2001).

Identifying and developing good measures of individual performance can be an extremely difficult and challenging process. It is difficult because it means translating an overall business strategy into measures that capture what each person should be doing in order for the business to accomplish its strategic goals. Large organizations must take their corporate strategies and translate them into measures for thousands and thousands of individuals. Unless this is done well, it can mean that employees are motivated to behave in the wrong ways with respect to the strategic agenda of the business (Kerr, 1975).

In addition to being strategically aligned, performance measures and standards need to be sufficiently objective and credible so that employees feel they are being measured fairly. If they do not perceive the measures to be fair and valid, they will have little hope that good performance will lead to rewards, and as a result, little motivation. Here too knowledge work presents a particularly difficult challenge because its outcomes may be difficult to specify in advance and hard to quantify.

Valid measurement of individual performance is feasible only when the work that individuals do is relatively independent. Independent work allows for the direct measurement of an individual's productivity without having to be concerned with the complexities of what he is responsible for and what other people are responsible for in the production of a product or delivery of a service. When the work of individuals is highly interdependent, it is often difficult to sort out who is responsible for what; as a result, measuring the performance of each individual becomes difficult or impossible.

Individual performance measurement is particularly difficult when individuals work in teams, as they often do in knowledge work organizations (Lawler et al., 2001). Teamwork requires great cooperation and mutual support, so that the impact of individual performance on output can be difficult to establish and measure (Mohrman et al., 1995). Often cooperation and teamwork can only be measured by members of the group and in a subjective manner. Finally, in many organizations that do knowledge work, individuals are on several teams, and as a result it is difficult to identify individual accountabilities and responsibilities during a particular time period.

Merit Pay

The most popular form of individual pay for performance is merit pay. Performance measurement is perhaps the most obvious and most frequently cited problem with merit pay. Often, adequate measures of individual performance do not exist, so valid performance judgments cannot be made. Organizations usually rely on supervisors to sort out how well individuals perform and determine what their pay should be. The hope is that supervisors can disentangle the effects of job content changes, the actions of others, luck, and their own likes and dislikes to make accurate and valid judgments of how well individuals have performed during a period of time. This hope is rarely realized (Smithers, 1998). Managers bring their own biases and information-processing problems to the task of performance appraisal, and so the appraisals are often flawed. Instead of creating sense out of a very complex situation, they add to the confusion and complexity of identifying and accurately measuring individual performance.

It is possible to create performance management systems that can help supervisors do a reasonably good job of evaluating individual performance. But this can only occur when the right work structures and measurement tools are available and supervisors are trained and required to do good job performance evaluations (Lawler, 2000). Often when merit pay is used, these conditions do not exist. As a result the supervisor evaluations of performance that form the basis for the merit pay actions are full of errors and bias. Thus, they are an extremely poor foundation on which to base pay for performance.

The challenges involved in operating an effective merit pay system do not end with finding good performance measurers and measures. Even when they exist, merit pay may not be an effective motivator or retainer of excellent employees. There is a fundamental flaw in merit systems. Increases usually become a permanent part of an individual's pay—an entitlement or annuity that may not reflect current performance but performance over a number of years of organizational membership. This is not an enormous problem if an individual's performance is stable from year to year. For some individuals it is, but performance often varies considerably over a person's working life. This is particularly likely to be true in knowledge work settings where technologies change and knowledge becomes obsolete.

The annuity problems with merit increases are closely related to a second big problem with pay delivery in merit pay systems: the size effect. There is no ultimate scientific answer to how large a pay change needs to be in order to be a significant motivator of performance

(Worley, Bowen, & Lawler, 1992; Mitra, Gupta, & Jenkins, 1997). Sometimes very small increases can be powerful motivators if they are seen as a form of recognition and accomplishment. That said, a good guess is that in order to be meaningful from a financial and lifestyle point of view, merit pay increases must reach at least the 5 percent level and may need to exceed 10 percent in order to be truly motivating and energizing. A large pay increase may be particularly needed to motivate knowledge workers if, as is often speculated, they are concerned with many things in addition to how much they are paid.

In low-inflation environments, pay increase budgets of even 5 percent are difficult to justify. Indeed, during the 1990s pay increase budgets in the United States averaged around 4 percent. This meant that the very best performers were getting perhaps 6 or 7 percent increases, whereas average performers were getting 3 to 4 percent. The difference between 4 percent and 6 percent is not the kind of difference that is likely to produce a great motivation based on the desire to earn more money. Of course, a recognition factor may come into play, so that individuals who get the highest raises feel significantly rewarded simply because they are told that they are top performers and have been given the top raise.

Incentive Pay
There are a variety of approaches to rewarding individual performance with onetime payments or bonuses. Without question, the two most popular are piecework and sales incentive or commission plans. Both pay individuals a prescribed amount for each unit of work they do. Under some conditions these plans can be quite successful. The problems with them are in some ways the opposite of those with merit pay—that is, they frequently become too-powerful motivators of what is rewarded and measured. A company may get more of the behavior it rewards, but less than it wants of the things it does not reward. Not surprisingly, there is evidence that when these plans are in place, individuals develop knowledge about how to "beat" the system and rarely share knowledge about how to improve performance (Whyte, 1955).

Individual incentive plans focus on establishing a clear line of sight between a particular kind of performance and a significant amount of money. This often happens when incentive plans are applied to jobs that involve independent work that can be measured accurately and when the plans make a onetime variable payment. The use of onetime payments is critical because it means that large amounts of money can be paid without creating an annuity effect. Effective incentive plans require not only good measures but also performance standards and specification of payment amounts for performance at different levels. This is often impossible to do with knowledge work, and as a result these plans generally are not effective in knowledge work settings.

An increasingly popular form of variable pay uses the results of a performance appraisal to determine the amount of the bonus paid to individuals. In essence, this approach can eliminate one of the biggest failings of merit pay: not enough money being available to motivate individuals. It does this by eliminating the annuity feature of merit pay, thus freeing up dollars to be used for variable pay. Often, bonus plans are installed in organizations by gradually decreasing the merit budget and increasing the amount of money paid out in variable bonuses to individuals. With a discretionary bonus-pay approach, changes in base pay usually result from promotions or perhaps from changes in the value of jobs in the marketplace. In the case of person-based pay, they can come from changes in the person's skills, knowledge, and competencies. Rewards for performance are given strictly in terms of a variable bonus amount. The amount of bonus pay is often relatively small for lower-level jobs (5 to 10 percent) but can be 100 percent or more of salaries for higher-level management and key technical jobs.

A bonus-pay approach can be an effective way to reward individual excellence as well as to retain excellent performers. It is particularly effective in retaining new employees because they can almost immediately obtain a high pay level, a critical issue in the case of knowledge workers whose skills are hard to come by. It also makes it possible to reduce the total compensation of poor performers quickly. Finally, it can make very clear the relationship between a performance appraisal and the amount of pay.

Bonus pay may be the most effective way to reward contract employees. Often, short-term employees are not interested in the success of the organization or in other organizational rewards. As a result, they are difficult to motivate. One possible solution is to offer them short-term cash incentives. This may be particularly effective when knowledge workers are employed to produce a well-specified product with a clear deadline.

What the bonus approach does not do is ensure that supervisors do a good job of judging the performance of their subordinates, which is essential for this approach to be effective. Indeed, if performance is not appraised accurately, the approach may be much more destructive than merit pay because the appraisal makes such an important difference in how much people are paid. Thus, it puts a great deal of pressure on what is often the weakest link in many companies' reward system: the appraisal. Some of the problems with appraisal systems are unsolvable; others are simply caused by organizations not doing what the large amount of research on performance management suggests they need to do to create an effective system (Smithers, 1998). For example, many systems lack well-developed behavioral measures, do not properly train the participants, and are not clear about how the results will be used.

Rewarding Teams

There are a number of different ways to reward performance when work teams are involved. One is to reward the individual team members for their performance. A second is to reward the teams for their performance. A third is to reward team performance indirectly by rewarding organizational performance. Additional options can be created by using a combination of the first three.

Perhaps the most common way to reward the members of work teams in knowledge work settings is to appraise their individual performance. Instead of rewarding the team as a whole, organizations simply add a dimension to the performance appraisal of individuals that focuses on how good a team member they are. This usually counts toward their overall appraisal score and determines the amount of pay increase or bonus they get. In essence, it continues the individual pay-for-performance practices of most organizations but adapts them slightly to a team environment.

However, in several ways, rewarding individuals for being good team members creates conflicting motivations that can cancel each other out. This approach asks individuals to compete for a given amount of money but changes the basis of competition by including performance as a team member. In other words, individuals end up competing with other team members to be the most helpful, cooperative, best contributor. This keeps the performance focus on the individual rather than on the team and does little to get individuals to focus on how effectively their team is performing. The impact of this on behavior has not been well researched, but it seems unlikely to produce cohesive behavior (Sundstrom, 1999). Lack of cohesive team behavior can be a real problem in knowledge work situations where true group products are desired—for example, (software) programs, new technology products, and consulting reports (Mohrman et al., 1995).

The most powerful way to motivate team performance is to establish objectives and metrics for successful team performance and link rewards to team success. Performance pay in the form of salary increases or bonuses can then be distributed equally to team members based on the results of a team performance appraisal. In order for team performance pay to work, there must be clear and explicit objectives, accepted measures, and good feedback. Particularly when it comes to team dynamics and work methods, a good guess is that rewarding the team as a whole will lead to more knowledge development and sharing than will rewarding individuals.

A mature work team may be able to use a peer evaluation process to reward individuals for their contributions to the team's overall performance. The decision process is more likely to be effective if team members assess team performance before they assess individual performance so that team performance sets the framework for appraising individual performance (Mohrman et al., 1995). By having teams evaluate individuals and divide up a pool of money that originally was generated by the effectiveness of the team, individuals are rewarded for being cooperative in producing the bonus pool but still are primarily rewarded as individuals. This approach may be a good fit in knowledge work where team members have the knowledge and information to judge each other's performance and the work is not highly interdependent. However, further research is needed on how it affects the conflict level in teams and their cohesiveness.

A second way of linking pay to team performance is through the use of special reward and recognition programs. Unlike appraisals with goals and formula-driven approaches, these programs reward exceptional performance after it has occurred on an unscheduled basis. This approach fits well in situations where the output of a team is difficult to specify in advance because it is doing creative work. Although there is relatively little research on how effective these plans are, there is evidence that they are growing in popularity (Lawler et al., 2001).

The use of gainsharing, goal sharing, profit sharing, and stock plans will be discussed in the next section. They constitute the third major approach to providing rewards for team performance. They often suffer from a poor line of sight but can be effective in motivating team performance and may be the best choice if the work of two or more teams is highly interdependent. As a general rule, the greater the interdependence between work teams, the more pay-for-performance systems should be based on organizational performance (Lawler, 2000).

Organizational Rewards

The main advantage of pay plans that reward organizational performance is the ability to align individual rewards with the strategic performance of the business (Gerhart, 2000; Lawler, 2000). This alignment is often better and more easily created at the organizational level than at the team or individual level because there are fewer measurement problems at the organizational level. An organization's key strategic objectives usually can be and are translated into regularly collected corporate, financial, and operational measures. This creates the possibility of relating reward amounts directly to the degree to which organizational objectives are accomplished. With team and individual pay-for-performance plans, the organizational objectives often must be converted into appropriate behaviors at the individual and group levels and measures developed for them.

In many respects the main advantage of paying for organizational performance is also the main problem with it. It is often difficult for individuals to see how their behavior relates to measures of organizational performance, especially in large organizations and when complex financial measures are used. This is the other side of the coin with respect to paying individuals based on organizational goals and performance. Just as it is hard for managers to translate strategic goals into individual measures of performance, it is often difficult for individuals to see how their behavior directly affects whether the organization accomplishes its strategic objectives. Thus, they may not be motivated to share their knowledge or develop new knowledge in the right areas.

Because of their common impact throughout an organization, rewards for organizational performance can have a positive impact on the culture. They can help focus the organization on a common set of goals and create a sense of the importance of individuals supporting each other and working together. Again, there is some similarity here to the impact of team-based reward systems, but organizational reward systems have an impact on the total organization's culture.

Depending on how the rewards are paid out and how large they are, organizational reward systems can affect attraction and retention. They can have a positive effect on retention if individuals believe the plans will continue to pay off. They can be particularly effective in retention if they are paid out in ways that require continued organizational membership.

Because they reward a large number of people in a common manner, organizational pay-for-performance systems can have the effect of integrating an organization. They end up creating a common fate for the entire workforce, and this can have a positive effect on the degree to which people cooperate across a wide variety of functions and units. In this respect they are like team-based incentives but on a much larger scale. They are able to integrate teams, plants, and total organizations, not just groups. It is also possible that they may encourage knowledge sharing and the use of knowledge developed by others. There is some research evidence to support this in the work done on gainsharing plans.

Gainsharing Plans

The best-known gainsharing plan is the Scanlon plan. Much of its initial implementation occurred in the steel industry during the 1940s and 1950s. In the 1960s and 1970s it spread to a number of different types of manufacturing establishments and some nonmanufacturing locations. However, gainsharing plans usually do not focus on knowledge workers and are not used by organizations that primarily do knowledge work.

In order to create a meaningful line of sight, gainsharing plans tend to focus on organizational units of less than a thousand employees and measure performance outcomes that are controllable by the workforce. The most difficult issue with gainsharing plans involves maintaining their impact over time. As is true with other pay-for-performance plans, particularly critical is establishing the standard against which current performance is compared in order to calculate the bonus. Gainsharing plans emphasize the importance of basing it on past performance and keeping it the same unless there are big changes in products, technology, or capital investment. The rationale for this is simple and sensible: if the standard is raised every time employees improve performance, they will quickly lose their incentive to improve performance. They will realize that they are in fact working themselves out of an incentive every time they improve. In short, no good deed will go unpunished. Gainsharing advocates argue that as long as performance is above standard, both sides win; therefore, it is reasonable to continue to pay employees bonuses when their performance exceeds its historic level. It is hard to disagree with the rationale underlying the idea of a fixed historic standard—but it is difficult to apply to organizations that change rapidly. Thus, it often is difficult to apply in knowledge work organizations.

A number of studies have looked at the success of gainsharing plans. All report positive results. Typical of the findings is the conclusion that approximately 80 percent of the gainsharing plans in the United States have produced positive financial performance results and have lasted at least three to five years (Bullock & Lawler, 1984). Many of the gains come from individuals and teams suggesting work method improvements. Because of the incentive, new ideas are generally shared and used.

Gainsharing is not for every organization. It seems to fit best in relatively stable operations where medium- to small-size organizational units can be identified that have good performance measures. Stability is important because it makes setting a historic standard easier and makes it worthwhile to develop the sometimes complex and extensive measures that are part of the payout formula. Organizations also need to be willing to engage in at least some form of employee involvement that shares business information, educates employees in the economics of business, and encourages suggestions. It does not fit most rapidly changing knowledge work organizations, but because it can support knowledge development and sharing it may be appropriate for some of them.

Profit Sharing

Profit sharing is the oldest and most commonly used bonus-based approach to rewarding organizational performance. In 1999, 70 percent of Fortune 1000 companies operated profit-sharing plans. This represents virtually no change from the percentage that had profit-sharing plans in 1987 (Lawler et al., 2001).

Most profit-sharing plans use the publicly reported earnings of a company as the measure of performance that determines the size of the bonus payment made to organization members. Usually some minimum level of earnings has to be achieved in order for there to be a payout; earnings above this level fund a bonus pool that is divided among the eligible employees. In most profit-sharing plans not all employees are covered (Lawler et al., 2001). The payouts to employees may come in the form of a cash bonus, or they may fund a retirement account. They are usually paid out based on a percentage of an employee's salary. In some plans, individuals get different percentage amounts based on their performance.

Profit-sharing plans have a number of strengths and weaknesses. Perhaps their greatest weakness is their effect on employee motivation. In large and medium-size companies it is extremely difficult to establish a line of sight between employee behavior and corporate profitability (Lawler, 2000). As a result profit-sharing plans usually do not have a significant impact on individual or organizational performance (Lawler, 1990). Simplifying and taking out uncontrollable factors when measuring earnings can help, but this is not likely to make a significant difference in the line of sight of most employees. The one exception is very senior managers. They have more control over the reported earnings of the company, and their incentive opportunity is often much greater than it is for lower-level employees. Therefore, the incentive effect of profit sharing may be more significant for them.

Profit sharing, like any other variable pay plan, is not universally attractive to all employees. It introduces risk into an individual's compensation package and therefore is unlikely to be attractive to someone who cannot tolerate risk and who is suspicious of how large organizations operate and deal with their employees. Again, the fact that it is attractive only to some individuals may not be a problem. It may even be an advantage if it helps attract and retain the kind of employees who will fit an organization's culture.

Perhaps the main advantage of profit-sharing plans is their impact on an organization's culture and the way people think about the organization. When a profit-sharing plan covers most members of an organization, there is the potential for it to stimulate interest in the organization's financial results and to create a culture where attention is focused on performance. In other words, although profit sharing may not be terribly motivating in the sense of driving people to work harder, it may motivate them to pay attention to financial results and try to understand the business. This effect occurs because employees want to understand what their bonus is likely to be, where it comes from, and how it is computed. The effect on employees can be a better understanding of the organization and thus more knowledgeable and profit-focused decision-making behavior. Unfortunately, there is very little evidence showing the extent to which profit sharing has an effect on how knowledge is developed and used in organizations.

Stock Plans

Stock plans have become increasingly popular, and that trend is likely to continue. Today most organizations have some form of stock plan for their employees. In 1999, for example, 87 percent of the Fortune 1000 companies had stock option plans, most covering only senior executives (Lawler et al., 2001). Stock ownership can be a way to retain individuals, to motivate them, and to create a culture of ownership. Despite the ups and downs of the stock market, stock ownership plans have great appeal today because of the importance of human capital in knowledge work organizations, the creation of more high-performance organizations, the increased desire of the workforce to participate in the success of their company, and the favorable tax treatment these plans receive in the United States.

There are a variety of ways to reward employees with stock in their corporation. One way is simply to give it to them. A second is to allow them to buy stock at a substantially reduced price, either directly or in one or more retirement vehicles. Employees also can be granted stock options that give them the right to buy stock at a certain price. If the price of the stock at the time the option can be exercised is higher than the current exercise price, an employee has an incentive to buy the stock but little incentive to hold onto it once the purchase is completed. In fact there is good reason to believe that employees usually exercise their options as soon as they can (assuming the stock price is the above-option price) and immediately sell most or all of the stock they purchase.

Broad-based stock option plans are becoming much more popular, particularly in high-technology companies. Studies suggest that between 10 and 15 percent of all large corporations have broad-based stock option plans (Lawler et al., 2001). Virtually every technology company that is based in the United States has made liberal use of them for years in part because they seem to be particularly attractive to knowledge workers.

The effect of stock plans on motivation is likely to be slightly less than the effect of profit sharing because the line-of-sight problem is even more severe. Stock prices depend on more than just the somewhat-controllable financial performance of the company. They depend on how the stock market evaluates the earnings and the future of the company, and they depend on the economy. These factors are less controllable by the company than the company's earnings are. Thus, even for senior managers, the line of sight for the value of their company's stock may be muddled.

The strength of stock as a motivator comes from the amount of reward that can be earned. The amount that can be gained from stock programs as a result of improvement in an organization's stock price is virtually unlimited, while in many plans the risk is small. Thus, there is a real possibility that at the very senior levels of management in large companies where large stock option grants are common, they are an effective motivator. This is unlikely to be true for employees who have only a few hundred shares of stock and a much weaker line of sight.

Stock plans have the most negative impact when they make only senior executives wealthy. Surprisingly, there is little or no research on the impact of executives making hundreds of millions of dollars as a result of their stock option grants while the rest of the organization does not participate in the plans. An educated guess, however, is that this creates an enormous division between people at the top and everybody else in the workforce (Lawler, 1990). This gap can make it difficult for top-level managers to talk credibly about shared mission and importance of everyone working together to create a more effective organization. It also can lead executives to manipulate the books of corporations, as happened in the cases of Enron and Tyco.

Finally, some studies suggest that it is difficult for executives to work together in teams when they have dramatically different compensation amounts and pay structures (Bloom, 1999). This makes good sense, because the executives will not all be motivated to accomplish the same goals and objectives, and indeed there may be considerable resentment because of the different compensation levels.

Because stock options do not have to be exercised if the stock price of the company drops, they have a potentially different effect on their holders than direct stock ownership has. When employees and executives own stock in their company there is both an upside potential and a downside potential; with stock options there is only an upside. If the stock goes up, the employees can be big winners; if it goes down, they simply lose the opportunity to make extra money. In contrast, with stock ownership individuals can suffer significant losses on an ongoing basis; thus the problem of individuals not caring once their stock options are well under water (have no value) does not occur. Given this reality it is reasonable to assume that most employees and executives would rather receive stock options than stock, particularly if, as is often true, the stock they receive has to be held for a period of time.

The evidence on broad-based stock ownership as motivator is relatively clear. There is no reason to believe that in most large organizations the ownership of a relatively small number of shares is likely to drive employee behavior (Blasi, 1988; Blinder, 1990). Thus, although granting small numbers of shares to employees can be a rewarding event for employees and appreciated by them, it is unlikely to operate as an effective performance motivator. The same is true for employees owning stock in the company through their retirement plan or another vehicle. Stock tends to motivate only when the organization is relatively small and there is significant employee involvement in its operations. Relatively small size helps because it creates a sense that collective effort by employees can influence the performance of the company, and ultimately, the price of the stock. Involvement is crucial because it provides the understanding of and ability to influence organizational performance that must be in place for a line of site to exist. This is consistent with the line-of-sight argument as it applies to profit sharing and gainsharing.

The use of stock options and stock ownership is a particularly interesting issue in attraction and retention. Particularly in high-tech companies, it has become common to offer stock options when firms try to attract knowledge workers. In many ways this can create a win-win situation. When the stock market is performing well, there is good reason to believe that employees may value stock options at a level that is greater than their cost. Thus, it is very much in the interest of companies to offer stock options because it is a cheap way to attract employees. It is particularly cheap for companies in the United States to offer options because the accounting principles do not require companies to reduce their earnings as a result of making option grants. A growing number of companies, however, are doing just this.

Options are very attractive to employees because they can receive them and not pay taxes on them until they are exercised. Options can play an important role in retention because they often are not exercisable for several years after they are granted. Thus, if the stock performs well, individuals have strong incentive to stay until they can exercise their options. There is little research on how effective options are as a retention device, but my guess is that with knowledge workers they can be a powerful one. Clearly, options can be a win for the company and possibly a win for employees. Of course, their attractiveness and impact are substantially reduced by poor stock market performance.

Over time, both parties do have to pay for options. Employees have to pay taxes, and companies either have to buy stock and give it to employees or issue new stock and suffer a dilution of their equity capital because there are more shares outstanding. The latter issue is becoming a sticky one with investors. As companies have granted more and more options (some have issued options equal to over 25 percent of the stock that is held by investors), investors have become more and more concerned about the impact of options on their share of the equity in companies. Increasingly, investors are questioning and in some cases voting against the issuance of additional options and shares because they see too large a dilution of their ownership position. There also is growing pressure on companies to account for the cost of options when they are issued.

Overall, the impact of plans that give stock to most or all employees on the relationship between employees and companies is probably similar to the impact of profit-sharing plans. They do put employees who are on the plans in the same situation as investors and thus can create a positive alignment of interests among these two stakeholder groups. They also can encourage employees to learn more about the business and how the investment community looks at their company. However, because the impact of stock on the motivation of most members is relatively weak to nonexistent, the effect of stock ownership on an organization's performance is bound to be more indirect than direct.

Conclusion

Reward systems clearly can have an impact on how successful organizations are in developing knowledge-based approaches to obtaining and sustaining competitive advantage. Knowledge-based organizations need to use different reward system practices than production organizations. Picking the right set of reward system practices, however, is not a simple matter. It needs to take into account the nature of an organization and the type of work it does.

Exhibit 10.1 shows the main reward system approaches that have been reviewed here as well as their most likely impact in knowledge-based organizations. Most have areas of weakness. The one that shows the greatest positive impact is person-based pay. This is hardly surprising because it can encourage individuals to learn and develop skills as well as build a culture of knowledge development and skill development. Of course, by itself it does not significantly affect motivation to perform well. It needs to be combined with a performance-based pay system in order to develop a complete reward system for a knowledge-based organization.

Exhibit 10.1. Impact of Pay Systems.

	Motivation	Attraction	Retention	Knowledge Culture
Job-based	Negative	Weak positive	Weak positive	Negative
Person-based	Positive	Positive	Positive	Positive
Individual merit	Neutral	Neutral	Weak positive	Negative
Team bonus	Positive	Weak positive	Weak positive	Positive
Gainsharing	Positive	Weak positive	Positive	Positive
Profit sharing for top only	Positive for top	Positive for top	Positive for top	Negative below top
Profit sharing, broad-based	Little impact except for top	Weak positive	Weak positive	Positive
Ownership for top only	Positive for top	Positive for top	Positive for top	Negative below top
Ownership broad-based	Little impact except for top	Positive	Positive	Positive

The pay-for-performance systems that come out with the most positive pictures are the ones that reward team and organizational performance. Specifically, team bonuses and broad-based stock and bonus plans all have relatively favorable outcomes for knowledge-based organizations. Which of them make the most sense in a particular organization is truly a matter of business strategy and the kind of technology and organization design that are present in it. None of them are necessarily the right answer in all situations. In small organizations, for example, profit sharing might be quite powerful, whereas in a large one it might make sense either not to have profit sharing at all or to complement it with team and gainsharing bonuses. They can compensate for the weak line of sight, which is the case with a profit-sharing plan in a very large organization.

It is worth pointing out that a great deal more research needs to be done on the impact of reward systems on managing knowledge. Most of the research on reward systems is focused on traditional manufacturing or service organizations that do not rely on knowledge for competitive advantage. Some of the conclusions that are based on this research may not apply to knowledge-based situations.

Particularly needed is research on the impact of knowledge- and skill-based pay plans. They have been researched in the manufacturing environment, but little has been done in knowledge work settings. There is the long history of research on technical ladders, but these were never focused on skill development in the way that plans need to be in order to support knowledge being a source of competitive advantage. Much needed is research on the assessment of an individual's knowledge, the willingness of individuals to transfer knowledge to others, and how this behavior can be supported by a knowledge-based reward system. This is the area where I/O psychology has a lot to offer, particularly if it broadens its horizons to include the impact of knowledge assessment and development on organization culture and business strategy.

Finally, research is needed on the effects of collective reward systems—team, stock option, and other plans that reward everyone— on knowledge organizations. Do they increase the willingness of individuals to develop and share knowledge? Do they affect its development of social capital and implicit knowledge? Although there is a great deal of research on reward systems, these new questions have not been answered. Much of the research on rewards was done on traditional topics in traditional organizations. What is needed now is research on knowledge-based organizations that addresses the key determinants of their effectiveness.

References

Barney, J. B. (1991). Firm resources and sustained competitive advantage. *Journal of Management, 17,* 99–129.

Barney, J. B. (2001). Is the resource-based "view" a useful perspective for strategic management research? Yes. *Academy of Management Review, 26,* 41–56.

Bartol, K. M., & Locke, E. A. (2000). Incentives and motivation. In S. L. Rynes & B. Gerhart (Eds.), *Compensation in organizations* (pp. 104–147). San Francisco: Jossey-Bass.

Blasi, J. R. (1988). *Employee ownership.* New York: Ballinger.

Blinder, A. S. (1990). *Paying for productivity.* Washington, DC: Brookings Institution.

Bloom, M. (1999). The performance effects of pay dispersion on individuals and organizations. *Academy of Management Journal, 42,* 25–40.

Bullock, R. J., & Lawler, E. E. (1984). Gainsharing: A few questions, and fewer answers. *Human Resource Management, 23*(1), 23–40.

Davenport, T. H., & Prusak, L. (1998). *Working knowledge: How organizations manage what they know.* Boston: Harvard Business School Press.

Gerhart, B. (2000). Compensation strategy and organizational performance. In S. Rynes & B. Gerhart (Eds.), *Compensation in organizations: Current research and practice* (pp. 151–194). San Francisco: Jossey-Bass.

Hitt, M. A., Keats, B. A, & DeMarie, S. M. (1998). Navigating in the new competitive landscape: Building strategic flexibility and competitive advantage in the 21st century. *Academy of Management Executive, 12,* 22–42.

Jenkins, G. D. Jr., Ledford, G. E. Jr., Gupta, N., & Doty, D. H. (1992). *Skill-based pay: Practices, payoffs, pitfalls and prospects.* Scottsdale, AZ: American Compensation Association.

Jenkins, G. D. Jr., Mitra, A., Gupta, N., & Shaw, J. D. (1998). Are financial incentives related to performance? A meta-analytic review of empirical research. *Journal of Applied Research, 83,* 777–787.

Kerr, S. (1975). On the folly of rewarding A while hoping for B. *Academy of Management Executive, 9*(2), 7–14.

Lawler, E. E. III. (1971). *Pay and organizational effectiveness: A psychological view.* New York: McGraw-Hill.

Lawler, E. E. III. (1990). *Strategic pay: Aligning organizational strategies and pay systems.* San Francisco: Jossey-Bass.

Lawler, E. E. III. (1994). From job-based to competency-based organizations. *Journal of Organizational Behavior, 15,* 3–15.

Lawler, E. E. III. (1996). *From the ground up: Six principles for building the new logic corporation.* San Francisco: Jossey-Bass.

Lawler, E. E. III. (2000). *Rewarding excellence.* San Francisco: Jossey-Bass.

Lawler, E. E. III. (2001). The era of human capital has finally arrived. In W. Bennis, G. M. Spreitzer, & T. G. Cummings (Eds.), *The future of leadership* (pp. 14–25). San Francisco: Jossey-Bass.

Lawler, E. E. III., & Jenkins, G. D. Jr. (1992). Strategic reward systems. In M. D. Dunnette & L. M. Hough (Eds.), *Handbook of industrial and organizational psychology* (Vol. 3; 2nd ed.; pp. 1009–1055). Palo Alto, CA: Consulting Psychologists Press.

Lawler, E. E. III, Mohrman, S. A., & Benson, G. (2001). *Organizing for high performance.* San Francisco: Jossey-Bass.

Milkovich, G. T., & Newman, J. M. (1996). *Compensation* (5th ed.). Burr Ridge, IL: Irwin.

Mitra, A., Gupta, N., & Jenkins, G. D., Jr. (1997). A drop in the bucket: When is a pay raise a pay raise? *Journal of Organizational Behavior, 18,* 117–137.

Mohrman, S. A., Cohen, S. G., & Mohrman, A. M. Jr. (1995). *Designing team-based organizations: New forms for knowledge work.* San Francisco: Jossey-Bass.

Smithers, J. M. (Ed.). (1998). *Performance appraisal.* San Francisco: Jossey-Bass.

Spencer, L. M., & Spencer, S. M. (1993). *Competence at work.* New York: Wiley.

Sundstrom, E. (1999). *Supporting work team effectiveness.* San Francisco: Jossey-Bass.

Whyte, W. F. (Ed.). (1955). *Money and motivation: An analysis of incentives in industry.* New York: HarperCollins.

Worley, C. G., Bowen, D. E., & Lawler, E. E. III. (1992). On the relationship between objective increase in pay and employees' subjective reactions. *Journal of Organizational Behavior, 13,* 559–571.

Zingheim, P. K., Ledford, G. E. Jr., & Schuster, J. R. (1996). Competencies and competency models: One size fits all? *ACA Journal, 5*(1), 56–65.

CHAPTER 11

Retaining Knowledge by Retaining Technical Professionals

Implications of the Unfolding Turnover Model and the Job Embeddedness Construct

Steven D. Maurer
Thomas W. Lee
Terence R. Mitchell

The theme and title of this volume emphasize that management of knowledge workers is key to competitive advantage in knowledge-based organizations. In this chapter, we focus on a specific aspect of this management issue: retaining knowledge workers. We thus respond to others in this volume who have specifically noted that the intellectual capital of knowledge workers is more mobile than other competitive resources (DeNisi, Hitt, & Jackson, Chapter One, this volume) and that such workers are often—if not constantly—shopping for job opportunities in a normally favorable sellers' market (Pulakos, Dorsey, & Borman, Chapter Six).

In this discussion we presuppose that knowledge workers are professional employees (Pulakos et al., Chapter Six) who provide competitive advantage through their ability to apply existing knowledge and learning capacity to the creation and application of ideas. Our focus is on a particular class of knowledge workers: technical professionals who tend to work in the core areas of technical organizations. Although much of this chapter is probably applicable to a variety of occupational groups, we focus on technical professionals because in a worldwide knowledge-based economy these workers are both the source and the embodiment of many organizations' core competency—knowledge. Further, it seems logical to assert that a firm's ability to create and sustain competitive advantage in a knowledge-based economy is inextricably linked to its ability to retain the technical professionals most responsible for creating and using knowledge capital.

We begin the chapter by considering the characteristics of technical professionals and the unique dimensions of the employment context affecting them. Next, we introduce and briefly describe the unfolding model of voluntary turnover and the job embeddedness construct as recent developments in the literature on turnover. Finally, we discuss the implications of these advancements for researchers and HR practitioners interested in managing knowledge retention by retaining the technical professionals who create and use proprietary information.

Technical Professionals: A Definition

For better than two decades, the term *technical professional* has been used in studies of scientists and engineers (Gutteridge, 1978). Consistent with these studies, we propose that such workers have three main characteristics. First, they have earned at least a bachelor's degree in computer sciences, engineering, or related physical sciences (for example, chemistry, physics, biology, geology, mathematics) and they work as scientists or engineers. Consistent with the description of science and engineering workers used in the Scientists and Engineers Statistical Data System (SESTAT) survey of technical workers, we define these workers as people educated in engineering, physical, and life sciences, but not those trained as technicians, computer programmers, and data processing specialists (National Science Foundation, 1999). Second, their work tasks are generally consistent with the Bureau of Labor Statistics description of engineering workers in the *Occupational Outlook Handbook* (2002), which states that they "apply the theories and principles of science and mathematics to research and develop economical solutions to technical problems." In practice, this means that these employees usually work in areas such as engineering, design, project management, technical support, or R&D. Finally, a significant proportion of them are truly professional employees. According to the consensual definition of *professional*, they may be characterized as possessing expertise in a body of abstract knowledge, having the autonomy to make choices in both the means and ends of their work, and having a commitment to the work and the profession, identity with the profession and other professionals, a code of professional ethics, and commitment to maintaining standards among colleagues (Kerr, Von Glinow, & Shriesheim, 1977; Miller, 1986).

To consider turnover among technical professionals, we make four basic assumptions about their employment context. First, we assume that these workers are continually faced with the need to upgrade and maintain their technical expertise. That is, based on assertions that the "half-life" of a bachelor's level education in some technical fields is no more than three years (Miljus & Smith, 1987), we assume that technical professionals are primarily concerned with the adverse career effects of technical obsolescence and are driven to maintain their technical human capital through calculated career and educational choices.

Second, we assume that the decisions of technical professionals are affected by a dynamic and volatile labor market where, for instance, engineers with a bachelor's of science degree are presently paid significantly more and than graduates in other fields (Bureau of Labor Statistics, 2002). Based on evidence that the supply of engineers is continuing to decrease while future demand for engineering and physical science professionals will grow to four times that of all other occupations (National Science Foundation, 2000), it would seem that present HR practices such as six-figure signing bonuses, employee pirating, and "gaudy" perquisites (such as massage therapy sessions, tickets to sports events, professional leaves, and so on) will continue to have a significant impact on job-change decisions.

Third, because they are professionals, we assume they may be affected by inherent conflicts between their professional and organizational interests. Von Glinow (1988) refers to these conflicts as "tension points" that, among other things, cause distinctions between professional and organizational commitment and often motivate individuals to balance their ethical standards and obligations with the demands of a job. Of interest here is the argument that these tension points are unique to the interests of professional employees and may be significant factors in destabilizing the employment relationship when professional and employer loyalties collide.

Finally, we assume that many of these workers are employed to create, apply, and manage technical knowledge to advance the interests of their employers. Because they usually work in areas such as R&D, product design, technical sales, project management, and technical support, they are exposed to proprietary knowledge that may be critical to the employer's success and at the same time is highly marketable to other, prospective employers. Thus, the roles filled by these employees make them vulnerable to misappropriation (inadvertent or otherwise) of proprietary information and unusually susceptible to the influence of competitors eager to gain advantage through employment enticements.

The Unfolding Model of Voluntary Turnover

Research on voluntary turnover has yielded a vast literature that has been estimated to include over a thousand studies (Hom & Griffeth, 1995). Because several current, readable, and thorough reviews of that literature already exist (see Griffeth, Hom, & Gaertner, 2000; Hom & Griffeth, 1995; Maertz & Campion, 1998), we do not provide a review here. Instead we summarize the specific research on the unfolding model and the embeddedness construct as recent developments that inform our later propositions and speculations on the retention of technical professionals.

Lee, Mitchell, and colleagues (Lee & Mitchell, 1994; Lee, Mitchell, Wise, & Fireman, 1996; Lee, Mitchell, Holtom, McDaniel, & Hill, 1999) sought to integrate and extend employee turnover research by proposing an unfolding model of voluntary turnover. In this model, an individual is theorized to make the decision to leave a company by following one of four prototypical processes or decision paths. In three of the decision paths, leaving is precipitated by a shock—an event that prompts the person to think about leaving. In Path One this shock triggers a preexisting plan of action, a kind of psychological script that results in the person's quitting. For example, a person may plan to leave and then actually quit after completing two years on the job, getting accepted to law school, or having a child. With such shocks neither work affect (for example, job satisfaction) nor job search and evaluation activities play a strong role in the departure decision. In Path Two, a shock prompts a very strong (usually negative) reaction that results in an almost immediate decision to quit. For instance, the person may discover that the firm is intentionally engaging in repugnant practices—such as destroying the environment, engaging in illegal insider stock trading, or encouraging the addiction of children to tobacco products—and this results in an abhorrent reaction and an immediate quit. Note that with these shocks there may or may not be a role for work affect (for example, organizational commitment), but there is no role for search and evaluation of work alternatives.

In the third decision path, the shock prompts relative dissatisfaction and a subsequent job search and evaluation. For example, a person might be quite happy with his job, but if he learns about a better opportunity or hears that a coworker received a substantial pay increase when she left, that might make him more dissatisfied with his current situation. After this kind of shock, dissatisfaction, search, and evaluation occur. Finally, Path Four is not initiated by a shock at all; instead, it follows the traditional, well-researched and well-understood process of affect-induced leaving (for example, Hom & Griffeth, 1995). Thus, shocks prompt leaving on three of the four paths but it is important to note that not all leaving is precipitated by a shock.

In the unfolding model, a shock is theorized to be a very distinguishable event that jars a person into making a deliberate judgment about a job and the possibility of quitting voluntarily (Lee & Mitchell, 1994). Individuals perceive these events to be positive or negative. For example, an anticipated job offer that includes a sizable pay increase would be a positive event. In contrast, a missed promotion opportunity would be negative (for example, an unexpected denial of tenure and promotion from assistant to associate professor, or being bypassed for promotion from associate professor to professor). Most important, the event generates information or has meaning about a person's system of beliefs and images. In this sense, the shock is sufficiently jarring that it cannot be ignored. It is important to note that not all events are shocks. Unless an event leads to deliberations about leaving the job, it is not a shock.

Job Embeddedness

The unfolding model helps us understand how and why people decide to leave their jobs. Based on the previous summary, there are several ways to leave, and job satisfaction is not the only or perhaps even the best predictor of that decision. What is less obvious is that the decision to stay with an organization is not just the obverse of the decision to leave. That is, the factors that precipitate leaving may differ substantially from those that reinforce staying. However, there has been much less work on the process of staying on a job. Maertz and Campion (1998, p. 75) note, for example, that "relatively less turnover research has focused specifically on how an employee decides to remain with an organization and what determines this attachment."

Based on the ideas discussed in the preceding section, Mitchell, Holtom, Lee, Sablynski, and Erez (2001) articulated a construct and developed a measure called *job embeddedness*. Two well-known bodies of research initially informed their thinking. These were Kurt Lewin's field theory (Lewin, 1951) and the research on the embedded figures test (Witkin, Dyk, Faterson, Goodenough, & Karp, 1962). Embedded figures are immersed in their background. They are attached or linked in various ways and integrated with their surroundings. Similarly, Lewin suggested that we see ourselves enmeshed in a network of forces and connections. The self may be loosely or strongly attached to various factors. The attachments may be few or many, close or distant, strong or weak. Someone who is deeply embedded will have many strong and close attachments, whereas the opposite would be true for the weakly embedded person. In addition, although the level of embeddedness could be the same, the *content* of the connections or attaching factors could vary substantially. We believe that three main factors contribute to job embeddedness: the extent to which people have strong attachments to people or groups on the job and in their community, the extent to which they fit or are a good match with the job and the community, and the degree to which they would have to give up or sacrifice things if they left their job. We label these factors *links,* *fit,* and *sacrifice.*

Links

We define links as the formal or informal connections an individual has with other individuals or groups either on or off the job. One can visualize these links as strands that form a web of attachments to friends, family, teams, community groups, and so on. We believe the sheer number of these links is an important reason for choosing to stay on a job. Although some links are obviously more important than others, we focus here on the overall level of connectedness represented by links.

There is research that supports these ideas, but most of it focuses on relationships at work. Price and Mueller (1981), for example, reported that being happy or satisfied with one's coworkers was a factor that decreased turnover. Similarly, Reichers (1985) argued that commitment to groups, teams, and other individuals at work could contribute to overall commitment and reduce turnover. Following this line of thinking, Becker (1992) added commitment to top management, supervisors, and unions. Among technical professionals, for example, a person might stay because of certain work relationships—perhaps the opportunity to work with "the best and the brightest" or to collaborate with others who share a passion for the work.

Relationships off the job also have an impact on an individual's likelihood of staying with or leaving a job. Abelson (1987) and Blegen, Mueller, and Price (1988) showed that both kinship responsibilities and number of children improved retention. Lee and Maurer (1999) found that having children in the home and being married made a stronger contribution to the prediction of turnover than organizational commitment. There are also nonfamily links that are important, such as membership in sports or social clubs and church membership. For instance, Reichers (1985) showed that one dimension of her "constituent commitments" included commitment to the community. Later, Cohen (1995) revealed that outside activities, including hobbies and church activities, solidified retention. Thus, technical professionals working and living in a community heavily populated by similar types of knowledge workers (for example, Los Alamos, New Mexico, or Silicon Valley) may be particularly linked to the area's social and cultural attractions.

Links can influence retention in at least two ways. First, the sheer number of links pressures an individual to stay. Thinking about a job change could cause major and minor reverberations in that person's web of relationships. The second impact is more direct. People who are friends and close to us can bring pressure (or "normative influences") to bear that will influence deliberations or thoughts about leaving a job. Among technical professionals, for example, other project team members (who may be few or many, or whose own work might be dependent on someone else's research) may exert considerable normative pressures to stay until an assigned task is completed (Lee & Maurer, 1997).

Fit

Our fit construct is also meant to represent a broad and nonaffective factor that contributes to job embeddedness. *Fit* is defined as the individual's compatibility with work and nonwork settings. It is our contention that a person's overall feeling of fit or compatibility will influence retention. More specifically, the better the fit, the less likely the person is to leave.

A large body of research is now available on the topic of person-organization fit. Schneider's (1987) important initial contribution suggested that organizations tend toward homogeneity and that people who do not fit will leave. His more recent work (Schneider, Goldstein, & Smith, 1995; Schneider, Smith, Taylor, & Fleenor, 1998) supports this theory. There is homogeneity of the personalities of leaders in organizations and industries. Although not reviewed here, these data (along with many other social psychological studies) clearly confirm the old adage that "birds of a feather flock together." The greater the misfit, the more likely a person is to leave.

How to influence or increase fit has also been studied. Westaby (1999) has argued that better training opportunities and experiences increase fit. Both Kristof-Brown, Bono, and Laurer (1999) and Cable and Parsons (1999) show that the process of socializing new employees can strongly influence fit and subsequent retention. Werbal and Gilliland (1999) argue that the person's fit with his or her work group should be considered in the selection process. Thus, there is strong evidence that fit develops early for new recruits and that placement, socialization, and training can all be important (Cable & Judge, 1996, 1997).

Unfortunately, there has been essentially no research on dimensions of fit that pertain to off-the-job factors. We suspect, however, that external fit perceptions are an integral part of embeddedness. Included would be one's fit with the type and size of city where one works, its location, its climate and amenities, and the activities that are available. For example, is there a major research university nearby? Does the location allow for active participation in professional or technical societies? We hasten to add, however, that just as for links, the idea of fit is nonaffective and can be independent of how a person feels about his or her job. One can fit in well at IBM but not in New York State, or vice versa. We believe that good fit, both on and off the job, increase retention.

Sacrifice

The sacrifice dimension is meant to capture the things that someone must relinquish or give up when leaving a job. It is the perceived loss of material or psychological benefits that are currently available or may be available in future. When we leave an organization we may lose interesting projects or pleasant perks. Financial factors that are not portable, such as stock options or defined benefit plans, may cause a person to reconsider leaving. In most cases, these relatively obvious financial sacrifices are built into existing measures of job satisfaction or organizational commitment. Most job satisfaction measures (for example, Meyer & Allen, 1997) include terms about sacrificing benefits. Having to give up such things has been known to reduce a person's tendency to leave (Gupta & Jenkins, 1980; Shaw, Delery, Jenkins, & Gupta, 1998). In many cases, these factors can be easily quantified and compared with other job alternatives.

What is less obvious and infrequently measured are two other types of organizational factors that might have to be given up. First, structural and institutional dimensions are important, such as opportunities for advancement, job training, and job stability (for example, sacrificing a firm's policy that encourages a programmer to maintain computer skills). In an era of downsizing, takeovers, and mergers, job stability and future opportunities may be important factors in any turnover decision (for example, sacrificing opportunities to work on challenging technical problems). Second, there are numerous more subtle factors, which might be labeled personal investments. People acquire knowledge that is institutionally unique that helps them cope, function, and succeed in that organization. Various subtle benefits accrue to those who stay. Their office location improves. Their time logged toward obtaining a developmental sabbatical increases. People around them have come to know their strengths and weaknesses. These dimensions are far less quantifiable and are not likely to occur in other employment opportunities. Thus, they often are seen as things that people have to give up if they leave. It is this type of sacrifice that we hope to capture with job embeddedness.

Just as for links and fit, sacrifice contains an off-the-job component. It is obviously more significant if a person has to move geographically. That individual must give up the obvious attachments (links) as well as various possessions or contextual factors, such as home, community, and perhaps geographical location. There are also personal investments, such as the excellent athletic tickets or seats at the ballet that it took twenty years to acquire. The individual may face more traffic or miss the beautiful views he or she used to enjoy on the way to work. Such off-the-job factors are basically untouched by the current turnover literature but we feel are important in embedding an employee in a current job.

Implications for Research and Practice

How might the unfolding model and elements of the job embeddedness construct be of help in managing the retention of key contributors who, by definition, are technical professionals "whose loss would pose a threat to the company" (Gomez-Mejia, Balkin, Milkovich, 1990, p. 66)? Because of the relative newness of these turnover concepts, this discussion draws from their documented relevance to other professions, such as nurses (Lee et al., 1996) and accountants (Lee et al., 1999), and an earlier article on their application to engineers (Lee & Maurer, 1997) to speculate on their practical and research implications for managing turnover among technical professionals.

Implications of the Unfolding Model

A clear inference of the unfolding model approach to managing technical professional turnover is that HR strategies should focus on managing shocks and scripts at work in turnover "hot spots." Thus, a logical first step is to identify turnover problem areas based on specific dimensions such as operational division (for example, R&D, engineering, technical support, and so on), job title (project engineer, research scientist, and so on), technical field (such as chemical engineering versus chemistry), or educational level (MBA, Ph.D., and so on). Once identified, key contributors in these areas might then be queried to gain insights into which HR strategies to employ to affect salient scripts and shocks "typical" of such workers. In order to inform these efforts, we submit that the unfolding model's view of voluntary turnover focuses on the following three operational and research questions.

How Can HR Policies Be Used to Manage Scripts of Key Contributors?

Presently, turnover researchers have yet to document scripts important to technical professionals or to consider script-based methods for either hiring persons whose scripts are consonant with employment opportunities or forging HR strategies that promote the key contributor's ability to enact scripts internally (rather than through departure). Because women, minorities, and foreign nationals increasingly earned technical degrees during the 1990s (National Science Foundation, 2000), many technical professional workers may be operating from "protected class" scripts (for example, plans for starting a family, plans to return to their homeland, and so on) that are legally and pragmatically unusable for screening purposes. However, it is also likely that many more typical technical professional scripts (professional goals, educational plans, career planning goals) may be quite useful for hiring persons whose personal scripts fit the employer's job or career opportunities. In practice, this task could be accomplished by recruiting from sources, such as educational programs or fields or universities, that are likely to yield persons with fitting scripts and by using screening devices such as situational interviews (Latham, Saari, Purcell, & Campion, 1980) to select candidates whose scripts might lead to job or career choices consistent with the employer's job offerings.

In addition to using scripts to screen technical professionals, such information might also prove to be useful in designing and implementing HR strategies that would allow key contributors to satisfy their scripts by staying with their present employer. For instance, given the documented importance of career issues to technical professionals (Allen & Katz, 1992; Bailyn & Lynch, 1983) and the impact of career-related scripts (for example, a chance to go to graduate school) on the quit decisions of professional nurses (Lee et al., 1996) and accountants (Lee at al., 1999), it is logical that script-driven career development efforts might be a particularly effective means of enabling technical professionals to act out their career scripts in the organization. Existing studies indicate that flexible programs will be needed to support engineers, for example, whose scripts tend to lead to distinctly different professional, managerial, or project-oriented career tracks (Allen & Katz, 1986, 1995). What is needed now is detailed script information that can be used both to inform script-based career development programs and to enable employers to aid key contributors in framing and pursuing scripts compatible with the employer's available job or career opportunities. To gain this information, efforts might begin by extending existing studies of the successful and failed dual career ladder programs (Moore & Davies, 1977; Moravec, 1993) in order to detect script information actually used by employees in responding to dual career program offerings.

How Can HR Strategies Be Used to Manage Shocks Affecting Technical Professionals?

In addition to scripts, the unfolding model is significant for its distinguishing among various shocks as prime movers of quit decisions. Because these shocks are disruptive events that would cause an individual to invoke a script that leads to a preplanned departure (Path One), quit without an available alternative (Path Two), or quit to pursue an available alternative (Path Three), it becomes important to consider HR strategies for managing the various shocks likely to affect technical professionals. Here we consider the first three decision paths of the unfolding model and relevant characteristics of the technical professionals (and their labor market) to examine research and methods potentially useful to managing shock events that either "push" or "pull" the individual into a quit decision.

"Push" Shocks. These shocks lead to turnover by either causing the employee to invoke a preexisting script (Path One) or initiate an immediate quit decision in response to an abhorrent event (Path Two). In either case, the main practical and scientific issue is that of discerning how to prevent employees from being pushed into action through a triggering shock.

Because Path One shocks compel behavior in response to preexisting scripts, it follows that much of the previous discussion on efforts to understand and control the kinds of scripts of those hired can also be used to manage the probability of triggering such shocks. A potentially fruitful area of inquiry and practice here might be to investigate further how realistic job previews might be used to "inoculate" (Wanous, 1980, 1992) new hires against the triggering potential of normal practices (for example, typical promotion timetables, timing and magnitude of pay rate adjustments). Similarly, knowledge of scripts can be used to explore whether long-term employment contracts might effectively preclude triggering of time-related shocks such as a planned departure date ("I'm only going to work here until I complete this project").

In adopting this approach, existing studies of technical professionals have provided insights that can be used to affect probable scripts and events that would trigger a Path One push decision. For instance, evidence that technical professionals must strive continually to update their technical competence (Younger & Sandholtz, 1999) suggests that such workers are likely to be greatly affected by preplanned educational scripts. Knowledge of this fact can be used to anticipate educational or developmental milestones and substantiate programs such as in-house courses, technical distance education programs (for example, National Technological University), and professional society continuing education offerings to preclude the triggering of such scripts. Also, for the nearly one-third of all engineers who aspire to management careers

(Allen & Katz, 1995), career development procedures (noted earlier) for creating realistic scripts should be joined with sequential training opportunities to prevent shocks associated with a management-oriented developmental script. We propose that a main task facing researchers and practitioners alike is to use such basic research insights to isolate initiating (that is, "push") triggers in technical professional scripts and systematically examine how HR strategies might be used to diminish their salience in the perceptions and decisions of key contributors.

To understand and act upon the push forces affecting Path Two quit decisions, it is necessary to identify the specific abhorrent triggering events for technical professionals. Existing research has suggested at least three possible sources of such shocks. For instance, researchers have noted that graduates of science and engineering programs often lack job experience (Rynes, Heneman, & Schwab, 1980) and are thus subject to "job reality" shocks in their early job experiences. Similarly, research suggests that some shocks may be the product of intense decision-making conflicts in situations where the economic or operational interests of management may be severely at odds with the technical professional's concerns about the profession's legal, ethical, and technical standards (Kleingartner & Anderson, 1987). Finally, some shocks can be traced to what Von Glinow (1988) calls the "fundamental tensions" between organizations and technical professionals caused by HR methods that are poorly designed and are grossly insensitive to these individuals' needs and expectations.

Based on these insights, we believe that research and practitioner attention should be given to at least three issues. First, realistic job previews (RJPs) (Wanous, 1980) designed to present extensive information on specific job duties, technical responsibilities, and shorter-term career opportunities should be examined for their ability to preclude abhorrent job-career shocks among recent graduates. Such efforts should focus specifically on technical professional workers and the factors likely to be particularly disturbing to them. The goal should be to consider how preemployment RJP methods might be used to convey specific information about the role and autonomy of technical professionals in making critical decisions. The end product of this effort would be to promote preemployment RJP information strategies that would enable new hires to set realistic expectations and attenuate the potential abhorrent effects of career and decision-making events.

In addition to researching methods for preventing triggering shocks, attention should be given to specific mechanisms for lessening the intensity of shocks when they arise. For instance, in dealing with shocks arising from conflict in making important technical decisions, it makes sense to consider the degree to which formal grievance procedures or an internal professional standards board might effectively diminish the adverse effects of procedural or distributive fairness concerns in making such decisions.

Finally, both research and practical concerns would be well served by efforts to understand better how to design HR policies and methods that are less likely to violate the needs and demands of key contributors. Performance appraisal is suggested as a particularly fruitful area for such inquiry by Schainblatt (1982, p. 58), who surveyed practices used to evaluate the productivity performance of scientists and engineers and concluded: "There are no currently used systems for measuring the productivity of scientific and engineering groups without substantial flaws." To address this issue it would seem prudent to investigate specifically how the "shock potential" of the performance appraisal process might be diminished among technical professionals by incorporating factors such as professional standards and technically competent evaluators into the performance measurement process. Similarly, given the apparent dominance of management by objectives (MBO) as a means of measuring technical productivity (Meinhart & Pederson, 1989) and the conflicts noted with use of MBO as a productivity measure in technical organizations (Sherwin, 2000), research is needed to document whether the potential shock reduction characteristics of an MBO system (for example, user involvement in the goal-setting process, specific use of technical criteria) are outweighed by the factors likely to induce perceptual shocks among key contributors (for example, unreasonable or ambiguous standards, lengthy time horizons needed to measure technical contributions).

"Pull" Shocks. In the first and second decision paths, the shock event "pushes" the individual into action. In Path Three, the impetus is a "pull" initiated by an attractive alternative. For an employer who

wants to prevent the loss of knowledge created by key contributors, this path is particularly important because it is precisely the knowledge characteristics of such key individuals that make them targets for competitors. Because Path Three decisions unfold more slowly than in Paths One and Two, the strategy and related research questions should focus less on *preventing* "pull" shocks that are highly prevalent in technical labor markets (Shaw et al., 1998) and more on strategies for *influencing* the way in which key contributors might evaluate attractive alternatives. In light of the fact that technical professionals are faced with a continuous need to upgrade and maintain technical expertise (Younger & Sandholtz, 1999) in a financially lucrative job market, it makes sense for employers to consider strategies for dealing with the professional growth and financial enticements of competing firms.

Logically, career development and training practices could be used to help technical professionals see that their career and professional objectives may be met without changing jobs. For instance, design and implementation of a comprehensive career growth program based on sophisticated HR planning methods, dual career ladders, formal evaluation systems (for example, assessment centers), content-valid performance appraisals, and active counseling by managers, mentors, and HR staff could greatly diminish the actual and perceived need to advance a career through job hopping. This effect could be reinforced by on-the-job programs that offer technical professionals the ability to engage simultaneously in several different projects and the opportunity to bid for projects they want to work on. Similarly, technical training opportunities might be provided through firm-specific courses or free access to commercially available programs presented by professional societies, local training firms, or distance education providers. At the extreme, this strategy might also offer sabbaticals or tuition reimbursement programs for individuals seeking to attend graduate programs and courses in their field.

As for financial inducements, the most tempting approach to dealing with Path Three shocks would be to adopt a market leader wage strategy and be prepared to match or exceed competitor offers to key contributors. However, the surprisingly limited growth rate shown in longitudinal wage data of engineering and scientific employees (National Science Foundation, 1999) indicates that relatively few individuals might respond to such a "bidding war" approach. Moreover, it is probable that attempts to meet individual wage offers may induce inflationary havoc in the wage structure, and perhaps worse, increase possible Path Two shocks because of gross pay inequities (wage inversions) across individuals (Lee & Maurer, 1997). Instead, employers might concentrate on the perceived procedural justice of the pay system by ensuring that the pay and benefits package is continually updated, consistently administered, and effectively communicated. HR managers could preempt the appeal of competing offers by publishing wage data in a way that emphasizes the employer's competitiveness. To support this strategy, the employer should make sure that technical managers and HR personnel are given pay information that will allow them to respond quickly and effectively to questions about competing offers.

Implications of Job Embeddedness

For HR managers, the embeddedness construct calls attention to methods and processes that improve an individual's fit and links with his or her employer while increasing the costs of departure. Although the concept of embeddedness refers to both organizational and community ties, it is logical to expect that community ties (identity with community groups, sports teams, friendships, and so on) are personal preferences that are, at best, indirectly affected by employer policies. Thus, this discussion focuses on organizational job embeddedness and how this perception might be influenced by HR strategies designed to increase the fit, link, and sacrifices of technical professionals.

How Can HR Strategies Be Used to Manage Organization-Job Fit?

Organizational fit refers to the degree to which employees perceive that they are technically and psychologically suited to both a job and an organization (Mitchell et al., 2001). For HR practitioners seeking to increase this perceived match, this definition directs attention to methods that will enhance the organization and job fit of new hires and reinforce this connection over time. In dealing with technical professionals, it has long been known that engineers and other technical graduates at the beginning stages of their career often have relatively limited job information with which they can determine their compatibility with available openings (Rynes et al., 1980). Assuming this problem persists, a practical and scientific challenge in hiring recent graduates is to devise effective strategies for conveying the information that each individual needs to pursue and select the job best suited to his or her talents. A possible strategy was offered in a national survey of engineering graduates by Maurer, Howe, and Lee (1992). In that study, principles of service marketing were used to examine how information sources and the type of information offered in campus interviews affected the search decisions of graduating engineers. Of particular relevance to the organizational fit concept is that information on the match between job requirements and the applicants' skills significantly affected the applicants' decision to interview with an employer. Also, their concerns about both job (short-term) and career (long-term) match were among the most important factors in their search process. Later, Maurer and Howe (1995), using a marketing approach and consumer behavior decision models, found that the quality and credibility of the information about job or organizational match (among other factors) were more important to applicants' attraction to an employer than who the actual recruiter was (that is, a line manager or engineer rather than an HR representative).

In addition to such relatively recent efforts, existing research has also suggested a variety of preemployment methods for conveying information that candidates need to be able to self-select into suitable jobs or organizations. The realistic job preview (RJP) (Wanous, 1992), perhaps the most prominent and viable of these approaches, is particularly relevant because this method predicts that applicants with choice options (such as technical professionals) will use highly specific information about job duties and activities to self-select into jobs for which they are well-suited and will avoid other jobs. However, as we noted in our discussion of RJPs as a vehicle for reducing shocks, research has yet to examine the degree to which this method may be specifically relevant to technical professionals. We believe that this method may be particularly useful to fostering fit among key contributors because such workers have the skills to pursue numerous job options and may be particularly affected by RJP information about the fit between their skills and career and job opportunities.

Another obvious preemployment method for increasing fit is the employment interview. Given the potential usefulness of organization-job fit as a selection criterion (Werbel & Gilliland, 1999), it makes sense to consider how interviews may be used to increase organizational or job fit. Maurer, Sue-Chan, and Latham (1999) have argued that the job-specific critical incident scenarios posed in situational interviews convey realistic information likely to affect a person's perceptions of his or her suitability to the real demands of a job. If so, then this advantage, along with evidence of the superior predictive validity of situational interviews over other interviewing methods (McDaniel, Whetzel, Schmidt, & Maurer, 1994), suggest that this method may be particularly useful for increasing fit by simultaneously promoting better decisions by both interviewers and job applicants. As of this writing, these advantages await future research to test the actual suitability of situational interviews to technical professional hiring processes and their true viability as a means of conveying information that is relevant to the job.

In addition to strategies to ensure better fit at the hiring stage, we noted earlier that certain posthire strategies can improve technical professionals' perceptions of the match between the organization's interests and their own. Because career development is by definition a process by which organizational needs are matched to employee strengths and interests (see Gutteridge, Leibowitz, & Shore, 1993), it is almost axiomatic that an effective career development system and its core processes (for example, self-assessment, career planning, training and development opportunities) should be employed as the primary structure for enhancing fit perceptions. However, despite the appeal of this notion, numerous questions remain about the strategies and technologies for enacting an effective career development program among technical professionals. An example of the complexity of this problem is provided in a study of dual ladder systems among some twenty-five hundred engineers and scientists in eleven U.S. and European firms. Results of that study (Allen & Katz, 1992) showed that the ability of individuals to meet their needs by pursuing either a managerial or a technical career path is affected by a complex and dynamic array of educational, age, and socialization factors that may actually decouple and estrange technical professionals from one another and the organization. Clearly, for employers seeking to retain key contributors by maintaining their perceived fit to the organization, such findings illustrate the need for great care in career development implementation as well as theory-based research to understand and explain exactly how these programs might affect the fit perceptions of technical professionals.

How Can HR Strategies Be Used to Manage Links to the Organization?

According to Mitchell et al. (2001), links are the perceived connections between a person and other people or groups in an organization. Hence, the goal of HR managers concerned with building links is to find ways to improve the means by which key contributors develop close ties to groups in the firm and to the firm itself.

Because technical professionals tend to work in project teams or design and development groups such as R&D teams (Mankin, Cohen, & Biksen, 1997), HR managers need to understand how to improve their link to these groups. Existing research offers two insights. First, research on project teams reveals that the technical competency and professionalism of team members are critical to the technical professional's perceptions of team loyalty and commitment (Thamhain & Wilemon, 1987). This suggests that practices that allow individuals to participate in selecting project team members (for example, group interviews) and that enhance cohesion around professional standards (for example, team-building interventions) may prove particularly effective.

Second, research shows that technical professionals are often driven by the need to advance their skills and professional identity by working on increasingly sophisticated and important projects (Allen & Katz, 1995). Thus, it is reasonable to expect that links to groups might be improved if key contributors are allowed to choose to participate in high-visibility project groups that are likely to advance both their technical skills and the firm's recognition of them as contributors important technical objectives. Indeed, team-based strategies adopted by knowledge firms such as WRQ, a software development company, have been shown to increase the networking bond that links workers to the people and professional opportunities offered by an employer (Lublin, 2000).

Employers might also enhance professional ties to the organization by recognizing professional accomplishments; professional recognition has been shown to be important to technical professionals (Kleingartner & Anderson, 1987). Perhaps the simplest approach is to use firm-specific vehicles such as the company newsletter or companywide recognition ceremonies to publicize and celebrate professional accomplishments. Research conducted among other knowledge workers—CPAs—suggests that this might also be accomplished through a mentor system that gives new hires a chance to work under the tutelage of persons recognized in the organization as professionally competent (Terry, 1994). Finally, it is logical for both practitioners and researchers to investigate the degree to which financial support for visible professional activities (for example, sponsorship to professional societies, travel support to professional conferences) might enhance the technical professional's sense of obligation to, and identity with, his or her present employer.

How Can HR Strategies Be Used to Manage Sacrifices Associated with Quitting?

As already noted, sacrifice refers to the cost people have to pay if they leave a job. As they have done with other key workers, employers have "upped the ante" on job change among technical professionals by offering financial incentives for longevity such as retention bonuses, retirement funds, stock options, and "golden handcuffs" (Shaw et al., 1998) and more subtle rewards such as longevity-based mini-sabbatical leaves, a pleasant organizational environment, funds to personalize offices, an atrium, lovely views, exercise facilities, and massages (Shaw et al., 1998; Shellenbarger, 1997). Although such strategies do attract and retain technical professionals, their value when it comes to perception of sacrifice is limited in a labor market where competing firms are both willing and able to offer the same or better enticements.

Under such market conditions, a more direct strategy for increasing perceived sacrifice may be to affect adversely the workers' ability to transfer knowledge or ideas gained in their present job to another employer. Although patents, common law principles, and professional codes of ethics already impose some legal and ethical constraints, HR managers can also employ procedures that protect trade secrets (as proprietary information) and therefore increase the probability that the technical professional may have to sacrifice some portion of his or her stock-in-trade—technical knowledge—in changing employers.

To date, relatively little has been written about how employers can make it legally risky for technical professionals hoping to market their knowledge to prospective employers. In one of the rare attempts to address this issue, Maurer and Zugelder (2000) reviewed trade secret law in high-tech industries and presented three strategies for increasing knowledge-based sacrifices in changing jobs. First, employers may require technical professionals to sign nondisclosure agreements, which stipulate that the employee cannot, without specific permission, disclose or use confidential information during or after present employment. Although common law already prohibits divulging trade secrets, such an agreement has proven to be an important factor considered by the courts in deciding the ability of employers to prevent the application of trade secrets in technical areas such as the manufacture of intraocular lenses (*Surgidev Corp. v. Eye Technology Inc.*, 1986), the programming of CAD software (*Vermont Microsystems Inc. v. Autodesk Inc.*, 1996), and the use of the chemical formula for a polytetrafluoroethylene (PTFE) release agent (*Mangren R&D v. National Chemical Co.*, 1996).

Second, employers could require technical professionals to sign a "covenant not to compete" agreement to increase the sacrifice perceptions of those who wish either to transfer their knowledge to a competing employer or to create a new business in competition with an existing employer. Such preemployment agreements can impose a sacrifice through geographical and timing standards that reasonably restrict where and when (that is, the length of time after quitting) trade secret information can be competitively employed.

Finally, "assignment of inventions" agreements can be created to require the employee to assign to the employer all interests in inventions that arise from his scope of employment. Although the so-called Peck Rule (*Standard Parts v. Peck,* 1924) has long established that employers have a "shop right" to inventions made on the job, an assignment of inventions agreement increases the risk of leaving by specifically limiting the ability to use knowledge of key inventions.

These legal devices, as well as practices such as exit and entry interviews that remind departing employees of their inability to use trade secrets and guard against hiring a trade-secret risk, HR managers can increase the perception that an employer can and will take steps to limit the employee's ability to use elsewhere knowledge gained on the job. However, research has yet to document whether taking such steps truly affects the sacrifice perception. Based on our initial studies of the embeddedness construct and the fact that technical professionals are inherently concerned with the ability to protect and expand their cache of technical knowledge, we speculate that it would be very useful to examine how these and other strategies might affect the individual's perceived sacrifice in making a job change.

Conclusion

In this chapter we have argued that the ability to retain the creators of technical knowledge—technical professionals—is of critical importance to knowledge-based organizations. We have used elements of the unfolding model and the job embeddedness construct to present a variety of HR options and related research issues to be considered in accomplishing this task. In all of these we have embraced three critical, but scientifically tenuous, assumptions. First, we have presupposed that the employer's strategic goal is to manage turnover among key contributors rather than simply prevent turnover among all technical workers. Thus, we assume that turnover among some (that is, less critical) workers is essential and even desirable to enable the employer to infuse the organization constantly with new talent. However, we propose that research is needed to establish whether and how turnover among technical professionals actually affects the viability of knowledge-based firms.

Second, we have asserted that educational preparation, professional standards, and labor market factors affect the decision processes of technical professionals in unique ways. Thus we submit that a very basic empirical question is whether our ideas about turnover and retention actually apply to them. To answer this question we believe that, at a minimum, a conceptual replication of the existing research in work groups of technical professionals is needed to establish the degree of confidence that both practitioners and researchers might place in our comments here. Finally, we have supposed that it is in the best interests of both individual employers and society as a whole that firms take steps to constrain the movement of technical professional workers. However, in the new economy, the information age, or the technology era—as the present environment has been variously described—it may be that the interests of employers would ultimately be better served by the economic growth and synergy of ideas gained through a highly mobile technical professional workforce. This is a question awaiting clarification by macroeconomists and social theorists. In the interim, we simply argue that knowledge-based firms will instinctively strive to maintain their most productive technical professionals and that success in doing so is key to competitive advantage in the idea economy of the twenty-first century.

References

Abelson, M. A. (1987). Examination of avoidable and unavoidable turnover. *Journal of Applied Psychology, 72*, 382–386.

Allen, T. J., & Katz, R. (1986). The dual ladder: Motivational solution or managerial delusion. *R&D Management, 16*, 185–197.

Allen, T., & Katz, R. (1992). Age, education, and technical ladder. *IEEE Transactions on Engineering Management, 39*(3), 239–245.

Allen, T., & Katz, R. (1995). The project-oriented engineer: A dilemma for human resource management. *R&D Management, 25*, 129–140.

Bailyn, L., & Lynch, J. T. (1983). Engineering as a lifelong career: Its meaning, its satisfactions, its difficulties. *Journal of Occupational Behavior, 4*, 263–283.

Becker, T. E. (1992). Foci and bases of commitment: Are there distinctions worth making? *Academy of Management Journal, 35*, 232–244.

Blegen, M. A., Mueller, C. W., & Price, J. L. (1988). Measurement of kinship responsibility for organizational research. *Journal of Applied Psychology, 73*, 402–409.

Bureau of Labor Statistics. (2002). *Occupational outlook handbook, 2002–03.* Washington, DC: Superintendent of Documents, U.S. Government Printing Office.

Cable, D. M., & Judge, T. A. (1996). Person-organization fit, job choice decision, and organizational entry. *Organizational Behavior and Human Decision Processes, 67*, 294–311.

Cable, D. M., & Judge, T. A. (1997). Interviewers' perceptions of person-organization fit and organizational selection decisions. *Journal of Applied Psychology, 82:* 562–577.

Cable, D. M., & Parsons, C. K. (1999, August). *Establishing person-organization fit during organizational entry.* Paper presented at the annual meeting of the Academy of Management, Chicago.

Cohen, A. (1995). An examination of the relationships between work commitment and nonwork domains. *Human Relations, 48,* 239–263.

Gomez-Mejia, L. R., Balkin, D. B., & Milkovich, G. T. (1990). Rethinking rewards for technical employees. *Organizational Dynamics, 1,* 62–75.

Griffeth, R. W., Hom, P. W., & Gaertner, S. (2000). A meta-analysis of antecedents and correlates of employee turnover: update, moderator tests, and research implications for the next millennium. *Journal of Management, 26,* 463–488.

Gupta, N., & Jenkins, G. D. (1980). *The structure of withdrawal: Relationships among estrangement, tardiness, absenteeism, and turnover.* Springfield, VA: National Technical Information Service.

Gutteridge, T. G. (1978). Labor market adaptations of displaced technical professionals. *Industrial & Labor Relations Review; 31,* 460–473.

Gutteridge, T. G, Leibowitz, Z. B., & Shore, J. E. (1993). *Organizational career development: Benchmarks for building a world-class workforce.* San Francisco: Jossey-Bass.

Hom, P. W., & Griffeth, R. W. (1995). *Employee turnover.* Cincinnati, OH: South-Western.

Kerr, S., Von Glinow, M. A., & Shriesheim, J. (1977). Issues in the study of professionals in organizations: The case of scientists and engineers. *Organizational Behavior and Human Performance, 18,* 329–345.

Kleingartner, A., & Anderson, C. S. (1987). *Human resource management in high technology firms.* San Francisco: New Lexington Press.

Kristof-Brown, A., Bono, J. E., & Laurer, K. J. (1999). *Learning to fit it: How socialization affects perceived and actual person-environment fit.* Paper presented at the annual meeting of the Society for Industrial and Organizational Psychology, Atlanta.

Latham, G. P., Saari, L. M., Purcell, E. D., & Campion, M. A. (1980). The situational interview. *Journal of Applied Psychology, 65,* 422–427.

Lee, T. W., & Maurer, S. D. (1997). The retention of knowledge workers with the unfolding model of voluntary turnover. *Human Resource Management Review, 7,* 247–275.

Lee, T. W., & Maurer, S. D. (1999). The effects of family structure on organizational commitment, intention to leave and voluntary turnover. *Journal of Managerial Issues, 11,* 493–513.

Lee, T. W., & Mitchell, T. R. (1994). An alternative approach: The unfolding model of voluntary employee turnover. *Academy of Management Review, 19,* 51–89.

Lee, T. W., Mitchell, T. R., Holtom, B. C., McDaniel, L., & Hill, J. W. (1999). Theoretical development and extension of the unfolding model of voluntary turnover. *Academy of Management Journal, 42,* 450–462.

Lee, T. W., Mitchell, T. R., Wise, L., & Fireman, S. (1996). An unfolding model of voluntary employee turnover. *Academy of Management Journal, 39,* 5–36.

Lewin, K. (1951). Field theory in social science. In D. Cartwright (Ed.), *Name-field theory in social science: Selected theoretical papers.* New York: HarperCollins.

Lublin, J. (2000, September 12). In hot demand, retention czars face tough job at some top firms. *Wall Street Journal,* p. B1.

Maertz, C. P., & Campion, M. A. (1998). Twenty-five years of voluntary turnover research: A review and critique. *International Review of Industrial and Organizational Psychology, 13,* 49–81.

Mankin, D., Cohen, S. G., & Biksen, T. K. (1997). Teams and technology: Tensions in participatory design. *Organizational Dynamics, 26,* 63–76.

Maurer, S. D., & Howe, V. L. (1995). Comparing personnel representatives and line managers as recruiters: An application of the Elaboration Likelihood Model of persuasive communication. *Journal of High Technology Management Research, 6,* 243–259.

Maurer, S. D., Howe, V. L., & Lee, T. W. (1992). Organizational recruiting as marketing management: An interdisciplinary study of engineering graduates. *Personnel Psychology, 45,* 807–833.

Maurer, S. D., Sue-Chan, C., & Latham, G. P. (1999). The situational interview: A research review and agenda for future inquiry. In R. W. Eder & M. A. Harris (Eds.), *The employment interview: Theory, research, and practice* (2nd ed.). Thousand Oaks, CA: Sage.

Maurer, S. D., & Zugelder, M. T. (2000). Trade secret management in high technology: A legal review and research agenda. *Journal of High Technology Management Research, 11,* 155–174.

McDaniel, M. A., Whetzel, D. L., & Schmidt, F. L., & Maurer, S. (1994). The validity of employment interviews: A comprehensive review and meta-analysis. *Journal of Applied Psychology, 79,* 599–616.

Meinhart, W. A., & Pederson, J. A. (1989). Measuring the performance of R&D professionals. *Research Technology Management, 32,* 19–21.

Meyer, J. P., & Allen, N. J. (1997). *Commitment in the workplace.* Thousand Oaks, CA: Sage.

Miljus, R. C., & Smith, R. L. (1987). Key human resource issues for management in high tech firms. In A. Kleingartner & C. Anderson (Eds.), *Human resource management in high technology firms* (115–131). San Francisco: New Lexington Press.

Miller, D. B. (1986). *Managing professionals in research and development.* San Francisco: Jossey-Bass.

Mitchell, T. R., Holtom, B. C., Lee, T. W., Sablynski, C. J., & Erez, M. (2001). Why people stay: Using job embeddedness to predict voluntary turnover. *Academy of Management Journal, 44,* 1102–1121.

Moore, D. C., & Davies, D. S. (1977). The dual ladder: Establishing and operating it. *Research Management, 20,* 14–19.

Moravec, M. (1993). How BPX implemented dual-career ladders. *Research Technology Management, 36,* 39–44.

National Science Foundation. (1999). *Characteristics of scientists and engineers in the United States, 1999* (NSF 99–337). Arlington, VA: National Science Foundation, Division of Science Resources Studies, Scientists and Engineers Statistical Data System (SESTAT).

National Science Foundation. (2000). *Science and engineering indicators, 2000* (SENIEF; NS 1.28/2). Washington, DC: National Science Board.

Price, J. L., & Mueller, C. W. (1981). A causal model of turnover for nurses. *Academy of Management Journal, 24,* 543–565.

Reichers, A. (1985). A review and reconceptualization of organizational commitment. *Academy of Management Review, 10,* 465–476.

Rynes, S. L., & Boudreau, J. W. (1986). College recruiting in large organizations: Practice, evaluation, and research implications. *Personnel Psychology, 39,* 729–758.

Rynes, S. L., Heneman, H. G. III, & Schwab, D. P. (1980). Individual reactions to organizational recruiting: A review. *Personnel Psychology, 53,* 529–542.

Schainblatt, A. H. (1982). How companies measure the productivity of engineers and scientists. *Research Management, 25,* 58–66.

Schneider, B. (1987). The people make the place. *Personnel Psychology, 40,* 437–453.

Schneider, B., Goldstein, H. W., & Smith, D. B. (1995). The ASA framework: An update. *Personnel Psychology, 48,* 747–775.

Schneider, B., Smith, D. B., Taylor, S., & Fleenor, J. (1998). Personality and organizations: A test of the homogeneity of personality hypothesis. *Journal of Applied Psychology, 83,* 462–470.

Shaw, J. D., Delery, J. E., Jenkins, G. D., & Gupta, N. (1998). An organization-level analysis of voluntary and involuntary turnover. *Academy of Management Journal, 41,* 511–525.

Shellenbarger, S. (1997, August 13). Rooms with a view and flexible hours draw talent to WRQ. *Wall Street Journal,* p. B1.

Sherwin, D. (2000). A review of overall models for maintenance management. *Journal of Quality in Maintenance Engineering, 6,* 138–164.

Terry, P. (1994, July). CPA firms try to stop revolving door for women. *Journal of Accountancy,* pp. 8–12.

Thamhain, H. J., & Wilemon, D. L. (1987). Building high performing engineering project teams. *IEEE Transactions on Engineering Management, 34,* 130–137.

Von Glinow, M. A. (1988). *The new professionals.* New York: Ballinger.

Wanous, J. P. (1980). *Organizational entry.* Reading, MA: Addison-Wesley.

Wanous, J. P. (1992). *Organizational entry* (2nd ed.). Reading, MA: Addison-Wesley.

Werbel, J. D., & Gilliland, S. W. (1999). The use of person-environment fit in the selection process. In G. Ferris (Ed.), *Research in personnel and human resource management* (Vol. 17). Greenwich, CT: JAI Press.

Westaby, J. D. (1999). *Organizational practices for increasing retention: A look across organizations.* Paper presented at the annual meeting of the Society for Industrial and Organizational Psychology, Atlanta.

Witkin, H. A., Dyk, R. B., Faterson, H. F., Goodenough, D. R., & Karp, S. A. (1962). *Psychological differentiation.* New York: Wiley.

Younger, J., & Sandholtz, K. (1999). Helping technical professionals build successful careers. *Journal of Coatings Technology, 71,* 59–64.

PART 5

Measuring Knowledge-Based Resources

CHAPTER 12

Assessing the Culture and Climate for Organizational Learning

Lois E. Tetrick
Nancy Da Silva

In their introductory chapter to this volume, DeNisi, Hitt, and Jackson emphasize that strategic management of knowledge-based resources is crucial for an organization to gain and sustain a competitive advantage in today's environment. It has been recognized that an organization's success in managing knowledge depends in part on a culture or climate that is conducive to knowledge acquisition and development (Gnyawali & Grant, 1997).

This chapter discusses one specific capability by which an organization can leverage its knowledge-based resources: an organizational climate that promotes organizational learning. First, we briefly examine the concepts of knowledge management and organizational learning. We then discuss general measures of organizational culture and climate with dimensions that are particularly relevant to organizational learning, and follow that with a discussion of measures that have been specifically developed to assess organizational learning. We conclude the chapter by discussing implications of assessing the culture for organizational learning and future research directions.

Knowledge Management and Organizational Learning

Knowledge management, although often equated with information technology systems, as Fiol asserts in Chapter Three of this volume, is a general term describing the mechanism by which organizations can manage the content, accumulation, and life cycle of knowledge (Siemieniuch & Sinclair, 1999). The broader definition of the term appears similar to the definition of organizational learning. For example, Fiol and Lyles (1985) defined organizational learning as a process of improving actions through understanding and knowledge. According to Garvin (1993), a learning organization can create, acquire, and transfer knowledge, and with this new knowledge, it can then change its behaviors in order to improve organizational performance. Therefore, as Hult, Nichols, Giunipero, and Hurley (2000) suggest, organizational learning—or at least the development of a culture for organizational learning—is a key strategy for gaining competitive advantage through knowledge management.

Types of Learning

Gnyawali and Grant (1997) describe four types of learning in an organization and discuss how these different types may serve as strategies for acquiring knowledge resources. First, they state, there are two primary methods by which organizational members can learn: *knowledge acquisition* involves the acquisition, distribution, and interpretation of already existing knowledge that is external to the learning unit, whereas *knowledge development* is the development of new knowledge that occurs in a learning unit primarily through processes such as dialogue and experience. By combining these two strategies for increasing knowledge in the organization and varying the emphasis on each, Gnyawali and Grant propose four types of learning: reinventive learning, formative learning, adjustive learning, and operative learning. (See Figure 12.1.)

Reinventive learning refers to the ability of individuals in an organization to change their existing perception and understanding of the organization. In other words, reinventive learning occurs when organizational members are able to alter their beliefs, views,

Figure 12.1. Type of Learning Resulting from Knowledge Acquisition and Development Strategies.

| | | Knowledge Acquisition | |
		High emphasis	Low emphasis
Knowledge Development	High emphasis	Reinventive learning	Formative learning
	Low emphasis	Adjustive learning	Operative learning

and assumptions about the way the organization operates. This type of learning emphasizes both knowledge acquisition and knowledge development. It is similar to Argyris and Schön's (1996) concept of double-loop learning and to Senge's (1990) concept of generative learning. Fiol and Lyles (1985) define double-loop learning as the ability of organizational members to adjust the overall rules and norms in the organization. Double-loop learning involves continual investigation into how the organization goes about defining and solving problems (McGill, Slocum, & Lei, 1992). Reinventive learning has the same goal.

Formative learning focuses on the creation of new, shared mental models based on experimental processes. The emphasis is on knowledge development; there is less emphasis on knowledge acquisition. Cnyawali and Grant (1997) suggest that formative learning resembles Weick's (1993) notion of learning as sense-making and Levitt and March's (1988) interpretative schemas.

Adjustive learning focuses on refining an existing understanding of how the organization operates. The greater emphasis is on knowledge acquisition, with less emphasis on knowledge development. This kind of learning involves changing specific activities or behaviors without actually changing the underlying values or norms (Argyris & Schön, 1996). It is most similar to first-order learning

(Fiol & Lyles, 1985), single-loop learning (Argyris & Schön, 1996), and learning as adaptation (Senge, 1990).

Finally, *operative learning* focuses on validating existing knowledge. Therefore, it does not really emphasize either knowledge acquisition or knowledge development. The main concern in operative learning is to reduce errors and accumulate experience to facilitate increased operating efficiency.

Defining Organizational Learning

There are several definitions and conceptualizations of organizational learning, including those presented in the previous paragraphs, and there is no agreed-upon or universal perspective on the phenomenon. Crossan, Lane, White, and Djurfeldt (1995) pointedly articulate the reason for the lack of conformity: most organizational learning researchers either explicitly or implicitly frame their definitions and concepts based on a set of assumptions about the following three dimensions: level of analysis, cognition and behavior, and learning-performance relationship. That is, in general, organizational learning researchers tend to make implicit assumptions about the level of learning, the nature of learning, and the outcomes of learning. Researchers with different assumptions create divergent definitions and concepts. This divergence then leads to different and potentially inconsistent ways to operationalize and measure organizational learning. Lundberg (1995) and Crossan et al. (1995) discuss these issues in detail, but because we focus here on measures of culture and climate for organizational learning, we provide only a brief review of them.

Individual Versus Organizational Level of Analysis

Based on an extensive review of the organizational learning literature, Crossan et al. (1995) discuss a series of influential papers and note the level of analysis on which the different authors base their conceptualizations of organizational learning. For example, they argue that Garvin (1993) and Senge's (1990) conceptualizations are focused primarily at the individual level, whereas Stata (1989) and Duncan and Weiss (1979) define organizational learning at the group level. Fiol and Lyles (1985) and Levitt and March (1988) discuss organizational learning at the organizational level.

Although some theorists use the term *organizational learning* to refer to individual learning, few argue that the individual should be the only level of analysis (March & Olson, 1975; Simon, 1991). Most researchers acknowledge that organizational learning is a product of the extent to which organizational members interact and share experiences and knowledge. This shared form of knowledge is greater than the sum of individual learning (Fiol & Lyles, 1985). Thus, individual learning is a necessary but not sufficient condition for organizational learning to occur (Lundberg, 1995). The information must be distributed to the organizational members, resulting in a shared organizational interpretation of it (Slater & Narver, 1995). Lipshitz, Popper, and Friedman (2000) differentiate individual and organizational learning as follows: individual learning is essentially a cognitive process, whereas organizational learning is essentially a social process. Inkpen and Crossan (1995) also differentiate between individual and organizational learning, suggesting that different learning processes occur at the individual, group, and organizational levels. The key processes are interpreting (at the individual level), integrating (at the group level), and institutionalizing (at the organizational level). As Inkpen and Crossan point out, this conceptualization of organizational learning is similar to Nonaka's (1994) notion of knowledge creation, where knowledge begins at the individual level and moves to the group and then the organizational level. Thus, the creation of knowledge is an upward spiral process.

Cognitive Versus Behavioral Emphasis

As noted by Fiol and Lyles (1985), Lundberg (1995), and Crossan et al. (1995), organizational learning theorists need to distinguish between cognitive and behavioral learning. Most researchers agree that if there is a change in thought processes (that is, cognition) and in behavior, then learning has occurred. But not everyone agrees that a change in thought processes without a change in behavior is actually learning (Crossan et al., 1995). Inkpen and Crossan (1995) resolve this debate by presenting a contingency view of learning. Rather than focusing on whether learning involves either cognitive or behavioral changes, the authors suggest six types of learning that can occur depending on whether there is a cognitive or behavioral change. Researchers need to acknowledge this issue—whether organizational learning encompasses cognitive change, behavioral change, or both. It is fundamental in defining organizational learning and the definition that guides research.

Relationship Between Learning and Performance

Many organizational learning theorists argue that learning organizations will have a competitive advantage over other organizations that do not have the ability to acquire and apply new knowledge effectively (for example, Lundberg, 1995; Slater & Narver, 1995). Yet there is little empirical evidence relating organizational learning to organizational performance (for example, Jacobs, 1995). In fact, Crossan et al. (1995) argue that in the short run organizational learning may actually have a negative impact on performance, because individuals have to discard familiar practices and start using unfamiliar ones. Conversely, good performance may not necessarily be an indication that learning has occurred because many factors affect organizational performance, such as downturns experienced by competitors.

As Crossan et al. (1995) suggest, the relationship between organizational learning and organizational performance may be a complex, indirect relationship and thus not easily tested. But another possible reason for the paucity of evidence is that there simply have been few empirical studies conducted to test the link between organizational learning and organizational performance. One reason for this lack is that very few instruments have been developed to assess organizational learning.

To advance the field of organizational learning, researchers need to examine the organizational learning process to "develop an understanding of how changes in cognition, either incremental or transformational, relate to changes in behavior at the individual, group, and organizational levels and how the changes impact performance" (Crossan et al., 1995, p. 355). The next section covers two areas: the issues that need to be considered when measuring organizational learning—or more specifically, when measuring a culture that promotes organizational learning, assuming that the culture affects the effectiveness of organizational learning (McGill et al., 1992), and general measures of culture and climate that are particularly relevant to organizational learning.

Organizational Culture and Climate and Organizational Learning

The literature on knowledge management and organizational learning emphasizes the importance of communities of practice, personal relationships, and shared meaning, as discussed by DeNisi et al. (Chapter One, this volume), Fiol (Chapter Three), and Noe, Colquitt, Simmering, and Alvarez (Chapter Eight). Developing and maintaining shared meaning and values are at the core of the literature on organizational culture and climate (James & Jones, 1974; Schein, 1990; Schneider & Reichers, 1983). A review of the literatures on organizational learning and on culture and climate suggests several dimensions on which measures might be based: level of climate or culture, such as artifacts and behavior patterns, espoused beliefs and cognition, and underlying assumptions and values; level of analysis, such as individual, group, or organization; and method of assessment, such as observation, interview, and survey. Figure 12.2 illustrates these dimensions. This framework will be used to discuss how to assess the relationship between organizational culture or climate and organizational learning.

Figure 12.2. Framework for Assessing Organizational Climate and Culture.

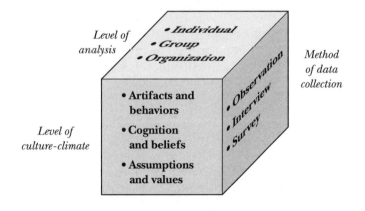

Defining Organizational Culture
Versus Organizational Climate

Schein (1990, p. 111) defined organizational culture as "(a) a pattern of basic assumptions, (b) invented, discovered, or developed by a given group, (c) as it learns to cope with its problems of external adaptation and internal integration, (d) that has worked well enough to be considered valid, and therefore (e) is to be taught to new members as the (f) correct way to perceive, think, and feel in relation to those problems." Drawing on the organizational learning and knowledge management literatures, some theorists have suggested that organizational culture is actually synonymous with organizational knowledge and learning. For example, Gruenfeld and Fan (1999) described group culture as the tacit knowledge of the group's practices, and Levine and Moreland (1999) described shared knowledge as the cognitive component of culture. Therefore, there appears to be an inherent link between knowledge management, organizational learning, and organizational culture.

According to Schein (1990), there are three levels of organizational culture. These levels overlap with the debate about the cognitive versus behavioral emphasis of organizational learning. Schein's first level of organizational culture is made up of observable artifacts and patterns of behavior, the second level includes the espoused values and beliefs held by members of the organization, and the third includes their basic underlying assumptions and values. Schein suggested that the first level—symbols and artifacts—although tangible, is often difficult to interpret because observers may not react to these artifacts in the same way as members of the organization. In contrast, he felt that the second level—espoused values—could be assessed through interviews, questionnaires, and survey instruments. As for the third level, Schein indicated that it is difficult to assess the basic underlying assumptions, and assessment can only occur through intensive observation and dialogue with individuals in the organization. Therefore, assessment of organizational culture varies according to the level of culture and the method of data collection (see again Figure 12.2). Most theorists would consider the appropriate level of analysis for assessing organizational culture to be the organization, although some would also include the group or subunit level of analysis.

Organizational climate, too, has been defined as the shared perceptions of the members of an organization. These shared perceptions describe the organizational environment and are considered to be consistent with the organization's value system (Denison, 1996; Rentsch, 1990). James and James (1989) suggested that climate perceptions represent meaning, or the stored mental schemas of individuals. Therefore, climate reflects knowledge about the organization. Climate has been conceptualized at two levels of analysis—organizational climate and psychological climate (James & Jones, 1974). *Psychological climate* refers to individuals' perceptions of the situation. *Organizational climate* is a situational attribute and is most often operationalized as the aggregate of individual perceptions, providing there is agreement among the group of individuals' perceptions. Most climate measures, unlike culture measures, have relied on quantitative survey data (Denison, 1996), and consistent with the definition of climate, most focus on beliefs, cognition, or behavior.

There is continuing debate about the distinction between the concepts of culture and climate. One of the historical distinctions was based on the methods used for assessment, with culture usually being assessed qualitatively and climate being assessed quantitatively. However, this distinction has blurred as culture is increasingly being measured quantitatively as well (Denison, 1996).

Measures of General Dimensions of Culture and Climate

Despite the early approach to organizational culture, which eschewed attempts to determine universal dimensions, several measures of organizational culture have been developed to quantify the level or strength of an organization's culture (Denison, 1996). Ashkanasy, Broadfoot, and Falkus (2000) reviewed the literature on measures of organizational culture and identified three instruments that focus on patterns of behavior consistent with Schein's first level of culture. Of the three, they found only Cooke and Lafferty's Organizational Culture Inventory to be reliable, with evidence of consensual, construct, and criterion validity. This inventory identifies three types of cultures: passive-defensive, aggressive-defensive, and constructive (Cooke & Szumal, 2000). The passive-defensive culture is characterized by strong approval norms, conventional norms, and dependence norms. The aggressive-defensive culture is characterized by strong oppositional norms, power norms, competitive norms, and perfectionistic norms. Both of these cultures are inconsistent with organizational learning. In contrast, the constructive culture, which is characterized by achievement norms, self-actualizing norms, humanistic-encouraging norms, and affiliative norms, is consistent with organizational learning.

Ashkanasy et al. (2000) also identified fifteen instruments that assessed organizational culture at Schein's second level of espoused beliefs and values. Of these, only O'Reilly, Chatman, and Caldwell's (1991) measure of value fit based on a Q-sort was considered to have demonstrated reliability and consensual, construct, and criterion validity. It should be noted, however, that the Q-sort approach has been criticized for collapsing across distinct dimensions (Edwards, 1993; Ryan & Schmit, 1996). O'Reilly, Chatman, and Caldwell's measure included fifty-four items that reflected personal and organizational values to determine fit between an individual's values and the organization's values. Some of the organizational values that are of particular relevance to this chapter are flexibility, adaptability, innovativeness, willingness to experiment, risk taking, autonomy, free sharing of information, achievement orientation, and opportunities for professional growth.

Finally, Ashkanasy et al. (2000) described their own Organizational Culture Profile. This instrument provides a descriptive profile of organizations based on ten behavioral dimensions of organizational culture that are consistent with Schein's (1990) first and second levels. The ten dimensions are leadership, structure, innovation, job performance, planning, communication, environment, humanistic workplace, development of the individual, and socialization on entry. The innovation and development-of-the-individual dimensions are particularly relevant to learning organizations.

Ashkanasy et al. (2000) did not find any general organizational culture measures that assessed Schein's (1990) third level of culture, the basic underlying assumptions of organizational members. This is not surprising, however, because Schein considered that this level of culture could be assessed only through in-depth observation and dialogue with members of an organization and not by quantitative instruments.

As for organizational climate, in 1981 Cook, Hepworth, Wall, and Warr presented a review of measures. They identified twenty-six measures, most of them global measures of organizational climate. Some of the dimensions included in these measures were autonomy, communication, flexibility, innovation, openness, risk, and trust. Ten years later, Koys and Decotiis (1991) presented the results of their review of the psychological climate literature, which located eight summary dimensions: autonomy, cohesion, fairness, innovation, pressure, recognition, support, and trust. These dimensions are consistent with many of the dimensions of other measures of climate—as well as culture for that matter (Denison, 1996)—and the dimensions of fairness, trust, and innovation appear to be especially relevant for knowledge management and organizational learning.

Measures of Dimensions of Organizational Subcultures and Specific Climates

The measures described in the preceding paragraphs focus on the organization as the level of analysis, although it is conceivable that with appropriate modifications they could be used to assess group or team culture. But some researchers have examined the culture of a specific domain or a particular type of organization rather than dimensions that apply to all organizations. For example, Major (2000) described the culture of high-performance organizations as flexible and adaptable, with continuous learning and self-development, information sharing, and teamwork. Zeitz, Johannesson, and Ritchie (1997) presented evidence of five dimensions of organizational culture that support total quality management: job challenge, cohesion, communication, innovation, and trust. It is interesting to note that these dimensions are not all that different from the general dimensions of organizational culture discussed earlier, and they appear to be relevant to organizational learning.

In addition to examining cultures supporting certain types of organizations, the culture and climate literature has been extended from the organizational level to subgroups or subcultures. For example, Schneider and Reichers (1983) suggested that climate can be differentiated depending on whether one is referring to the global climate of an organization or to subclimates. This perspective is based on the proposition that individuals make sense of a set of psychologically related events in the work environment. These events are usually considered to be more proximal to individuals and may or may not relate to a more global assessment of the organizational climate. Further, it has been acknowledged that specific climates may emerge, such as a climate for service (Schneider, Parkington, & Buxton, 1980), a climate for safety (Zohar, 1980), a climate for creativity (Amabile, Conti, Coon, Lazenby, & Herron, 1996; Isaksen, Lauer, & Ekvall, 1999), and a climate for innovation (Agrell & Gustafson, 1994; Anderson & West, 1996; Burningham & West, 1995; Scott & Bruce, 1994). Climates for creativity and innovation are especially relevant to knowledge management and organizational learning, so we will briefly discuss measures that assess them before going on to discuss assessment of the culture or climate for organizational learning.

Climate for Creativity

Creativity, the generation of novel and useful ideas, has been identified as an important factor in organizational learning and knowledge management (see Oldham, Chapter Nine, this volume). A search of the literature found two measures of climate for creativity in organizations. These were Amabile et al.'s (1996) KEYS measure and Isaksen et al.'s (1999) Situational Outlook Questionnaire (SOQ), which is based on the work of Ekvall and colleagues in Sweden. These two measures appear to overlap somewhat, although the dimensions do not clearly map directly onto each other. Both instruments include freedom and challenging work as dimensions of climate for creativity. Both also incorporate the factors of time pressure and political struggles in the organization as impediments to creativity. Trust and openness are included in both measures, although trust and openness is a specific dimension of the SOQ but part of the work group support dimension of the KEYS.

Climate for Innovation

Whereas creativity is the generation of novel and useful ideas, innovation is the implementation of these ideas (Amabile et al., 1996). Scott and Bruce (1994) conceptualized the psychological climate for innovation as including support for innovation from supervisors and team members as well as adequate resources. Support for innovation includes the extent to which people view the organization as open to change, supportive of new ideas, and tolerant of diversity. Resource adequacy is similar to Amabile et al.'s (1996) dimension of sufficient resources and Isaksen et al.'s (1999) dimension of idea time, because resource adequacy incorporates both sufficient materials and information and adequate time.

A second measure of climate for innovation that specifically focuses on the team level was developed by Anderson and West (1996). The Team Climate Inventory includes four factors: team or group vision (shared team objectives, organizational relevance of team objectives, usefulness of objectives, clarity of team objectives, and negotiated vision); task orientation; participation and safety (information sharing, participation, cohesiveness, and open group processes); and support for innovation (verbal encouragement for innovation and engaged support for innovation). This factor structure was replicated by Burningham and West (1995) as well as by Agrell and Gustafson (1994), who used a Swedish version of this inventory. Scores on the Team Climate Inventory were related to external ratings of group innovation (Burningham & West, 1995) and creativity (Agrell & Gustafson, 1994).

Assessing the Culture or Climate for Organizational Learning

In order for organizational learning to be effective, several authors (for example, McGill et al., 1992) note that an organization must have a climate or culture that encourages openness and trust among its members. The preceding sections described measures that contain organizational culture and climate dimensions that are theoretically related to knowledge management and organizational learning. However, they were not designed to assess the culture for knowledge management and organizational learning specifically, and so they may not assess all the relevant aspects or provide direct tests of organizational learning theories. In this section we present methods developed specifically to assess organizational learning. It should be noted that the empirical literature on culture and climate has a much longer history than that on investigating organizational learning, so evidence for the validity of these approaches is not nearly as extensive. Indeed, all of the approaches for assessing organizational learning that we identified, including those presented here, need further research to support their reliability and validity. Our inclusion of an assessment approach in this section does not indicate our support for it. Also, readers should note that we chose not to include measures of individual learning, such as in Kraiger and Cannon-Bowers (1995), or knowledge engineering and technology, such as in Macintosh, Filby, and Kingston (1999) and Milton, Shadbolt, Cottam, and Hammersley (1999). Instead, we chose to focus on measures of culture and climate for knowledge management and organizational learning. We present the assessment approaches based on whether we saw them as primarily qualitative or quantitative.

Dimensions of Culture and Climate for Organizational Learning

Several dimensions of organizational climate and culture have been identified as important in the literature on knowledge management and organizational learning. These include innovation (Janz, Colquitt, & Noe, 1997), experimentation, risk taking, and creativity (Bokeno & Gantt, 2000), a climate of openness and continuous education (DiBella & Nevis, 1998), acceptance of failure, trust, and a high value on learning (Hoffmann & Withers, 1995; Huseman & Goodman, 1999). Unfortunately, there have been relatively few empirical studies to test these theoretical propositions. In fact, there have been very few empirical studies, even of a descriptive nature, on knowledge management or organizational learning (Tsang, 1997).

In 1997, Redding listed twenty-one learning organization assessment instruments. These instruments focused on individual, team, and organizational levels of learning; almost all of them purported to measure culture; and they varied based on whether they were self-administered or expert-administered and whether they were self-scored, expert-scored, or either. A search of the literature turned up only one or two empirical studies reporting use of one of these instruments, although based on Redding (1997), they were available for use in organizations. In our search, we identified some additional assessment instruments or procedures. The assessment techniques reflect the various perspectives and disciplines—and their respective methodological approaches—that have been interested in organizational learning or learning organizations (Easterby-Smith, 1997).

We have chosen to highlight a few of the organizational learning assessment approaches to provide readers with a full perspective on the methods shown earlier in Figure 12.2. The methods of data collection vary, including interviews, observation, group exercises, and surveys. Readers are referred to Sackmann (1991) for a concise summary of the advantages and disadvantages of each method. Given the nascent state of assessments of organizational learning, we suggest that a convergent approach using multiple approaches building on their respective strengths may be most useful.

Qualitative Approaches

Lipshitz, Popper, and Oz (1996) and Lipshitz and Popper (2000) describe the identification of organizational learning mechanisms (OLMs) in two very different organizations: the Israeli defense forces and a hospital. OLMs are "institutionalized structural and procedural arrangements that allow organizations to systematically collect, analyze, store, disseminate, and use information relevant to the performance of the organization" (Lipshitz & Popper, 2000, p. 345). For example, physicians' rounds were identified as one OLM operating in the hospital units studied. The method used to identify OLMs was semistructured interviews. The structure was provided by tutorials on organizational learning. After the interviews, teams integrated the results and then presented the results to the larger unit. This approach was based on the organizational or subunit level of analysis, although it could also be used to look at teams.

Sackmann (1991, 1992) also took a qualitative approach to investigating organizational learning. She described her approach as an inductive approach reflecting a compromise between a detailed ethnography and a questionnaire. She conducted fifty-two interviews with members of an organization, including top management. The interviews were not completely unstructured; instead, they focused on the issue of innovation in the organization. In addition, she made observations in the organization and analyzed internal documents to see if they converged with the content analysis of the interviews. A framework of cultural knowledge that included dictionary knowledge, directory knowledge, recipe knowledge, and axiomatic knowledge developed by Sackmann (1992) was used for the content analysis of the interviews. This approach primarily focused on the organizational and group level of analysis.

Quantitative Approaches

Edmondson (1999) presented a model of team learning in which she introduced the construct of team psychological safety. She defined this as "a shared belief held by members of a team that the team is safe for interpersonal risk taking" (p. 350). Oldham (Chapter Nine) as well as DeNisi et al. (Chapter One) indicate that a safe, nonjudgmental climate is important for the strategic management of knowledge-based resources. According to Edmondson, team psychological safety is a critical factor in team learning. Through a multimethod study, she developed a measure of this new construct. First, she conducted interviews and observed team meetings. Based on this information, she developed a questionnaire, which she then administered to the teams. The intraclass correlations supported aggregating the team members' responses to the psychological safety items to signify a team-level climate measure. Interviewers independently rated the teams, and these ratings were compared with the team psychological safety measures. Last, observations and follow-up interviews were carried out after the survey was completed, providing some evidence for the validity of the measure.

Da Silva, Tetrick, Jones, Slack, Latting, and Beck (1999) developed a measure to assess the climate for organizational learning based on Senge's (1990) disciplines of organizational learning: personal mastery, management of mental models, team learning, shared vision, and systems thinking. The practice of these disciplines can be viewed as an individual-level phenomenon or aspects of the psychological climate. It is also possible, and certainly implied by Senge, that at least the disciplines of team learning, shared vision, and systems thinking could meaningfully occur at the team, group, and organizational levels. Da Silva et al. (1999) and Tetrick et al. (2000) did not examine the climate for organizational learning at these levels. Like Edmondson's (1999) measure of team psychological safety, the disciplines of organizational learning instrument yielded a "climate for" measure that exhibited adequate reliability and the dimensionality suggested by the theory. Some evidence for validity was provided based on discriminant and convergent validity with other constructs, such as sense of community and learning goal orientation.

DiBella and Nevis (DiBella, 1997; DiBella & Nevis, 1998) took another assessment approach. The Organizational Learning Inventory is based on their research program that has identified seven learning orientations—such as internal versus external knowledge source and individual versus group learning focus—and ten facilitating factors—such as concern for measurement, climate of openness, and a systems perspective. The assessment involves an exercise in which a group of people from a particular unit, such as a department or work group, work with a facilitator to reach a consensus on their learning profile based on the learning orientations and facilitating factors. As part of the group consensus exercise, the unit also identifies its unique resources and capabilities. Thus, this approach is structured by the exercise in the framework of the learning orientations and facilitating factors dimensions. But the group generates the actual learning profile through an interactive social process rather than an empirical aggregation of group members' responses.

Watkins and Marsick developed the Dimensions of the Learning Organization Questionnaire (DLOQ). Watkins and Marsick (1993, 1996a, 1996b) believe that a learning organization develops if the organization takes seven complementary actions, as follows: creates continuous learning opportunities, promotes inquiry and dialogue, encourages collaboration and team learning, establishes systems to capture and share learning, empowers people toward a collective vision, connects the organization to its environment, and uses leaders who model and support learning at the individual, team, and organizational levels.

These seven imperatives constitute seven dimensions of the DLOQ instrument. Several empirical studies have been conducted with the original forty-three-item instrument (Watkins, Yang, & Marsick, 1997; Yang, Watkins, & Marsick, 1998), but a reduced twenty-one-item version has been shown to possess better psychometric properties (Ellinger, Ellinger, Yang, & Howton, 2000). In addition, Ellinger et al. asked midlevel managers at U.S. manufacturing firms to complete the DLOQ, and their responses were found to be correlated with perceptual and objective organizational performance outcomes.

The final quantitative measure of organizational learning we will present here is the Organizational Learning Capacity (OLC) instrument developed by Hult (Hult & Ferrell, 1997; Hult, 1998; Hult et al., 2000). This measure is based on both theoretical writings (for example, Senge, 1990; Slater & Narver, 1995) and case studies. Team orientation, systems orientation, learning orientation, and memory orientation are the four dimensions it measures.

Several studies have used the OLC and examined its relationship to customer satisfaction, relationship commitment, and cycle time performance in strategic sourcing processes (Hult, 1998; Hult et al., 2000). Like the other organizational learning measures, the OLC exhibited adequate reliability and evidence of its dimensionality suggested by the theory.

In concluding this section, we wish to point out that these measures are for the most part still in development. As more evidence accumulates for the validity of these assessment procedures, they may be able to present a clearer link between strategically changing the organizational culture or climate and enhancing knowledge management and organizational learning. Unfortunately, because the measures are based on different theoretical approaches and methods of data collection, it is not known if there will be a convergence of dimensions or techniques that are most useful.

Implications and Directions for Future Research on Organizational Learning

Several studies have examined organizational learning in relation to individual-level outcomes such as job stress, perceived well-being, and employee job performance (Da Silva et al., 2002; Mikkelsen, Saksvik, & Ursin, 1998; Tetrick et al., 2000). However, in order for an organization to have a competitive advantage, knowledge resources derived from organizational learning must be used in a manner that improves performance at the organizational level (DeNisi et al., Chapter One). The following is a brief overview of some of the research relating organizational learning to organizational performance.

As we mentioned earlier, most organizational theorists assume that organizational learning leads to improved organizational performance (Lundberg, 1995). For example, Slater and Narver (1995) state that generative learning or double-loop learning is "frame-breaking" and more likely to lead to competitive advantage than adaptive or single-loop learning. Dodgson (1993) asserts that when the environment is uncertain, organizational learning is a method of improving productivity and innovation. There is some research suggesting that organizational learning is related to organizational performance (for example, Ellinger et al., 2000). However, it has been suggested by some that equating organizational learning with performance may be oversimplifying the relationship (Crossan et al., 1995). In fact, Hamel and Prahalad (1993) point out that organizational learning may not be a sufficient condition for success; rather, the organization must be capable of learning more efficiently than its competitors. Thus, comparative studies examining organizational learning across organizations in an industry need to be conducted so we can understand better the relationship between organizational learning and performance. Such research would also inform practitioners about the most effective strategies for developing a culture for organizational learning.

We also need to understand better the obstacles to organizational learning. For example, Argyris and Schön (1978) discuss how organizational politics can impede organizational learning. Elmes and Kassouf (1995) discuss how an organization can prevent organizational learning, such as by establishing aggressive deadlines. When they work under extreme time pressures, employees are not able to reflect on what they are doing or communicate effectively with their colleagues. Amabile et al. (1996) suggest that excessive workload pressures undermine creativity. Future research needs to examine the extent to which such aspects of the organizational culture may undermine organizational learning.

It is also possible that learning does not always lead to improved behavior (Levitt & March, 1988). In some situations organizations may learn incorrectly or learn something that is incorrect (Huber, 1991). Hedberg (1981) suggested that organizations may have a more difficult time discarding knowledge than acquiring new knowledge. Individuals and organizations tend to keep documentation beyond its usefulness, and organizational routines tend to be enveloped in organizational structures and systems (Easterby-Smith, 1997). Thus, when an organization is faced with a rapidly changing environment, unlearning information may be extremely important to its survival. Future studies need to examine the problem of unlearning (see also Fiol, Chapter Three).

Another issue that has been discussed in the literature is whether there are boundary conditions to organizational learning. For example, Cohen and Levinthal (1990) discuss the concept of absorptive capacity, which suggests that in order for an organization to be successful in acquiring and assimilating new knowledge it needs prior related knowledge. Research by Pennings, Barkema, and Douma (1994) support this notion. These authors found that when firms were expanding, the successful firms were those whose expansion efforts were closely related to their core skills and those that had past experiences with diversification.

Another way to expand or gain knowledge, as discussed by Deeds in Chapter Two, is by acquiring or merging with other firms. Research has been conducted that supports the potential for learning in mergers and acquisitions (for example, Barkema & Vermeulen, 1998; Vermeulen & Barkema, 2001). Alliances are another type of strategic action that may affect organizational learning (Hitt, Dacin, Levitas, Arregle, & Borza, 2000; Lane & Lubatkin, 1998; Parkhe, 1991). For example, Parkhe (1991) linked organizational learning with the longevity and effectiveness of an organization's global strategic alliances.

Inkpen and Crossan (1995) used the framework of organizational learning to examine joint ventures between American and Japanese companies. Based on their findings, they discussed the multilevel, dynamic, cross-cultural nature of organizational learning in this context. For example, unlike their Japanese counterparts, American managers were preoccupied with short-term issues and reluctant to engage in experimental learning when performance benefits were not clearly identifiable. These findings raise the issue of whether organizational learning is culture-specific. Researchers such as Shibata, Tse, Vertinksy, and Wehrung (1991) suggest that certain national cultures, such as Japan's, have a greater tendency toward organizational learning practices than their American counterparts. Senior Japanese managers placed considerable emphasis on encouraging innovation, taking risks, and facilitating information flow. Thus, future cross-cultural studies in organizational learning need to be conducted to explore the issue of cultural specificity further.

Although there is a growing body of research on organizational learning and performance, there is still a paucity of research that directly addresses the multiple levels at which learning may occur. If research is to inform theory and practice on developing organizational cultures for organizational learning, it needs to incorporate cross-level analyses. It would seem especially important to link dimensions of the culture or climate for organizational learning to the various operationalizations of knowledge, as Boudreau discusses in Chapter Thirteen of this volume.

Conclusion

Some empirical research that has been conducted suggests that organizational learning can be linked to individual and organizational level outcomes. Unfortunately, the conceptual definitions of organizational learning and the associated assessments of the culture and climate for organizational learning have not been consistent. We recommend that researchers consider the levels of culture and climate, the levels of analysis, and the methods of data collection, as presented in Figure 12.2, as a framework for continuing work on assessing the culture and climate for organizational learning. Research is needed to help us understand the mechanisms and context in which organizational learning affects individuals, groups, and organizations, but we need some consistent way of examining differences in studies that are based on different conceptualizations and different operationalizations of it.

References

Agrell, A., & Gustafson, R. (1994). The Team Climate Inventory (TCI) and group innovation: A psychometric test on a Swedish sample of work groups. *Journal of Occupational and Organizational Psychology, 67,* 143–151.

Amabile, T. M., Conti, R., Coon, H., Lazenby, J., & Herron, M. (1996). Assessing the work environment for creativity. *Academy of Management Journal, 39*(5), 1154–1184.

Anderson, N., & West, M. A. (1996). The team climate inventory: Development of the TCI and its applications in teambuilding for innovativeness. *European Journal of Work and Organizational Psychology, 5*(1), 53–66.

Argyris, C., & Schön, D. A. (1978). *Organizational learning: A theory of action perspective.* Reading, MA: Addison-Wesley.

Argyris, C., & Schön, D. A. (1996). *Organizational learning II: Theory, method, and practice.* Reading, MA: Addison-Wesley.

Ashkanasy, N. M., Broadfoot, L., E., & Falkus, S. (2000). Questionnaire measures of organizational culture. In N. M. Ashkanasy, C.P.M. Wilderom, & M. F. Peterson (Eds.), *Handook of organizational culture and climate* (pp. 131–145). Thousand Oaks: Sage.

Barkema, H. G., & Vermeulen, F. (1998). International expansion through start-up or acquisition: A learning perspective. *Academy of Management Journal, 41*(1), 7–26.

Bokeno, R. M., & Gantt, V. W. (2000). Dialogic mentoring. *Management Communication Quarterly, 14*(2), 237–270.

Burningham, C., & West, M. A. (1995). Individual, climate, and group interaction processes as predictors of work team innovation. *Small Group Research, 26*(1), 106–117.

Cohen, W. M., & Levinthal, D. A. (1990). Absorptive capacity: A new perspective on learning and innovation. *Administrative Science Quarterly, 35,* 128–152.

Cook, J. D., Hepworth, S. J., Wall, T. D., & Warr, P. B. (1981). *The experience of work: A compendium and review of 249 measures and their use.* Orlando: Academic Press.

Cooke, R. A., & Szumal, J. L. (2000). Using the Organizational Culture Inventory to understand the operating cultures of organizations. In N. M. Ashkanasy, C.P.M. Wilderom, & M. F. Peterson (Eds.), *Handbook of organizational culture & climate* (pp. 147–162). Thousand Oaks: Sage.

Crossan, M. M., Lane, H. W., White, R. E., & Djurfeldt, L. (1995). Organizational learning: Dimensions for a theory. *International Journal of Organizational Analysis, 3*(4), 337–360.

Da Silva, N., Tetrick, L. E., Jones, A. P., Slack, K. J., Latting, J. K., & Beck, M. H. (1999, April). *Development of an organizational learning assessment instrument: An examination of its dimensionality and correlates.* Paper presented at the annual conference of the Society for Industrial and Organizational Psychologists, Dallas.

Da Silva, N., Tetrick, L. E., Slack, K. J., Etchegaray, J. M., Latting, J. K., Beck, M. H., & Jones, A. P. (2002, April). *Employees' psychological climate for organizational learning and supervisory performance.* Paper presented at the annual conference of the Society for Industrial and Organizational Psychologists, Toronto, Canada.

Denison, D. R. (1996). What *is* the difference between organizational culture and organizational climate? A native's point of view on a decade of paradigm wars. *Academy of Management Review, 21*(3), 619–654.

DiBella, A. J. (1997). Gearing up to become a learning organization. *Journal for Quality and Participation, 20*(3), 12–14.

DiBella, A. J., & Nevis, E. C. (1998). *How organizations learn: An integrated strategy for building learning capability.* San Francisco: Jossey-Bass.

Dodgson, M. (1993). Organizational learning: A review of some literatures. *Organization Studies, 14*(3), 375–394.

Duncan, R., & Weiss, A. (1979). Organizational learning: Implications for organizational design. In L. L. Cummings & B. M. Staw (Eds.), *Research in organizational behavior* (Vol. 1; pp. 75–123). Greenwich, CT: JAI Press.

Easterby-Smith, M. (1997). Disciplines of organizational learning: Contributions and critiques. *Human Relations, 50*(9), 1085–1113.

Edmondson, A. (1999). Psychological safety and learning behavior. *Administrative Science Quarterly, 44,* 350–383.

Edwards, J. R. (1993). Problems with the use of profile similarity indices in the study of congruence in organizational research. *Personnel Psychology, 46,* 641–666.

Ellinger, A. D., Ellinger, A. E., Yang, B., & Howton, S. W. (2000). An empirical assessment of the relationship between the learning organization and financial performance. In D. H. Redmann (Ed.), *Outstanding papers from the 2000 annual Academy of Human Resource Development conference.* Raleigh-Durham, NC: Academy of Human Resource Development.

Elmes, M. B., & Kassouf, C. J. (1995). Knowledge workers and organizational learning: Narratives from biotechnology. *Management Learning, 26*(4), 403–422.

Fiol, C. M., & Lyles, M. A. (1985). Organizational learning. *Academy of Management Review, 10*(4), 803–813.

Garvin, D. A. (1993, July-August). Building a learning organization. *Harvard Business Review,* pp. 78–91.

Gnyawali, D. R., & Grant, J. H. (1997). Enhancing corporate venture performance through organizational learning. *International Journal of Organizational Analysis, 5*(1), 74–98.

Gruenfeld, D. H., & Fan, E. T. (1999). What newcomers see and what old-timers say: Discontinuities in knowledge exchange. In L. L. Thompson, J. M. Levine, & D. M. Messick (Eds.), *Shared cognition in organizations: The management of knowledge* (pp. 245–265). Hillsdale, NJ: Erlbaum.

Hamel, G., & Prahalad, C. K. (1993, March-April). Strategy as stretch and leverage. *Harvard Business Review*, pp. 75–84.

Hedberg, B. (1981). How organizations learn and unlearn. In P. C. Nystrom & W. H. Starbuck (Eds.), *Handbook of organizational design.* London: Cambridge University Press.

Hitt, M. A., Dacin, M. T., Levitas, E., Arregle, J., & Borza, A. (2000). Partner selection in emerging and developed market contexts: Resource-based and organizational learning perspectives. *Academy of Management Journal, 43*(3), 449–467.

Hoffmann, F., & Withers, B. (1995). Shared values: Nutrients for learning. In S. Chawla & J. Renesch (Eds.), *Learning organizations: Developing cultures for tomorrow's workplace* (pp. 463–474). Portland, OR: Productivity Press.

Huber, G. P. (1991). Organizational learning: The contributing processes and the literatures. *Organization Science, 2*(1), 88–115.

Hult, G.T.M. (1998). Managing the international strategic sourcing process as a market-driven organizational learning system. *Decision Sciences, 29*(1), 193–216.

Hult, G.T.M., & Ferrell, O. C. (1997). Global organizational learning capacity in purchasing: Construct and measurement. *Journal of Business Research, 40,* 97–111.

Hult, G.T.M., Nichols, E. L., Jr., Giunipero, L. C., & Hurley, R. F. (2000). Global organizational learning in the supply chain: A low versus high learning study. *Journal of International Marketing, 8,* 61–83.

Huseman, R., & Goodman, J. P. (1999). *Leading with knowledge: The nature of competition in the 21st century.* Thousand Oaks, CA: Sage.

Inkpen, A. C., & Crossan, M. M. (1995). Believing is seeing: Joint ventures and organization learning. *Journal of Management Studies, 32*(5), 595–618.

Isaksen, S. G., Lauer, K. J., & Ekvall, G. (1999). Situational outlook questionnaire: A measure of the climate for creativity and change. *Psychological Reports, 85,* 665–674.

Jacobs, R. (1995). Impressions about the learning organization: Looking to see what is behind the curtain. *Human Resource Development Quarterly, 6*(2), 119–122.

James, L. A., & James, L. R. (1989). Integrating work environment perceptions: Explorations into the measurement of meaning. *Journal of Applied Psychology, 74*(5), 739–751.

James, L. R., & Jones, A. P. (1974). Organizational climate: A review of theory and research. *Psychological Bulletin, 81*(12), 1096–1112.

Janz, B. G., Colquitt, J. A., & Noe, R. A. (1997). Knowledge worker team effectiveness: The role of autonomy, interdependence, team development, and contextual support variables. *Personnel Psychology, 40*(4), 877–904.

Koys, D. J., & Decotiis, T. A. (1991). Inductive measure of psychological climate. *Human Relations, 44*(3), 265–285.

Kraiger, K., & Cannon-Bowers, J. A. (1995). Measuring knowledge organization as a method for assessing learning during training. *Human Factors, 37*(4), 804–816.

Lane, P. J., & Lubatkin, M. (1998). Relative absorptive capacity and interorganizational learning. *Strategic Management Journal, 19*(5), 461–477.

Levine, J. M., & Moreland, R. L. (1999). Knowledge transmission in work groups: Helping newcomers to succeed. In L. L. Thompson, J. M. Levine, & D. M. Messick (Eds.), *Shared cognition in organizations: The management of knowledge* (pp. 267–296). Hillsdale, NJ: Erlbaum.

Levitt, B., & March, J. G. (1988). Organizational learning. *Annual Review of Sociology, 14,* 319–340.

Lipshitz, R., & Popper, M. (2000). Organizational learning in a hospital. *Journal of Applied Behavioral Science, 36*(3), 345–361.

Lipshitz, R., Popper, M., & Friedman, V. (2000). *A multi-facet model of organizational learning.* Haifa, Israel: University of Haifa, Department of Psychology.

Lipshitz, R., Popper, M., & Oz, S. (1996). Building learning organizations: The design and implementation of organizational learning mechanisms. *Journal of Applied Behavioral Science, 32*(3), 292–305.

Lundberg, C. C. (1995). Learning in and by organizations: Three conceptual issues. *International Journal of Organizational Analysis, 3*(1), 10–23.

Macintosh, A., Filby, I., & Kingston, J. (1999). Knowledge management techniques: Teaching and dissemination concepts. *International Journal of Human Computer Studies, 51,* 549–566.

Major, D. A. (2000). Effective newcomer socialization into high-performance organizational cultures. In N. M. Ashkanasy, C.P.M. Wilderom, & M. F. Peterson (Eds.), *Handbook of organizational culture & climate* (pp. 355–368). Thousand Oaks, CA: Sage.

March, J. G., & Olson, J. P. (1975). The uncertainty of the past: Organizational learning under ambiguity. *European Journal of Policy Research, 3*(2), 147–171.

McGill, M. E., Slocum, J. W., & Lei, D. (1992). Management practices in learning organizations. *Organizational Dynamics, 21*(1), 5–17.

Mikkelsen, A., Saksvik, P. O., & Ursin, H. (1998). Job stress and organizational learning climate. *International Journal of Stress Management, 5*(4), 197–209.

Milton, N., Shadbolt, N., Cottam, H., & Hammersley, M. (1999). Towards a knowledge technology for knowledge management. *International Journal of Human Computer Studies, 51,* 615–641.

Nonaka, I. (1994). A dynamic theory of organizational knowledge. *Organization Science, 5,* 14–37.

O'Reilly, C. A. III, Chatman, J., & Caldwell, D. F. (1991). People and organizational culture: A profile comparison approach to assessing person-organization fit. *Academy of Management Journal, 34*(3), 487–516.

Parkhe, A. (1991). Interfirm diversity, organizational learning, and longevity in global strategic alliances. *Journal of International Business Studies, 22*(4), 579–601.

Pennings, J. M., Barkema, H., & Douma, S. (1994). Organizational learning and diversification. *Academy of Management Journal, 37*(3), 608–640.

Redding, J. C. (1997, August). Hardwiring the learning organization. *Training and Development Journal,* pp. 61–67.

Rentsch, J. R. (1990). Climate and culture: Interaction and qualitative differences in organizational meanings. *Journal of Applied Psychology, 75,* 668–681.

Ryan, A. M., & Schmit, M. J. (1996). An assessment of organizational climate and P-E fit: A tool for organizational change. *International Journal of Organizational Analysis, 4,* 75–95.

Sackmann, S. A. (1991). Uncovering culture in organizations. *Journal of Applied Behavioral Science, 27*(3), 295–317.

Sackmann, S. A. (1992). Culture and subcultures: An analysis of organizational knowledge. *Administrative Science Quarterly, 37*(1), 140–162.

Schein, E. H. (1990). Organizational culture. *American Psychologist, 45*(2), 109–119.

Schneider, B., Parkington, J. J., & Buxton, V. M. (1980). Employee and customer perception of service in banks. *Administrative Science Quarterly, 25,* 252–267.

Schneider, B., & Reichers, A. E. (1983). On the etiology of climates. *Personnel Psychology, 36,* 19–39.

Scott, S. G., & Bruce, R. A. (1994). Determinants of innovative behavior: A path model of individual innovation in the workplace. *Academy of Management Journal, 37*(3), 580–607.

Senge, P. M. (1990). *The fifth discipline: The art and practice of the learning organization.* New York: Currency Doubleday.

Shibata, G., Tse, E., Vertinksy, I., & Wehrung, D. (1991). Do norms of decision-making styles, organizational design and management affect performance of Japanese firms? An exploratory study of medium and large firms. *Managerial and Decision Economics, 12*(2), 135–146.

Siemieniuch, C. E., & Sinclair, M. A. (1999). Organizational aspects of knowledge lifecycle management in manufacturing. *International Journal of Human Computer Studies, 51,* 517–547.

Simon, H. A. (1991). Bounded rationality and organizational learning. *Organization Science, 2*(1), 125–134.

Slater, S. F., & Narver, J. C. (1995). Market orientation and the learning organization. *Journal of Marketing, 59*(3), 63–74.

Stata, R. (1989). Organizational learning: The key to management innovation. *Sloan Management Review, 30*(3), 63–74.

Tetrick, L. E., Da Silva, N., Jones, A. P., Etchegaray, J. M., Slack, K. J., Latting, J. K., & Beck, M. H. (2000, April). *Organizational learning: Does it lead to employee well-being?* Paper presented at the annual conference of the Society for Industrial and Organizational Psychologists, New Orleans.

Tsang, E.W.K. (1997). Organizational learning and the learning organization: A dichotomy between descriptive and prescriptive research. *Human Relations, 50*(1), 73–89.

Vermeulen, F., & Barkema, H. (2001). Learning through acquisitions. *Academy of Management Journal, 44*(3), 457–476.

Watkins, K. E., & Marsick, V. J. (1993). *Sculpting the learning organization: Lessons in the art and science of systemic change.* San Francisco: Jossey-Bass.

Watkins, K. E., & Marsick, V. J. (1996a). Adult educators and the challenge of the learning organization. *Adult Learning, 7*(4), 18–20.

Watkins, K. E., & Marsick, V. J. (Eds.). (1996b). *In action: Creating the learning organization.* Alexandria, VA: American Society for Training and Development.

Watkins, K. E., Yang, B., & Marsick, V. J. (1997). Measuring dimensions of the learning organization. In R. Torraco (Ed.), *Proceedings of the 1997 annual Academy of Human Resource Development conference* (pp. 543–546). Atlanta: Academy of Human Resource Development.

Weick, K. E. (1993). *Sense-making in organizations.* Thousand Oaks, CA: Sage.

Yang, B., Watkins, K. E., & Marsick, V. J. (1998). Examining construct validity of the dimensions of the learning organization questionnaire. In R. Torraco (Ed.), *Proceedings of the 1998 annual Academy of Human Resource Development conference* (pp. 83–90). Oak Brook, IL: Academy of Human Resource Development.

Zeitz, G., Johannesson, R., & Ritchie, J.E.J. (1997). An employee survey measuring total quality management practices and culture. *Group & Organization Management, 22*(4), 414–444.

Zohar, D. (1980). Safety climate in industrial organizations: Theoretical and applied implications. *Journal of Applied Psychology, 65,* 96–102.

CHAPTER 13

Strategic Knowledge Measurement and Management

John W. Boudreau

The strategic value of human capital, knowledge, and talent is now well established. The other chapters in this volume attest to their essential roles in organizational value creation, uniqueness, and competitiveness. This chapter focuses on measuring knowledge. Because most research in industrial/organizational psychology and even in human resource management has focused on measuring knowledge at the individual level—competencies, skills, abilities, understanding, and so on—this chapter will focus on measuring it at more aggregate levels and on the connection between knowledge measures and the competitive value proposition of organizations.

Knowledge is increasingly important to competitive advantage (DeNisi, Hitt, & Jackson, Chapter One, this volume; Evans & Wurster, 1998, 1999; Rayport & Sviokla, 1995; Seely-Brown & Duguid, 2000), so information *about* knowledge—knowledge measurement—becomes even more critical. As Boudreau and Ramstad (in press) have noted, human capital measures, including knowledge mea-

Note: Thanks to Benjamin D. Dunford, Wendy R. Boswell, and Peter M. Ramstad for their assistance in preparing this chapter. And thanks a second time to Benjamin Dunford for his particularly helpful contributions to the network paragraphs in the section on measuring knowledge enablers. HC BRidge^{TM} is a trademark of the Boudreau-Ramstad Partnership.

sures, not only help HR leaders to make good decisions (Boudreau, 1991, 1996) but also send important signals to constituents such as financial analysts (Low & Seisfeld, 1998), prospective and actual employees (Cappelli, 2000), and shareholders. Measuring knowledge systematically supports better decision making about human capital and signals to others that knowledge is valued.

However, simply creating knowledge measures does not achieve these goals (Boudreau & Ramstad, in press). Researchers need to look past merely developing measures to develop measures that connect talent to strategic success. Such rich and articulated connections, supported by measurement, explain the effectiveness and prominence of decision systems such as finance and marketing (Boudreau & Ramstad, 1999, 1997). Thus, knowledge measurement should articulate, test, and reinforce connections between knowledge and competitive advantage. DeNisi et al. (Chapter One, this volume) similarly note that competitive advantage depends not simply on possessing resources but on how those resources are exploited.

There is no shortage of knowledge measures or consulting products (toolboxes, navigators, scorecards, dashboards, and so on) that propose to measure intellectual capital, knowledge, or learning (for example, Bontis, Dragonetti, Jacobsen, & Roos, 1999; DiFrancesco & Berman, 2000; Sveiby, 1997; Roos & von Krogh, 1996; Petrash, 1996; "A Viking," 1998; Low & Seisfeld, 1998; Stewart, 1998; Barsky & Marchant, 2000). A recent survey of senior executives in 158 companies found that 80 percent had knowledge management (KM) efforts, 60 percent expected to use KM throughout the enterprise within five years, 25 percent had a chief knowledge officer, and 21 percent had a KM strategy (Hackett, 2000).

Yet the definition of the word *knowledge* remains elusive (Crossan, Lane, & White, 1999; Dodgson, 1993; Fisher & White, 2000) and a "black box" of intervening variables affects how knowledge can be enhanced and how it contributes to organizational success (for example, Argote, Ingram, Levine, & Moreland, 2000; Collins, 2000). Boudreau and Ramstad (in press) adopted a new metaphor—a bridge of linking elements—to replace the black box. This bridge is shown in Figure 13.1. The details of this framework are covered elsewhere (Boudreau, Dunford, & Ramstad, 2001; Boudreau & Ramstad, in press), but its principles will help to articulate the purposes of this chapter and its conclusions.

Figure 13.1. HC BRidge™ Framework.

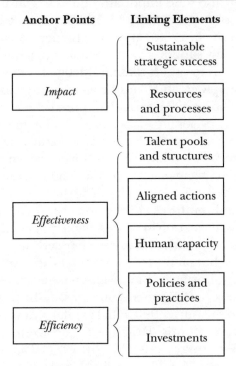

Note: Copyright 1999, 2002 by John W. Boudreau and Peter M. Ramstad (PDI). All rights reserved.

Chapter Goals

The editors of this volume suggested that this chapter explain how to design strategically appropriate measures to assess the role of knowledge in the organization's value chain. As noted, I/O psychology measures knowledge primarily at the individual and the HR-program level. In the framework shown in Figure 13.1, I/O and HR research have generally focused on the elements of *effectiveness,* particularly individual differences (human capacity) and HR or I/O initiatives (HR policies and practices) and their associated relationships (DeNisi et al., Chapter One). Some studies relate knowledge-based HR practices directly to financial outcomes, but measuring knowledge at aggregated levels has not been a primary focus. The linking elements of the *impact* portion of the HC BRidge™ model (talent pools and structures, resources and processes, strategic success) have not been central to I/O research either. As DeNisi et al. point out, there are fruitful research and practical opportunities to understand not only the traditionally studied individual differences related to knowledge (*human capacity* in the figure) but the tasks and context that enable their contribution to competitive advantage (*effectiveness* and *impact* in the figure).

However, measures that vividly reflect these linking elements do exist in other disciplines, such as accounting, economics, psychology, political science, and operations management. This chapter will encourage a broadening of measurement in I/O and HR research by illustrating such measures. This is particularly necessary to reflect elements including not only knowledge capital but social capital and reputational capital (DeNisi et al., Chapter One). Future researchers, managers, and consultants may consider integrating the traditional focus of I/O—the individual and the intervention—and the traditional paradigms—cognitive psychology and organizational behavior—with emerging knowledge at more aggregate levels and from a wider array of disciplines.

Aggregated Units of Analysis, Competitive Value-Chain Context, and Pivotal Roles

Three related themes are helpful in organizing and developing the research implications of knowledge measurement.

First, these measures focus on *aggregated units of analysis*—which include groups of individuals—from profit centers, alliance partners, and firms to regions and economies.

Second, these measures strive to articulate the link between knowledge and the strategic value proposition of the organization, or the *value-chain context*. The term *value chain* refers to the system of processes (as shown in Figure 13.1) that support competitive and strategic success. For example, to measure the knowledge embodied in organizational learning curves reflecting production efficiency, it is necessary to identify key measures of production efficiency and how they fit into the particular value chain being examined. I/O research may find value in measures that more closely link knowledge outcomes to the value context of organizations.

Third, focusing on the value chain and the role of knowledge in it highlights the importance of talent pools, as shown in Figure 13.1, and particularly the idea of *pivotal roles* (Boudreau & Ramstad, in press). Pivotal roles are played by those individuals whose performance or quality differences have the greatest impact on organizational value and competitiveness. The measures described in this chapter are frequently constructed specifically to focus on the organizational units, teams, or jobs most likely to affect competitive advantage. For example, research on patent and patent citations has often identified areas of research and types of researchers likely to be particularly relevant to certain markets or production processes.

This chapter will describe two general roles in I/O research for the measures discussed here: (1) as higher-level dependent variables that can help validate knowledge effects usually measured at the individual or intervention level of analysis, and (2) as moderator or mediator variables that can help explain why the effects of HR interventions on knowledge may vary with the context or serve as intervening variables between HR interventions, individual differences, and higher-level knowledge outcomes. The chapter excludes literature focusing primarily on general principles of individual learning, cognition, and traditional HR research on knowledge, skills, and abilities because other chapters in this volume discuss those issues.

A Framework for Knowledge Measurement: Stocks, Flows, and Enablers

Fisher and White (2000, p. 245) noted that "the literature and research on organizational learning are so fragmented that there is no widely accepted model or theory." The definition of knowledge is elusive (see also Walsh & Ungson, 1991; Dodgson, 1993). Crossan et al. (1999, p. 522) noted that despite more than thirty years of attention to organizational learning, there is "little convergence or consensus on what is meant by the term." Thus, we are limited by the lack of a universal approach to multidisciplinary knowledge measures. Still, this also creates opportunities. Precisely *because* they have not been widely integrated, these measures span a diverse set of theoretical and empirical perspectives.

Walsh and Ungson (1991) recognized that knowledge resides in organizational memory, manifested in "retention facilities," including individuals, culture, transformations, structures, and ecology. Dodgson (1993) and others have noted that research on knowledge can focus on outcomes of learning, the processes of learning, and the structures and strategies that enhance learning (p. 377). DeNisi et al. (Chapter One) note that knowledge must include "what employees have mastered as well as their potential for adapting and acquiring new information." Deeds (Chapter Two) also employed the stock-flow concept, noting that it can be usefully combined with the concept of tacit knowledge. Thus, this chapter will use a three-category organizing framework for knowledge measures: *stocks, flows,* and *enablers.*

Stocks may be defined as the existing level of knowledge at a point in time. For example, Argote and Ingram (2000) suggest that knowledge is held in three basic "reservoirs" or elements of organizations—members, tools, and tasks—as well as their connections and networks. Fiol (Chapter Three, this volume) noted that the importance of retiring knowledge that has outlived its usefulness has been underrated.

Flows may be defined as the movement of knowledge between entities, including individuals, organizations, or organization levels. This includes notions of knowledge transfer, organizational learning, group interaction, and information flows through networks. Nahapiet and Ghoshal (1998) correctly noted that the nature of knowledge transfer mechanisms, including social networks, must be considered part of an organization's knowledge resources. Conner and Prahalad (1996) suggested that knowledge acquisition, transfer, and use are significant reasons for the existence of firms. Fiol (Chapter Three) notes that knowledge flows should be conceived not only as "pipelines" that reflect traditional movement of disembodied knowledge but also as "rivers" that reflect the myriad personal and social inflows and outflows of knowledge, and the unpredictability of its flow patterns. Though the river metaphor is much less common in research and practice, this chapter will describe measures of such social and personal processes, including elements of the community that nurtures knowledge.

Enablers are investments—processes, structures, and activities established by organizations to change or maintain knowledge stocks or influence knowledge flows. Argote and Ingram (2000, p. 153) suggest that knowledge about the network (for example, who knows whom, which members can use what tools, and so on) is likely to be important and that collective knowledge can be measured through task sequences, software, and production processes. Knowledge can be "tacit," or difficult to move. This kind of knowledge is embodied in the existence of common meanings or interpretation systems (Walsh & Ungson, 1991; Kogut & Zander, 1992). Thus, knowledge can be measured through enabling mechanisms, including organization design, alliances, network design, transactive memory, membership in cooperative initiatives, regional clustering, absorptive capacity, research and development, and HR practices.

Exhibit 13.1 organizes the knowledge measures discussed here according to these three categories. One way to use the exhibit as a research guide is to consider that the enablers facilitate the knowledge flows, which change the knowledge stocks. Perhaps even more interesting is to consider the measures in Exhibit 13.1 as oriented primarily to the impact part of Figure 13.1, whereas the HR practices and individual differences that are the typical focus of I/O reside in the effectiveness part of the figure. Thus, traditional I/O research might add the variables in the exhibit to enhance context and connections to outcomes. The next sections will illustrate the measures shown in the exhibit and suggest how they can serve as dependent variables and as moderator-mediator variables.

Measuring Knowledge Stocks

Stock measures provide a snapshot of the *level* of knowledge in an organization at a particular time. They reflect knowledge but also organizational performance (for example, survival or cost) and individual attributes (education and experience) as proxies for knowledge.

Accounting and Intangibles and Financial Statement Augmentation

It is fitting to begin with measures that emanate directly from accounting statements, because such statements are often considered the ultimate measure of strategic success. Accounting-based knowl-

Exhibit 13.1. Knowledge Measures.

Stocks	Flows	Enablers
Accounting	Changes in performance between units or firms	Geographic and political proximity
Augmenting financial statements		International and domestic organizational and alliance design
Patents or publications and their citation patterns	Type of alliance reorganization	
	Perceived knowledge flows between units and alliance partners	R&D expenditures
Organization experience and competitive rivalry		Absorptive capacity
Learning curves	Movement of routines, tools and ideas, including patents	Network attributes (strength, intensity, structure, communication, individual movement)
Unit-level competencies, education, experience, and job requirements	Perceived information exchanged or awareness of knowledge available in other units	Tacitness
"High-performance" work systems	Collaboration and information sharing between colleagues	
	Analysis of work products for sources of ideas and information	

edge measures strive to reconcile the difference between the *market value* of a firm's shares and the *book value* of the assets recorded in financial statements. Lev and Zarowin (1999, p. 362) present data showing that "overall results indicate a weakening of the association between market values and accounting information (earnings, cash flows, and book values) over the past twenty years," prompting proposals to augment financial statements with more information about so-called intangible assets. This type of measurement has been termed *financial statement reconciliation* (Boudreau & Ramstad, in press). The logic is that knowledge investments (the costs of a new organizational design, training programs, hiring of R&D employees, general R&D, and so on) are traditionally subtracted as accounting expenses, yet their benefits may accrue over time. Thus, the accounting system fails to reflect their value as assets. This argument was first made in human resource accounting (Flamholtz, 1999).

Baruch Lev has coined the term *knowledge-based earnings*. As described in *CFO* magazine (Mintz, 1999), knowledge-based earnings are calculated by first forecasting corporate earnings three years into the future. Then, the earnings due to traditional assets are estimated by assuming a level of expected return (for example, 7 percent for tangible assets) and multiplying that percentage by the amount of traditional assets on the books. Subtracting the estimated earnings from traditional assets from the total forecasted earnings leaves a residual amount called *knowledge capital earnings*. To transform this earnings amount into the level of knowledge assets, one must assume a rate of return on knowledge assets (*CFO* used 10.5 percent), and then divide estimated knowledge capital earnings by this percentage, to estimate the total knowledge-based assets. *CFO* publishes a compendium of company comparisons called the "Knowledge Capital Scorecard" annually (for example, Osterland, 2001).

Financial statement augmentation (Boudreau & Ramstad, in press) refers to measures that add human capital indicators to traditional financial information (for example, Skandia Corporation, 1996). Indicators may be as diverse as total training expense, number of employees under age thirty, and number of patents (Barsky & Marchant, 2000; Batchelor, 1999; Dzinkowski, 1999, 2000; Flamholtz, 1999; Lewis & Lippitt, 1999; Lynn, 1998; Roslender, 2000; Sveiby, 1997). But there is no standard format, so such reports may contain virtually anything an organization considers relevant or noteworthy. Skandia includes over one hundred measures in its intellectual capital report (Edvinsson & Malone, 1997), including replacement and acquisition costs, development of cross-functional teams, external relationships, information technology investments, and adoption of industry quality standards. Human resource accounting (Flamholtz, 1999) measures acquisition cost, replacement value, or the discounted value of expected future salaries.

Implications for I/O and HR Research

Accounting tries to reconcile the gap between traditional reporting and the growing importance of knowledge and intangibles. The "residual" approach takes what is accounted for traditionally and subtracts it from the estimated total value to reveal intangible value; the "augmentation" approach adds to traditional accounting reports measures that are presumed to reflect knowledge.

In terms of aggregated units, accounting approaches often require standard financial statements, which presume an entity of sufficient size to have accounting records and transactions. In terms of competitive and value-chain context, the measures are rather generic. They usually do not describe the mechanisms through which organizations create value or focus on how knowledge interacts with the value-creation processes. Rates of return are often estimated using averages within industries, and competitive processes are assumed to be reflected in the overall financial position. In terms of pivotal roles, these measures seldom identify which roles might most affect value through performance or quality differences. Though some financial statement augmentations attempt to report knowledge-based activities for key groups (for example, training for research scientists or the number of employees with qualifications in certain technologies), the links between roles and value are not explicitly identified.

For I/O researchers, accounting measures provide high-level dependent variables, such as the level of knowledge assets and returns from those assets. One can imagine studies asking, "Do knowledge-enhancing interventions or changes in individual knowledge levels relate to changes in the accounting levels or returns from knowledge assets?" Current HR strategy research often calculates relationships between HR practices and traditional financial ratios (see Boudreau & Ramstad, in press, for a review). Perhaps financial results adjusted to reflect intangibles provide an even more appropriate dependent variable. Do knowledge-based interventions relate more strongly to accounting estimates of intangible assets than to traditional accounting outcomes?

I/O research and theory might contribute to financial statement augmentation by suggesting which human capital numbers should be used. Financial augmentation usually reports training expenditures, numbers of employees, and human resource activities meant to indicate investments in knowledge-based assets. Theories and findings from I/O research on knowledge might well identify the most appropriate expenditures or activities to report.

Accounting-based measures may provide fruitful moderating and mediating variables. Knowledge-enhancing I/O and HR interventions may differ in their effectiveness depending on the rate of return to knowledge in the organization. Organizations with strong financial returns to knowledge may be more receptive to knowledge interventions, thus enhancing their effects. Similarly, the information reported in financial augmentation statements (for example, number of training programs, number of employees with advanced degrees, and so on) might be used to detect organizational receptivity to knowledge-based initiatives.

Patents, Publications, and Citations

Disciplines as diverse as strategic alliances, network analysis, industrial/organizational economics, and international relations have used patents to measure knowledge. Patented ideas represent the result of government scrutiny and endorsement of originality and usefulness. Patents are an outcome of knowledge, but can also represent part of the stock of knowledge because they are protected ideas that the firm has exclusive rights to use. Closely related to patents is the amount and pattern of research publications generated and used by an organization. Publications are not protected like patents, but like patents they reflect an external judgment (of the scientific field) that ideas are original and useful. Publications and patents can be objectively traced to an organization. Moreover, patent and publication citations provide valuable insights into the sources and patterns of knowledge used, as we shall see.

There is surprisingly deep information available about patents. Deng, Lev, and Narin (1999) describe a database of U.S. patents and citations that measures not only the number of patents but their citations. Citations of scientific studies in patent applications indicated the "basic" knowledge embodied there. The number of patents, citation impact, and science links were positively related to market-to-book value and stock returns. Sjoholm (1996) measured cross-border patent citations as knowledge flows between nations. Adams (1990) measured total knowledge in an industry as the number of scientific articles from that industry in each of nine scientific fields, weighted by the number of scientists allocated to each industry-field combination. Spencer (2000) examined archival data on articles published by researchers in Japanese and U.S. firms, measuring publication *volume* (number of articles), *quality* (number of times scientists in outside organizations cited the research), and *breadth* (number of different organizations whose scientists cited the work). Sorensen and Stuart (2000) used archival patent data to indicate innovation (citations to newer technology) and knowledge close to the existing core (self-citations). Hall, Jaffe, and Trajtenberg (2000) noted problems of noise in patent data and provide several methods for estimating patent quality. They found financial returns more highly correlated with citation-weighted patents than simple patent quantity.

Implications for I/O and HR Research

Patents, publications, and citations reflect aggregated units of analysis, with a focus on the level of the firm or business unit. Rich archival data across firms and industries offers significant opportunities. Moreover, because patents, publications, and citations are also associated with individuals, these measures offer I/O researchers measures that could potentially span units of analysis from individuals to business units and organizations. Several studies have found patent and citation-based measures to relate to financial outcomes, enhancing the strategic rationale for these measures. In terms of value-chain context, patents and publications can be classified by particular fields and groups of knowledge workers (for example, R&D scientists), and thus can be explicitly linked to different areas of the value chain and to different competitive processes. For example, Jaffe (1986) explicitly linked patent citations to particular competitive processes in R&D. Patents are also quite useful in identifying and describing pivotal roles and talent pools. They reflect the fields of expertise of individuals, and citation records can trace which knowledge roles have had the most significant impact on the knowledge base and in which business processes.

Thus, I/O research could use patents and publications as dependent variables, examining whether they are affected by knowledge-enhancing interventions, offering externally verified evidence of the effect of individual or program-level knowledge changes. Because patents, publications, and citations can be also be so specifically linked to the value chain of business processes, they offer useful intervening variables that may help to explain the links between knowledge changes at the individual or program level and eventual organizational returns. Finally, levels and patterns of patents and publications might provide useful moderator variables to explain contextual differences. For example, firms with a large number of highly cited and strategically relevant patents might benefit more from knowledge-enhancing interventions or from enhancements in individual knowledge, because the "platform" for using such knowledge is already very high.

Organization Experience, Rivalry Patterns, and Learning Curves

Measures of organization experience reflect the time and volume of production or services offered. The idea is that as organizations operate, they gain knowledge. DeNisi et al. (Chapter One) note that such knowledge can come from competitors and customers, as well as from access to experienced employees. Data on organization experience are often available through archival directories. For example, Baum and Ingram (1998) used the *Manhattan Classified Directory/Yellow Pages,* the *Annual Directory of the Hotel Association of New York City,* and the *Hotel and Travel Index,* to track "life history" information on 558 hotels operating in New York from 1898 to 1980. Industry experience was the number of rooms offered over time. Industry experience was found to matter early in the life cycle, through learning from similar hotels.

Organization experience is also measured by exposure to competition. Ingram and Baum (1997) constructed measures of competitive experience for hotel chains, including geographic dispersion of units and industry competitive intensity as the number of hotel failures over time. Barnett, Greve, and Park (1994) applied this method using the *Bankers Directory,* which codes the existence and assets of banks, their place of operation, and events such as foundings, dissolutions, and mergers. They measured bank experience in terms of density of rivals and branches. Barnett and Hansen (1996) found that banks were more likely to fail if they had more exposure to varied rivals early in their history. In an international context, Barkema, Shenkar, Vermeulen, and Bell (1997) gathered data on the number of domestic joint ventures and international subsidiaries at the time of entry into a new country.

Learning curves provide a particular interpretation of production experience, reflecting the reduction in unit costs and tangible process improvements that come with experience in specific production processes. Arrow (1962) first suggested that the "very activity of production gives rise to problems for which favorable responses are selected over time" (p. 156). Epple, Argote, and Devadas (1991) provide helpful definitions and derivations of learning curve indices, and Darr, Argote, and Epple (1995) provide vivid descriptions of the social processes of learning curves, such as how an innovation in placing pepperoni on pizzas was learned by other pizza stores. Learning curves are estimated using archival production data from business units (for example, pizza stores, production plants, production shifts). Darr et al. (1995) and Darr and Kurtzburg (2000) obtained data on pizzas sold and production costs from regional offices of pizza franchise corporations. Epple et al. (1991) and Epple, Argote, and Murphy (1996) gathered data from two work shifts in one truck production plant. Hoopes and Postrel (1999) measured reduced glitches, or preventable process problems caused by a lack of coordination.

Implications for I/O and HR Research

In terms of aggregated units of analysis, organization experience and rivalry can clearly be measured at the level of the firm, and perhaps even more usefully at the level of the business unit, division, production process, or work shift. Detailed directories in many industries are excellent archival sources that might be used to verify individual perceptions of rivalry or experience. One can even imagine measuring individual differences, such as whether employees have worked in business units or industries with more or less rivalry and competition. This might enhance more typical measures of organizational tenure or number of jobs held. In terms of the value-chain context, rivalry and competition measures are less specific because they reflect the number and age of entire business units rather than specific business processes in the value chain. However, learning curve measures address this shortcoming, focusing on specific key manufacturing or other processes and process quality. Similarly, measures of industry experience and rivalry do not reflect pivotal roles because of their focus on business units, and learning curves per se provide little information about particular roles or talent pools. However, learning curve research often gathers qualitative data suggesting how particular employees actually learned or implemented process improvements (for example, how pizza store employees shared their knowledge about pepperoni placement), potentially allowing researchers to determine which roles are key in knowledge transfer.

Thus, in I/O research, organization experience measures, as well as learning curve measures, offer additional dependent variables. For example, one effect of changes or differences in knowledge among individuals or HR programs might be changes in the survival or successful entry into more competitive environments. Research questions might include these: Do firms or business units with knowledge-enhancing HR practices tend to have more industry experience? Does enhanced knowledge among individual employees or the existence of knowledge-enhancing HR practices relate to accelerated learning-curve progress? Industry experience and learning curves may also have significant value as moderators and mediators in I/O and HR research. For example, individual knowledge and knowledge sharing about successful competitive practices might be more valued and more related to financial performance among firms facing highly competitive environments because competition makes innovation more valuable. The relationship might even be nonlinear (a ceiling effect) if highly competitive environments present such significant day-to-day challenges— particularly for firms with little experience—that HR practices and individual knowledge changes are simply not used or transferred. Businesses or units that are "early" in the learning curve might benefit more from interventions designed to enhance individual ability to receive knowledge, whereas those further into the learning curve process might benefit most from interventions that enhance knowledge sharing.

Unit-Level Competencies, Education, Experience, and Job Requirements

Clearly, this category encompasses a wide variety of attributes, such as cognitive ability, training results, performance ratings, and competencies (Lado & Wilson, 1994). The measurement of competencies is a field in itself, with a vast array of products and technologies that generally focus on the individual level. Many of them are covered in other chapters of this volume.

This section focuses on measures of these attributes at the level of jobs, production processes, firms, and industries. Much of this research emanates from labor economics, with roots in the concepts of human capital (Becker, 1964). For example, Leigh and Gifford (1999) used the National Longitudinal Survey of Youth (NLSY), which asked workers about the amount and type of training they had and who paid for it. Coff (1999) calculated the knowledge intensity of industries using reported education and training required for jobs. Cappelli (1993) used data from Hay Associates on job attributes, including know-how, problem solving, and accountability. Tomlinson's (1999) survey asked "whether the person's job required that they 'kept on learning new things'" (p. 437). Cappelli's (1996) survey asked, "Have the skills required to perform production jobs adequately risen over the last three years?" Cappelli (1993, 1996) suggests that the skill level of industries and organizations can be assessed in several ways, including *Dictionary of Occupational Titles* job analyses, "production functions" (the level or type of capital spending), and "work organization," indicated by the presence of high-performance HR practices.

Implications for I/O and HR Research

Aggregated units of analysis are probably the most distinguishing features of these measures. They emanate from the presumption that certain work demands, job requirements, or occupational titles (such as engineer) indicate the presence of individual-level knowledge, allowing unit-level experience and education to be measured directly rather than by aggregating individual-level attributes. I/O researchers might use such measures when individual-level data are unavailable, difficult to obtain, or unreliable. These measures do not specifically incorporate the value-chain context or pivotal roles, but they often choose to focus on particular jobs or work areas, suggesting which areas are critical to organizational value creation.

These variables might offer alternative dependent variables in I/O research designs. For example, in addition to tracking the immediate effects of HR interventions on individuals, researchers might also measure whether managers perceive that work requirements have changed, or whether the jobs involved begin to attract more knowledge workers (such as engineers or scientists). They also may provide useful moderator or mediator variables to explain contextual variance. For example, these measures could identify business units with rising knowledge demands, and those units might be more likely to exhibit strong effects of knowledge-enhancement interventions because their work environment is becoming more demanding.

Measuring Knowledge Flows

A distinguishing feature of organizational learning, as opposed to individual learning, is that it occurs through transfer of routines, culture, and processes—through collective interpretation (Cohen, 1991). Crossan et al. (1999) defined *organizational learning* as movement of knowledge through and between individual, group, and organizational units. DeNisi et al. (Chapter One) noted that continuous organizational learning may be particularly difficult for competitors to duplicate. Knowledge flows can be measured by tracking changes in the measures of knowledge stocks described in the previous section. Patent citations, for example, reflect the quality of knowledge but also indicate who has used prior developed knowledge (Hall et al., 2000; Mowery, Oxley, & Silverman, 1996; Almeida, 1996; Spencer, 2000). Relative changes in learning curves can indicate knowledge movement (for example, Baum & Ingram, 1998). Argote and Ingram (2000) defined knowledge transfer as "the process through which one unit (for example, group, department, or division) is affected by the experience of another" (p. 151).

In I/O and HR research, knowledge transfer is usually defined as applying knowledge from one setting (for example, the classroom) to another (on-the-job behavior). This same principle has been fruitfully applied to knowledge movement between organizations, business units, and groups and teams, as this section will illustrate. One group of measures focuses on business units and alliance partners; another focuses on groups and teams.

Knowledge Flows Between
Units and Alliance Partners

Business alliances are often formed to obtain knowledge (DeNisi et al., Chapter One). Deeds (Chapter Two) noted that the ability of a firm to develop and manage cross-boundary individual and firm relationships and learn from its prior experiences will be important to its competitive position, and is likely to increase. For example, in the pharmaceutical-biotechnology industry, Rothaermel and Deeds (2001) documented over twenty-two hundred active alliances. Deeds also noted that alliances are only one form of hybrid organization; such forms include simple licensing agreements, complex alliances in which multiple parties cross-license technologies and contribute to joint R&D, and multiparty joint ventures in which a jointly owned organization is set up to pursue a new market or technology. He noted that evidence suggests a positive effect of alliances on R&D performance and organizational productivity, as well as the tendency for alliances to have difficulty in their "adolescence," much as marriages do. This section will thus illustrate measures of knowledge and knowledge transfer that focus on organizational units, particularly international and alliance partners.

Downes and Thomas (2000) used the number of expatriates as a proxy for national market-specific knowledge and knowledge about international management. Shenkar and Li (1999) surveyed managing directors of Shanghai enterprises about three types of knowledge sought and offered to the potential partners: management skills, marketing skills, and technological know-how. Zahra, Ireland, and Hitt (2000) measured technological learning in international joint ventures by surveying managers about the *breadth* (for example, learned many different skills versus a few skills), *depth* (how well the company has learned or mastered new skills), and *speed* (how fast the company learned). Simonin (1999) had experts rate agreement with attributes describing prior alliances, such as "technology/process know-how easily transferable" (p. 606). Gupta and Govindarajan (2000) surveyed subsidiary presidents to learn whether seven specific knowledge types were received or supplied by the subsidiary, the parent corporation, or other subsidiaries. These seven types were marketing know-how, distribution know-how, packaging design and technology, product designs, process designs, purchasing know-how, and management systems and practices.

A paradox of knowledge flows is that although they can enhance learning *within* organizations, movable knowledge is also more easily appropriated by outsiders. This has been called *spillover* (for example, Van Meijl & van Tongeren, 1999). The effects of spillover are very different from useful internal knowledge transfer but the measures are similar; the difference is that spillover focuses on undesirable movement between *competing* organizations. Jaffe, Trajtenberg, and Fogarty (2001) measured spillover by the citation of research and patents produced in competing organizations. Almeida and Kogut (1999) measured spillover as the movement of major patent holders. Lane and Lubatkin (1998, p. 468) asked market researchers to consider particular industry alliances and to estimate "which partner benefited most from knowledge spillovers."

Knowledge flows have also been measured using data from archival secondary sources. Dussuage, Garrette, and Mitchell (2000) measured whether alliances were reorganized, taken over by one party, continued without change, or dissolved, defining the first two as representing "greater capability acquisition" (p. 104). Deeds (Chapter Two) and DeNisi et al. (Chapter One) note that premature turnover among key top managers or technical knowledge holders in an acquired company may indicate lost knowledge.

Knowledge Flows Between Individuals and Groups

Measures of knowledge flows between individuals reflect the concept of knowledge communities and that knowledge work is about social connections and interpretations (Fiol, Chapter Three). Some knowledge flow measures have focused on the degree to which individuals disclose information. Appleyard (1996) asked respondents whether they provided information to colleagues. Lawson and Lorenz (1999) observed collaboration between university professors and company scientists. Bouty (2000) conducted interviews with thirty-eight researchers working in France, measuring information exchanges with other scientists. McEvily and Zaheer (1999) surveyed top managers about their participation in assistance or user groups and whether they sought advice from individuals outside the firm. Inkpen and Dinur (1998) qualitatively evaluated how explicit was the knowledge shared between American and Japanese auto parts joint ventures.

Shared reality—convergence in group member judgments of ambiguous stimuli (Sherif, 1936)—can also indicate knowledge transfer. Levine, Higgins, and Choi (2000) noted that it can be embodied in beliefs, team mental models (Cannon-Bowers, Salas, & Converse, 1993), collective mind (Weick & Roberts, 1993), and transactive memory (Moreland, Argote, & Krishnan, 1996). Most measures focusing on this concept arose from experimental studies of groups. Moreland and Myaskovsky (2000) surveyed experimental subjects who constructed radios, asking, "How much do you think the other members of this group know about your radio-building skills?" "How similar are the skills in this work group?" and "How much do you know about the skills of others in this group?" Levine et al. (2000) measured the convergence recollections of whether certain nonsense words had appeared in a list. Stasser, Vaughan, and Stewart (2000) observed whether subjects mentioned information that had been shared with everyone or given only to one person in the group. Paulus and Yang (2000) measured the frequency of repeated ideas after a brainstorming session. Gruenfeld, Martorana, and Fan (2000) counted ideas contained in individual and group essays to examine how "outsiders" affect idea generation.

In the field, Bouty (2000) interviewed French researchers, coding anecdotes to reveal shallow exchanges (discussing published papers, products, and general scientific information and giving names and addresses) versus deeper exchanges (sharing scientific and technical information, giving contacts and recommendations, sharing ideas about works in progress, giving product samples, and pre-reviewing papers). Fiol (Chapter Three) describes a Paris-based advertising company that has employees rate the quality of information on their internal corporate Web site, moving highly rated information to positions with top billing.

Implications for I/O and HR Research

The knowledge flow measures illustrated here focus on aggregated units of analysis that are either business units and alliance partners or groups and teams. Measures focused on business units rely primarily on surveys of unit leaders regarding perceived information flows, with a few attempts to use archival data. Measures focusing on groups and teams also rely on surveys, but more often actually measure how shared knowledge appears in work products and team results. Though such measures are usually applied in experimental settings, their similarity to the patent citation information discussed earlier is quite striking. Both measure the use of knowledge from different sources in work products. Experimental studies provide very deep insights into the precise nature of individuals and situations that lead to knowledge use, whereas unit-level studies often provide access to objective archival data (for example, actual citations) as well as identify work groups according to their likely impact on organizational value. This point brings us to the issues of value-chain context in business processes and pivotal roles in talent pools. Many of the unit-level flow measures relate very specifically to particular value-enhancing alliances and even provide specific competitive scenarios, which respondents are asked to consider. They generally focus on particular talent pools (such as R&D scientists) or frame their questions around particular business processes or goals (forming an alliance or inventing a new product or service).

Unit-level knowledge flow measures may provide higher-level outcomes to validate and calibrate I/O research results. It is interesting to consider the implications of applying both the experimental methods and the archival or business unit survey methods in one study. The experimental methods would enhance understanding of group-level interactions, and their results might be compared with perceived unit communication, actual citation of work in publications or patents, and so on. For example, information is likely to be differentially known to different groups in the field, suggesting the possibility of tracking whether that information is used in final products or reports, just as experimental studies have done. These measures also may provide moderator or mediator variables. I/O and HR interventions to enhance knowledge sharing may be more effective when unit-level measures reveal positive managerial perceptions of the conditions for knowledge flows between alliances because the environment for sharing is more supportive.

Measuring Knowledge Enablers

Enablers facilitate changes in knowledge stocks and flows. The fact that enablers are present does not necessarily mean that they are actually used or that knowledge is generated or moved. Still, enablers are included here because virtually every theory and concept of knowledge notes that enabling mechanisms are essential. For example, DeNisi et al. (Chapter One) note Pfeffer and Sutton's (2001) admonishment that a key role of leadership is "to help build systems of practice that produce a more reliable transformation of knowledge into action" (p. 261). Fiol (Chapter Three) differentiates enablers (formal technologies and structures) from drivers (informal and social trusting communities). Here, the term *enabler* will encompass both ideas. Thus, enablers illustrate unique measurement opportunities and are promising candidates for moderator or mediator variables for I/O psychology and HR researchers.

Geographic and Political Proximity

Several authors have measured physical, personal, or political proximity as knowledge enablers. Maskell and Malmberg (1999) assert that smaller firms benefit from close geographic proximity by sharing knowledge and other resources. Torstensson's (1999) measure of membership in cooperative institutions (such as the European Union) predicted country growth. Capello's (1999) survey measured "location advantages" (for example, proximity to airports and to cultural or industrial centers). Zahra et al. (2000) measured "international diversity" using secondary sources and surveys of managers on the number of countries generating products or revenues.

International and Domestic Organizational and Alliance Design

Measures focusing on international organizational design include the number of domestic and international joint ventures (Barkema et al., 1997). Dyer and Nobeoka (2000) used archival and survey data to map a particularly comprehensive set of interactions among Toyota's supplier network, including subsidies to the network, meetings and committees, problem-solving teams combining Toyota and supplier employees, employee transfers to suppliers, free information access, open access to supplier plants, and perceived benefits of sharing knowledge. Finally, Hitt, Dacin, Levitas, Arregle, and Borza (2000) used a policy-capturing survey of executives in 202 firms, presenting thirty hypothetical case studies that varied fourteen potential alliance partner criteria, including "complementary capabilities," "unique competencies," "market knowledge–access," "intangible assets," "managerial capabilities," and "willingness to share expertise."

Some measures exploit archival information on financial and reporting structures. Darr and Kurtsberg (2000) measured pizza stores in terms of strategy, customers, and geography. Barnett et al. (1994) divided banks into branch and "unit" structures. Powell, Koput, and Smith-Doerr (1996) used the BIOSCAN database to measure the extent and centrality of formal agreements among different biotechnology firms and various partners.

Fiol (Chapter Three) noted that organization structures can be measured in terms of their complexity, number of levels, and level of specificity. She also noted that organizational structures may be subordinate to social processes in explaining knowledge flows.

Research and Development (R&D) Expenditures

Archival records of R&D spending provide an economic indicator of knowledge required in jobs, industries, or countries (for example, Berman, Bound, & Griliches, 1994; Bhagat & Welch, 1995; Lane & Lubatkin, 1998; Torstensson, 1999; Zahra et al., 2000). Helfat (1997) used a rich measure of R&D expenditures from the U.S. Department of Energy database, including total R&D for the twenty-six largest U.S. energy firms and the breakdown of R&D expenditures by type of business.

Absorptive Capacity

The capacity to absorb new knowledge can be associated with organizations, units, and partners (Cohen & Levinthal, 1990). Absorptive capacity measures overlap with some of the knowledge stock measures noted earlier, because having prior knowledge aids assimilation and exploitation of new knowledge (for example, Cohen & Levinthal, 1989, regarding R&D). Deeds (Chapter Two) noted that absorptive capacity, and the proximity between the knowledge bases of two alliance partners, may determine which sort of alliance arrangements (licenses, mergers, and so on) will be most effective.

Helfat (1997) measured a firm's absorptive capacity for coal gasification in terms of the level of complementary R&D already being done. Van den Bosch, Volberda, and De Boer (1999) described publishing firms moving into multimedia, defining their absorptive capacity in terms of their prior related knowledge as well as the organizational form (function, division, and matrix) and combinative capabilities (systems, coordination, socialization). Lane and Lubatkin (1998) measured the absorptive capacity of pharmaceutical companies forming alliances with biotechnology start-ups, using archival data on publication patterns. They calculated the overlap in the research communities where publications by alliance partners appeared. Measures included the total overlap of publication communities, overlap in basic knowledge (biochemistry), overlap in specialized knowledge (neurology, endocrinology, and so on), and percentage of research communities in a scientific discipline in which the partner is active. They also measured organizational "knowledge-processing similarity," such as formalization and centralization, incentive pay, and emphasis on scientific publications in the firm.

The Network

Attributes of individual and organizational networks are clearly a key enabler of knowledge flows. Wasserman and Faust (1994) provide an excellent treatment of many of the main approaches, including methods based on graph theory, matrix analysis, and so on. For example, strong versus weak ties (Granovetter, 1973) can be measured through affective reactions about relationships between individuals or groups (Hansen, 1999, p. 94). "Structural holes" describe network points that fill unique gaps (Burt, 1995).

Kogut (2000) applied these concepts to the interaction patterns among Toyota suppliers. Collins (2000) measured network size, range, and strength of ties by asking top managers to list contacts from nine external categories (suppliers, customers, financial institutions, and so on) and four internal categories (sales, R&D, and so on) and then to rate the relationships on dimensions such as frequency, duration, and intensity. Appleyard (1996) surveyed the importance of nine sources of technical information: one's colleagues in the company; technologists at other companies; equipment vendors; materials suppliers; customers; benchmarking studies; presentations at conferences; journals, books, and so on; and patents. Subramaniam and Venkatraman (2001) surveyed senior managers about the frequency of their telephone, fax, and e-mail exchanges to and from overseas managers. Hage and Hollingsworth (2000) noted that there are "numerous sets of data from which one may obtain measures of the connectedness/communication among actors, such as the European Commission's (1997) Community Information Survey and from the National Science Foundation in the U.S." (p. 986).

Networks can be traced through movement of individuals. Almeida and Kogut (1999) examined the actual movement of patent holders, and Capello (1999) interviewed Italian managers about the previous employment and training of technicians and their turnover.

Fiol (Chapter Three) notes the importance of trust in enabling knowledge. Glaeser, Laibson, Scheinkman, and Soutter (2000) found that attitude surveys predicted trustworthy behavior much better than trusting behavior. The World Values Survey contains a set of items tapping trust at an economic institutional level; it has been applied in over twenty countries (for example, Knack & Keefer, 1997).

Tacitness

"We know more than we can tell" (Polanyi, 1966, p. 4). Knowledge's tacitness refers to the effort required to move it (Almeida & Kogut, 1999). Tacitness is an enabler because it affects the ease of knowledge transfer and the effectiveness of other enablers (for example, DeNisi et al., Chapter One; Lam, 2000; Lawson & Lorenz, 1999). Tacitness can be harmful when it restricts desired knowledge flow between groups, but it can also be valuable in making knowledge difficult for competitors to copy (Teece, Pisano, &

Shuen, 1997; Barney, 1991). Definitions of tacitness abound. Several authors (Gupta & Govindarajan, 2000; Helfat, 1997; Kogut & Zander, 1992) distinguish "know-how" (procedures) as distinct from "know-what" (facts). Spender (1996) defined three types of tacit knowledge: *conscious* is codified at the individual level, *automatic* is completely implicit, and *collective* is held by the community or group.

Zander and Kogut (1995) surveyed engineers about specific innovations in their firm, obtaining ratings of codifiability (embedded in manuals, software, and documents), teachability (easily learned or taught), complexity (changing physical characteristics, shape, dimensions, and assembly), and system dependence (impossible for one person to know everything, frequent interpersonal contact required). Simonin (1999) surveyed managers about the degree to which alliance partner technology was "easily codifiable in written instructions" and "know-how more explicit than tacit." Tan and Libby (1997) defined tacit managerial knowledge as "knowledge of traits and behaviors related to managing self, others, and career" (p. 105). They asked accounting firm partners and their employees to react to a set of scenarios, with tacitness indicated by larger deviations between employees' and partners' ratings. Subramaniam and Venkatraman (2001) had respondents rate information from overseas partners in several ways: simple versus complex; easy versus difficult to document, communicate, and understand from written reports; obvious versus subtle to competitors; and easy versus hard to identify without personal experience.

Implications for I/O and HR Research

In terms of aggregated units of analysis, enabler measures span the widest range, from very specific (the communication of specific items of information by individuals or the use or citation of particular ideas in work products) to more general (geographic proximity or organization design). The value chain context is well developed in these enabler measures because they frequently reflect deep understanding of company strategies, and archival and financial data that illuminate key competitive aspects or results. For example, R&D expenditures and absorptive capacity measures are often constructed to focus on particular competitive innovations or business processes. The relevance of existing knowledge for assimilating new knowledge is certainly recognized in I/O theories of individual knowledge transfer, and the measures described here illustrate practical ways to apply the concept to organizations and business units, incorporating the value chain. Pivotal roles are also evident in the measurement of network attributes, such as identifying individuals who fill "structural holes." For example, Fisher and White (2000) noted that the turnover of such individuals may have negative implications for networks that go well beyond those individuals' job performance. This may offer one mechanism by which the loss of individuals can significantly affect a firm's intangible resources and competitive advantage (DeNisi et al., Chapter One).

The enabler measures noted here present opportunities for I/O researchers. Perhaps their most obvious role would be as moderators or mediators in traditional I/O research. The nature of organizational design and alliances, the tacitness of knowledge, and the degree to which current knowledge provides a framework for absorbing new competitive knowledge would all seem likely to influence the effects of HR and I/O knowledge interventions. Moreover, because many of the measures are based on archival information, this provides an opportunity to tap additional constructs relatively unobtrusively. Even the survey measures described here could be incorporated into many I/O studies. The concept of tacitness seems particularly relevant to I/O research on knowledge transfer.

Some of these enablers may also provide useful high-level dependent variables. For example, R&D expenditures might be expected to rise in areas where firms are targeting investments in employee knowledge. If this is not happening, it might signal missed opportunities to capitalize on such investments. Where HR interventions are aimed at increasing knowledge communication and clarity, we might expect to see increases in measures of absorptive capacity and decreases in measures of tacitness.

Conclusion

This chapter distinguished measures as stocks, flows, and enablers. These distinctions may prove useful to future researchers. Enablers and flows are likely intervening or moderating factors, and they may help researchers understand or explain additional cross-context variation in the effects of HR and I/O variables on organizational outcomes. Knowledge stocks may prove useful as high-level dependent variables as well as important moderators or mediators, particularly when the outcome variables reflect overall organizational financial results.

These distinctions between stocks, flows, and enablers may also prove useful in identifying which measures in Exhibit 13.1 are most likely to be affected by the HR practices, I/O interventions, and individual differences that are the focus of the other chapters in this volume. Certain HR practices or individual differences may be linked more closely to some categories than others. For example, training in group processes should probably manifest itself in an increased flow of knowledge, although it may or may not increase the stock of knowledge. In contrast, incentives for creativity might be most likely to affect knowledge stocks (for example, patents and cited papers) rather than flows or enablers.

Earlier sections noted that traditional HR and I/O research focuses at the HR program and individual level (*effectiveness* in Figure 13.1) and could be extended to encompass the logic of business processes and competitive context (*impact* in Figure 13.1). Also, the research that produced the measures described here could benefit from understanding the HR and I/O practices and individual differences that affect the phenomena they measure. Most I/O readers have already recognized potential improvements in psychometric properties (single-item measures, perceptions of only single subjects, and so on). I/O principles of units of analysis might also suggest improvements, such as validating the assumption that the existence of certain jobs ("scientist" or "expatriate") indicates associated knowledge ("scientific principles" or "global awareness").

Most of the research using higher-level knowledge measures makes an implicit assumption that organizations can create the teams or other design elements, with little discussion about how to do so. There is great potential in testing these assumptions. For example, research on networks has suggested that certain personality types might be associated with those filling "structural holes" (Burt, Jannotta, & Mahoney, 1998).

Such integration will require I/O and HR researchers to understand and more explicitly measure industry and competitive context. This does not mean simply adding financial outcomes to traditional variables such as HR practices or skill levels, but rather articulating the logical links between knowledge and pivotal roles within talent pools and structures, business processes, and aggregated strategic outcomes. The measures described here show that this is possible. R&D expenditures have been specifically weighted for their relevance to particular manufacturing processes. Shared ideas are not merely counted but are logically related to changes in production costs over time (learning curves). The field of knowledge management provides ample evidence that such a bridge is possible. Exhibit 13.1 illustrates some of the rich and varied measures that might help us realize the potential.

References

Adams, J. D. (1990). Fundamental stocks of knowledge and productivity growth. *Journal of Political Economy, 98*(4), 673–702.

Almeida, P. (1996). Knowledge sourcing by foreign multinationals: Patent citation analysis in the U.S. semiconductor industry. *Strategic Management Journal, 17,* 155–165.

Almeida, P., & Kogut, B. (1999). Localization of knowledge and the mobility of engineers in regional networks. *Management Science, 45*(7), 905–917.

Appleyard, M. (1996). How does knowledge flow? Interfirm patterns in the semiconductor industry. *Strategic Management Journal, 17,* 137–154.

Argote, L., & Ingram, P. (2000). Knowledge transfer: A basis for competitive advantage in firms. *Organizational Behavior and Human Decision Processes, 82*(1), 150–169.

Argote, L., Ingram, P., Levine, J. M., & Moreland, R. L. (2000). Knowledge transfer in organizations: Learning from the experience of others. *Organizational Behavior and Human Decision Processes, 82*(1), 1–8.

Arrow, K. J. (1962). The economic implications of learning by doing. *Review of Economic Studies, 29*(3), 155–173.

A Viking with a compass. (1998, June 6). *Economist,* p. 64.

Barkema, H. G., Shenkar, O., Vermeulen, F., & Bell, J. H. (1997). Working abroad, working with others: How firms learn to operate international joint ventures. *Academy of Management Journal, 40,* 426–442.

Barnett, W. P., Greve, H. R., & Park, D. P. (1994, Summer). An evolutionary model of organizational performance. *Strategic Management Journal, 15,* 11–28.

Barnett, W. P., & Hansen, M. T. (1996). The red queen in organizational evolution. *Strategic Management Journal, 17,* 139–158.

Barney, J. B. (1991). Firm resources and sustained competitive advantage. *Journal of Management, 17,* 99–120.

Barsky, N. P., & Marchant, G. (2000). The most valuable resource–measuring and managing intellectual capital. *Strategic Finance, 81,* 58–62.

Batchelor, A. (1999, February). Is the balance sheet outdated? *Accountancy, 123,* 81.

Baum, J., & Ingram, P. (1998). Population-level learning in the Manhattan hotel industry, 1898–1980. *Management Science, 44,* 996–1016.

Becker, G. S. (1964). *Human capital: A theoretical and empirical analysis, with special reference to education.* New York: Columbia University Press.

Berman, E., Bound, J., & Griliches, Z. (1994). Changes in the demand for skilled labor within U.S. manufacturing: Evidence from the annual survey of manufacturers. *Quarterly Journal of Economics, 109,* 367–397.

Bhagat, S., & Welch, I. (1995). Corporate research and development investment: International comparisons. *Journal of Accounting and Economics, 19,* 443–470.

Bontis, N., Dragonetti, N. C., Jacobsen, K., & Roos, G. (1999). The knowledge toolbox: A review of the tools available to measure and manage intangible resources. *European Management Journal, 17*(4), 391–403.

Boudreau, J. W. (1991). Utility analysis for decisions in human resource management. In M. D. Dunnette & L. M. Hough (Eds.), *Handbook of industrial and organizational psychology* (Vol. 2; 2nd ed.; pp. 621–745). Palo Alto, CA: Consulting Psychologists Press.

Boudreau, J. W. (1996). The motivational impact of utility analysis and HR measurement. *Journal of Human Resource Costing and Accounting, 1*(2), 73–84.

Boudreau, J. W., Dunford, B. B., & Ramstad, P. (2001). The human capital "impact" on e-business: The case of Encyclopedia Britannica. In N. Pal & J. M. Ray (Eds.), *Pushing the digital frontier: Insights into the changing landscape of e-business.* New York: AMACOM.

Boudreau, J. W., & Ramstad, P. M. (1997). Measuring intellectual capital: Learning from financial history. *Human Resource Management, 36*(3), 343–356.

Boudreau, J. W., & Ramstad, P. R. (1999). Human resource metrics: Can measures be strategic? In P. Wright, L. Dyer, J. Boudreau, & G. Milkovich (Eds.), *Strategic human resources management in the twenty-first century* (Supplement 4; pp. 75–98). G. R. Ferris (Ed.), *Research in personnel and human resource management.* Greenwich, CT: JAI Press.

Boudreau, J. W., & Ramstad, P. M. (in press). Strategic I/O psychology and the role of utility analysis models. In W. Borman, D. Ilgen, & R. Klimoski (Eds.), *Handbook of psychology* (Vol. 12; chap. 9). New York: Wiley.

Bouty, I. (2000). Interpersonal and interaction influences on informal resource exchanges between R&D researchers across organizational boundaries. *Academy of Management Journal, 43*(1), 50–65.

Burt, R. S. (1995). *Structural holes: The social structure of competition.* Boston: Harvard University Press.

Burt, R. S., Jannotta, J. E., & Mahoney, J. T. (1998). Personality correlates of structural holes. *Social Networks, 20,* 63–87.

Cannon-Bowers, J. A., Salas, E., & Converse, S. A. (1993). Shared mental models in expert team decision making. In J. J. Castellan, Jr. (Ed.), *Individual and group decision making: Current issues* (pp. 221–246). Hillsdale, NJ: Erlbaum.

Capello, R. (1999). Spatial transfer of knowledge in high technology milieu: Learning versus collective learning processes. *Regional Studies, 33*(4), 353–365.

Cappelli, P. (1993). Are skill requirements rising? Evidence from production and clerical jobs. *Industrial and Labor Relations Review, 46*(3), 515–521.

Cappelli, P. (1996, May-June). Technology and skill requirements: Implications for establishment wage structures. *New England Economic Review,* pp. 139–155.

Cappelli, P. (2000, January-February). A market-driven approach to retaining talent. *Harvard Business Review, 78,* 103–111.

Coff, R. (1999). How buyers cope with uncertainty when acquiring firms in knowledge-intensive industries: Caveat emptor. *Organization Science, 10*(2), 144–162.

Cohen, M. D. (1991). Individual learning and organizational routine. *Organization Science, 2*(1), 135–139.

Cohen, W. M., & Levinthal, D. (1989). Innovation and learning: The two faces of R&D. *Economic Journal, 99,* 569–596.

Cohen, W. M., & Levinthal, D. A. (1990). Absorptive capacity: A new perspective on learning and innovation. *Administrative Science Quarterly, 35*(1), 128–153.

Collins, C. (2000, August). *Strategic human resource practices and the development of organizational social capital.* Presentation made at the Academy of Management conference, Toronto.

Conner, K. R., & Prahalad, C. K. (1996). A resource-based theory of the firm: Knowledge versus opportunism. *Organization Science, 7*(5), 477–501.

Crossan, M. M., Lane, H. W., & White, R. E. (1999). An organizational learning framework: From intuition to institution. *Academy of Management Review, 24*(3), 522–537.

Darr, E. D., Argote, L., & Epple, D. (1995). The acquisition, transfer, and depreciation of knowledge in service organizations: Productivity in franchises. *Management Science, 41,* 1750–1762.

Darr, E. D., & Kurtzberg, T. R. (2000). An investigation of partner similarity dimensions on knowledge transfer. *Organizational Behavior and Human Decision Processes, 82*(1), 28–44.

Deng, Z., Lev, B., & Narin, F. (1999, May-June). Science and technology as predictors of stock performance. *Financial Analysts Journal, 55*(5), 20–32.

DiFrancesco, J. M., & Berman, S. J. (2000). Human productivity: The new American frontier. *National Productivity Review, 19*(3), 29–37.

Dodgson, M. (1993). Organizational learning: A review of some literatures. *Organization Studies, 14*(3), 375–394.

Downes, M., & Thomas, A. S. (2000). Knowledge transfer through expatriation: The U-curve approach to overseas staffing. *Journal of Managerial Issues, 12*(2), 131–149.

Dussuage, P., Garrette, B., & Mitchell, W. (2000). Learning from competing partners: Outcomes and durations of scale and link alliances in Europe, North America, and Asia. *Strategic Management Journal, 21*(2), 99–126.

Dyer, J., & Nobeoka, K. (2000). Creating and managing a high-performance knowledge-sharing network: The Toyota case. *Strategic Management Journal, 21,* 345–367.

Dzinkowski, R. (1999). Managing the brain trust. *CMA Management, 73,* 14–18.

Dzinkowski, R. (2000). The measurement and management of intellectual capital: An introduction. *Management Accounting, 78,* 32–36.

Edvinsson, L., & Malone, M. (1997). *Intellectual capital.* Cambridge, MA: Harvard Business School Press.

Epple, D., Argote, L., & Devedas, R. (1991). Organizational learning curves: A method for investigating intraplant transfer of knowledge acquired through learning by doing. *Organization Science, 2*(1), 58–71.

Epple, D., Argote, L., & Murphy, K. (1996). An empirical investigation of the microstructure of knowledge acquisition and transfer through learning by doing. *Operations Research, 44*(1), 77–87.

Evans, P., & Wurster, T. S. (1998). Strategy and the new economics of information. *Harvard Business Review, 75,* 70–83.

Evans, P., & Wurster, T. S. (1999, November-December). Getting real about virtual commerce. *Harvard Business Review,* pp. 85–94.

Fisher, S. R., & White, M. A. (2000). Downsizing in a learning organization: Are there hidden costs? *Academy of Management Review, 21*(1), 244–251.

Flamholtz, E. G. (1999). *Human resource accounting* (3rd ed.). New York: Kluwer.

Glaeser, E. L., Laibson, D. I., Scheinkman, J. A., & Soutter, C. L. (2000). Measuring trust. *Quarterly Journal of Economics, 115*(3), 811–847.

Granovetter, M. (1973). The strength of weak ties. *American Journal of Sociology, 6,* 1360–1380.

Gruenfeld, D. H., Martorana, P. V., & Fan, E. T. (2000). What do groups learn from their worldliest members? Direct and indirect influence in dynamic teams. *Organizational Behavior and Human Decision Processes, 82*(1), 45–59.

Gupta, A. K., & Govindarajan, V. (2000). Knowledge flows within multinational corporations. *Strategic Management Journal, 21,* 473–496.

Hackett, B. (2000, March). *Beyond knowledge management: New ways to work and learn.* New York: The Conference Board.

Hage, J., & Hollingsworth, J. R. (2000). A strategy for the analysis of idea innovation networks and institutions. *Organization Studies, 21*(5), 971–1004.

Hall, B., Jaffe, A., & Trajtenberg, M. (2000). *Market value and patent citations: A first look.* Working paper No. 7741, National Bureau of Economic Research, Washington, DC.

Hansen, M. T. (1999). The search-transfer problem: The role of weak ties in sharing knowledge across organizational subunits. *Administrative Science Quarterly, 44,* 82–111.

Helfat, C. E. (1997). Know-how and asset complementarity and dynamic capability accumulation: The case of R&D. *Strategic Management Journal, 18*(5), 339–360.

Hitt, M., A., Dacin, M. T., Levitas, E., Arregle, J. L., & Borza, A. (2000). Partner selection in emerging and developed market contexts: Resource-based and organizational learning perspectives. *Academy of Management Journal, 43*(3), 449–467.

Hoopes, D. G., & Postrel, S. (1999). Shared knowledge, glitches, and product development performance. *Strategic Management Journal, 20,* 837–865.

Ingram, P., & Baum, J. A. (1997). Opportunity and constraint: Organizations' learning from the operating and competitive experience of industries [Special issue]. *Strategic Management Journal, 18,* 75–98.

Inkpen, A. C., & Dinur, A (1998). Knowledge management processes and international joint ventures. *Organization Science, 9*(4), 454–479.

Jaffe, A. B. (1986). Technological opportunity and spillovers of R&D: Evidence from firms' patents, profits, and market value. *American Economic Review, 76*(5), 984–1001.

Jaffe, A. B., Trajtenberg, M., & Fogarty, M. S. (2001). *Knowledge spillovers and patent citations: Evidence from a survey of inventors.* Working paper, National Bureau of Economic Research, Washington, DC.

Knack, S., & Keefer, P. (1997). Does social capital have an economic pay-off? A cross-country investigation. *Quarterly Journal of Economics, 112*(4), 1251–1288.

Kogut, B. (2000). The network as knowledge: Generative rules and the emergence of structure. *Strategic Management Journal, 21,* 405–425.

Kogut, B., & Zander, U. (1992). Knowledge of the firm, combinative capabilities, and the replication of technology. *Organization Science, 3*(3), 383–397.

Lado, A. A., & Wilson, M. C. (1994). Human resource systems and sustained competitive advantage: A competency-based perspective. *Academy of Management Review, 19*(4), 699–727.

Lam, A. (2000). Tacit knowledge, organizational learning, and societal institutions: An integrated framework. *Organization Studies, 21*(3), 487–513.

Lane, P. J., & Lubatkin, M. (1998). Relative absorptive capacity and interorganizational learning. *Strategic Management Journal, 19,* 461–477.

Lawson, C., & Lorenz, E. (1999). Collective learning, tacit knowledge, and regional innovative capacity. *Regional Studies, 33*(4), 305–317.

Leigh, D. E., & Gifford, K. D. (1999). Workplace transformation and worker upskilling: The perspective of individual workers. *Industrial Relations, 38*(2), 174–191.

Lev, B., & Zarowin, P. (1999). The boundaries of financial reporting and how to extend them. *Journal of Accounting Research, 37*(2), 353–383.

Levine, J. M., Higgins, E. T., & Choi, H. (2000). Development of strategic norms in groups. *Organizational Behavior and Human Decision Processes, 82*(1), 88–101.

Lewis, E. E., & Lippitt, J. W. (1999). Valuing intellectual assets. *Journal of Legal Economics, 9,* 31–48.

Low, J., & Seisfeld, T. (1998, March-April). Measures that matter. *Strategy and Leadership, 26*(2), 24–29.

Lynn, B. (1998). Intellectual capital. *CMA Magazine, 72,* 10–15.

Maskell, P., & Malmberg, A. (1999). Localized learning and industrial competitiveness. *Cambridge Journal of Economics, 23,* 167–185.

McEvily, B., & Zaheer, A. (1999). Bridging ties: A source of firm heterogeneity in competitive capabilities. *Strategic Management Journal, 20,* 1133–1156.

Mintz, S. L. (1999, February). Seeing is believing. *CFO Magazine, 15*(2), 29–34.

Moreland, R. L., Argote, L., & Krishnan, R. (1996). Socially shared cognition at work: Transactive memory and group performance. In J. L. Nye & A. M. Brower (Eds.), *What's social about social cognition? Research on socially shared cognition in small groups* (pp. 57–84). Thousand Oaks, CA: Sage.

Moreland, R. L., & Myaskovsky, L. (2000). Exploring the performance benefits of group training: Transactive memory or improved communication? *Organizational Behavior and Human Decision Processes, 82,* 117–133.

Mowery, D. C., Oxley, J. E., & Silverman, B. S. (1996). Strategic alliances and interfirm knowledge transfer [Winter special issue]. *Strategic Management Journal, 17,* 77–91.

Nahapiet, J., & Ghoshal, S. (1998). Social capital, intellectual capital, and the organizational advantage. *Academy of Management Review, 23*(2), 242–266.

Osterland, A. (2001, April 1). Decoding intangibles. *CFO,* pp. 57–62.

Paulus, P. B., & Yang, H. (2000). Idea generation in groups: A basis for creativity in organizations. *Organizational Behavior and Human Decision Processes, 82,* 76–87.

Petrash, G. (1996). Dow's journey to a knowledge value management culture. *European Management Journal, 14*(4), 365–373.

Pfeffer, J., & Sutton, R. I. (2001). *The knowing-doing gap: How smart companies turn knowledge into action.* Boston: Harvard Business School Press.

Polanyi, S. (1966). *The tacit dimension.* New York: Doubleday.

Powell, W. W., Koput, K. W., & Smith-Doerr, L. (1996). Interorganizational collaboration and the locus of innovation: Networks of learning in biotechnology. *Administrative Science Quarterly, 41*(1), 116–136.

Rayport, J. E., & Sviokla, J. J. (1995, November-December). Exploiting the virtual value chain. *Harvard Business Review, 73,* 75–86.

Roos, J., & von Krogh, G. (1996). The epistemological challenge: Managing knowledge and intellectual capital. *European Management Journal, 14*(4), 333–337.

Roslender, R. (2000). Accounting for intellectual capital: A contemporary management accounting perspective. *Management Accounting, 78,* 34–37.

Rothaermel, F., & Deeds, D. (2001). More good things are not necessarily better: An empirical study of strategic alliances, experience effects, and innovative output in high technology startups. In M. A.

Hitt, C. Lucier, & B. Shelton (Eds.), *Strategy in the entrepreneurial millenium*. New York: Wiley.

Seely-Brown, J., & Duguid, P. (2000, May-June). Balancing act: How to capture knowledge without killing it. *Harvard Business Review, 78*(3), 73–80.

Shenkar, O., & Li, J. (1999). Knowledge search in international cooperative ventures. *Organization Science, 10*(2), 134–143.

Sherif, M. (1936). *The psychology of social norms*. New York: HarperCollins.

Simonin, B. L. (1999). Ambiguity and the process of knowledge transfer in strategic alliances. *Strategic Management Journal, 20*, 595–623.

Sjoholm, F. (1996). International transfer of knowledge: The role of international trade and geographic proximity. *Welrwirtschaftliches Archives, 132*, 97–115.

Skandia Corporation. (1996). *Power of innovation: Skandia Navigator* (Supplement to interim report). Stockholm, Sweden: Skandia Corporation.

Sorensen, J. B., & Stuart, T. E. (2000). Aging, obsolescence, and organizational innovation. *Administrative Science Quarterly, 45*(1), 81–112.

Spencer, J. (2000). Knowledge flows in the global innovation system: Do U.S. firms share more scientific knowledge than their Japanese rivals? *Journal of International Business Studies, 31*(3), 521–531.

Spender, J. C. (1996, Winter). Making knowledge the basis of a dynamic theory of the firm. *Strategic Management Journal, 17*, 5–9.

Stasser, G., Vaughn, S. I., & Stewart, D. D. (2000). Pooling unshared information: The benefits of knowing how access to information is distributed among group members. *Organizational Behavior and Human Decision Processes, 82*(1), 102–116.

Stewart, T. (1998). *Intellectual capital: The new wealth of organizations*. New York: Doubleday.

Subramaniam, M., & Venkatraman, N. (2001). Determinants of transnational new product development capability: Testing the influence of transferring and deploying tacit overseas knowledge. *Strategic Management Journal, 22*(4), 359–378.

Sveiby, K. E. (1997). *The new organizational wealth*. San Francisco: Berrett-Koehler.

Tan, H., & Libby, R. (1997). Tacit managerial knowledge versus technical knowledge as determinants of audit performance in the field. *Journal of Accounting Research, 35*, 97–113.

Teece, D. J., Pisano, G., & Shuen, A. (1997). Dynamic capabilities and strategic management. *Strategic Management Journal, 18*(7), 509–533.

Tomlinson, M. (1999). The learning economy and embodied knowledge flows in Great Britain. *Journal of Evolutionary Economics, 9*(4), 431–452.

Torstensson, R. M. (1999). Growth, knowledge transfer, and European integration. *Applied Economics, 31*(1), 97–106.

Van den Bosch, F.A.J., Volberda, H. W., & De Boer, M. (1999). *The meaning of patent citations: Report of the NBER/Case Western Reserve survey of patentees.* Cambridge, MA: National Bureau of Economic Research.

Van Meijl, H., & van Tongeren, F. (1999). Endogenous international technology spillovers and biased technical change. *Agriculture Economic Systems Research, 11*(1), 31–48.

Walsh, J. P., & Ungson, G. R. (1991). Organizational memory. *Academy of Management Review, 16,* 57–91.

Wasserman, S., & Faust, K. (1994). *Social network analysis: Methods and applications.* Cambridge, UK: Cambridge University Press.

Weick, K., & Roberts, K. (1993). Collective mind in organizations: Heedful interrelating on flight decks. *Administrative Science Quarterly, 38,* 357–381.

Zahra, S. A., Ireland, R. D., & Hitt, M. A. (2000). International expansion by new venture firms: International diversity, mode of market entry, technological learning, and performance. *Academy of Management Journal, 43*(5), 925–950.

Zander, U., & Kogut, B. (1995). Knowledge and the speed of the transfer and imitation of organization capabilities: An empirical test. *Organization Science, 6*(1), 76–92.

PART 6

Conclusion

CHAPTER 14

Managing Human Resources for Knowledge-Based Competition
New Research Directions

Susan E. Jackson
Michael A. Hitt
Angelo S. DeNisi

Modern organizations face a constantly changing environment. To thrive or merely survive in such an environment, they have to develop substantial management capabilities, one of which is effective knowledge management. That, in turn, requires developing a human resource management system that enhances the organization's ability to gain and use knowledge resources. Changes in the basic contours of the competitive landscape mean that some of our existing knowledge about human resource management is becoming obsolete. Research that adequately addressed the needs of organizations facing the competitive conditions of the past does not adequately address many issues faced today.

The preceding chapters have described many aspects of human resource management systems that influence an organization's knowledge management capability—including the design and structure of work (Deeds, Chapter Two; Fiol, Chapter Three; Mohrman, Chapter Four; Oldham, Chapter Nine), staffing (Pulakos, Dorsey,

& Borman, Chapter Six; Davis-Blake & Hui, Chapter Seven; Maurer, Lee, & Mitchell, Chapter Eleven), training and development (Noe, Colquitt, Simmering, & Alvarez, Chapter Eight), rewards (Lawler, Chapter Ten), organizational culture and climate (Tetrick & Da Silva, Chapter Twelve), and measurement practices (Boudreau, Chapter Thirteen). Through a combination of these practices, organizations can develop new HR architectures to ensure that they have the human capital they need to achieve their strategic objectives (Lepak & Snell, Chapter Five).

In the strategic HRM literature, several models have been proposed to explain how human resource management systems contribute to a firm's competitive advantage (for example, see Arthur, 1994; Becker & Huselid, 1998; Jackson & Schuler, 1995). One such model is referred to as the *behavioral perspective* (Schuler & Jackson, 1987). According to the behavioral perspective, human resource management practices are an organization's primary means for energizing and directing employee behaviors. Employee behaviors, in turn, are presumed to be among the factors that ultimately determine organizational effectiveness. Although many external forces beyond the control of individual employees have significant consequences for the ultimate survival and success of the firm, the aggregated effects of individual employee behaviors are the primary determinants of the organization's success or failure in the long term. Thus, identifying the needed employee behaviors is the first task in developing HR systems that support knowledge-based competition. Having identified the required behaviors, employers must then make sure that employees have the appropriate competencies, are motivated, and have opportunities to engage in the behaviors. Thus, these are the four primary tasks of any HRM system (Jackson & Schuler, 2002; Schuler, Jackson, & Storey, 2001).

In this chapter, we use the four primary HRM tasks to organize our discussion of the preceding chapters. For each task, we attempt to identify HR practices that employers are adopting to manage knowledge effectively. We also identify additional research that would be useful for developing an improved understanding of how HR practices can help manage knowledge resources effectively. Throughout our discussion, we assume that *all* elements of an HR system may be relevant to accomplishing *each* of the four tasks. This basic framework is illustrated in Figure 14.1.

Figure 14.1. Creating an HRM System for Knowledge-Based Competition.

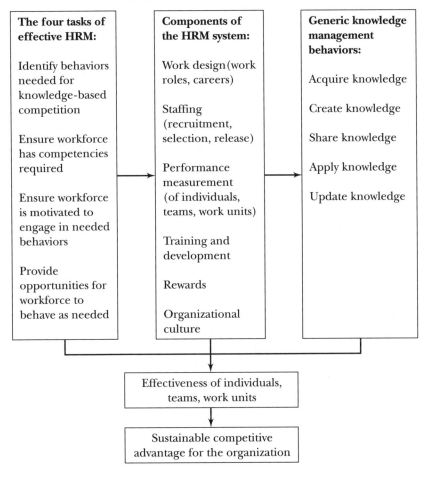

Knowledge-Based Competition

Industry Dynamics and Organizational Design

The four tasks of effective HRM:	Components of the HRM system:	Generic knowledge management behaviors:
Identify behaviors needed for knowledge-based competition	Work design (work roles, careers)	Acquire knowledge
	Staffing (recruitment, selection, release)	Create knowledge
Ensure workforce has competencies required		Share knowledge
	Performance measurement (of individuals, teams, work units)	Apply knowledge
Ensure workforce is motivated to engage in needed behaviors		Update knowledge
	Training and development	
Provide opportunities for workforce to behave as needed	Rewards	
	Organizational culture	

Effectiveness of individuals, teams, work units

Sustainable competitive advantage for the organization

Identifying Behaviors Needed for Knowledge-Based Competition

To design an HRM system that facilitates successful knowledge-based competition, it is necessary first to specify the behaviors needed in organizations pursuing knowledge-intensive strategies. Although empirical research is needed to verify the assertion that knowledge-based competition requires employees to engage in a set of idiosyncratic behaviors, a consensus is developing among management scholars that two categories of behaviors are needed for knowledge-based competition: generic knowledge management behaviors and firm-specific knowledge management behaviors.

It is widely assumed that the generic behaviors needed for effective knowledge-based competition are acquiring knowledge, creating knowledge, sharing knowledge, applying knowledge, and updating knowledge. In Chapter Six, Pulakos, Dorsey, and Borman offer definitions for most of these. Although it is important to support these behaviors among knowledge workers, the need to manage knowledge extends beyond this select group to include the entire workforce of an organization that is seeking competitive advantage in the knowledge-based economy.

Besides these generic behaviors, some firm-specific behaviors that reflect particular objectives and conditions are required. Industry-specific and market-specific behaviors—which lie between the two extremes of generic and firm-specific behaviors—may also be required. We do not describe these more specific behaviors in the present volume, nor do we assume that the tentative principles that apply to generic behaviors necessarily apply to behaviors that are specific to a particular firm, industry, or market. Our discussion in this chapter focuses on the generic behaviors needed for knowledge-intensive strategies.

Knowledge Acquisition

Most of the authors in this volume worked with the basic assumption that, ultimately, knowledge is an individual attribute (see DeNisi, Hitt, & Jackson, Chapter One). If knowledge is an individual attribute, then organizations have two general options for acquiring needed knowledge: they can help current employees acquire the needed knowledge or they can acquire new employees who already have the knowledge. Usually, organizations facilitate knowledge acquisition among employees through training and development programs (Noe et al., Chapter Eight). In some instances, however, current employees may lack the background or abilities necessary to acquire the needed knowledge, or it may take them too long to do so. In such circumstances, organizations may rely on mergers, acquisitions, strategic alliances (see Deeds, Chapter Two) and contract workers (see Davis-Blake & Hui, Chapter Seven) to obtain new members with the appropriate knowledge.

The tactics that organizations use to acquire new knowledge seem straightforward, yet none is foolproof. Thus, research is needed to identify the obstacles that organizations face when using these tactics and to develop solutions to overcome them. For example, rapid changes in the knowledge held by employees present a significant challenge to the design and implementation of training programs, which often impart specific knowledge. To develop such training programs, the developers must identify, encode, and transmit the knowledge content deemed most relevant. In knowledge-intensive environments where knowledge changes continuously, such "spoon feeding" of knowledge to employees is likely to be inefficient and ineffective. Rather than train employees in knowledge *content,* it may be more appropriate to develop their knowledge acquisition skills. Employees with effective knowledge acquisition skills can be encouraged to identify the knowledge they need and then develop personal strategies for acquiring that knowledge— strategies that may or may not require support from the organization. In addition to being more responsive to rapid changes in the knowledge environment, this approach to training may prove more effective in ensuring that employees obtain the elusive tacit knowledge that may determine an organization's success or failure.

Firms that seek to acquire knowledge resources externally also face obstacles. Although obtaining knowledge resources is a primary reason for many mergers and acquisitions (Vermeulen & Barkema, 2001), sometimes these knowledge resources are the first to leave the new organization (for example, Cannella & Hambrick, 1993). Some frameworks exist for understanding why executives depart under these conditions (for example, Walsh, 1988; Hambrick & Cannella, 1993), but additional research is required to determine whether these frameworks apply to other types of employees who possess critical knowledge, such as scientists or sales personnel with deep knowledge of particular customers (see Chapter Eleven).

Knowledge Creation

For knowledge-based competition, *unique* knowledge is particularly valuable. By applying their unique knowledge, organizations are able to offer products and services that competitors cannot match. Because of the value of unique knowledge, creative behaviors are widely acknowledged as essential to successful knowledge-based competition.

Creativity involves *bisociation*—the integration of complex matrices of information (Smith & Di Gregorio, 2002). Employees who are more creative integrate more advanced and unrelated information matrices. Of all the generic behaviors required for knowledge-based competition, creativity is probably the most widely studied. As Oldham (Chapter Nine) describes, such research suggests several issues that organizations need to address in order to create conditions that optimize employee creativity.

Most research on creativity and problem solving in organizations has assumed that employees understand the problems that must be solved. But in the everyday life of organizations, the search for solutions is only part of the total process. Knowledge-based competition requires more from employees than applying their knowledge to generate creative solutions to known problems. They also must identify the problems to be solved, articulate them in meaningful and compelling ways, and then gather new and relevant information that can be used to address them (for example, see Sheremata, 2000; Thomas, Sussman, & Henderson, 2001).

Given the importance of knowledge creation, research is needed to understand how organizations can foster it. Mohrman (Chapter Four) suggests that knowledge creation can be facilitated through the design of work—for example, by assigning tasks to work teams instead of to individuals. But empirical research is needed to develop principles for designing teams who can and will effectively identify the need for new knowledge and generate it. Also needed is research on how to supervise and manage such teams. For example, organizations may be able to increase creativity by teaching managers to provide developmental feedback, avoid close monitoring of employees, and create a supportive climate (Oldham, Chapter Nine; Tetrick & Da Silva, Chapter Twelve; Zhou, in press).

Knowledge Sharing

Acquiring or creating knowledge is critical for an organization to compete effectively in a knowledge-based economy, but these processes do not guarantee success. For the organization to benefit most from employees' knowledge, their knowledge must be shared. Knowledge sharing promotes widespread learning and minimizes the likelihood of wasting resources to solve the same problem repeatedly. Conversely, knowledge hoarding is widely viewed as a common dysfunctional behavior (see Lepak & Snell, Chapter Five).

The diffusion of knowledge throughout an organization has been referred to as *knowledge flow* (see Fiol, Chapter Three). When knowledge flows through an organization, it increases individual and organizational learning. Two types of knowledge flows usually found in organizations are feed-backward knowledge flows and feed-forward knowledge flows (Bontis & Crossan, 1999). Feed-backward knowledge flows occur when organizational practices provide employees with information that is useful in doing their work. Performance evaluation and career development activities generally support feed-backward knowledge flows, and these practices have been the focus of much research.

Feed-forward knowledge flows occur when the knowledge and experiences of individuals and work groups are used to inform strategic decisions. In comparison to the amount of research on understanding how to manage feedback processes, HR researchers have devoted relatively little attention to developing principles for managing feed-forward knowledge flows. Research on participation in decision making, suggestion systems, and quality circles should all be relevant to understanding feed-forward processes, but these topics have not claimed the attention of many researchers over the past decade. In the future, HR research could contribute to improving feed-forward knowledge flows by examining how practices such as staffing, training and development, performance management, and allocation of rewards can be used to support an organizational culture that promotes feed-forward knowledge flows.

To conduct studies of knowledge sharing, researchers will need to develop measures of knowledge-sharing behaviors. Boudreau (Chapter Thirteen) cites several examples of research that illustrates how this might be accomplished. Clearly, research on knowledge sharing is in its infancy, and creative approaches to measurement may be needed to advance our understanding of knowledge-sharing behaviors. In addition to the measurement approaches described by Boudreau, interested researchers will likely find it useful to adapt some of the methods that have been developed to study communication networks (for example, see Scott, 1991).

Knowledge Application

Knowledge that is available but never applied is of little use. Unless employees apply their knowledge appropriately, investments in knowledge acquisition and knowledge creation will produce little in return. To the extent that knowledge use is an intentional behavior, employees must not only possess the required knowledge but also *recognize* that they have the required knowledge, be motivated to use it, and believe that it is feasible to use it. Substantial evidence from laboratory studies of groups shows that people often fail to apply their knowledge to the problems they face (see Thompson, Levine, & Messick, 1999). Yet very little research addresses the question of how to ensure that the knowledge available in organizations is effectively used.

Research that examines the conditions that increase employees' use of available knowledge—both explicit and tacit—is clearly needed. Finding ways to increase employees' use of tacit knowledge may be especially challenging. Although employees are likely to recognize that they have various types of explicit knowledge, they may be less aware of their tacit knowledge. Thus, although the conditions that facilitate transfer of training in general may be useful for ensuring that employees apply their explicit knowledge, the same principles may not be effective for encouraging the use of tacit knowledge (for example, see Noe et al., Chapter Eight).

Motivational conflicts may also inhibit knowledge application. For example, knowledge workers may experience conflicts between their employers' expectations of appropriate uses of their knowledge and their own professional, legal, and ethical expectations (Maurer et al., Chapter Eleven). In addition, even when employees recognize that they have useful knowledge and are motivated to use it, they may run into obstacles. For example, contract workers may find it difficult to apply technical knowledge developed in other contexts to an organization's specific operations (Davis-Blake & Hui, Chapter Seven). Because it is increasingly important to ensure that an organization's available knowledge is actually used, research is needed to improve our understanding of the employment conditions that are most effective in ensuring that employees of all types apply the knowledge they bring.

Future research might also consider how decision-making processes should be structured to optimize the use of available knowledge. Is it inappropriate for individuals or teams to use all of their available knowledge under some conditions? For example, prior research has shown that individual performance feedback is not always effective, and may even be detrimental in some situations (see Kluger & DeNisi, 1996). When knowledge changes so rapidly, how can organizations ensure that their decision-making processes and management practices incorporate the most current knowledge while at the same time recognizing that this knowledge will quickly become obsolete?

Improving Our Understanding of Behaviors Needed for Knowledge-Based Competition

For knowledge-intensive organizations, an understanding of the knowledge management behaviors that are most critical to gaining a competitive advantage should serve as the foundation for building their human resource management system. Unfortunately, the job analysis and competency modeling tools in widest use today were *not specifically* developed to assess the importance or frequency of the complete set of generic knowledge management behaviors. Thus, continued reliance on these existing tools may inadvertently lead to inadequate specifications of the behavioral requirements of knowledge-intensive organizations. Over the past decade, I/O psychologists have developed job analysis and competency modeling tools tailored to service-based organizations;

using these tools yields information that is particularly helpful for HR systems in service organizations. Over the next decade, the development of analytical tools that are tailored to knowledge-intensive organizations could prove equally valuable. Importantly, tools are needed to identify not only individual-level knowledge management behaviors but also team-level and organizational knowledge management processes and routines.

For organizations that compete on the basis of knowledge, the five generic knowledge management behaviors—acquiring knowledge, creating knowledge, sharing knowledge, applying knowledge, and updating knowledge—provide a starting point from which to develop an organization-specific profile of knowledge management needs. For any particular organization, some of the behaviors listed may be relatively more important and others may be less important. For example, knowledge acquisition and creation may be more important for a firm that competes for customers on the basis of innovative products and services. Firms that seek to satisfy customers by providing the highest-quality products and services may find that knowledge sharing and application are more important as they strive for continuous incremental improvement. Firms implementing a strategy of mergers and acquisitions may put a greater priority on knowledge sharing across the boundaries that previously separated the combined companies. Of course, the knowledge management behavior profiles of an organization could be articulated more precisely by also considering how they differ for work carried out at each stage in the firm's value chain.

As these examples suggest, the profiles of firms' most valued knowledge management behaviors could serve as a basis for identifying organizations with similar objectives to be achieved through their HR systems. The ability to classify organizations according to their behavioral knowledge requirements would be useful for both research and practice. For example, studies in strategic management could assess the extent to which behavioral profiles predict future strategic moves. As for practice, the ability of managers to assess the similarities and differences in behavioral profiles could be useful for evaluating the attractiveness of potential alliance partners and for choosing organizations that might be useful for benchmarking. HR research studies might be conducted to evaluate whether various indicators of organizational effectiveness (as evaluated by employees, customers, managers, and shareholders) are associated with developing a closer match between organization-level profiles of required knowledge management behaviors and the knowledge management competencies of the workforce.

Ensuring Employees Have Competencies Required for Effective Knowledge Management Behavior

Psychologists use the term *competency* to refer to the knowledge, skills, personality characteristics, and attitudes that make it possible for employees to perform work tasks and roles (Jackson & Schuler, 2003). Here, we focus on the use of HR practices to ensure that an organization's workforce has the individual-level competencies required for successful knowledge-based competition. (Note that in the strategic management literature, the term *competency* is a firm-level concept that refers to capabilities or bundles of resources that contribute to achieving a competitive advantage; see DeNisi et al., Chapter One.) If an organization's stock of knowledge management competencies fits its behavioral requirements, then the workforce is capable of creating a competitive advantage. Consider, for example, the generic knowledge management behavior of knowledge acquisition. Over the past decade, changing information technologies have created many new ways for employees to acquire knowledge—they can search the Internet, use e-mail to communicate with experts, participate in distance learning, and so on. For organizations engaged in knowledge-based competition, having a workforce with the competencies to use these new knowledge acquisition tools is essential.

Several HR practices can be used to increase an organization's stock of relevant competencies. Clearly, the recruitment and selection of new organizational members influences the stock of competencies, as do training and development activities that promote learning. In addition, reward systems can provide incentives for employees to acquire valued competencies. Attending to the organizational culture can make it easier to recruit and retain employees who have the desired competencies, and competency assessment and measurement can be used to monitor competency stocks. Overall, it is likely that most of the basic approaches used to increase the employees' competencies in general also apply to increasing the stock of competencies that support knowledge management behaviors. Nevertheless, knowledge-intensive competition also poses some special challenges, as described next.

Managing Explicit and Tacit Competencies

For individual employees, changes in the knowledge management competencies that firms need create a demand for continuous learning, adaptation, and change (Noe et al., Chapter Eight). Keeping their stock of competencies current may require employees to update their technical knowledge, add new skills, shed obsolete attitudes, and so on. For knowledge-intensive organizations, a big challenge is ensuring that the competencies present in their workforce as a whole evolve to meet changing environmental conditions (see Lepak & Snell, Chapter Five).

Extensive research on learning processes, training techniques, and employee development provides a wealth of information that organizations can use to promote individual learning and change (for example, see Goldstein & Ford, 2002). However, it must be acknowledged that to a great extent these principles have been designed to address the development of "explicit" competencies—that is, competencies that can be articulated and codified. Similarly, many of the constructs that Pulakos et al. (Chapter Six) identified as useful predictors of knowledge workers' performance represent explicit competencies. Explicit competencies are amenable to formal and systematic management. They can be measured and transferred with relative ease. Technical knowledge and skills are examples of explicit competencies.

Unlike explicit knowledge and skills, tacit competencies are more difficult to articulate and measure, and so they are more difficult to manage. Creativity (or creative problem-solving ability) may be an example of a tacit competency. Some interpersonal skills and problem-sensing abilities may also be examples of tacit competencies. Tacit competencies are usually ignored by formal HRM practices. Because they are difficult to measure and teach, it has been assumed that they cannot (or should not) be managed. Of course, the ease of measuring and managing the competencies needed for knowledge management may have no relationship to their importance. Thus, research that illustrates effective approaches to measuring and managing tacit competencies should be given high priority.

Knowledge management scholars have argued that extensive interpersonal contact between teachers and learners provides the best means for transferring tacit knowledge (see Fiol, Chapter Three). Thus, one approach to managing tacit competencies may be to develop social networks that link together a broad cross section of individuals, including employees and others who are not members of the organization. If tacit competencies are transferred and learned implicitly and informally, then individuals who are embedded in strong social networks should be more likely to update their tacit competencies and add new ones as they become available. Focusing on the competencies of work teams and larger organizational units, which may be more easily measured, is one approach to addressing the conundrum of managing tacit competencies. Clearly, new research is needed to improve our understanding of how individuals and teams learn, update, and revise their tacit competencies.

Dynamic Nature of Knowledge Management Competencies

Recent studies of knowledge-based organizations highlight that managing knowledge resources is a dynamic process; for example, see the special issue of *Strategic Management Journal* on the knowledge-based view of the firm (Grant & Spender, 1996). The value of competencies currently held by an organization will diminish unless they are updated or changed (Lei, Hitt, & Bettis, 1996). The dynamic nature of knowledge is why organizations value it and consider it such an important strategic asset. Thus, organizations engaged in knowledge-based competition need HRM systems that promote the continuous evolution of competencies. Such systems must address the need for changes in individual competencies as well as changes in the organization's total stock of competencies.

Several chapters of this volume describe issues related to employee movement into, out of, and between organizations, and each is relevant to our understanding of the issues that must be addressed as organizations attempt to match the competencies of their workforce to their knowledge management requirements.

For example, Oldham (Chapter Nine) argues that employees who intend to remain with an organization are more likely to share their ideas with coworkers. Thus, encouraging employee retention (see Maurer et al., Chapter Eleven) is one way to increase the internal transfer of tacit competencies and ultimately build the organization's competency stocks.

As Davis-Blake and Hui describe (Chapter Seven), many firms use contract labor in order to acquire competencies temporarily. But contract labor generally cannot be used to fulfill all of the firm's needs. Ultimately, most organizations will want to increase their stock of workforce competencies by hiring new employees. Except under conditions of sustained growth, an organization's ability to hire new competencies depends partly on its ability to manage the outward flow of current employees. Thus, a useful direction for future research would be to develop analytical tools to help organizations assess and track *changes* in their *portfolio* of competencies. To be valuable, such tools must provide timely and comprehensive information yet also be cost-effective and easy to use. The conceptual work presented by Lepak and Snell (Chapter Five) should provide a helpful foundation for future research that addresses the need for such tools.

Motivating Employees to Engage in Knowledge Management Behaviors

Motivational forces influence the behaviors of employees as well as the effort they invest in those behaviors. Most psychological theories of motivation recognize that decisions about how to behave and how much effort to exert are influenced by both employee characteristics (including their competencies) and the work environment. In the preceding section, we noted that many elements of an HRM system can be used to ensure that an organization's workforce has the competencies necessary to contribute to knowledge-based competition. In this section we consider how HR practices can influence the likelihood that employees *will* engage in the knowledge management behaviors required. Our discussion is organized around three key issues: the decision to participate in the organization and its activities, initiative and self-direction, and making the effort.

Deciding to Participate

Although employment decisions are essentially voluntary for all U.S. employees, descriptions of knowledge-based competition often highlight the ability of knowledge workers to exercise their free will when deciding which organizations to join, which projects to work on, whether to participate in various informal communities of practice, and so on. The tight labor market conditions of the past decade and a tendency to equate knowledge work with highly technical work (although knowledge work is much broader) reinforced the belief that knowledge workers have relatively greater freedom to choose where, when, and how they work (see Chapter Eleven).

Clearly, employers need to understand how employees make decisions about whether to participate in various organizational roles and activities, yet these decision processes have received little attention. Some researchers have studied job applicants' reactions to employers' hiring practices and the consequences of these reactions for acceptance of job offers, but this work addresses only a small piece of the larger topic. Participants in research on job acceptance often are young professionals selecting their first full-time employers. Or perhaps they are more experienced employees making a decision about whether to accept an expatriate assignment. In a knowledge-based economy, decisions to participate extend far beyond accepting or rejecting job offers for full-time employment at home or abroad. For example, in Chapter Two Deeds explores employees' decisions to stay with or leave a company after it has been acquired. Given the prevalence of mergers and acquisitions in recent years, this is a critical knowledge retention issue for the acquiring firm. When high-quality employees leave, the new firm loses considerable value, making it more difficult for it to realize synergy from the merger.

After they agree to join an organization, employees of all types almost always have some discretion to engage in some tasks or to seek involvement in some projects and decline to participate in others. Employees may also decide whether to accept informal leadership and advocate roles, whether to participate as an instructor, who to mentor, and so on. Participation decisions such as these can influence the performance of the employee as well as others throughout the firm who are affected. Consider, for example, decisions about whether to participate in training programs, when to participate in such programs, which programs to choose, and how much knowledge to share with others during the course of training. In making such decisions, employees shape the development of their own portfolio of competencies and also affect the knowledge portfolios of others. Research that increases our understanding of how employees make these participation decisions will ultimately help to improve knowledge management in organizations.

Self-Direction

Having agreed to participate in an organization, project, or activity, employees attend to numerous environmental cues that influence their daily behavior. Job descriptions and work goals are among the most explicit cues to guide the *direction* of employee behaviors. In addition, employees learn behavioral norms by attending to the actions of others and the consequences of those actions—that is, they attend to the cues provided by the organization's culture (see Tetrick & Da Silva, Chapter Twelve). As Mohrman explains, however, knowledge-intensive organizations also rely on their employees being self-directed. In a dynamic knowledge environment, work cannot be fully specified; much must be left to employees' discretion and initiative. Employees are required to focus on the purpose and strategy of the larger system in order to know how to focus their own work (see Chapter Four). Conversely, knowledge workers expect their employers to give them considerable autonomy in carrying out their responsibilities.

How can HR practices direct employees' attention to the purpose and strategy of the larger system? The chapters in this volume suggest that well-designed compensation plans (Lawler, Chapter Ten), training programs (Noe et al., Chapter Eight), and measurement practices (Boudreau, Chapter Thirteen) can align the direction of employees' behaviors with the firm's strategic objectives. In addition, assessments of organizational climate and culture can be used to evaluate employees' perceptions of the behaviors and competencies that are valued (Tetrick & Da Silva, Chapter Twelve).

Although there is no shortage of conceptual work on designing HR practices that provide direction for employees, more empirical work is needed. In particular, we need research to demonstrate the practical steps that organizations can take to establish a line of sight between employee behaviors and the ultimate success of the organization (see Boswell, 2000). For example, one useful approach may be to involve employees in the design and implementation of HR practices. Employees' participation in the design of HR practices may improve their understanding of organizational goals as well as help to ensure that training programs, measurement practices, and compensation plans communicate the intended messages and provide appropriate incentives to obtain the competencies that the firm values.

New research on the use of goals may also be helpful. The motivational effectiveness of goals is well established (Locke & Latham, 1990). When people perform simple and routine tasks, specific performance goals appear to increase effort. But when people perform complex tasks and tasks that require them to learn strategies to enhance their performance, then "do your best" goals are more effective (Earley, Connolly, & Ekegren, 1989; Kanfer & Ackerman, 1989). Apparently, specific performance goals are ineffective for employees working on complex and novel tasks because they interfere with the experimentation and learning required to master such tasks. For knowledge-based organizations, goal setting may be most useful when it is used to promote learning (for example, see Winters & Latham, 1996). It would be helpful to examine how to use goals effectively in organizations that rely on self-directed employees who engage in continuous learning; such research would extend the usefulness of goal-setting theory in a new era of knowledge-based competition.

Making the Effort

The effort employees exert varies in two ways: the effort made at a point in time can be relatively great or small, and the total amount of time (such as hours per week) during which the effort is made can be relatively great or small. Two HRM practices that employers can use to encourage both types of effort are work design and rewards.

Work Design

Coincident with the evolution of the knowledge economy has been a shift in the design of organizations and jobs. As knowledge-based competition has intensified, so too has the prevalence of enriched, team-based jobs with many potentially motivating characteristics. Yet, as Mohrman (Chapter Four) explains, the design features that would seem to enhance the motivational quality of knowledge work (for example, significance, variety) may also contain the seeds from which motivational problems grow. For example, the collaborative and team-based nature of knowledge work should enhance employees' experience of task identity. However, the size and complexity of many such projects can be so great that knowledge workers actually find it difficult to identify with the project as a whole. Like assembly line workers, knowledge workers may sometimes find it difficult to see the connection between their own efforts and the organization's vision.

Work designs are changing in other ways as well. The boundary that separates an organization from its environment has long been recognized as permeable, but increasingly organizations are becoming boundaryless (Bowman & Kogut, 1995). As Deeds (Chapter Two) explains, alliances, joint ventures, mergers, and acquisitions all represent strategic actions that enable firms to change or reduce organizational boundaries between firms. As Fiol (Chapter Three) notes, information technologies help to sustain global communities of practice that connect people with common interests and knowledge, regardless of where they are employed. Simultaneously, the boundary that separates work from nonwork life is becoming less distinguishable. Because knowledge can be easily transmitted through space and time, knowledge work is more easily carried out at dispersed locations, including from the homes (Mohrman, Chapter Four; Oldham, Chapter Nine). And as employers have increased their reliance on contract labor, they are more accepting of having work performed off-site—for example, at the contract worker's home or another work site. For better or worse, knowledge work often permeates the lives of employees. One consequence of these changes is that it is no longer possible to ignore the ways in which conditions beyond an organization's formal boundaries can influence knowledge management behaviors. The "design" of an employee's nonwork life as well as the design of work in other organizations with which an employee has some contact can influence the employee's motivation to engage in the knowledge management behaviors of interest to an employer.

Rewards

Of all the HR tools available for managing employee motivation, recognition and rewards often are assumed to be the most powerful. Yet they are probably the least understood. Researchers continue to hold differing views about the effects of rewards on employees, despite many studies on the topic. Some of these differences in perspective are reflected in this volume. On the one hand, Lawler (Chapter Ten) asserts that contingent rewards serve the dual role of directing employees' attention to the most important aspects of their work and motivating them to exert maximal effort; as such, they can be effectively used to support the behaviors needed for knowledge-based competition. Lawler's arguments are consistent with research showing that organizations are more likely to achieve their stated goals when employees are rewarded for results that are consistent with those goals (that is, Montemayor, 1996; Shaw, Gupta, & Delery, 2002). On the other hand, Oldham (Chapter Nine) cautions that aggressively tying rewards to achieving creative outcomes may reduce rather than increase creative output. To avoid this problem, Oldham offers a counterintuitive suggestion: instead of immediately recognizing employee efforts by paying bonuses or offering other valued rewards, offer small rewards and give them only after considerable time has elapsed. Research that yields practical suggestions for how to develop effective reward systems in knowledge-based organizations is sorely needed. Similarly, research is needed to understand better how all elements of an organization's HR system affect the motivation of the workforce.

Providing Opportunities for Knowledge Management Behavior

Even if employees understand that knowledge management behaviors are valued in their organization, *and* they have the required competencies to engage in these behaviors, *and* they are motivated do so, they still may fail to manage knowledge effectively if there are no appropriate opportunities. In order to leverage the knowledge management capability of a workforce, organizations must make it easy for knowledge to flow into and through the organization. In the language of Boudreau (Chapter Thirteen), knowledge management is more likely to occur when it is enabled by the structural aspects of the environment. Similarly, Oldham's (Chapter Nine) discussion of the importance of workspace designs hints at the importance of designing appropriate opportunities for knowledge creation. Next, we consider two approaches that organizations have used to improve knowledge-sharing opportunities: electronic knowledge management systems and team-based organizational designs.

Electronic Opportunities

During the 1990s, installing new information and knowledge management systems was a popular way to provide more opportunities for employees to acquire, create, share, apply, and update their knowledge. Electronic knowledge management systems are intended to make it easier for employees to recognize that they face similar challenges, discover each other, discuss common problems, and collaborate in finding solutions. In practice, however, electronic knowledge management systems appear to have been more useful for knowledge storage and passive knowledge distribution than for stimulating employees to search for new knowledge and creatively apply it. Furthermore, most information technologies do not support any tacit knowledge management. For creativity, innovation, and tacit knowledge management, person-to-person exchanges seem more useful than document exchanges (Hansen, Nohria, & Tierney, 1999).

As the discussions of Fiol (Chapter Three) and Noe et al. (Chapter Eight) indicate, knowledge management technologies that simply reproduce ineffective communication patterns will not improve an organization's knowledge management practices. If bureaucratic procedures and organizational boundaries ensure that employees are likely to communicate with other people having similar and related knowledge, then the means of communication is of little consequence. Although an electronic information management system may make it easier for people to communicate when they are physically distant from each other, it is not likely to overcome communication roadblocks caused by administrative and structural barriers.

Few readers of this volume will conduct the type of research needed to improve the design of electronic knowledge management systems in general. But they may be particularly qualified to study the effective design of one type of electronic knowledge management system—namely, electronic HR systems. Through electronic HR systems, organizations can make profound changes in the knowledge that is available about their human resources. Electronic HR systems can also fundamentally change who has access to HR information and the way such information is used. Although electronic HR tools have been available for more than a decade, relatively few studies have investigated the many possible consequences of their use. For example, although several studies have examined computer monitoring as a method of performance appraisal, most have focused on how individual employees react to such monitoring, including changes in their stress levels and performance (for example, Aiello & Kolb, 1995; Amick & Smith, 1992; Chalykoff & Kochan, 1989). Similarly, research on computerized cognitive ability tests for selection (Mead & Drasgow, 1993), computer-based interviewing (Martin & Nagao, 1989), and computer-based attitude surveys (Lautenschlager & Flaherty, 1990) often assesses employee reactions to the technology or compares the results obtained using the new technology rather than older technologies. Although studies such as these are useful, they represent only first steps in the journey to understanding how new approaches to managing HR knowledge can influence employees and organizations. As HR knowledge is easier to create and access, what will employees and managers wish to acquire and create? How will empowered knowledge workers use such knowledge, and for what purposes? How will the availability of new HR knowledge change the social dynamics of teamwork and supervision?

Teamwork

Recognizing the limits of electronic knowledge management systems, organizations in knowledge-based competition have been quick to adopt team-based designs to increase opportunities for people to span boundaries that might otherwise hinder information flow (Bouty, 2000; Mohrman, Chapter Four). We agree that team-based structures are likely to create more opportunities for employees to engage in effective knowledge management. Nevertheless, much more research is needed—how can we ensure that the opportunities for knowledge management inside and between teams are optimized?

Knowledge-intensive organizations encourage the proliferation of cross-functional, multidisciplinary, and even interorganizational teams. These are not the familiar and static production-focused work teams found in modern manufacturing or routine service-delivery organizations. Employees working in knowledge-intensive organizations often have broadly defined work responsibilities that require them to participate as members of *several teams*. On one project an employee may serve as the team leader; on another, he or she may be called upon to serve as an expert adviser in a narrowly defined area. One project may require frequent meetings and close working relationships; another may require each person to make significant progress alone, with meetings of the whole team occurring only occasionally. Furthermore, these team structures are *dynamic*. As work requirements change, some new teams may be formed, other teams may be reconfigured or given new responsibilities, or a team may be disbanded. For knowledge-based organizations, it is assumed that a key advantage of team-based work is that it promotes the fluid movement of knowledge (Bontis & Crossan, 1999). That is, dynamic and flexible teams are a structural solution to the management challenge of ensuring that employees have many opportunities to acquire, create, share, apply, and update their knowledge.

Although research on improving work team functioning has increased during the past decade, much of that research has assumed a static view of work teams and does not reflect the fluid and dynamic nature of work in knowledge-intensive organizations. As several chapters in this volume emphasize, successful knowledge-based competition depends on the *mobility* of knowledge. Knowledge becomes mobile through human interaction. Therefore, it follows that human resource management practices can contribute to the success of knowledge-intensive organizations by identifying the optimal patterns of interactions needed for knowledge to become mobile, and encouraging and facilitating these interactions. Organizing employees into project teams may improve their opportunities to engage in effective knowledge management, but there is little understanding of how team design and team staffing influence knowledge sharing, creation, acquisition, application, and updating among team members or between teams.

Despite their increasing popularity, cross-functional teams do not always achieve their objectives. Staffing decisions may contribute to some of the problems. For example, a study of R&D teams found that high amounts of functional diversity interfered with teams' technical innovativeness as well as their performance against schedules and budgets (Ancona & Caldwell, 1992). Other studies have found that demographic diversity on teams can increase conflict and turnover rates (Jackson, May, & Whitney, 1995). Such findings suggest that poor staffing may create situations where team members have little opportunity for effective knowledge sharing. When team members have too little in common, they may be unable to use their diversity effectively—not because they lack basic knowledge management competencies or are unmotivated but because effective communication is difficult. Nahapiet and Ghoshal (1998) argued that effective knowledge exchange is most likely to occur when a social network exists to facilitate the exchange (see Noe et al., Chapter Eight). One implication is that those staffing teams should think about the social capital available. Because a team's social capital is likely to be at least partly related to the demographic characteristics of its members—their age, tenure, gender, ethnicity, and so on—attending to the team's social capital is fraught with difficulties, especially for HR researchers and practitioners. Nevertheless, HR practices that ignore the role of social capital may inadvertently detract from an organization's ability to increase its employees' knowledge management opportunities.

The composition of a team is not the only factor that can limit or foster knowledge management opportunities—connections between team members and others inside and outside the organization (external social capital) also play a role. For example, a study of R&D teams found that functionally diverse teams were most effective when members were well connected to an external network (Keller, 2001; see also Ancona & Caldwell, 1992). The external communications of team members also influence knowledge transfer between firms that enter into strategic alliances. Such alliances often spring from relationships forged by employees who represent their firms on the technical committees of cooperative technical organizations (CTOs). CTOs serve as a mechanism for members of an industry to collaborate and agree on technical standards for future products and services. In a study of firms that manufacture and service cellular products, participation in CTOs was related to a firm's subsequent involvement in strategic alliances among members of the CTO. Furthermore, the evidence indicated that subsequent strategic alliances were most likely when a firm's representative to the CTO was a long-standing member who had developed an extensive network of relationships with representatives from other firms (Rosenkopf, Metiu, & George, 2001).

Such findings remind us that a team does not function in a vacuum. Just as the composition of the team shapes opportunities for effective knowledge management behaviors, the external organizational landscape also shapes the team's knowledge management opportunities (Joshi & Jackson, in press; Tsai, 2002). Thus, when staffing teams, the question of who is *not* on a team may be as important as the question of who *is*. The development of HR practices that facilitate the creation of externally connected teams would appear to be useful. Again, however, more research is needed before prescriptions can be offered on how to design the "external" landscape of a team to profit from its opportunities for effective knowledge management.

Conclusion

Effectively managing human resources for knowledge-based competition requires adopting a strategic approach. A strategic approach to managing human resources recognizes that an organization's competitive environment and strategic imperatives should be reflected in its HR practices. It also recognizes that the only sustainable HR practices are those that simultaneously address the needs of employees and of employers. As described in Chapters One and Two, effective knowledge management has become a strategic priority for organizations in a wide range of industries. Likewise, many employees have begun to evaluate their employment conditions and opportunities based on the knowledge-enhancing opportunities they provide; employees are seeking work that supports their goal of building a personal knowledge base, which will enhance their employability in the longer term. Thus, both employers and employees would benefit from research that increases our understanding of how to use HR practices to improve the knowledge management capabilities of employees continuously.

In this chapter, we have argued that the design of effective knowledge management practices begins with the identification of knowledge management behaviors. Our discussion has focused on generic knowledge management behaviors that are generally cited in the extant literature: knowledge acquisition, knowledge creation, knowledge sharing, knowledge application, and knowledge updating. This list of behaviors should not be treated as definitive. Research is still needed to document the claim that these behaviors are particularly valuable to firms engaged in knowledge-based competition. In addition, we encourage research to identify the knowledge management behaviors needed to succeed in specific industries and markets. Methods for identifying important firm-specific knowledge management behavior should be developed.

Assuming that the behaviors needed for effective knowledge-based competition can be identified, research is required to improve our understanding of the individual competencies and conditions that support or discourage the behaviors. For researchers who wish to study the relationship between individual competencies and knowledge management behaviors, tacit competencies may pose a particular challenge. Because tacit competencies are difficult to identify and measure, they may be ignored. We hope that this tendency will be resisted, however, for tacit competencies also may prove to be the most valuable to both employers and employees. Furthermore, whereas sophisticated HR practices for managing explicit competencies already exist, there is a great need to develop equally sophisticated approaches for managing tacit competencies.

As for the contextual conditions that support or discourage effective knowledge management, we have briefly commented on factors that signal the importance and desirability of these behaviors; factors that motivate employees to engage in the behaviors, including conditions both in the employing organization and outside organizational boundaries; and electronic and social structures that may expand or constrain opportunities for effective knowledge management. Clearly, a complete discussion of the conditions that influence knowledge management behaviors is beyond the scope of this chapter and this volume. Our objectives here were more modest.

One goal of our discussion was to highlight the wide range of contextual conditions that HR researchers should look at as they strive to develop practices that support knowledge-based competition. A second objective was to emphasize that any particular HR practice can affect an employee in many different ways and to call for research that considers the *combined* effects of an organization's entire set of practices. To be effective, the elements that make up the total HR system should jointly encourage and support workforce effectiveness by ensuring that employees have the required competencies, are motivated to use them, and are given appropriate opportunities to engage in behaviors that contribute to competitive advantage.

In the traditional model of personnel management, each area of HR practice was closely tied to one or perhaps two particular tasks. For example, job analysis and competency modeling were viewed as relevant primarily for identifying the required behaviors. Staffing, training, and development practices were seen to be relevant primarily for ensuring that individual employees had the required competencies. Performance management and rewards were viewed as relevant primarily for managing motivation. The issue of whether employees had appropriate opportunities to engage in the behaviors required for the organization's success was often ignored or assumed as a given. By contrast, a strategic perspective assumes that all available HR practices can and should be used to ensure that the workforce understands the generic and firm-specific knowledge management behaviors needed, has the competencies that enable such behaviors, is motivated to engage in the required behaviors, and has appropriate opportunities to do so.

In closing this chapter, we wish to highlight the need for more integration of individual- and team-level and organization-level research traditions at all stages of the research endeavor—from the formulation of a research question through the design of the study to the final interpretations and conclusions. In other words, we hope readers will be motivated to acquire new knowledge from other fields, share their own expertise with researchers with different perspectives and methods, and work collaboratively with other researchers to generate new knowledge. We and the other chapter authors have attempted to engage in these same knowledge behaviors during the process of preparing this volume, and we have experienced the difficulties involved. Clearly, our efforts are only a first step, and much more work is needed. For organizations to compete effectively in the future, they must simultaneously manage knowledge at macro (organizational) and micro (individual and team) levels. Thus, they need to understand how knowledge management practices aimed at each organizational level—for example, in teams, between businesses—influence knowledge management at the other levels. Research that integrates available knowledge from the fields of strategic management, organizational theory, organizational behavior, and human resource management will be needed to come to this understanding. We hope that this volume serves as a catalyst for such research.

References

Aiello, J. R., & Kolb, K. J. (1995). Electronic performance monitoring and social context: Impact on productivity and stress. *Journal of Applied Psychology, 80,* 339–353.

Amick, B. C., & Smith, M. J. (1992). Stress, computer-based monitoring, and measurement systems: A conceptual overview. *Applied Ergonomics, 23,* 6–16.

Ancona, D. G., & Caldwell, D. F. (1992). Bridging the boundary: external activity and performance for organizational teams. *Administrative Science Quarterly, 37,* 634–665.

Arthur, J. B. (1994). Effects of human resource systems on manufacturing performance and turnover. *Academy of Management Journal, 37,* 670–687.

Becker, B. B., & Huselid, M. A. (1998). High performance work systems and firm performance: A synthesis of research and managerial implications. *Research in Personnel and Human Resource Management, 16,* 53–101.

Bontis, N., & Crossan, M. M. (1999, June). *Managing an organizational learning system by aligning stocks and flows of knowledge.* Paper presented at the Conference on Organizational Learning, Lancaster, United Kingdom.

Boswell, W. R. (2000). *Aligning employees with the organization's strategic objectives: Out of "line of sight," out of mind.* Unpublished doctoral dissertation, Cornell University, Ithaca, NY.

Bouty, I. (2000). Interpersonal and interaction influences on informal resource exchanges between R&D researchers across organizational boundaries. *Academy of Management Journal, 43,* 50–65.

Bowman, E., & Kogut, B. (1995). *Redesigning the firm.* New York: Oxford University Press.

Cannella, A. A., & Hambrick, D. C. (1993). Effects of executive departure of the performance of acquired firms. *Strategic Management Journal, 14,* 137–152.

Chalykoff, J., & Kochan, T. A. (1989). Computer-aided monitoring: Its influence on employee satisfaction and turnover. *Personnel Psychology, 40,* 807–834.

Earley, P. C., Connolly, T., & Ekegren, G. (1989). Goals, strategy development and task performance: Some limits on the efficacy of goal setting. *Journal of Applied Psychology, 74,* 24–33.

Goldstein, I. L., & Ford, J. K. (2002). *Training in organizations.* Belmont, CA: Wadsworth.

Grant, R. M., & Spender, J.-C. (1996, Winter). Knowledge and the firm [Special issue]. *Strategic Management Journal, 17.*

Hambrick, D. C., & Cannella, A. A. (1993). Relative standing: A framework for understanding acquired executive departure. *Academy of Management Journal, 36,* 733–762.

Hansen, M. T., Nohria, N., & Tierney, T. (1999, March-April). What's your strategy for managing knowledge? *Harvard Business Review, 77,* 106–116.

Jackson, S. E, May, K. E., & Whitney, K. (1995). Under the dynamics of diversity in decision-making teams. In R. A. Guzzo & E. Salas (Eds.), *Team effectiveness and decision making in* organizations (pp. 204–261). San Francisco: Jossey-Bass.

Jackson, S. E., & Schuler, R. S. (1995). Human resource management in the context of organizations and their environments. *Annual Review of Psychology, 46,* 237–264.

Jackson, S. E., & Schuler, R. S. (2002). Managing individual performance: A strategic perspective. In S. Sonnentag (Ed.), *Psychological management of individual performance* (pp. 371–390). New York: Wiley.

Jackson, S. E., & Schuler, R. S. (2003). *Managing human resources through strategic partnerships.* Cincinnati, OH: South-Western.

Joshi, A., & Jackson, S. E. (in press). Managing workforce diversity to enhance cooperation in organizations. In M. West, D. Tjosvold, & K. Smith (Eds.), *International handbook of organizational teamwork and cooperative working.* New York: Wiley.

Kanfer, R., & Ackerman, P. L. (1989). Motivation and cognitive abilities: An integrative aptitude-treatment interaction approach to skill acquisition. *Journal of Applied Psychology, 74,* 657–690.

Keller, R. T. (2001). Cross-functional project teams in research and new product development: Diversity, communications, job stress, and outcomes. *Academy of Management Journal, 44,* 547–555.

Kluger, A. N., & DeNisi, A. S. (1996). The effects of feedback interventions on performance: Historical review, meta-analysis, a preliminary feedback intervention theory. *Psychological Bulletin, 119,* 254–284.

Lautenschlager, G. J., & Flaherty, V. L. (1990). Computer administration of questions: More desirable or more social desirability? *Journal of Applied Psychology, 75,* 310–314.

Lei, D., Hitt, M. A., & Bettis, R. A. (1996). Dynamic core competences through meta-learning and strategic context. *Journal of Management,* 22, 549–569.

Locke, E. A., & Latham, G. P. (1990). *A theory of goal setting and work performance.* Englewood Cliffs. NJ: Prentice Hall.

Martin, C. L., & Nagao, D. H. (1989). Some effects of computerized interviewing on job applicant responses. *Journal of Applied Psychology,* 74, 72–80.

Mead, A. D., & Drasgow, F. (1993). Equivalence of computerized and paper-and-pencil cognitive ability tests: A meta-analysis. *Psychological Bulletin, 114,* 449–458.

Montemayor, E. F. (1996). Congruence between pay policy and competitive strategy in high-performing firms. *Journal of Management, 22,* 889–908.

Nahapiet, J., & Ghoshal, S. (1998). Social capital, intellectual capital, and the organizational advantage. *Academy of Management Review, 23*(2), 242–266.

Rosenkopf, L., Metiu, A., & George, V. P. (2001). From the bottom up? Technical committee activity and alliance formation. *Administrative Science Quarterly, 46,* 748–772.

Scott, S. (1991). *Social network analysis.* Thousand Oaks, CA: Sage.

Schuler, R. S., & Jackson, S. E. (1987, August). Linking competitive strategies with human resource management practices. *Academy of Management Executive, 1,* 207–219.

Schuler, R. S., Jackson, S. E., & Storey, J. (2001). HRM and its links with strategic management. In J. Storey (Ed.), *Human resource management: A critical text.* London and Boston: ITP.

Shaw, J. D., Gupta, N., & Delery, J. E. (2002). Pay dispersion and workforce performance: Moderating effects of incentives and interdependence. *Strategic Management Journal, 23,* 491–512.

Sheremata, W. (2000). Centrifugal and centripetal forces in radical new product development under time pressure. *Academy of Management Review, 25,* 389–408.

Smith, K. G., & Di Gregorio, D. (2002). Bisociation, discovery, and the role of entrepreneurial action. In M. A. Hitt, R. D. Ireland, S. M. Camp, & D. L. Sexton (Eds.), *Strategic entrepreneurship: Creating a new mindset* (pp. 129–150). Oxford, England: Blackwell.

Thompson, L. L., Levine, J. M., & Messick, D. M. (Eds.). (1999). *Shared cognition in organizations.* Hillsdale, NJ: Erlbaum.

Thomas, J. B., Sussman, S. W., & Henderson, J. C. (2001). Understanding "strategic learning": Linking organizational learning, knowledge management, and sense-making. *Organizational Science, 12,* 331–345.

Tsai, W. (2002). Social structure of "coopetition" within a multiunit organization: Coordination, competition, and intraorganizational knowledge sharing. *Organizational Science, 13,* 179–190.

Vermeulen, F., & Barkema, H. G. (2001). Learning through acquisitions. *Academy of Management Journal, 44,* 457–476.

Walsh, J. P. (1988). Selectivity and selective perception: An investigation of managers' belief structures and information processing. *Administrative Science Quarterly, 31,* 873–896.

Winters, D., & Latham, G. P. (1996). The effect of learning versus outcome goals on a simple versus a complex task. *Group and Organization Management, 21,* 236–250.

Zhou, J. (in press). When the presence of creative coworkers is related to creativity: Role of supervisor close monitoring, developmental feedback, and creative personality. *Journal of Applied Psychology.*

Name Index

Subject Index

A

ABB, 74–75

Absorptive capacity: defined, 11–12; as knowledge enabler, 382–383

Accounting, to measure knowledge stocks, 366–370

Acer, 81

Acquisition of knowledge. *See* Knowledge acquisition

Acquisitions. *See* Mergers and acquisitions (M&As)

Action learning, 217–218

Adaptation, in teams, 223

Adjustive learning, 335–336

Aggregated units of analysis: and knowledge measurement, 363; and measurement of knowledge flows, 379–380; and measurement of knowledge stocks, 371, 373, 375

Alliances. *See* Strategic alliances

American Management Association, 178–179, 197

AT&T, 183

Autodesk Inc., Vermont Microsystems Inc. v., 324

Autonomy, knowledge work design for, 108, 113–114

B

BDDP, 75

Behaviors: as approach to human resources management, 400; for knowledge acquisition, 402–404; for knowledge creation, 404–405; for knowledge sharing, 405–406; motivating employees to engage in, 412–417; providing opportunities for, 417–422

Bell Labs, 172

Biopharmaceutical industry, alternative strategies for knowledge acquisition by, 38–41

Bisociation, 404

Bonus pay, 287–288

Boundaries: capabilities for managing, when contracting, 189, 194–195; and organizational learning, 352; work design to cut across, 118

Boundary paradox, 90

British Petroleum, 101, 214–215

Bureau of Labor Statistics, 304, 305

C

Capabilities: defined, 9; knowledge-based, 13–16; strategic, 13; strategic alliances' role in development of, 44

Career development. *See* Professional development

Cisco Systems, 48, 54, 70, 72

Climate. *See* Organizational climate

Cohorts. *See* Employee cohorts

Collaboration, work design for, 103–104

Combination: defined, 211; as means of creating intellectual capital, 219; as mode of knowledge sharing, 214

knowledge enabler measures for, 367, 381–386; knowledge flow measures for, 367, 376–380; knowledge stock measures for, 366–376; and pivotal roles, 364; and value-chain context, 363–364

Knowledge sharing: behaviors for, 405–406; between contract and standard workers, 192; as dimension of performance, 165, 166–167; future research on, 235–236; and human capital management at individual level, 135–136; modes of, 214; predictor constructs for, 170

Knowledge stocks: accounting-based measures of, 366–370; competencies as measures of, 374–376; defined, 365; learning curves as measure of, 373, 374; measuring, 366–376; organization experience as measure of, 372, 373–374; patents and publications as measures of, 370–372; types of, 49–54, 57

Knowledge transfer: defined, 210, 376; future research on, 234, 235–236. *See also* Knowledge flows

Knowledge transmission, pipeline vs. river view of, 67–69, 71–72, 87–88, 89–90

Knowledge work: characteristics of, 97–102; role of trust in, 84–86; structural approach to, 76–77, 81–82; structures used to support, 82–84; technology as driver of, 70–73; technology used to support, 74–76. *See also* Knowledge management

Knowledge workers: attributes of, 105–106; job design for, 107–116; shortage of, 104–105. *See also* Contract workers; Employees; Technical professionals

Knowledge-based capabilities, 13–16

Knowledge-based competition: applications of I/O psychology in, 16–19; creating HRM system for, 400–401; identifying behaviors needed for, 402–409; universality of, 66. *See also* Competitive advantage

Knowledge-based earnings, 368

Knowledge-based resources: acquiring, 11–12; aggregating, 12–13; defined, 6, 9; importance of, 8, 9–10

Knowledge-intensive firms (KIFs), 66

L

Learning: action, 217–218; adjustive, 335–336; communities of, 218, 236; distance, 215–216; formative, 335; operative, 336; process, 101; reinventive, 334–335; work design for, 104. *See also* Organizational learning

Learning curves, as measure of knowledge stocks, 373, 374

Licensing, 41–42, 52, 55, 57

Links: HR strategies for managing, to organization, 322–323; as influence on job retention, 309–310

M

Managerial work, distinction between knowledge work and, 118

Mangren R&D v. National Chemical Co., 324

Matrix structures, 78

McKinsey & Company, 80

Measurement. *See* Knowledge measurement

Mergers and acquisitions (M&As): defined, 45; human capital management required in, 16–17; increased number of, 44–45; as knowledge acquisition strategy,

CABRINI COLLEGE LIBRARY
610 KING OF PRUSSIA RD.
RADNOR, PA 19087-3699

DEMCO